Viking Glass 1944-1970

Dean Six

With Pam Ochs and Rock Wilson

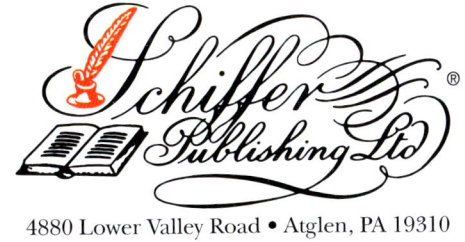

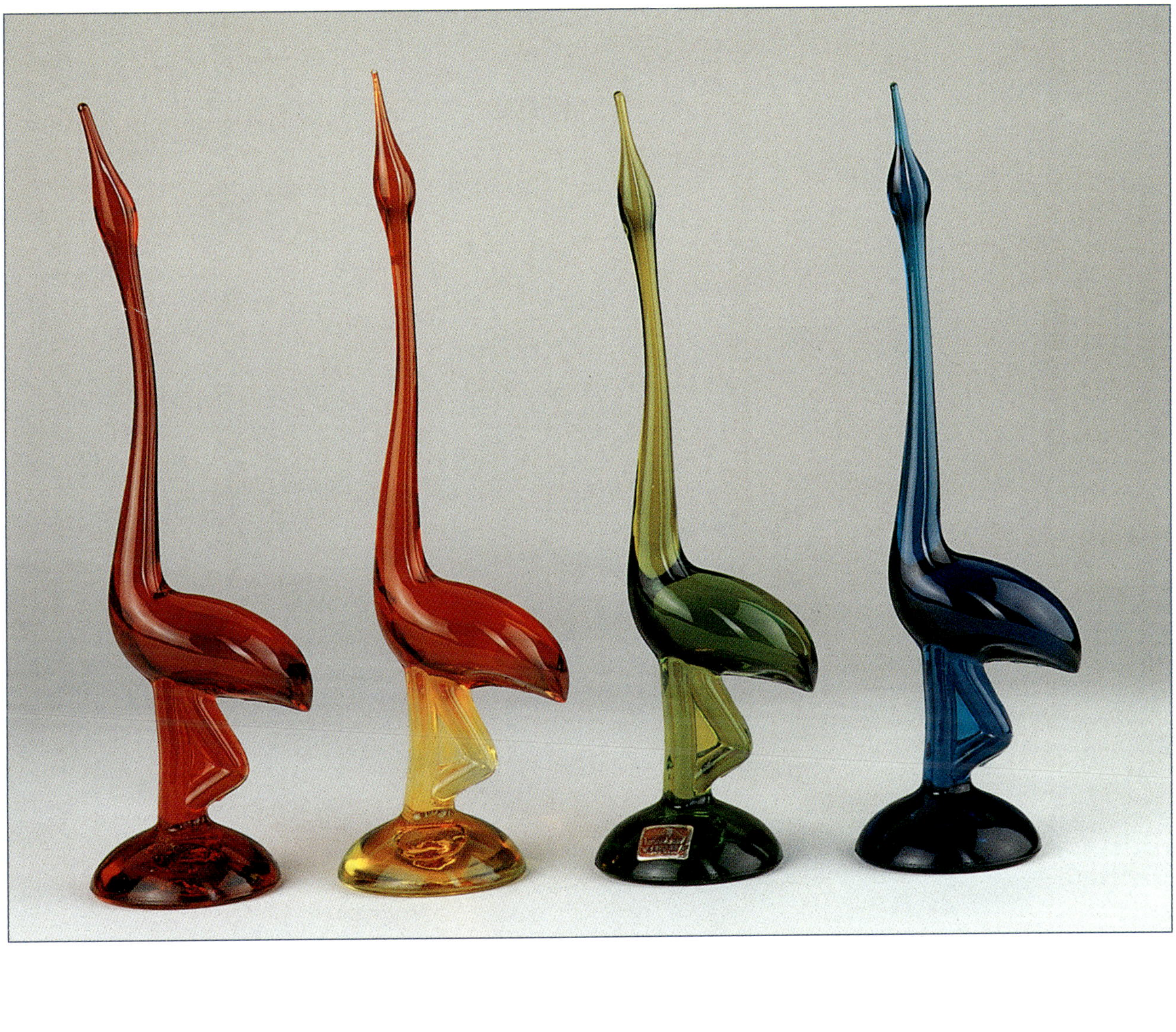

4880 Lower Valley Road • Atglen, PA 19310

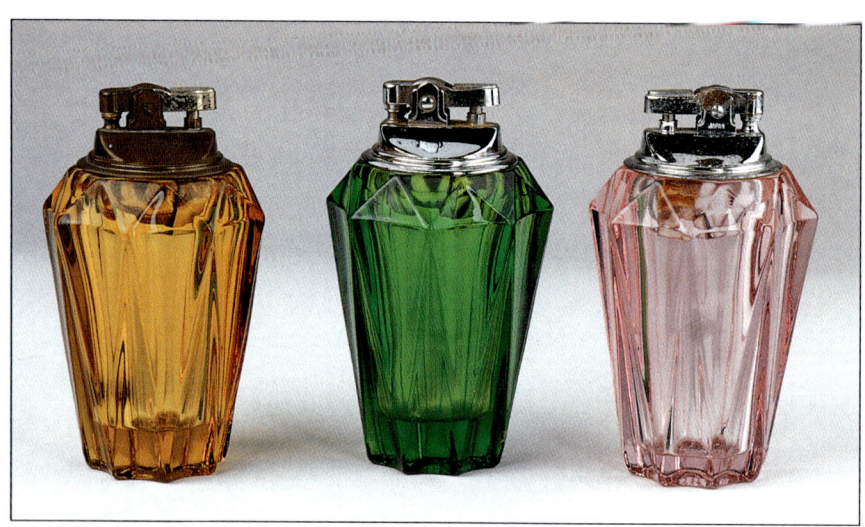

Designed by Ellen J. "Sue" Taltoan
Type set in Lydian BT/Lydian BT

ISBN: 978-0-7643-1859-7
Printed in India
5 4 3 2

Published by Schiffer Publishing Ltd.
4880 Lower Valley Road
Atglen, PA 19310
Phone: (610) 593-1777; Fax: (610) 593-2002
E-mail: Info@schifferbooks.com
Please visit our web site catalog at www.schifferbooks.com
We are always looking for people to write books on new and related subjects. If you have an idea for a book please contact us at the above address.

This book may be purchased from the publisher.
Please try your bookstore first.
You may write for a free catalog.

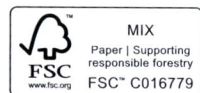

MIX
Paper | Supporting responsible forestry
FSC
www.fsc.org
FSC™ C016779

Contents

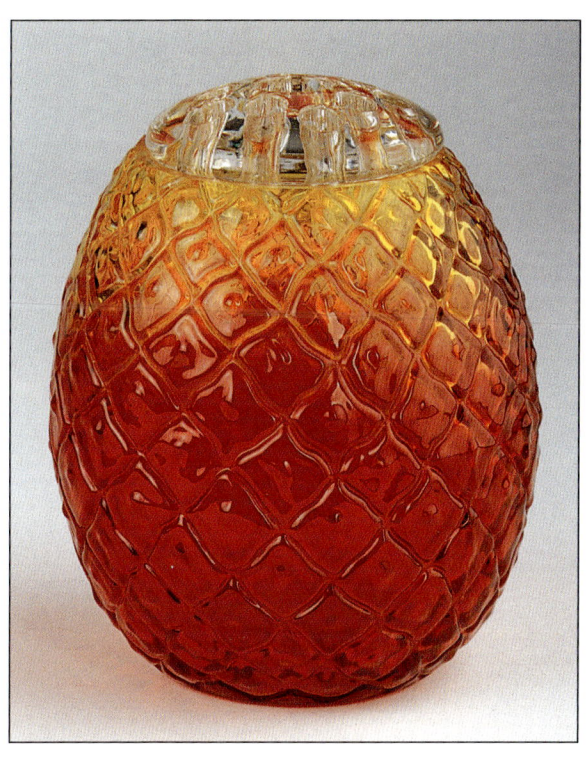

Acknowledgments

"I do not promote mischief, I inspire freedom"

Ian Conley

Each project we undertake in life has the potential to gain us new friends, affirm old friendships, and stretch our world in unexpected ways. This book was no different.

A book on Viking came about because I heard, repeatedly, questions about the products of this significant handmade glass house. Questions for which there was no readily available research material, no in print answers. If you think in terms of projects, as I do, an unanswered question can quickly evolve into a project. And a book is born.

This book is special in that a long-time friend and business partner, Rock Wilson, got excited about the quest for Viking Glass. He was soon burning with the acquisition fire that collectors know well. His quickness to see stylistic similarities, color, and design made his collection soar. In a year or so he had gathered dozens, literally hundreds, of pieces of Viking that have been borrowed and included in this book. His intrigue with chasing and finding helped keep me focused and excited. A special thanks to his daughter, Timber, who shared her Dad with this, at times, consuming project!

Pam Ochs was an expert on glass flower frogs and a nationally recognized dealer in fine handmade glass. She was often found at shows or her web site www.facets.net/classics. She supported the West Virginia Museum of American Glass, a favored project for me, in many ways. She gave rare catalogs, paper archives, and much-desired objects. When I inquired of her to help me understand Viking made flower frogs, her enthusiasm and willing spirit was irrepressible. In the months that followed, she and husband Nick made trips from their Florida home to West Virginia to share knowledge and glass. She employed her dogged research skills in discerning dates and production for Viking and kept me diligent. It was an unexpected shock when Pam passed away at the end of 2002. To her brilliant and gentle spirit this book is dedicated.

An amazing number of folks have stepped forward to inquire, advise, consult, share, ship, dust, sort, and generally support in any of a number of ways. Some of those are listed here. Regretfully, some may be missed. To all of you who have helped make this tribute to the glass made at Viking possible, in whatever way, my sincere thanks.

Eleanor & Kester Six
Tom & Neila Bredehoft
Jeff Conover
Mary Lou, Rock's Mom, who can indeed find Viking Glass!
Bob Page & Dale Frederiksen and Replacements, LTD.
Tom Bloom and Doug Gregg & Charles Street Antiques.
Gail Bardhan, The Rakow Library at the Corning Museum of Glass
Jeannine Burwell
Stephanie and Steve Seese
Samantha & Christopher Robin
Eric Hurst
Dick Schnacke
Nick Ochs
Jaime Robinson
Rachael Potts
Jill Spencer
Tom Felt
Lorraine Hawkins
Tim and Robin Cook
Butch and Sandy Nance
Bonnie S. Shannon of the City of New Martinsville and previously of Viking
Barb Minor and the Wetzel Chronicle
D. "Woody" Moore
Bruce Water, photographer of exceptional skill
West Virginia Museum of American Glass and its members, board, and supporters over time
Ian Conley
June McGinnis, eternally
Jeff Zimmerman, Robert Cross, Phyllis Cross, Goldie Smith, Franklin "Bud" Smith and Gladys Salisbury, all once employed at Viking and who cared enough to share their stories...

Pricing

Prices are often the hardest part of a book project. Locating objects to image, untangling product lines and numbers and dates, writing text to tell the story all seem relatively easy in contrast to *pricing*. I write from West Virginia, a few miles from New Martinsville and the place where Viking Glass was made. Prices for Viking here are not the same as the West Coast or a southern flea market. Introduce prices from e-bay, and it's like seeing the wind. One moment it seems to be here, the next it is certainly there. I tracked and logged e-bay Viking Glass prices for many months. And pattern prices were wildly erratic. The same piece would sell for $14 dollars in February and $38 in July. I thought I saw a trend! Then in August an identical object sold for $12. What trend?

What I have worked to include here is a SUGGESTED price range. I have quizzed dealers and collectors in other states when I can. But, at best, pricing is always a guide to value and no more. Should there be two or more collectors for an object in your area, sales and prices may reflect that. "Modern" may sell best in urban areas and less in some rural areas. Such localized and regional anomalies are common. Very common.

Please consider the prices offered in this text as informed suggestions of the price ranges pieces might bring on the open market. Pay what YOU deem an object is worth to you. Buy what you like, pay what seems reasonable. And reasonable is a terribly subjective term! Happy hunting!

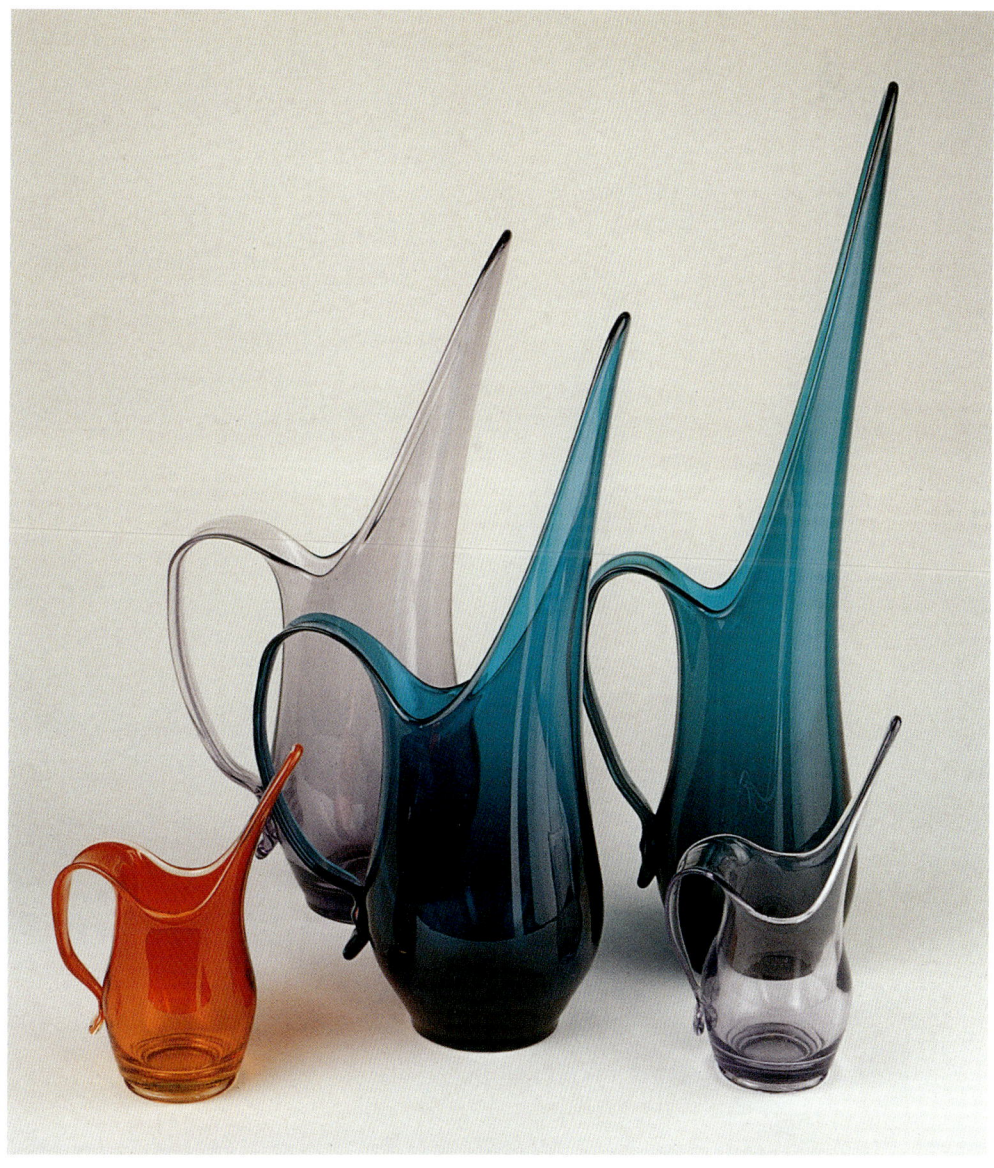

A Brief History

West Virginia as a Glass Capital: The Big Picture

Glass was first produced in western Virginia in the second decade of the 1800s in what is now West Virginia. It was then Charles Town, Virginia, now Wellsburg, West Virginia, where that first hot liquid glass was formed within our state. That site had the necessary coal for fuel to sustain the intense temperatures required to melt glass; it was near Pittsburgh, Pennsylvania, an early emerging glass production center from which experienced labor could be drawn, and it had one further advantage. Wellsburg was further west than Pittsburgh and it was on the Ohio River. The Ohio River was the lifeline from Pittsburgh west to the newly emerging nation, and Wellsburg was further down stream than Pittsburgh. This meant more water in summer to enhance navigation and a shorter, albeit possibly only slightly shorter, period of limited navigation due to the freezing river. Wellsburg flourished over time and the town became home to roughly forty hot glass-producing firms over almost 200 years. The last hot glass was produced in Wellsburg in 2001. From Wellsburg the glass industry grew across northwestern West Virginia and over time approximately 450 different concerns have produced hot glass in the Mountain State.

Wellsburg is a matter of a few short miles north of the town of New Martinsville, West Virginia, on the Ohio River. New Martinsville has been home to two glass factories utilized by five different companies over time. It is one of these sites, the New Martinsville Glass Manufacturing Co., that is the beginning of our Viking Glass story.

New Martinsville Glass Before Viking

New Martinsville Glass Manufacturing Company was chartered in 1900 in part due to the discovery of natural gas in the areas adjacent to the Ohio River. Gas promised cheap and dependable fuel for glass manufacturing and the proliferation of twentieth century glass factories in West Virginia is tied to the discovery and commercial availability of natural gas. Melting sand into a fiery liquid is a fuel intensive process.

The company was operating by 1901 but a fire, the eternal bane of glass houses, ceased production and the building was rebuilt. Fire took extensive tolls on New Martinsville Glass over time. Once recovering from the 1901 fire the factory was again damaged when a combination Ohio River flood and ensuing fire and subsequent explosions rocked the factory. The factory being surrounded by floodwater hampered the local fire department. The trade journal *China, Glass and Lamps* reported on their front page of 7 November 1901 "the New Martinsville Glass Manufacturing Company have a fine new factory here … and reasons to be proud of (it). It was built last summer and began operations last August. It is now running day and night, making just as fine of goods of this class as any made in the country. They are working 13 shops and could work more if they had room. They are already making preparations to enlarge and work on additions will be soon commenced."

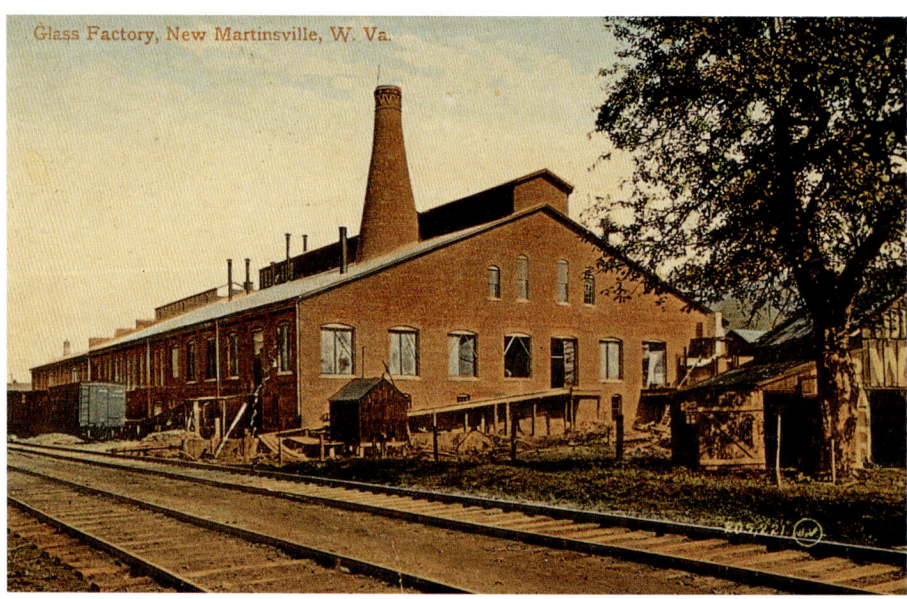

"Glass Factory, New Martinsville, W.Va." postcard postmarked July 1903. The original New Martinsville Glass Co. shortly after construction. This building was used as a part of the Viking complex until the factory closed in the 1990s.

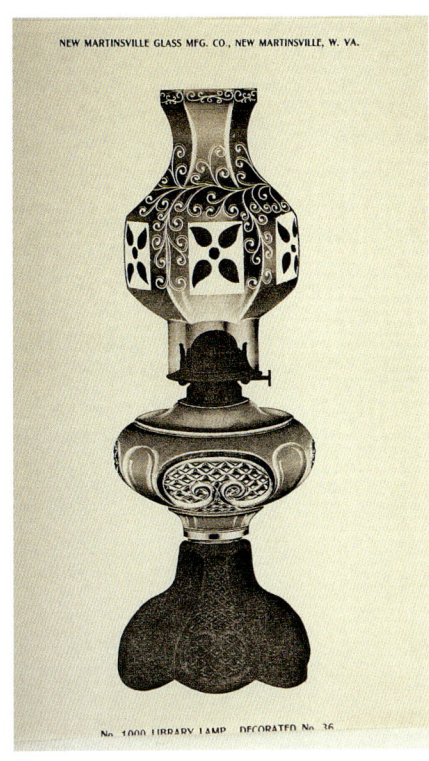

NEW MARTINSVILLE GLASS MFG. CO., NEW MARTINSVILLE, W. VA.

No. 1000 LIBRARY LAMP DECORATED No. 36

Original advertisement showing a large library lamp manufactured by New Martinsville Glass in the early 1900s. "No. 1000 Library Lamp decoration No. 36." Original hand colored image owned by the Historical Society of Western Pennsylvania.

"At present they make tumblers, goblets, tableware, lamps, ink wells, etc. but opal goods will be added as soon as new tanks are built. They are now filling an order for 750 gross of inkwells. (That's over 1/4 of a million ink wells! -Dean) There is a railroad siding the whole length of the factory building connecting with the Ohio River railroad. A wide porch extends along the entire side of the building and at present it is full of barrels of packed ware fifteen feet high ready for shipment. There are five or six carloads and they will be shipped at one."

"The main plant is operated by a 50-horse power gas engine and the mold shop is run by another gas engine of small capacity. They use natural gas here exclusively and have practically an inexhaustible supply. The gas field is only about four miles from the factory. The company employ(s) about 150 people at present. They have about four acres, all level and consequently plenty of room to spread out."

Operations were normalized at New Martinsville Glass and fires, flooding, and explosions seemed a thing of the past. In 1919 Ira M. Clark, "formerly general manager and sales manager of John B. Highbee Glass Co., of Bridgeville, Pa." was announced as the factory's general manager (*China, Glass and Lamps* 21 April 1919). Clark remained a principal player in the glass industry and was in part responsible for successes at New Martinsville until his death in 1937. Prior to Clark, the factory manager had been Jule Braun, formerly of D.C. Jenkins Glass of Kokomo, Indiana and earlier still Charles Rockhill had been the general manager of the company.

From the 1930s on, as America fell into the great Depression, New Martinsville Glass struggled. Pay for employees had been tendered in company paper script. Other glass companies had used script, long a common practice in the coal industry, at times. Script is essentially a voucher that replaced government legal tender and was backed and assured by the company and payable at the company office. Employees and perhaps others providing services and goods to New Martinsville Glass had been paid in company script, a strong indication of cash flow problems at New Martinsville Glass. In 1933 hard times forced New Martinsville Glass into court appointed receivership and Ira M. Clarke was appointed receiver to operate the factory. They continued to manufacture "tableware and decorate glassware." (*Crockery and Glass Journal*, March 1933)

In 1937 the death of long time general manager Ira Clark (*China, Glass and Lamps*, May 1937) and the compounding financial woes of some years took their toll and New Martinsville Glass filed for bankruptcy in the local Wetzel County Circuit Court. Frank C. Berger, the local sheriff as well as being a prominent local businessman, but not a glass man, was appointed receiver of the company. H.D. Barth and Fred Schlens continued to play a role in daily operations as they had under the direction of Ira Clark; Barth oversaw production and Schlens the business office. (*Crockery & Glass Journal*, June 1937) Fred Schlens was the son-in-law of Ira Clark. The plant and company assets were offered for sale at a public auction July 24th, 1937 but no bidders prevailed.

A second sale attempt was reported in the *Wetzel County Democrat* in July 1938 and bids of $44,000 were accepted. Winning bidders were Carl Schultz and R.M. Rice, both men from Connecticut. While these men were not local and had no direct experience at New Martinsville or in glass production they were reportedly involved with the popular and successful Silver City Glass Company of Meridian, Connecticut. Silver City was a firm that decorated glass produced by others; New Martinsville had been a supplier to Silver City. Operations resumed 15 August 1938, ending a receivership that had lasted six years and several receivers. (*China, Glass and Lamps*, August 1938)

The new owners created their own new company, retaining some of the familiar name. This seems to have been in hopes of gaining from the reputation and recognition New Martinsville Glass Manufacturing Co. had held in the market place. By late 1938 New Martinsville Glass Co. had begun production and New Martinsville Glass Manufacturing Co. was defunct. Perhaps more important than a change in name was that ultimate control now resided in New England and sales were connected to Silver City, albeit informally.

From 1938 until 1 June 1944 the factory was operated as New Martinsville Glass Co. A number of talented and well-connected glass industry people joined in the management. Harry Barth, who had been at the factory, returned as general manager for the new owners and proved an important player. C. F. Merritt succeeded Barth in 1940. Merritt had worked at New Martinsville Glass in the 1920s and had, immediately prior to returning, been in charge of the cutting department of Seneca Glass in Morgantown, West Virginia. (*China, Glass and Lamps*, August 1940). Recognizing the successes of Seneca as a major glass producing and cutting firm, one can easily imagine the influences and directions Merritt might seek to go while at New Martinsville. Orie (O.F.) Mossor came as general manager later and had also had early experience at New Martinsville. While away from New Martinsville Mossor is reported to have worked at Cambridge Glass in Ohio and at Duncan and Miller Glass in Washington, Pennsylvania, both highly reputable handmade glass houses. One can easily see there were few or no secrets in the glass industry circa 1940 and the similarity of product and design was surely due in part to this fluid relocation of skilled workers and management.

The years 1940-1941 saw dramatic changes at New Martinsville Glass and the beginnings of Viking Glass.

Viking Glass Emerges

"The plant of the New Martinsville Glass Co. is being completely revamped, remodeled and modernized in preparation for the entrance of the company during the upcoming year into an entirely different field of glass production, the manufacturing of hand-made, quality glassware of the Swedish type. It has also been revealed that the name of the company is to be changed in the near future to the Viking Glass Co. in order that its name will more closely identify (with the product). Some of the old lines will continue in production with the line of ware it will specialize in also...Under the leadership of Carl A. Schultz, who is president, and under the direction of O.F. Mossor, a practical glass technician of many years experience, who joined the company last spring as plant manager, the plant has been undergoing improvements." (*Retailing, Homes Furnishings*, Edition 29, December 1941)

This reference in 1941 is the earliest reference to the "soon-to-be" Viking Glass yet found in trade journals or elsewhere.

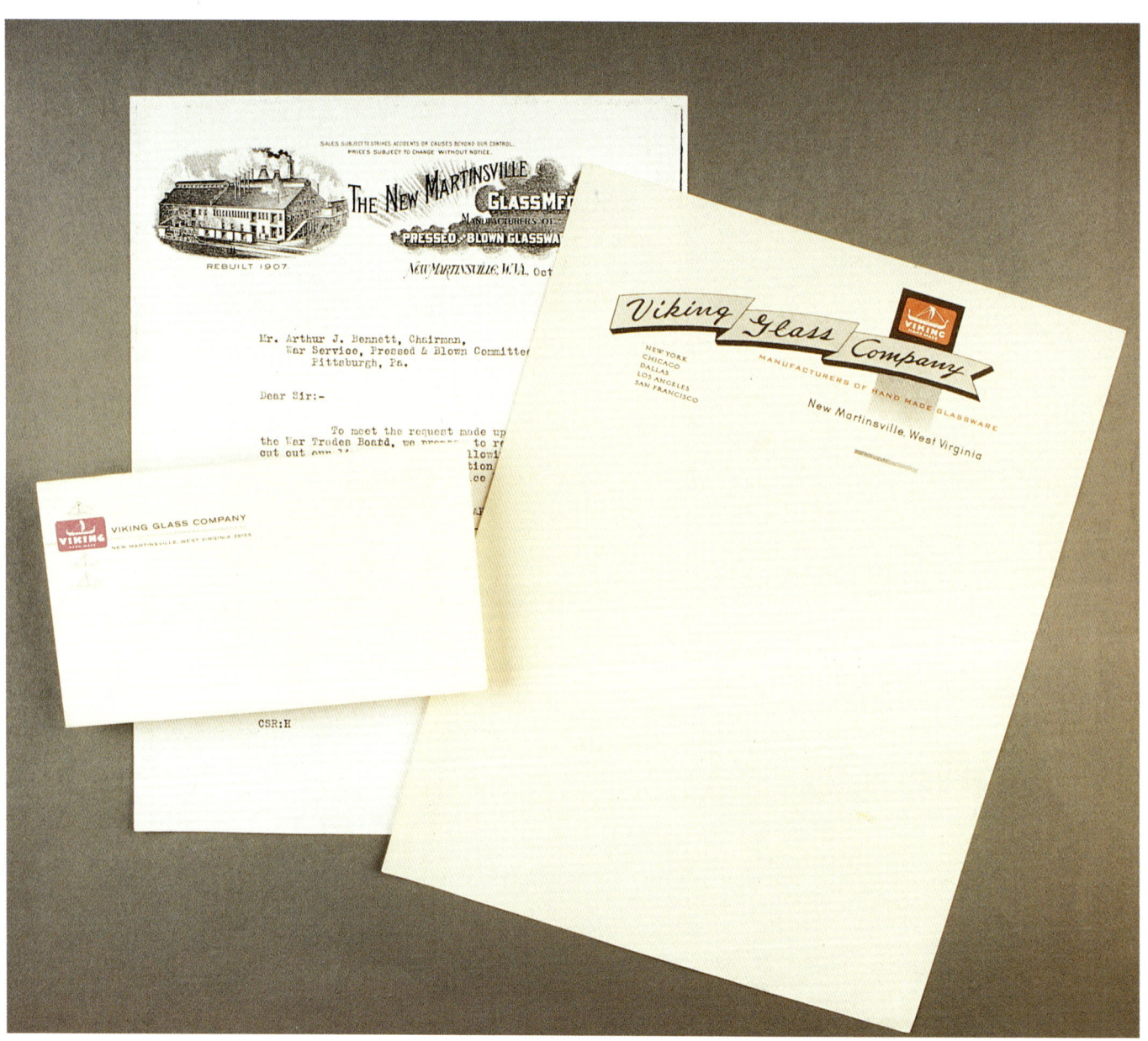

New Martinsville Glass letterhead of 1918 showing the factory and later letterhead used by Viking Glass.

Sanborn Co. Fire Map of the New Martinsville Glass Manufacturing Co. in 1913. Compare this to the postcard view to understand better the location of the railroad tracks and other details. Note the cooper's material shed (wood for making barrels), the decorating lehr, decorating room, and other clues to the products and processes of glass in 1913.

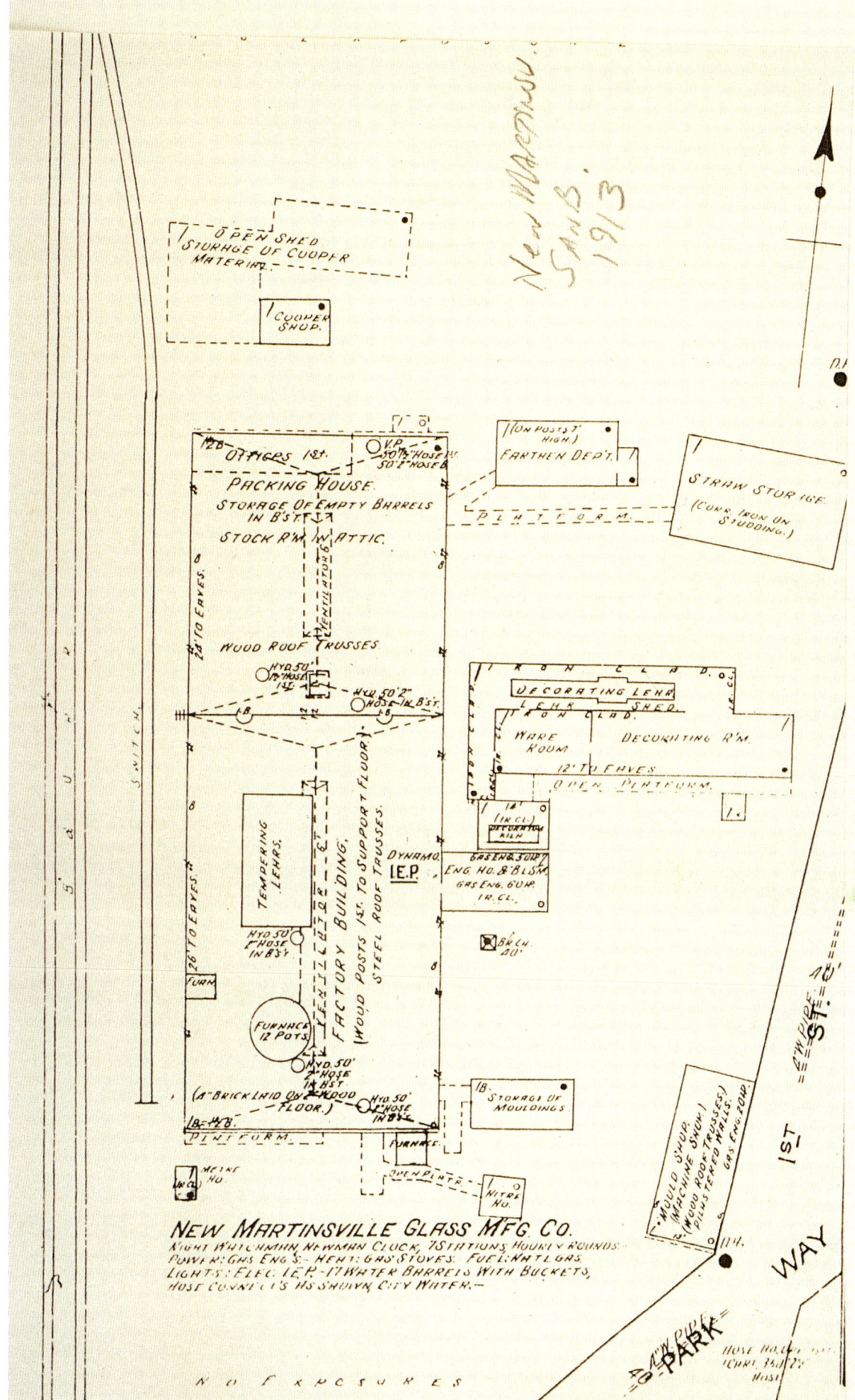

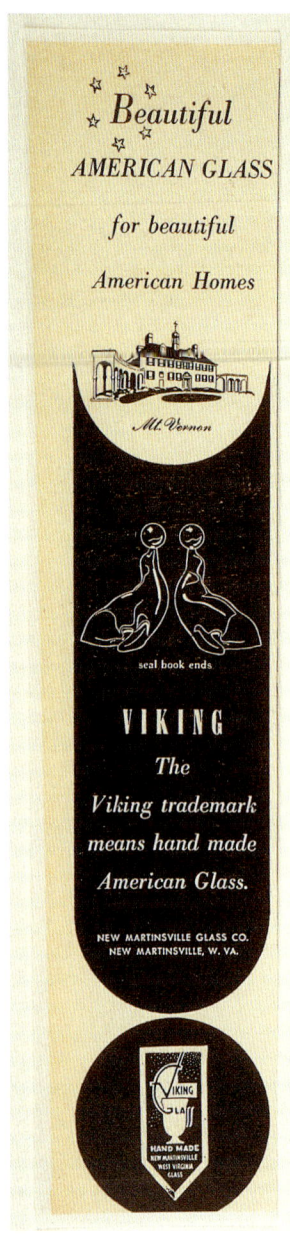

An early use of the Viking name is this New Martinsville Glass October 1942 ad from *China & Glass* promoting "heavy Viking crystal."

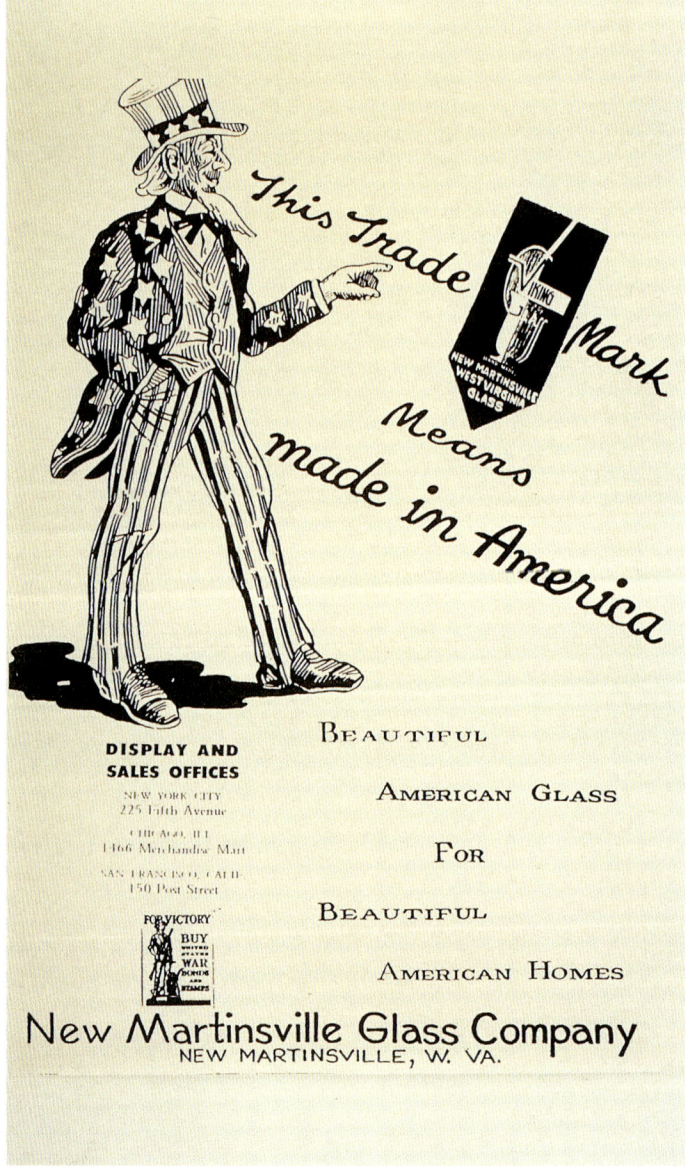

Uncle Sam adds his weight to the need to stress that Viking glass is American.

Amazingly the name change would not come quickly. Ad copy in *China & Glass* for October 1942 noted New Martinsville Glass Company offering "ball balancing seals modeled in the heavy Viking crystal." The name change process was underway, but the name was not yet changed. By July of 1943 ads began to appear marketing the Viking name, but as a trade name or product line name, seeking to establish some recognition or identity for the new Viking company. These ads appeared for several months in the second half of 1943 and talked not of a new company name but of a label to look for and a trademark that meant Made in America by hand. The world was at war and in America marketing "American Made" had more appeal than identifying with foreign products or designs. Viking glass was emerging driven by a strong national marketing campaign to insure the new "modern" glass was recognized as American hand made glass.

As if New Martinsville Glass were exploring two options, both Viking and Krystal Klear were used in advertising in the early years of the 1940s. In December of 1942 New Martinsville was placing two page advertisement spreads promoting the colorless, Krystal Klear line and "All that the name Implies" as a marketing slogan.

In January 1944 magazines carry a full-scale advertising campaign. It hits the media promoting and seeking to familiarize readers in the wholesale trade and glass industry with the Viking name. For each month in 1944 there is a full-page advertisement in *China & Glass*, a leading trade journal. These ads wisely tied American Glass, "handmade in America," to use in American homes. In the event the reader should fail to grasp the point most of these ads included a piece or selection of Viking Glass beside a recognizable American icon home, like George Washington's Mount Vernon, Thomas Jefferson's Monticello, etc. The bold message was "This Is American." Each ad still notes the company as New Martinsville Glass, but in small print. The large message is consistently American and Viking goes together. Amidst World War II this appeal of new and modern yet very American was the work of an exceedingly savvy, and costly, advertising campaign. In late 1944, Ferry-Hanly Co. of New York was selected for the New Martinsville/Viking advertising agency. (*Crockery & Glass Journal*, November 1944)

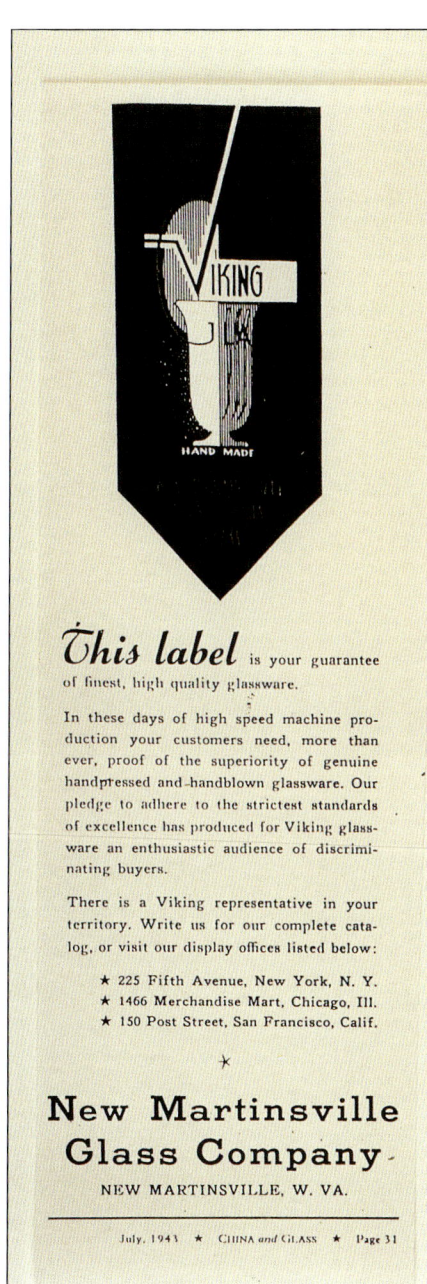

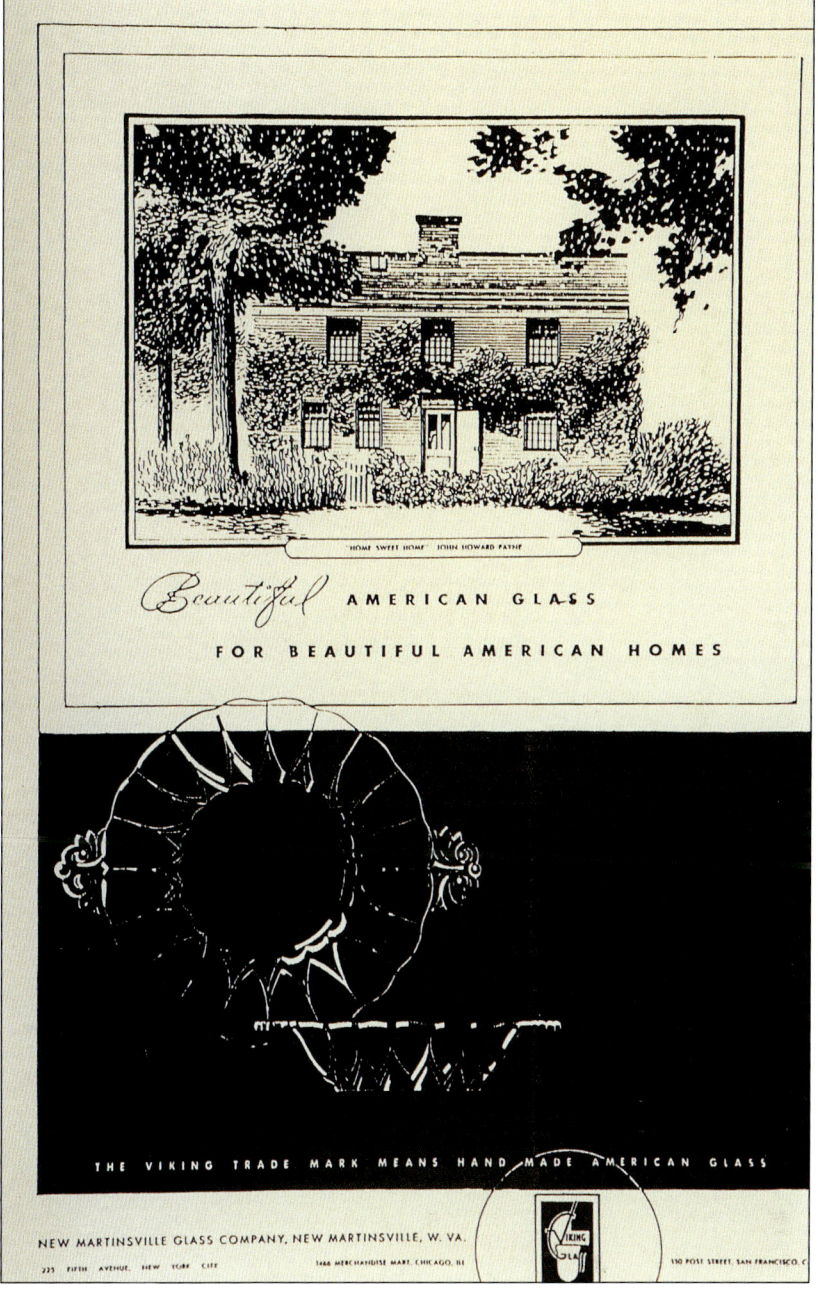

The promotion of the Viking Handmade trademark, noting permanent display and sales rooms in New York, Chicago, and San Francisco in 1943. "Viking" was from the earliest years widely distributed. *China and Glass*, July 1943.

One of a series tying the "handmade in America" theme to a strong identity with historical America. Showing the homes of famous Americans with "Viking" glass was intended to sell us on the American traditions and roots of this product while our country and the world was in the midst of a war.

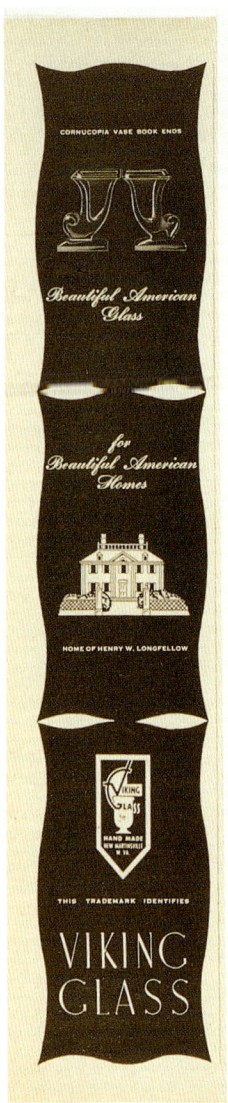

One in an extensive series of glass and historic homes advertisements. Shown here are the Cornucopia Vase bookends in heavy "Viking" crystal, the home of Henry W. Longfellow, and the caption "Beautiful American Glass for Beautiful American Homes." *House and Garden*, July 1944.

The public announcement of the name change came at last at the end of 1944, very likely tied to the hiring of the New York advertisement agency. A press release stated, "the New Martinsville Glass Company recently announced a change of name to the Viking Glass Company. (*Crockery & Glass Journal*, November 1944 and *Gift & Art Buyer*, November 1944) Reports are that the decision and vote by the company to change the name had taken place in June 1944 but advertisements had continued to run under the New Martinsville Glass name and the announcement had been delayed until almost the year's end. Recall the company had said in 1941 that it would soon be called Viking. The delay was surely, in part, due to the war.

One designer for Viking in the 1940s was Jay Ackerman. He had served Viking in the early 1940s and had other design clients in house wares and the appliance industry prior to WWII. It was announced in 1945 that he had been "re-appointed chief designer for Viking Glass Company." (*Retailing*, March 15, 1945 and *Crockery & Glass*, April 1945) In 1948 Robert Gruen was named the Viking designer. Gruen, of New York City, was noted as having glassware designs in the US that were displayed in the New York Metropolitan Museum of Art and elsewhere abroad. (*American Glass Review*, April 17, 1948)

As the decade turned and the

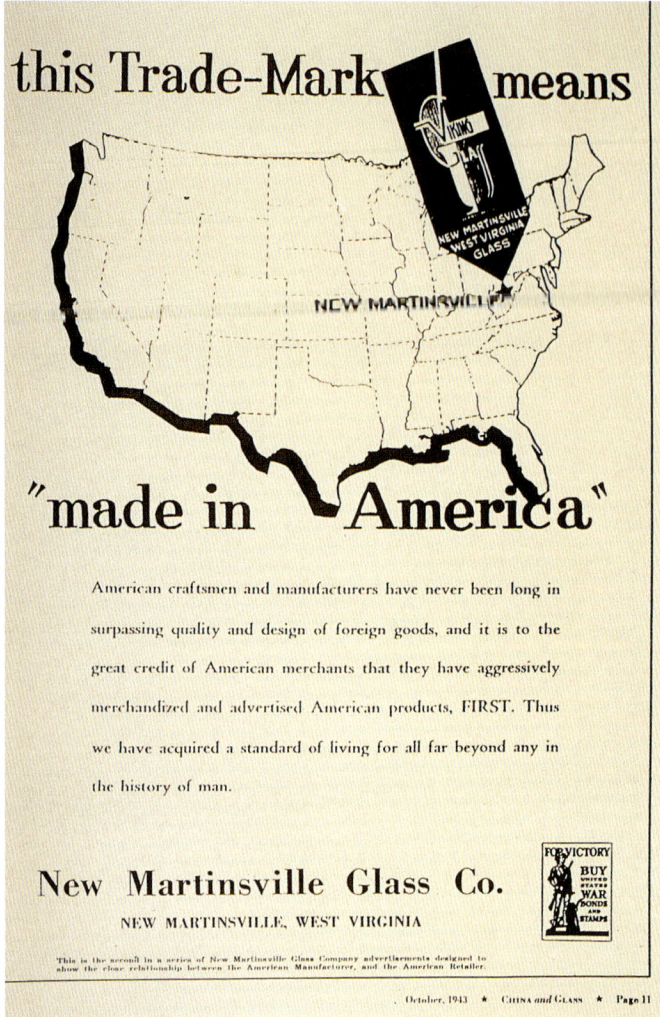

New Martinsville Glass apparently felt a compelling need to establish an American identity in the middle of World War II indicated by the numerous and extensive advertising campaigns they undertook to do so. Today it is difficult for many of us to imagine the disdain for things not American that then prevailed. Viking was working to overcome that. Here the "made in America" theme shows you clearly where in America! *China and Glass*, October 1943.

1950s saw America recover from a decade of war, indeed saw America soar, in a post war economy and into the period we call the baby boom, America spread her wings. In glassware, color supplemented and almost completely replaced the clear Swedish influenced crystal. *China, Glass and Decorative Accessories* reported "a trend to increasing variety of colors is indicated for the coming year by C. E. Willis, sales manager of the Viking Glass Company. This trend reflects the growing consumer interest in color, which has been widely noted and which has been specifically felt by the Viking organization. Colors for 1951 include, in addition to crystal, "evergreen," amber, ebony, cobalt blue, sky blue and ruby." (December 1950)

In 1953 the *Glass Factory Yearbook* reported Viking Glass employed "200 people making handmade tableware, smokers supplies, novelties and private mold work totaling a volume of $1,000,000 a year." The 1953 Viking price list of January is wonderfully revealing in its offering and notes. Particularly noteworthy is that "all stemware in Prelude Etching and Leaf Cutting is shipped FOB from Morgantown, W.Va." While it is only speculative, this suggests that the thin, blown and not pressed wares in the Viking lines were indeed made (and decorated) by one of the several Morgantown glass houses. This would be reasonable as Viking was predominately a pressed glass factory.

A closer look at that 1953 production reveals some of the earlier New Martinsville Glass crystal figurines remained in production. In production were the seal, ship bookends, squirrel with base, elephant, and wolfhound only. In the smoking supplies department twenty-seven different items appear in the price list. Georgian, a popular pattern made by many glass houses, was offered in a limited number of shapes: 9-oz. tumbler, 12-oz. tumbler and 4-oz. sherbet. What Georgian lacked that year in piece type variety it more than compensated for in color. In 1953 the three Georgian forms could be ordered in "crystal, amber, amethyst, evergreen, olive green, charcoal, colonial blue, harvest gold, and cherry-glo." Crackled items were also in the 1953 offerings but only in crystal and olive green. Crackle items were ashtrays, plate, shallow bowls, and crystal jugs with color handles.

Viking production, like that of most glass houses, included a significant amount of glass made in molds privately owned by someone else. These items, created at and by Viking, were generally sold as products labeled or know under the mold owner's name. No public connection to Viking glass was generally known. A major customer for this type of work was L.G. Wright glass; a glass jobber located a very short distance away in New Martinsville. Wright had been a salesman for New Martinsville Glass until its sale in 1938. Wright began his own glass marketing business around 1938, but his company never manufactured glass. Until the final closure of the factory decades later the L.G. Wright Glass Company remained a significant production contract for Viking. Others, many others, engaged the quality glass and workmanship at Viking to produce lighting goods, glass figurines, limited editions, commemoratives, and more. The private mold work done by Viking for an array of customers would constitute a big book in its own right. That production, acknowledged and important, is not dealt with in any depth here. This is a book largely about the products marketed by and as Viking Glass.

The year 1955 saw reports to the trade that Viking was expanding and improving their production capacities to address increases in sales. (Crockery & Glass Journal, August 1955) As production grew new designs were required to sustain continued growth. Over time a number of people created designs for Viking. The Astra line was designed by Dick Schnacke, a New Martinsville resident. Some others who were engaged as Viking designers in this era were Gail Docktor and, in the later 1970s, Bill Prindle.

In the late 1950s a man arrived at Viking whose reputation as a machinist still draws strong praise from his ex-coworkers. Billy Reinbeau's input was critical in developing the "spun mold" process at Viking. This was an important development at the time and remained so until the factory's closing in the 1990s, decades later. A spun mold used centrifical force to raise hot liquid glass up into the sides of a moving mold. The results were nearly abstract and very graceful fluid forms. Bowls, vases, and other "modern" forms at Viking would utilize spin molds for years to come. From the 1950s Flamenco and early Epic pieces to the small candle votive made by Dalzell-Viking at the end of the factory's production, spun mold technology was critical to Viking production.

Color complements form and design. It was critical to Viking's successes. Color is discussed elsewhere in this book but color at Viking was noted in the trade journals. The "brilliant reddish yellow cast which selenium produces in glass flashed at Viking Glass Co. is in the new decorative pieces it will show in January. C.E. Willis confirms the report frequently voiced in the trade that higher priced glass is wanted: Viking orders reflect this trading up trend, too. New collection emphasizes taller, more impressive objects: decanters, pitchers and vases." (Crockery & Glass Journal, December 1957)

Viking Glass, while heavily into promoting the image of American made, was also busy marketing beyond the states. Viking glass announced Canadian sales agency Bremner & Co. of Vancouver would serve in Alberta & British Columbia. Hopkins- Morgan of Toronto in all other provinces (China, Glass & Tableware, October 1959)

The year 1966 saw a return to the Georgian pattern as the eighteenth century panel cut look was given considerable publicity in ruby, avocado, honey, and bluenique. (China, Glass & Tableware, October 1966) Again Viking marketing focused on color and form as a joined push.

As America had largely abandoned formal dining and moved to informal patios, to dining in front of television sets, to backyard barbecues, and other informal dining arrangements a line of candles for the table and home, less formal than a crystal candelabra, was required. In 1967 Viking introduced "Glimmers," a line of candlelights in the old fairy light tradition. The original in this line, a diamond pattern, was available in a typically broad spectrum of color: clear or frosted in amberina, bluenique, thistle, crystal, honey, and avocado.

At the end of 1969 Viking introduced a set of mushrooms, four in size, and the transition to pop culture was complete. From post World War II elegant dinnerware to the trendy little symbol of psychedelic 1960s America or objects etched with the signs of the Zodiac, Viking was there. Modern, trendy, and cool.

For the purposes of this book 1970 is a turning point. No single event in the company history signals this as a turning point. However, by 1970 the glass-collecting world had emerged; collectors and not just decorators and hostesses were the consumers. The 1970 catalog included new directions and is the last production looked at in this book. As 1970 ended, so does this part of the story of Viking Glass, the rest of the tale waiting for another day.

Marketing, Catalogs, and The Viking Glass Booklets

Viking utilized a nation-wide network of independent sales representatives (reps) to market the glass. These firms generally maintained showrooms for the wholesale trade in major cities where the glass could be viewed and orders placed. Viking reps were called to an annual meeting in New Martinsville where they were presented with a showing of samples or prototypes of new glass for possible inclusion in the next year's line. They had a strong voice in the decision to include or exclude these samples from the coming years production. The pieces the reps liked appeared in the next Viking catalog. It is certainly true the reps were not always right.

Pieces made as samples but that were not "voted" into the line as marketable by the sales reps were often sold in the factory outlet store in New Martinsville. This selection of the design process resulted in some wonderfully unexpected and limited production objects. A piece was not likely made as a single unique object due to cost, likelihood of imperfection, etc. Instead, a small but not insignificant number of each possible line item was made for consideration. Today these "not put into production" pieces are out there on the secondary market, having been sold to the traveling and tourist public through the factory outlet. The factory outlet store opened in New Martinsville in 1958. Shops titled "factory outlets" later operated in Cambridge, Ohio, and other places.

Viking ex-employees have repeatedly told us that often a piece intended as a vase or bowl or some other form might become oddly shaped or somehow "flawed" in the art of hand crafting. A "mistake" such as this was seldom destroyed but completed if possible and sent to the outlet to be sold as a one-of-a-kind piece. This practice has not been unique to Viking over time and it explains the existence of an endless number of unique and interesting variations on the more recognizable production and "order filling" ware.

Viking used only paper labels to mark the glass. This was a significant marketing tool creating name identity. At the end of Viking's time, under the ownership of Dalzell-Viking, there were a few piece marked in the glass. We had hopes of creating a dating system for Viking found with paper labels intact. Dating production based on the color of the labels would have been a great help; there are several types and colors of labels and many people attributed various meanings to those. Several ex-employees, management folks, and the outlet manager all agreed the color of a label is no indication of age or any other designation. They agreed that putting a label on was important at times, but which label was not important. Apparently rolls of various colors and ages were abundant in the factory and used based more on access to a roll, any roll, of stickers. That the first and earliest paper labels were red and gold metallic looking is something everyone who had worked there agreed on. With time these may appear pink. We also heard of rolls of stickers being sold at the annual warehouse sales (thus possibly being later attached to anything) and of old rolls being found near the end of time and being both used and sold/given away. We have observed, and in some cases sadly purchased, interesting items with Viking paper labels that we later learned were not Viking but simply bore the label. The label message: buyers beware.

Price lists and catalogs are invaluable tools in identifying products and assigning time of production. Early Viking catalogs are loose leaf in a gray cover held together by three brass clips. This "loose leaf" nature creates apparent problems.

Of the early catalogs found and examined, which are four in number, all include the same initial title page which reads Treasured American Glass Created By Viking Glass. The reverse of the page is a "letter" from the company stating, "in 1902 the Viking Glass Company first opened its doors." Near the end of the letter it reads, "it is well to remember that in forty-five years Viking has grown…" From this one might assume, and others have, that forty-five plus two and this is a 1947 catalog. There surely were catalogs bearing this initial page for use in 1947. We believe, of the four catalogs bearing this identical text, none are from 1947. We viewed these catalogs, looking closely at which pages had been compiled into each loose leaf page binder. We matched those compilations of pages to the price lists and the trade journal notices of new products, what was in production at certain times, etc. We then can accurately date the early and seemingly complex catalogs we used to within a year or two and in some events to an exact year.

The earliest catalog we viewed is January 1948 with pages 40a, 40b, etc. to supplement it to 1949. The next is the January 1950 catalog, then the same catalog supplemented to 1951, and finally a 1956 catalog. This last catalog matches the price list dates for that year, removing doubt. Please see the bibliography notes for more on these and later catalogs used.

Viking used a booklet about how glass was made for decades as a major promotion and marketing tool. It was popular, and it seems to have worked amazingly well.

The first of these found bears a 1950 copyright. The 46-page booklet is titled, "…From American Sands and Artists' Hands." This tells a short history of glass but predominately explains the process of making handmade glass. It includes thirty-seven wonderful period black and white photos. Fred Gardner Company, Inc., a New York advertising agency, produced this booklet. (*China, Glass and Decorative Accessories*, September 1950)

In 1968 a new edition of forty-four pages was issued illustrating and describing how handmade glass was crafted. This edition was titled "Beauty is Glass from Viking." It had large photos and some color images (*China, Glass and Tableware*, November 1968)

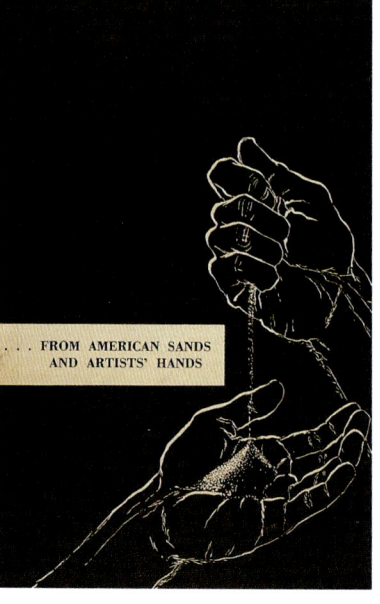

Shown is the 5-1/4" x 8-1/4" dramatic black and white cover to the heavily illustrated forty-six page 1950 booklet "…From American sands and Artist's Hands." A superb illustrated guide to handmade glass processes today as well as half a century ago. This edition is valued at $15-25.

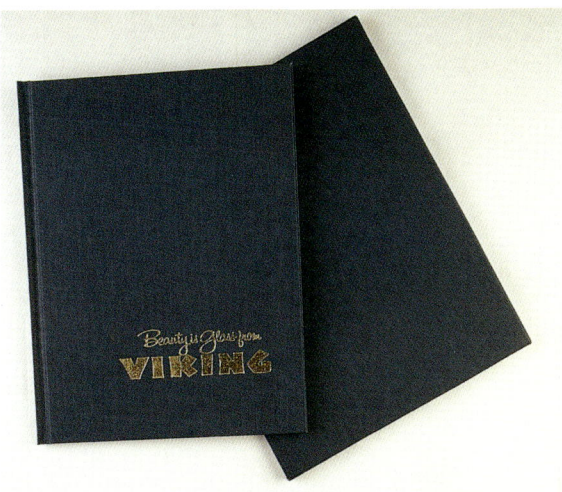

An elegant edition of the promotional book continued in use at Viking. This 8-1/2" x 11" 1967 version is shown here in a cloth bound and gold embossed cover with cloth bound slip cover. An obvious presentation piece intended to impress. Paperback edition, $6-12; as shown, $30-45.

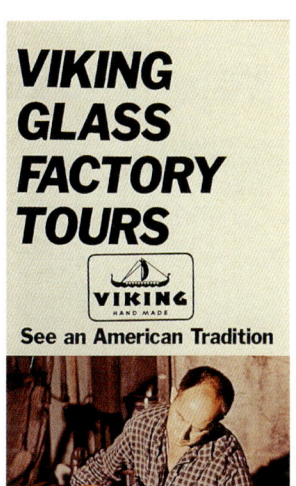

One of several folding pamphlets produced over time promoting the factory outlet and tours to "See an American Tradition." Collecting the paper memorabilia about glass is a growing part of the glass-collecting world. Illustrated is a highly skilled artisan hand finishing the oblong pressed Epic line bowl.

The most commonly found red paper label applied to Viking glass was used over several decades and is no specific indicator of time.

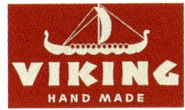

Viking was one of the leaders in elaborate educational materials produced to sell the glass. This ad notes the free booklet will be promoted in *Better Homes and Gardens, House and Garden,* and *Living for Young Homemakers. Crockery & Glass Journal,* October 1950.

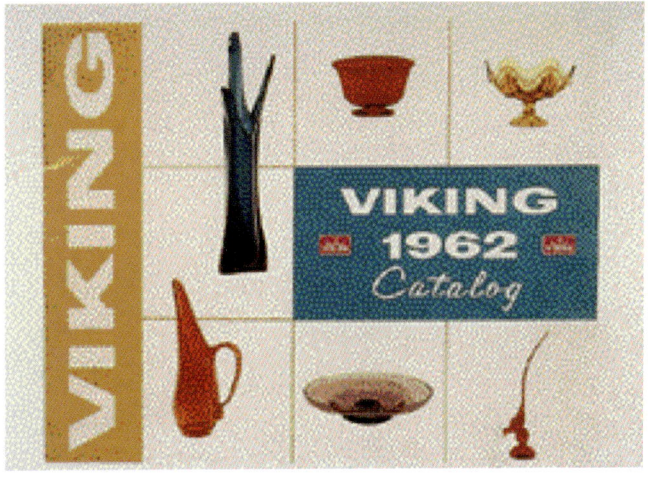

The cover to the 1962 Viking catalog shows products that make an extreme departure from the Victorian table lamps produced a short fifty years earlier and shown above in the example of the lamp.

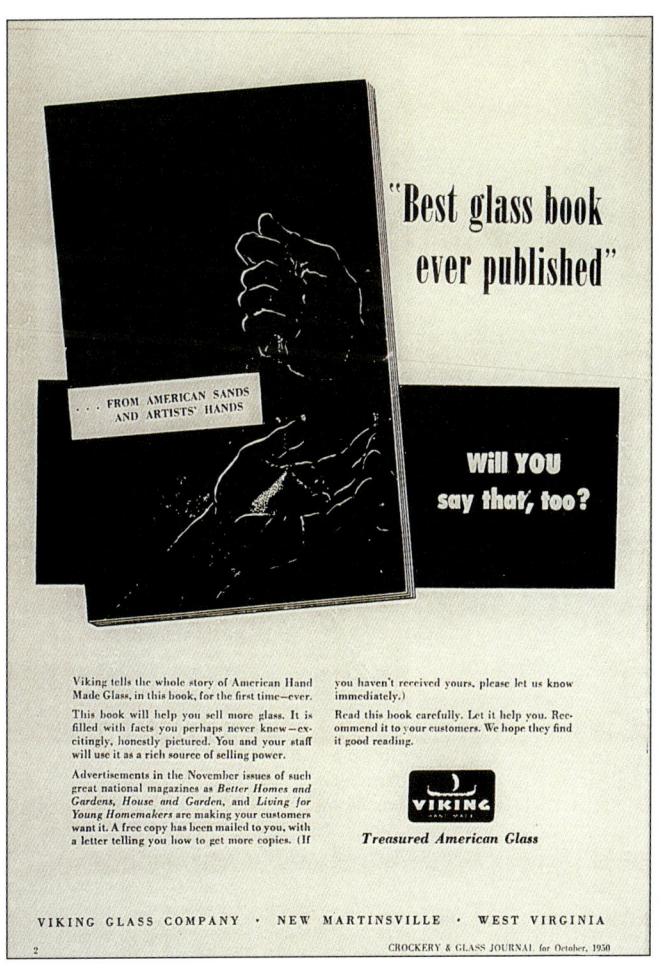

"Best glass book ever published"

Will YOU say that, too?

Viking tells the whole story of American Hand Made Glass, in this book, for the first time—ever.

This book will help you sell more glass. It is filled with facts you perhaps never knew—excitingly, honestly pictured. You and your staff will use it as a rich source of selling power.

Advertisements in the November issues of such great national magazines as *Better Homes and Gardens, House and Garden,* and *Living for Young Homemakers* are making your customers want it. A free copy has been mailed to you, with a letter telling you how to get more copies. (If you haven't received yours, please let us know immediately.)

Read this book carefully. Let it help you. Recommend it to your customers. We hope they find it good reading.

Treasured American Glass

VIKING GLASS COMPANY · NEW MARTINSVILLE · WEST VIRGINIA

CROCKERY & GLASS JOURNAL for October, 1950

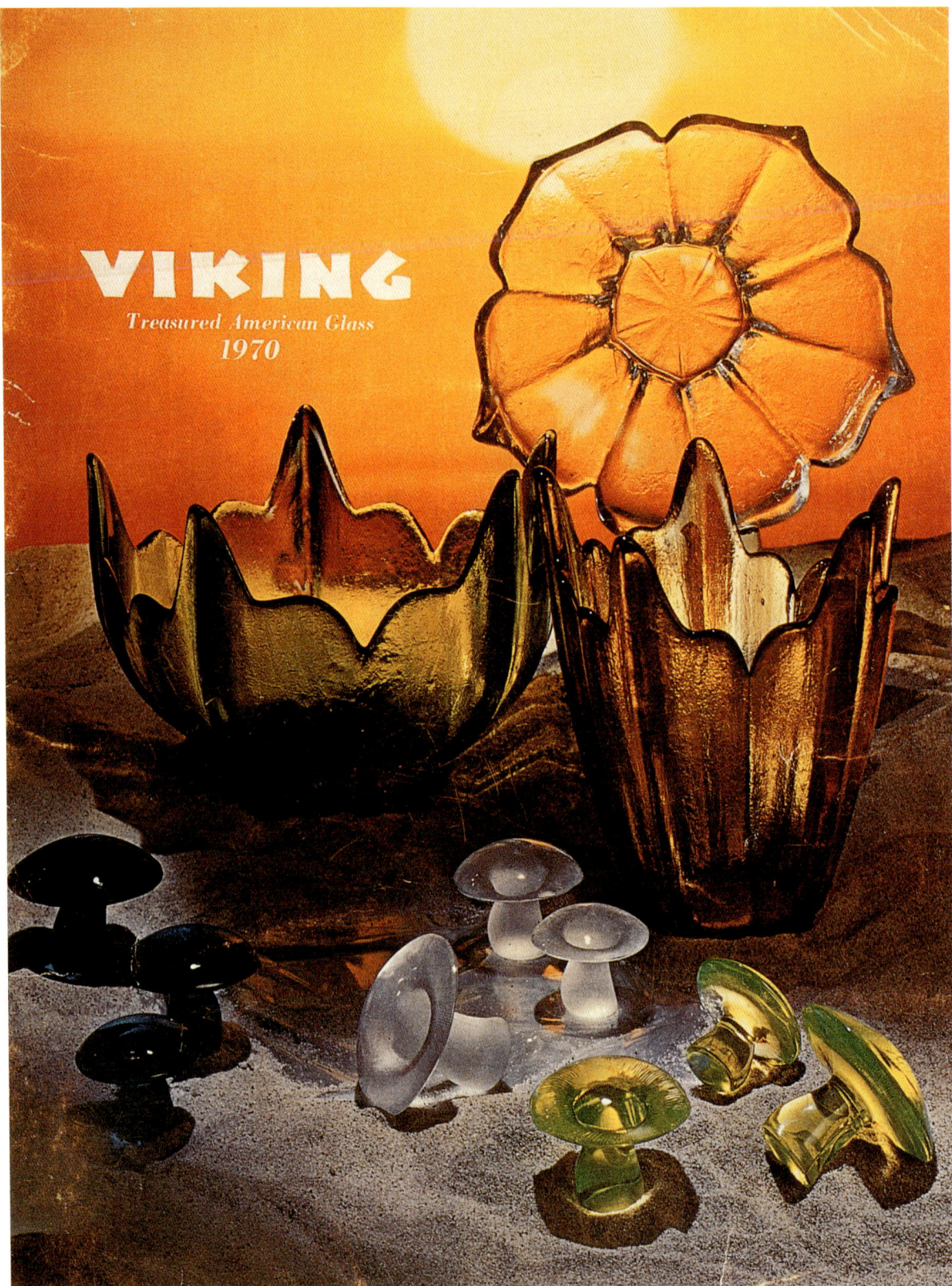

The cover to the 1970 catalog, the last year of Viking production covered in this book.

COLOR: The VIKING Magic of 1944-1970

Color was a flowing river of change at Viking. Thirty-three different color names have been identified as used by Viking in the twenty-five-year period of this book. A number of other descriptive color names are found in trade journals and in descriptions of Viking products. For this book I have avoided use of those descriptive only color references and included the color names as used by Viking Glass. When Viking began production, the style of product was the same or similar to that of the former New Martinsville Glass. A crystal glass, in the modern, heavy Scandinavian/Viking mode was the primary product. To date no reference to color is found in the mid- to late 1940s literature. This is not the same as saying no color was made. Recall that World War II had dramatically limited access to resources of all kinds across America. The possibility of Viking not having had access to color imparting chemicals in the 1940s is very likely, dictating a crystal dominated line of production. Couple this materials availability with the idea the company had marketed of modern, Swedish/ Viking looking heavy colorless crystal in 1940s advertisements, color was not dominant even if present in the production offering.

The 1940s era absence or limited use of color was shortly to change for Viking. The very first mention of color in the dozens and dozens of 1940s Viking ads found is for a punch set where the offering was for all crystal or crystal with cobalt or ruby cup handles. (*House Beautiful*, November 1948)

The 1950 company literature reviewed included crystal, sky blue, cobalt blue, ebony, evergreen, and ruby. The color pallet was limited to six colors. Included were two items in amber and crystal combination, a 5" sweetheart swan handled dish and a six" handled basket.

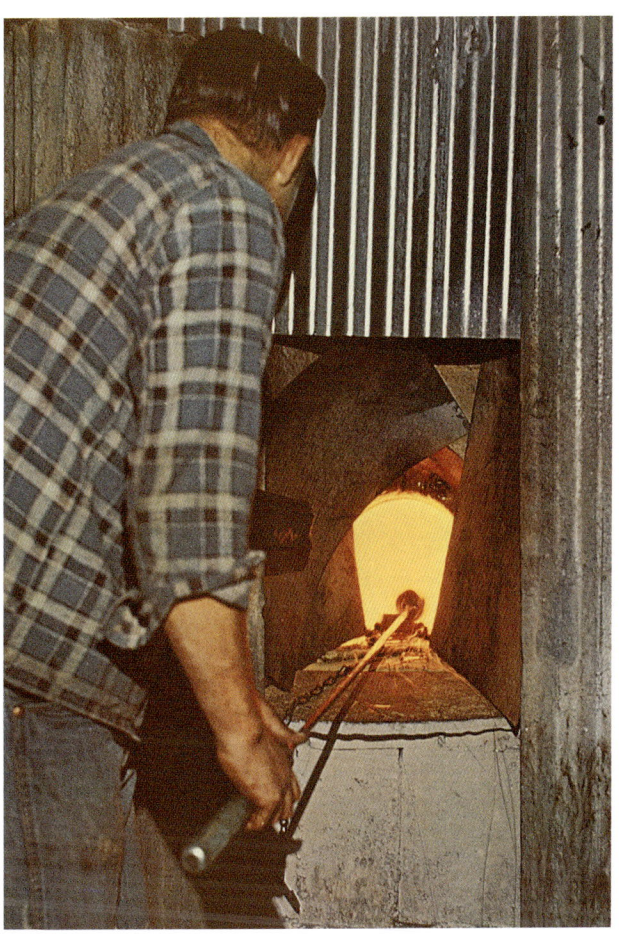

A captivating color image from one of the Viking promotional booklets shows the gatherer reaching into the 2,000 degree plus pot to gather molten glass that is then poured in the glass mold for pressing.

In 1953 the colors offered numbered eleven: amber, amethyst, charcoal, cherry glo, colonial blue, crystal, ebony, evergreen, harvest gold, olive green, and ruby.

By 1956 seventeen (17) colors appear in the company price list, an all time high for the number of Viking color offerings in the period of this book and possibly all times. Note that a color, once satinized, took on a new name and was counted as a different and distinct color. For filling orders and sales it indeed constituted a "new color." The colors in production as of 1956 were:

Amber, amethyst, amethyst mist, blue mist, charcoal, cherry glo, cherry pink, cobalt blue, colonial blue, crystal, ebony, emerald green (sometimes cited as just emerald), glamour gold, glamour green, gray mist (charcoal satinized), midnight (ebony satinized), and ruby.

Even with this wide 1956 selection, some of the most recognizable Viking colors like avocado, bluenique, honey and persimmon – all very popular in the 1960s – had not appeared yet.

By 1964 the color choices from Viking had fallen to a mere seven: amberina, avocado green, bluenique, crystal, honey, persimmon, and ruby. By 1968 the number was little changed, with the addition of Thistle bringing the offerings to eight. In 1969 Amberina and Thistle were discontinued and Lime Green had been added. Throughout the late 1950s, and into the 1970s period, amber and avocado were the popular decorating colors and interior choice for American homes. Accordingly these colors sold well in glass and certainly sold well in the Viking Glass line. Today it is amber and avocado, those originally popular colors, that are most easily found and generally most modestly priced.

In 1970, the last year covered in the scope of this book, ten colors were offered by Viking: avocado green, bluenique, brown, crystal, charcoal, cobalt, honey, lime, persimmon, and ruby.

Viking colors identified as used in the 1944-1970 period include:

Brown

BROWN is found mentioned in 1970; this is not amber but a true brown. See the yellow section below to explore amber production.

DRIFTWOOD is a brown slag looking milk glass illustrated in a 1957 catalog. It is a surface treatment fixed to the hot glass by oxidation.

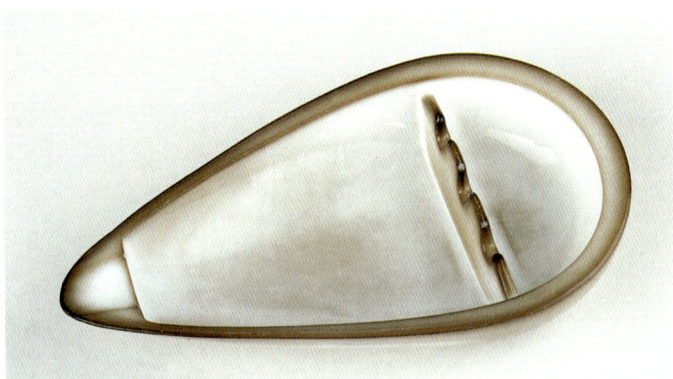

Driftwood color.

Blacks

EBONY, Viking's black glass, was produced from 1949 to 1956 by Viking and later reintroduced by Dalzell-Viking.

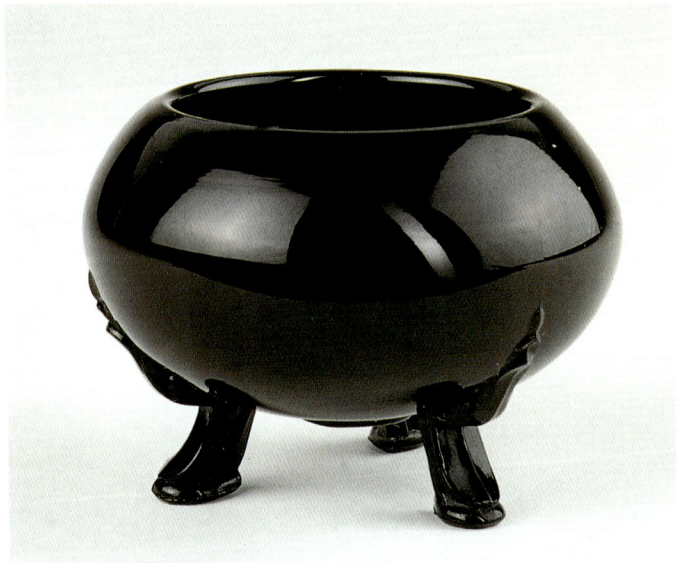

Ebony color.

MIDNIGHT Black Satin glass, a frosted product produced in 1954-1956 only.

CHARCOAL was made intermittently from 1953-1970. Collectors and dealers have incorrectly called this smoke, but it is a gray glass and not smoke-amber.

GRAY MIST, charcoal frosted or satin, and appeared only in 1956. Uncommon.

Blues

COBALT was begun in 1949 and was in and out of production through 1970. It was again popular with much of the later Dalzell-Viking production.

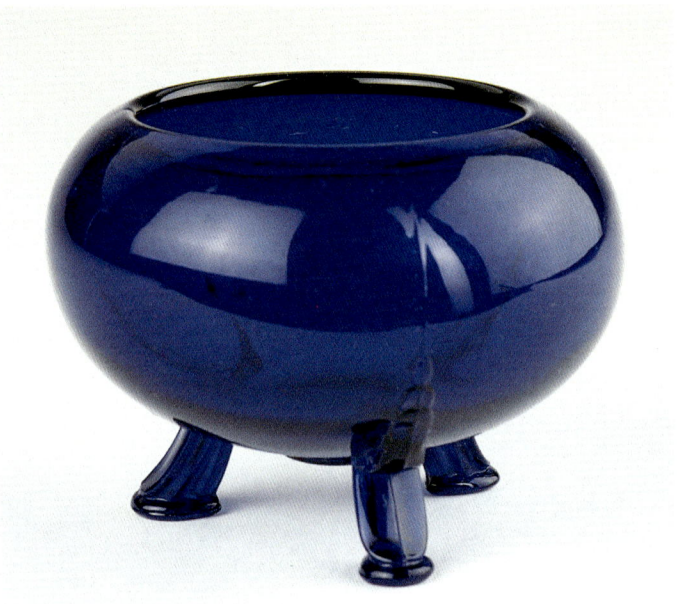

Cobalt blue color.

COLONIAL BLUE was made from 1953 or earlier and through at least 1956.

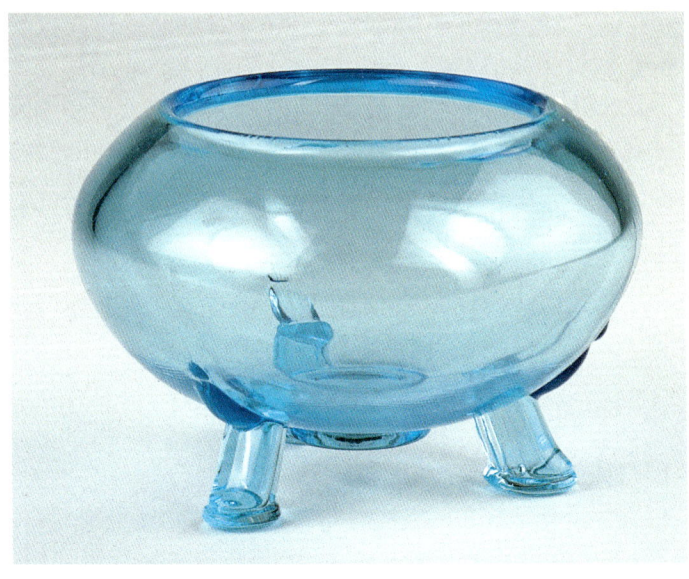

Colonial blue color.

BLUE MIST was produced in 1956 only and is a frosted or satin blue.

SKY BLUE was in production in the mid-1940s and until circa 1950.

BLUENIQUE is a created word to describe the unique coloration of a Viking vibrant blue introduced in 1958 that remained in production through 1970.

Crystal

From the earliest days, when New Martinsville first used the Viking brand name in the early 1940s, until the end of the factory's run, crystal was in active production for some objects.

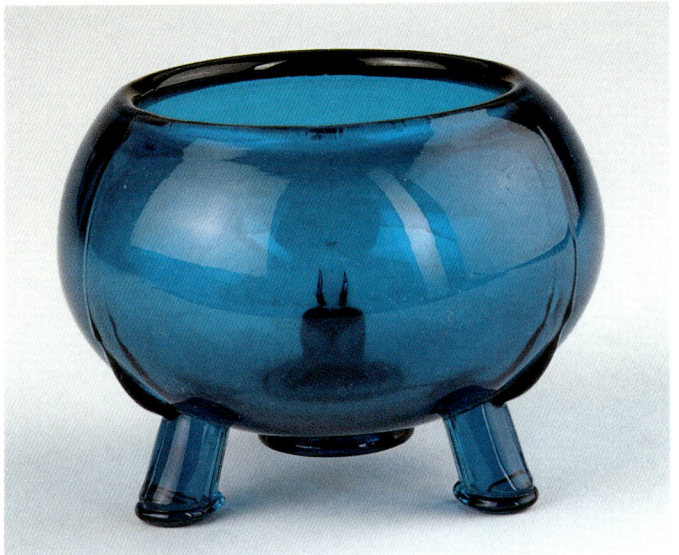

Bluenique color.

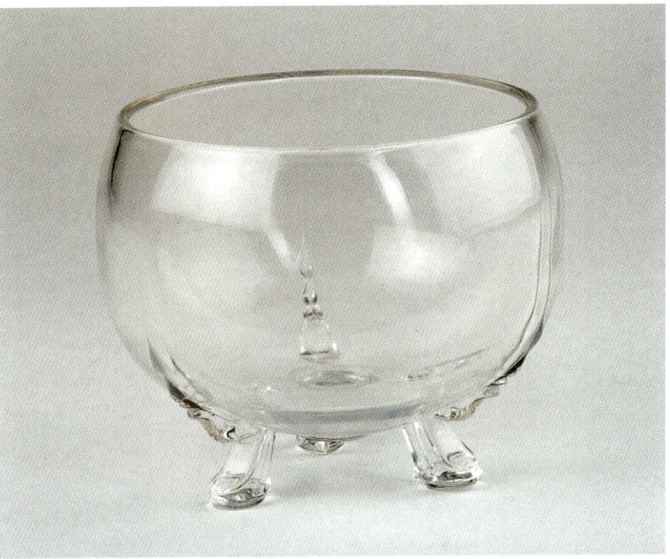

Crystal color.

BLUE MILK GLASS is an uncommon color for which the original Viking name is not presently know. Using the few pieces found in the color as indicators, it appears to date somewhere between 1955 and 1962.

Greens

EVERGREEN, a dark forest green, was introduced in 1949 and produced through at least 1953.

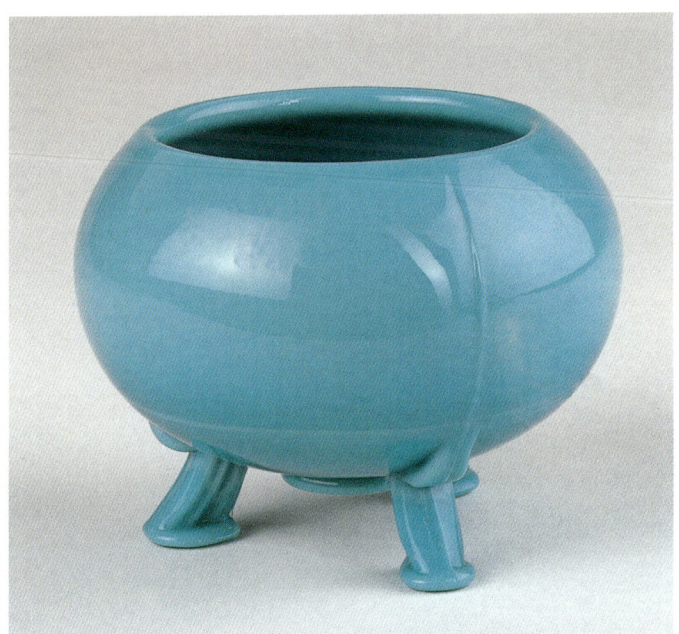

Blue milk glass color.

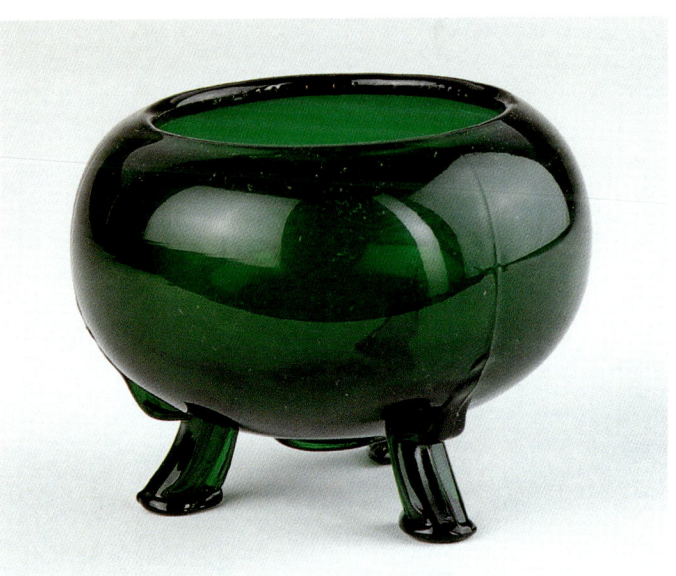

Evergreen color.

OLIVE GREEN is found only in the 1953 price list.

GLAMOUR GREEN is frosted or satin green and was made in 1956.

AVOCADO was made from 1964 until 1970.

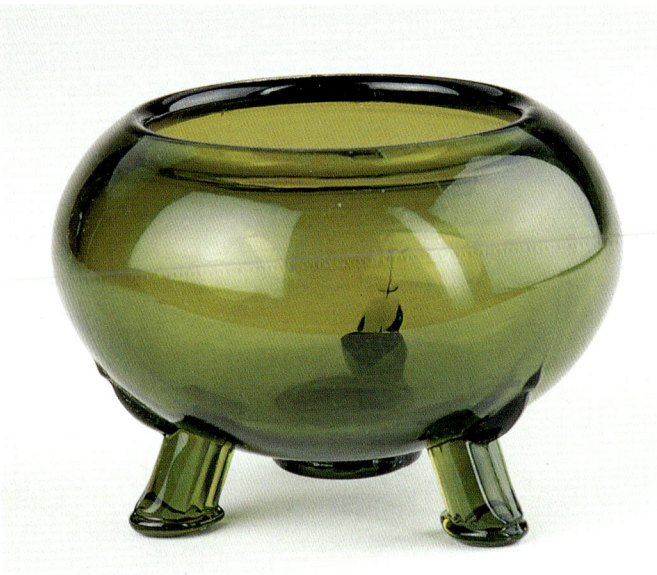

Olive green color.

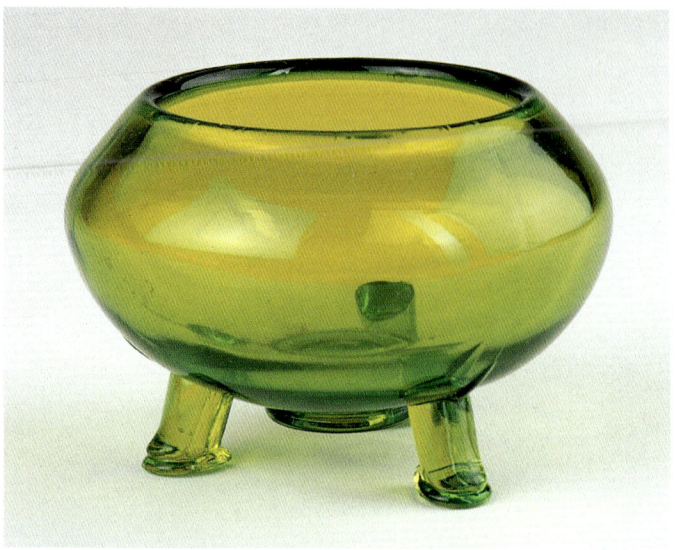

Avocado green color.

EMERALD GREEN is the name used for a brilliant, medium green from 1956 - 1959.

LIME was the new green introduced in 1969.

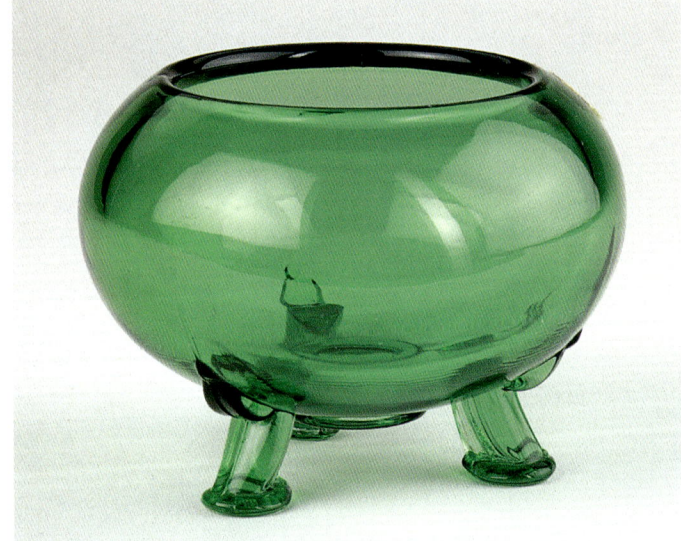

Emerald green color.

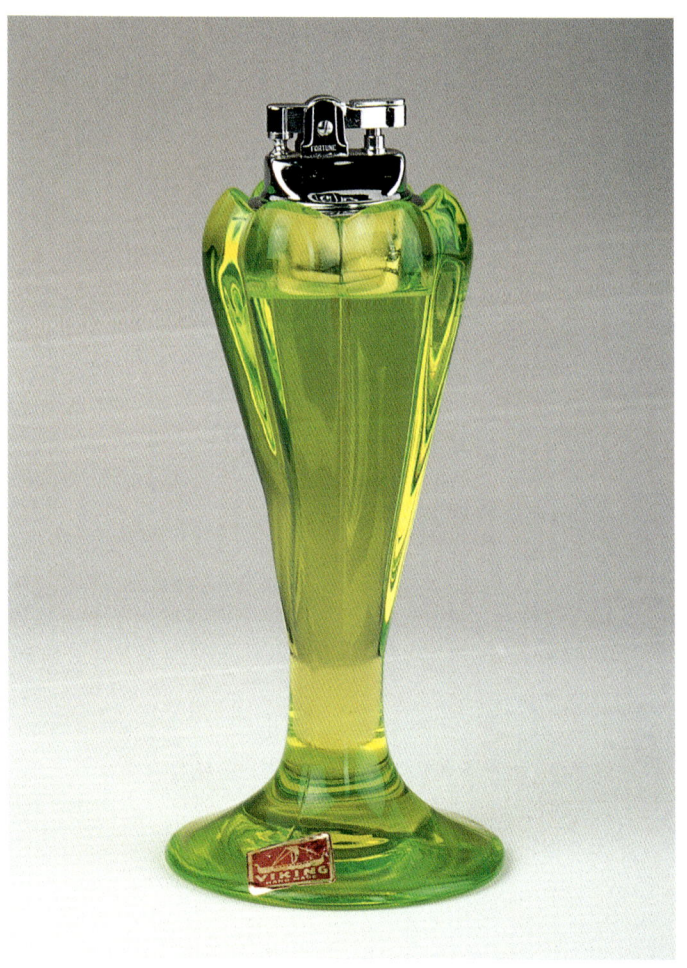

Lime Green.

NILE GREEN is found in the color production in 1964. In 1964, the same color becomes Viking Green.

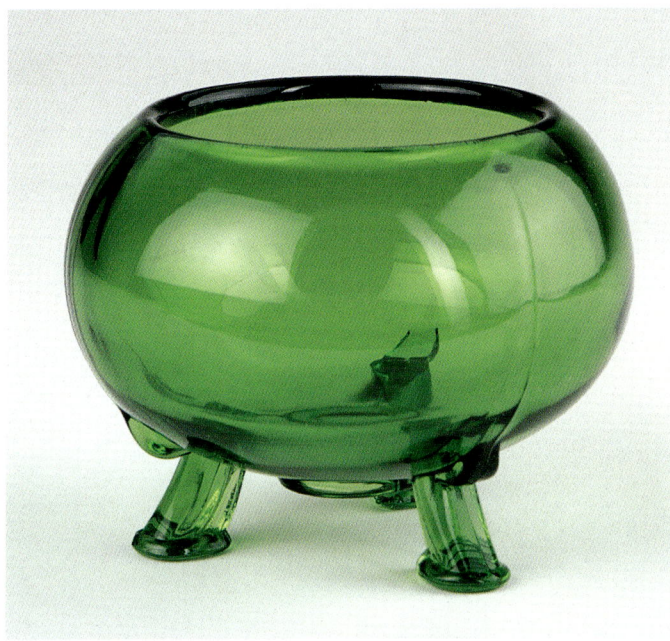

Nile green color.

VIKING GREEN is the 1964 renaming of the color Nile Green.

Milk Glass

MILK GLASS was the opaque white glass produced, beginning in 1958, through at least 1960 when it was still appearing in the catalog.

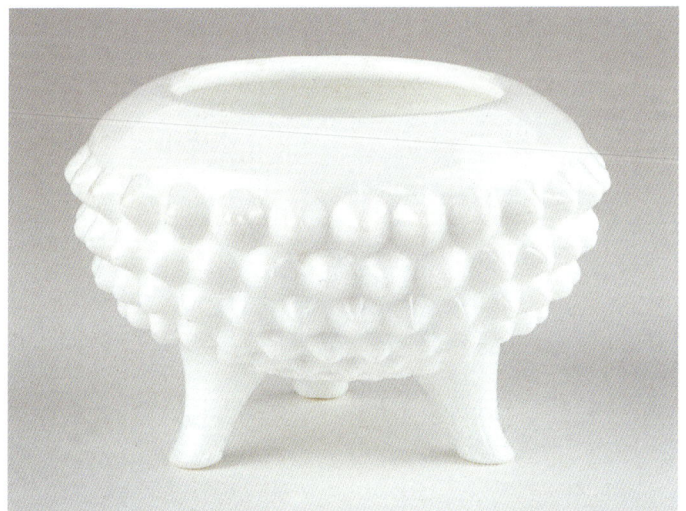

Milk glass color.

Oranges

AMBERINA is in the line from 1957 (C&GJ Dec 1957) through 1968 and is the historic shading of amber and orange-red. Do not confuse ruby glass that retains some vestiges of yellow-amber due to incomplete flashing to ruby with Amberina. Amberina requires two distinct color bands be present: yellow-amber to red-orange. Distinction between Amberina and second quality ruby can be difficult at times.

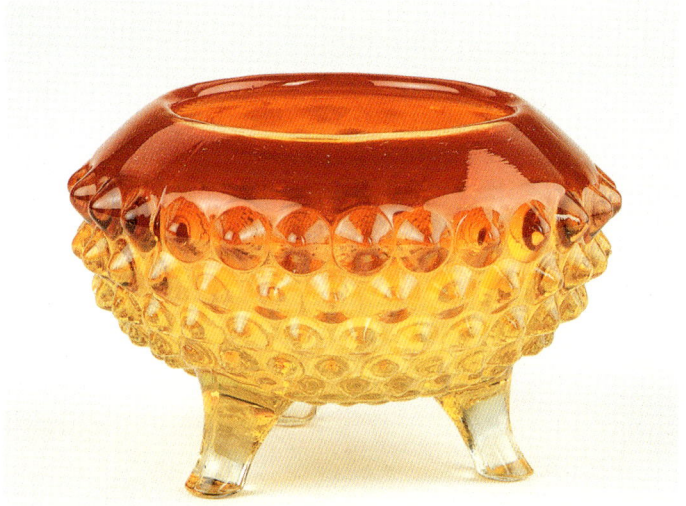

Amberina color.

PERSIMMON is one of Viking's most recognized colors of all times. It was produced from 1958 through 1970 and is a bright, almost radiant orange.

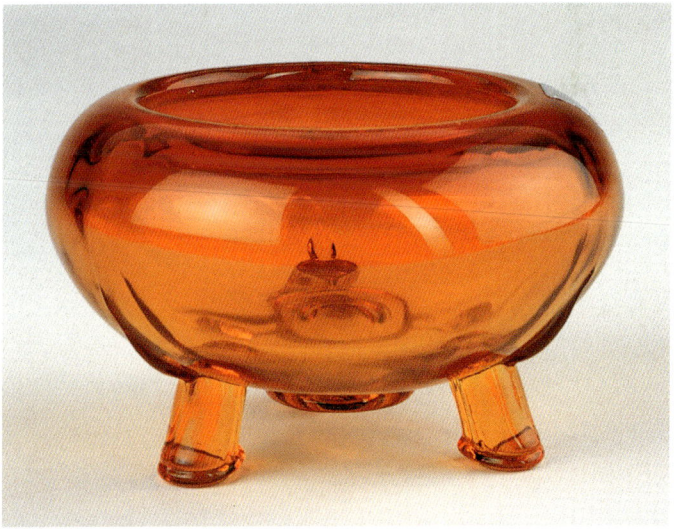

Persimmon color.

TAWNY is the term used in 1958 to describe Viking's Amberina.

Pinks
CHERRY GLO is a traditional pink made first in circa 1953.

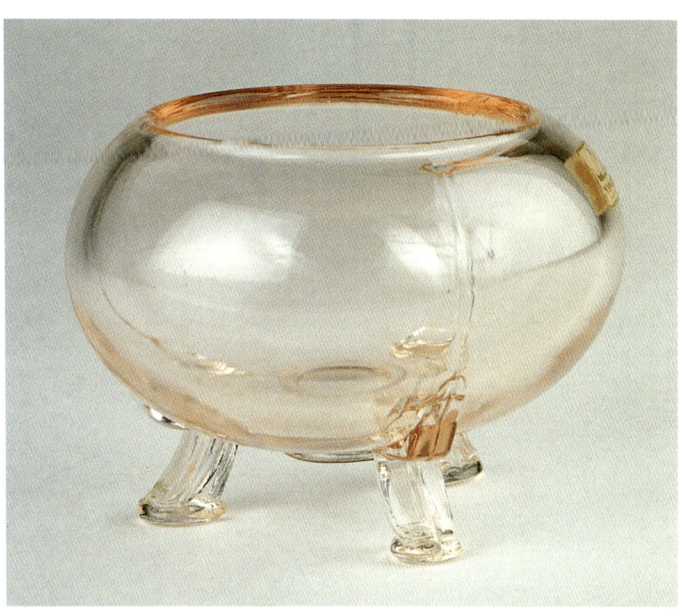

Cherry Glo color.

CHERRY PINK is a frosted or satin pink made from 1953-1956.

TEABERRY was a new color in 1961 and is a brilliant pink with a hint of violet found in very few items.

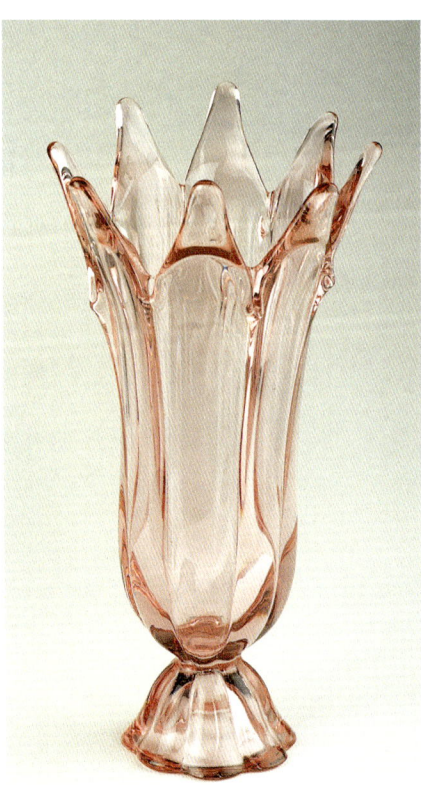

Teaberry color.

Purples
AMETHYST was produced from 1953 through 1958.

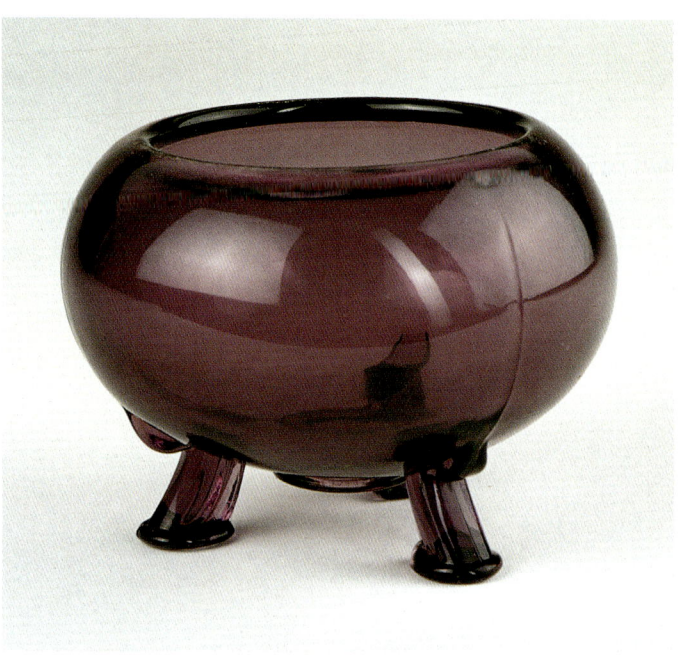

Amethyst color.

AMETHYST MIST was a satin or frosted amethyst made in 1956.

THISTLE was mentioned in trade journals in 1967 and on the 1968 price list. It is a brilliant yet soft hue and no doubt was named to reflect the almost pastel purple blossom of the thistle plant. Thistle was discontinued in 1969, making it a short production run and hard to find today.

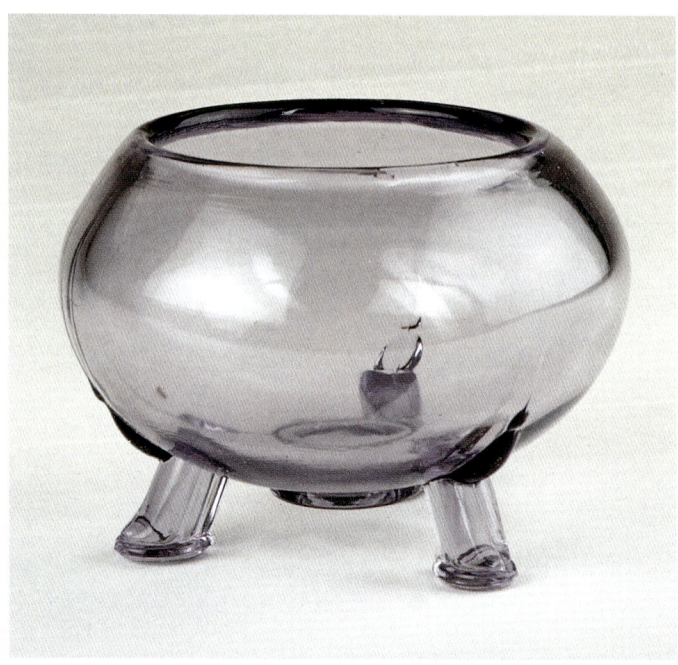

Thistle color.

Red

RUBY was made by Viking from 1949 throughout the period of this book and beyond.

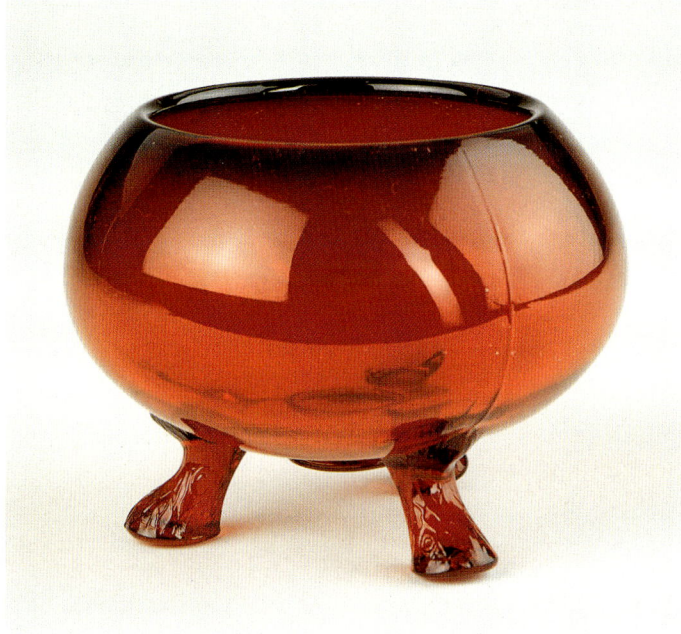

Ruby color.

Yellow

AMBER was made by Viking from 1950 on into the 1970s. While Viking was good at changing color names and keeping the same color, Amber seems to have changed color, becoming less dark and more of a topaz - amber around 1951. The color name, however, was not changed.

HARVEST GOLD was the name of a color introduced in 1953 – it is close to a Vaseline color in its tendency toward yellow and brightness. It has been called a bright canary yellow at times. It resembles the Morgantown Glass color Pineapple of roughly the same period.

Harvest gold color.

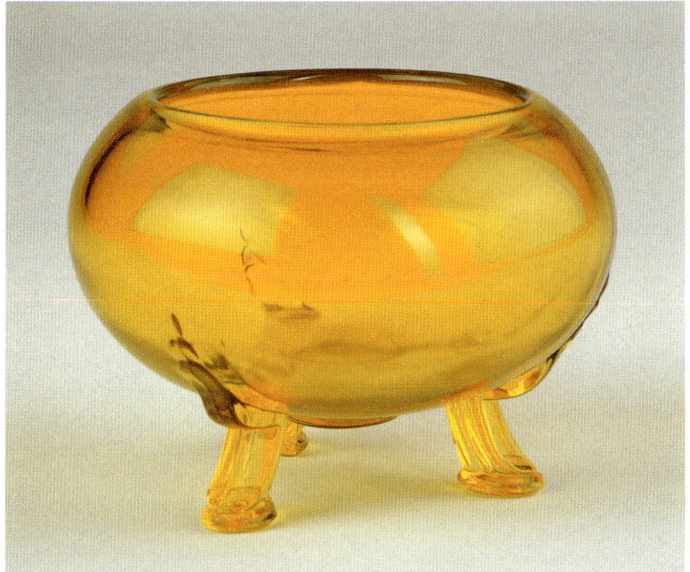

GLAMOR GOLD was the satin or frosted amber as listed on the 1956 price list.

HONEY was noted as new in 1961 and found through 1968.

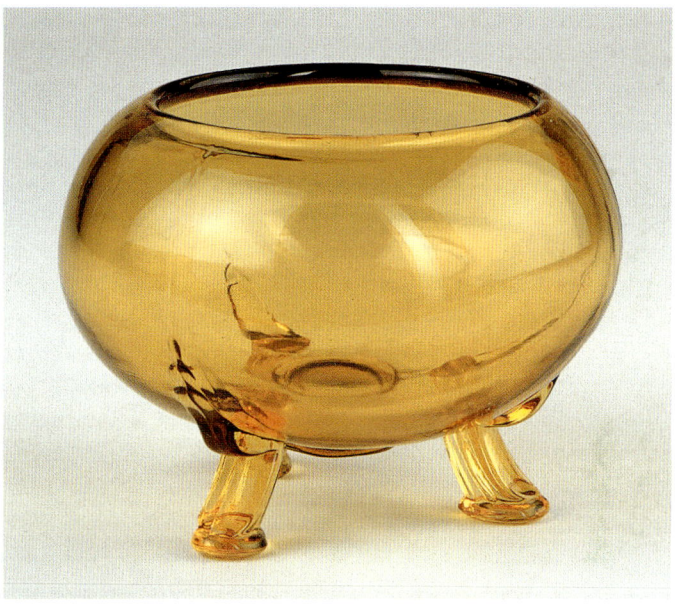

Honey color.

The Products by Shape

Animals and Figurals

Viking Glass's inheritance in 1944 included a legacy of pressed glass animals and figurals from New Martinsville Glass. Among the assets Viking assumes are the molds of New Martinsville Glass. Until the last days of Dalzell-Viking decades later, the use, re-use and re-re-use of these same molds prove a profitable asset for the glass companies that work from this same factory site regardless of the company name.

While the continued use of a number of glass animal and figural molds was a blessing to the profit margins of the company, it is a modern day curse to collectors. That an item would be in the line, out of the line, in again and out and so on, repeating that pattern over time, makes easy dating of Viking/New Martinsville/Dalzell-Viking animals very difficult. Here is an attempt to order and understand production periods for different shapes.

Viking never used some New Martinsville Glass Co. figural forms. The reasons are unknown, but Police Dog lamp base, Elephant forms cigarette box and incense burner, the figural woman flower frog, and others do not get reissued. Some others lay dormant for years only to be reissued much later. Additionally Viking made a significant number of glass animals using molds owned by others. This "private mold work" was a critical part of production and income for any glass house. At Viking the use of animal molds has always created interest. James Measell, in his book on New Martinsville Glass, cites passages from a mold shop logbook of privately owned molds coming, going, and being repaired at Viking. For the purposes of this book, these "Not Viking Products" are not listed. What follows is our best effort to create a simplified list of the Viking Animals of the 1944-1970 period:

Bear, baby #487, 3": 1945
Bear, mama #448, 4": 1945
Bear, papa #489, 4": 1945
Bird, ashtray #7030: 1970
Bird, long tail #1310, 12", Epic colors and crystal: 1961, 1970
Bird, long tail #1311, 9-1/2", Epic color and crystal: 1961, 1970
Bird, candy box and cover #3112, 6", Epic colors: c.1962, 1970
Bird on round base #6807 Epic colors: 1968
Cat #1322, 8", Epic colors and crystal: 1960s
Chicks #667, 1": 1945
Dog # 1323, 8", Epic colors and crystal: 1960s
Dog, police #733, 5", crystal only: 1945
Duck, small on round base #1316, 5": 1960s, 1970
Duck, small no base: 1960s

Duck, large #1317, 9", Epic colors: 1960s, 1970
Duck, candy box and cover #1313, 6", Epic colors: 1960s
Ducks, pair #6712 "fighting" Epic colors and crystal: 1968
Egret, long necked #1315, 9-1/2" to 12", Epic colors: early 1960s, 1970
Elephant #710, 5": 1945, out of line in 1948, back in 1950
Fish #1320, 10": early 1960s
Fish, ashtray #436, 4": 1945
Fish, angelfish #1301, 6-1/2": c.1960
Hen #669, 5", crystal only: 1945
Horse #1302 (from Paden City Glass Co. mold) crystal only
Mushroom, jumbo #6939 Epic colors and crystal: introduced late 1969
Mushroom, large #6942 Epic colors and crystal: introduced late 1969
Mushroom, medium #6941 Epic colors and crystal: introduced late 1969
Mushroom, small #6940 Epic colors and crystal: introduced late 1969
Owl #1318, 4-1/2"
Owl ashtray #6944 Epic colors: 1969
Owl Glimmer #6900 Epic colors: 1969
Pelican #761, 8" tall, crystal only: 1948, out of line in 1950
Pig, large #762, 4" x 6-1/2", crystal only: 1948
Pig, small #763, 1", crystal only: 1948
Porpoise #766, 6", crystal only: 1948, out of line in 1950, reintroduced much later
Rabbit, large #764, 5" x 2-1/2", crystal only: 1948
Rabbit, small (3 shapes) #765, 1": 1948
Rabbit, "thumper" #6008
Rooster #668, 7-1/2", crystal only :1945
Rooster #1321, 9-1/2", Epic colors :1960s
Seal, baby #435, 3-1/2" wide, crystal only: 1945
Seal, #452, 5" wide, crystal only: 1945
Seal, with candle ball #452, 5" wide, 7" tall, crystal only: 1945
Ship, bookend #3499, 5-1/2", crystal only: 1945, out of line in 1948, back in 1950
Squirrel with base #670, 5-1/2" tall, crystal only: 1945
Squirrel without base #674, 4-1/2" tall, crystal only: 1945
Stove, glimmer pot bellied #7000: 1970
Swan #1324, 6-1/2": early 1960s
Swan #6946: 1970
Swan handle, oval bowl #687/1S, 12-1/2": 1948
Swan handle, oval celery #951/1S, 10-1/2": 1948
Swan handle, oval pickle #956/1S, 7": 1948
Swan handle, dish #974, 5": 1950, 1955
Swan handle, bowl Princess pattern #5203/1S: 1952
Swan handle, bowl Princess pattern #5208/1S: 1952

Swan handle, bowl Princess pattern #5212/1S: 1952
Swan handle, bowl Princess pattern #5215/1S: 1952
Swan handle, ashtray #412/1S, 4": 1948
Wolfhound #716, 7", crystal only: 1945

    The dates after each object indicate only a specific time when we have verified that piece was in production. It does not reflect the only period of production but a reference as to period.

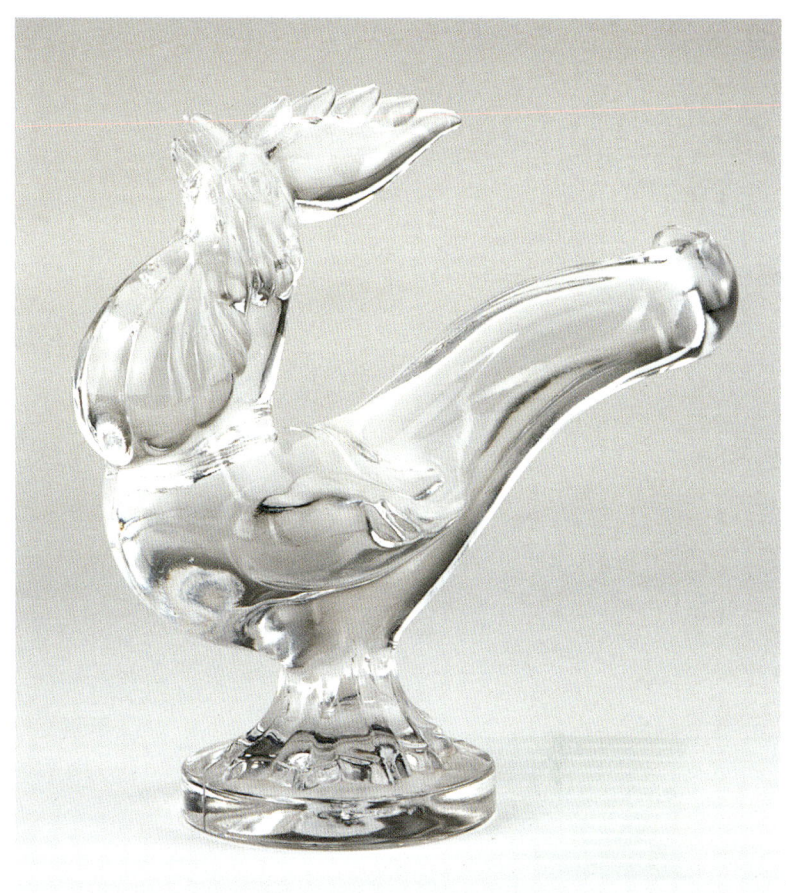

Rooster #668 crystal 7-1/2", $85-125.

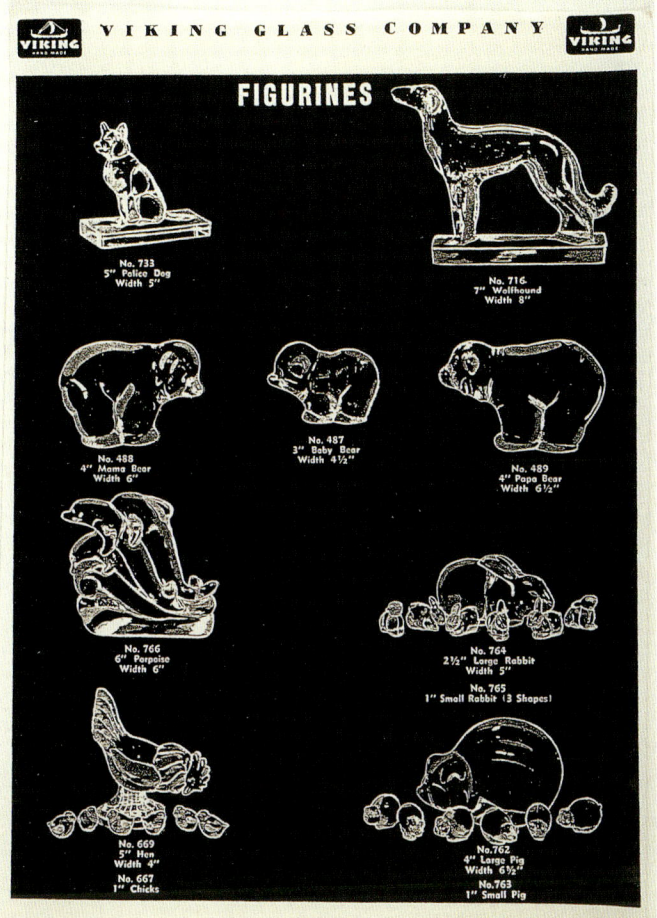

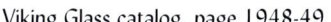

Viking Glass catalog, page 1948-49.

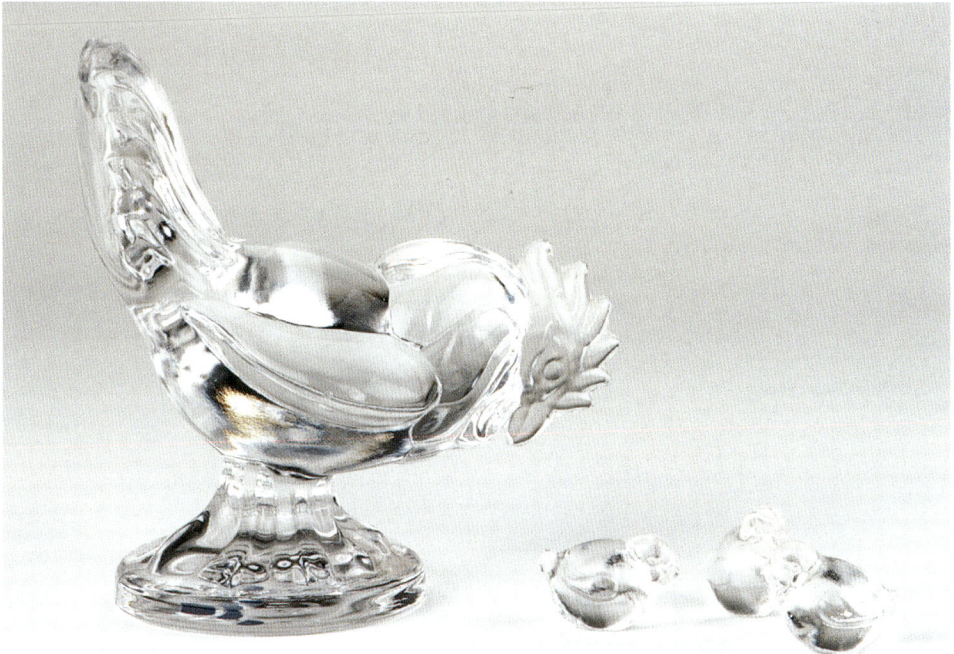

Hen #669 crystal 5", $65-90; three chicks #667 crystal 1", $35-45 each. *Collection of Bob Page.*

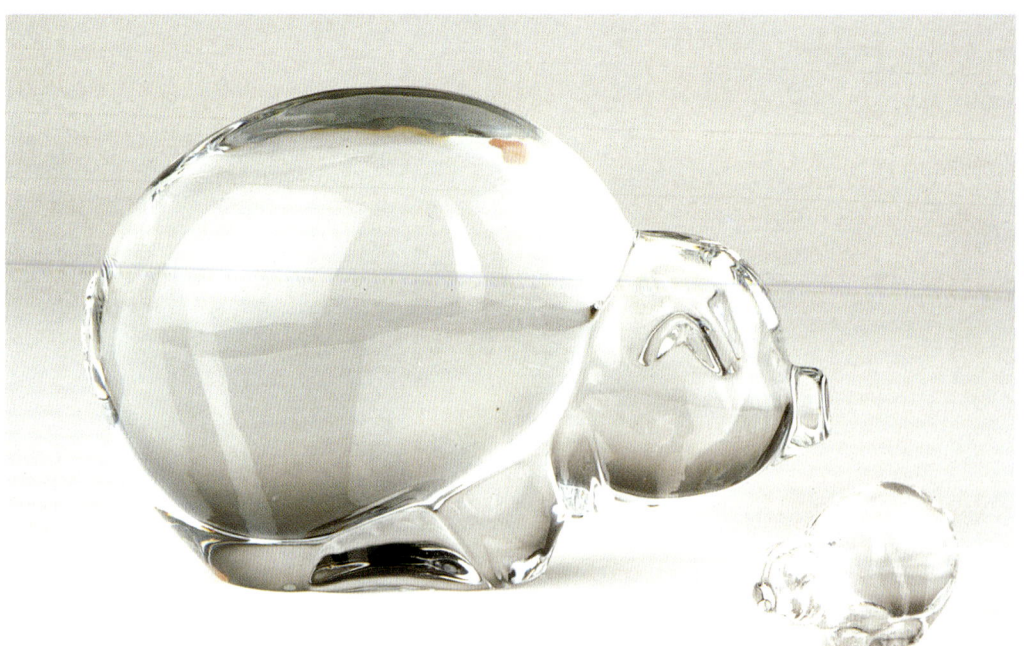

Large Pig #762 crystal 6-1/2",
$95-145; small pig #763 crystal
1", $45-65.

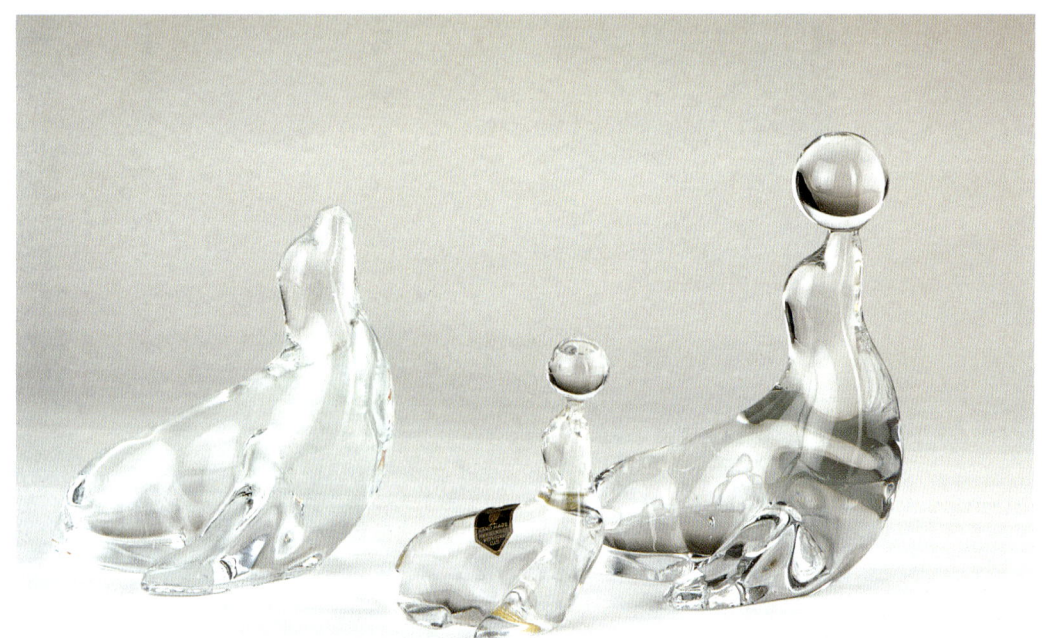

Large seal with no ball, a product made after the period of this book. Note the
variances in the tone of the crystal between this and the two others. Baby seal #435
crystal with original New Martinsville Viking label, $58-78; Large seal with ball #452
crystal 7", $75-95. Be alert to later reissues.

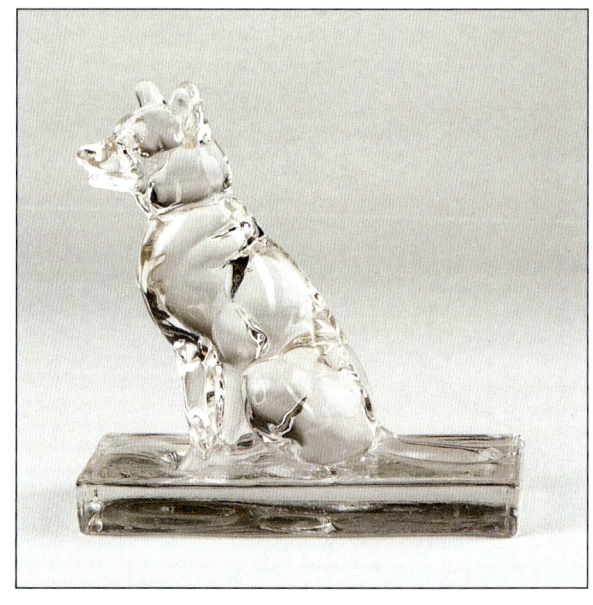

Police dog #733 crystal 5", $65-95.

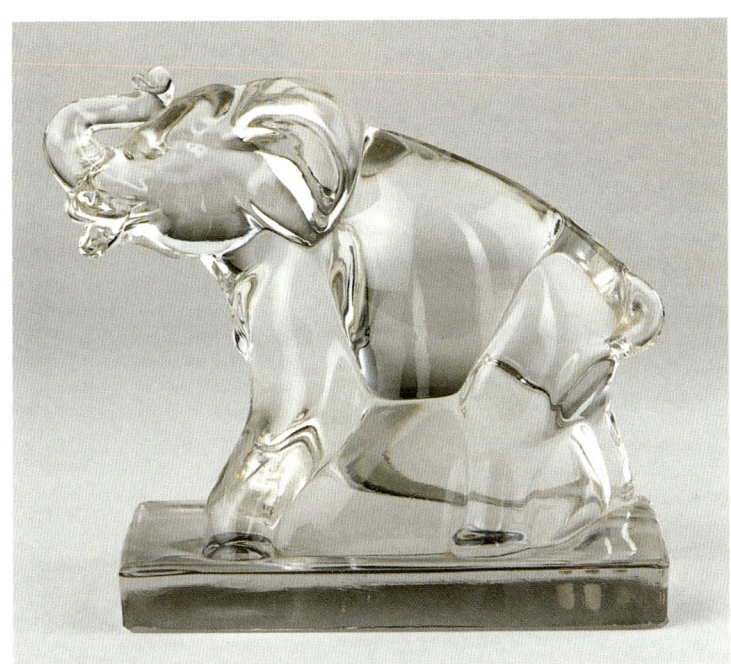

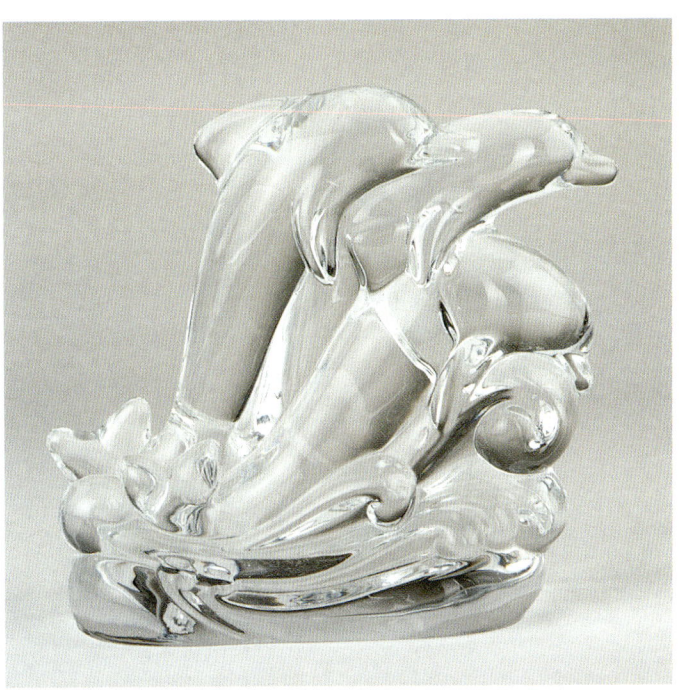

Elephant #710 crystal 5", $65-95. *Collection of Bob Page.*

Porpoise #766 crystal 5", $85-140. Heavily reissued later by Dalzell-Viking from the same mold. It is very hard to distinguish the early and late versions, most of those viewed by the authors appear to have been post 1980s.

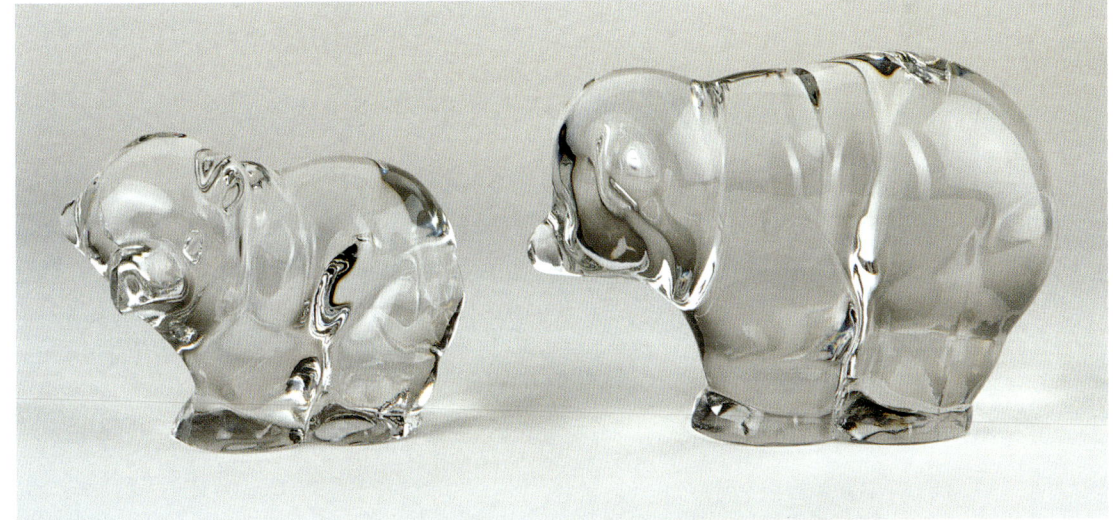

Mama bear #448 crystal 6", $140-165; Baby Bear #487 crystal 4-1/2", $45-68. Be alert to reissues from same mold; they are very difficult to distinguish from originals.

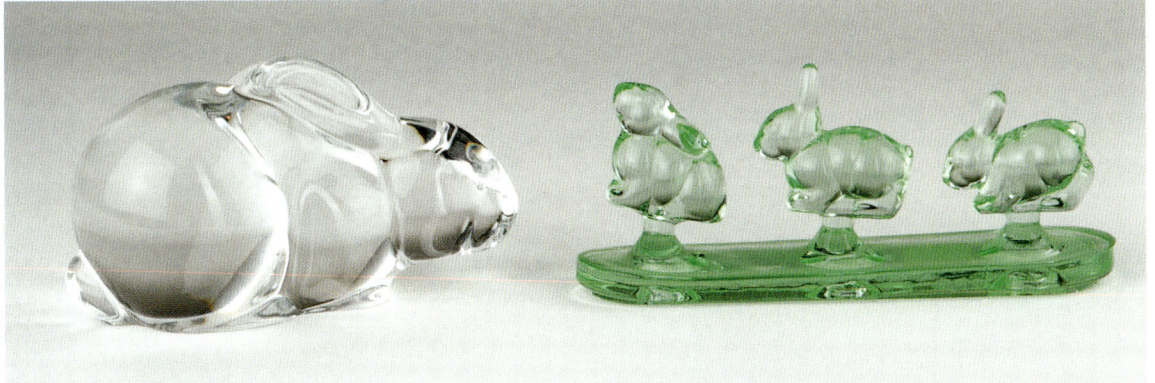

Large Rabbit #764 crystal 5", $145-180. Small rabbits shown as they were made/pressed and not intended to be sold. This transparent green color is post 1970. The small rabbits were pressed for the sake of economy of production as shown, then they were broken off the base and their bottoms ground to allow them to sit flat. Three positions, 1" each when separated by breaking off and bottoms ground for sale. Small rabbits in crystal, $45-68 each; as shown green and on base, $100-120.

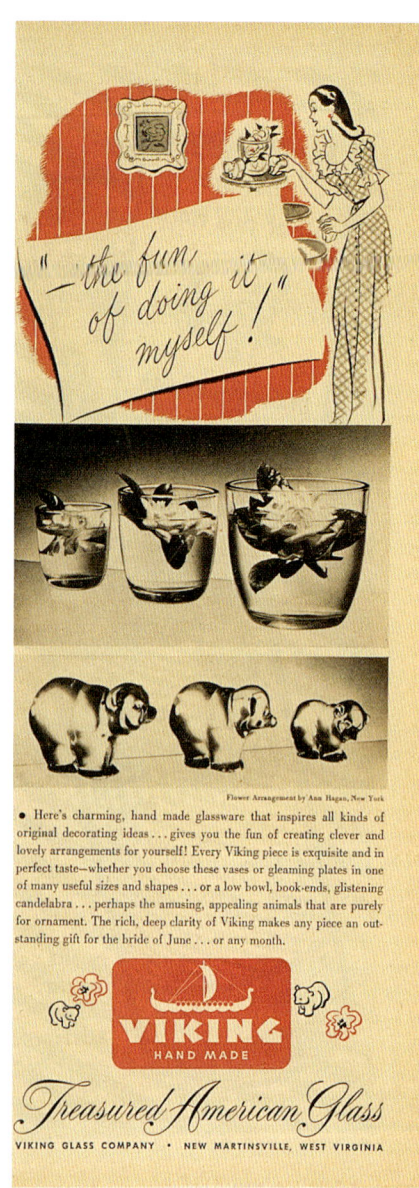

Advertisement for Viking showing heavy "Swedish styled" vases and the crystal bear family as "outstanding gifts for the bride …". *House and Garden*, June 1945.

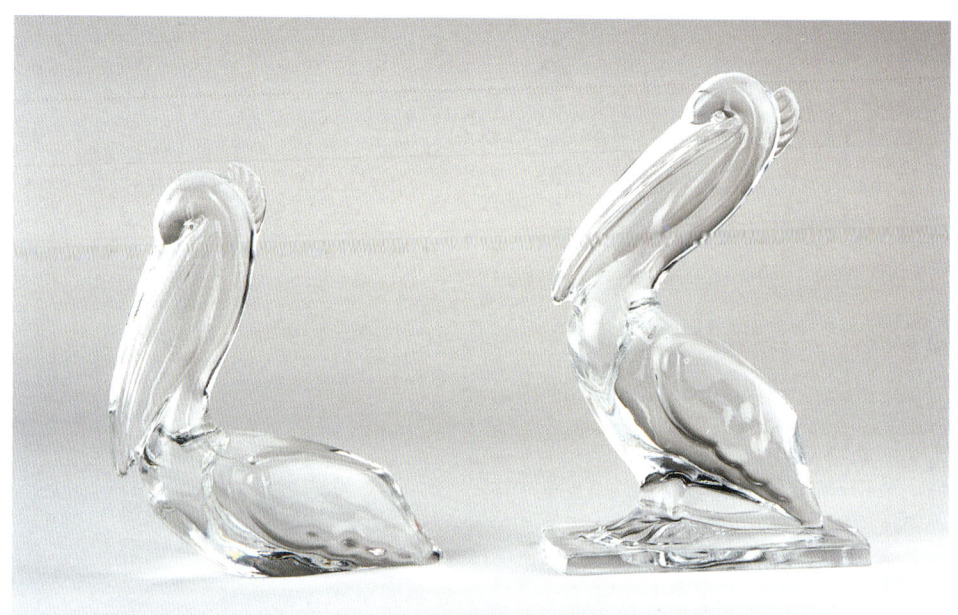

Pelican #761 crystal 8", $75-95. Pelican ground to create an uncommon "nesting" version. Possibly after 1970, $55-75.

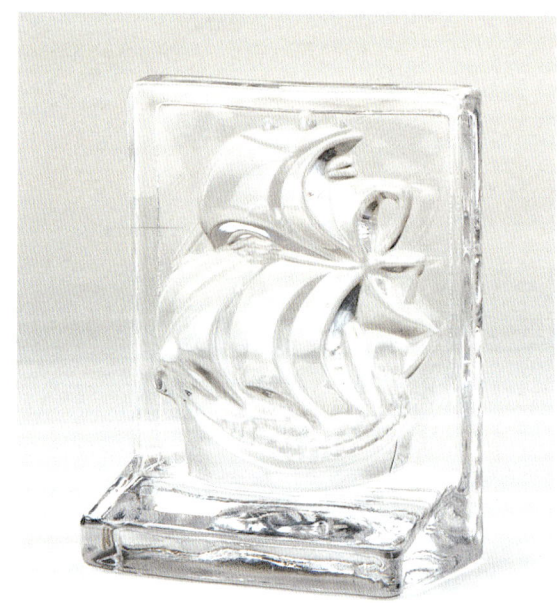

Ship Bookend #499 crystal 5-1/2", $40-55 each.

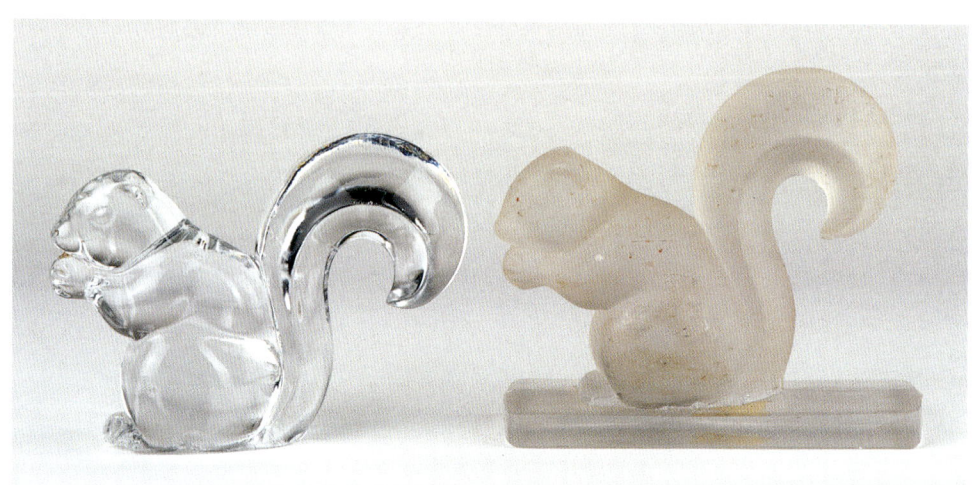

Squirrel #647 no base crystal 4-1/2", $45-65; Squirrel #670 with base crystal satin 5-1/2", $65-85.

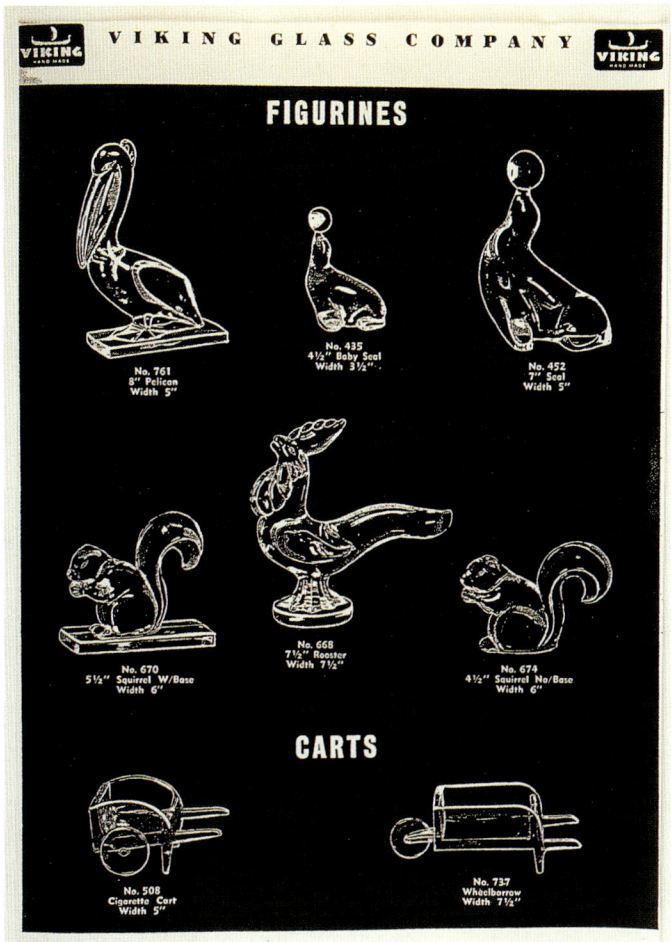

Viking Glass catalog page 1948-49.

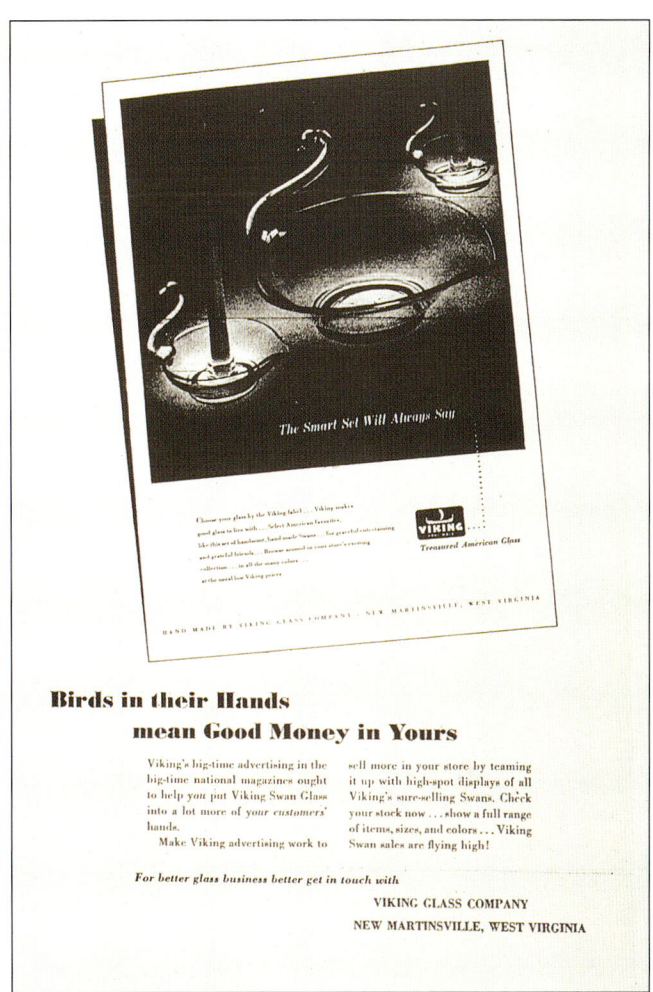

Advertisement featuring the large swan bowl and matching candlesticks. *Crockery, Glass & Decorative Accessories*, April 1950.

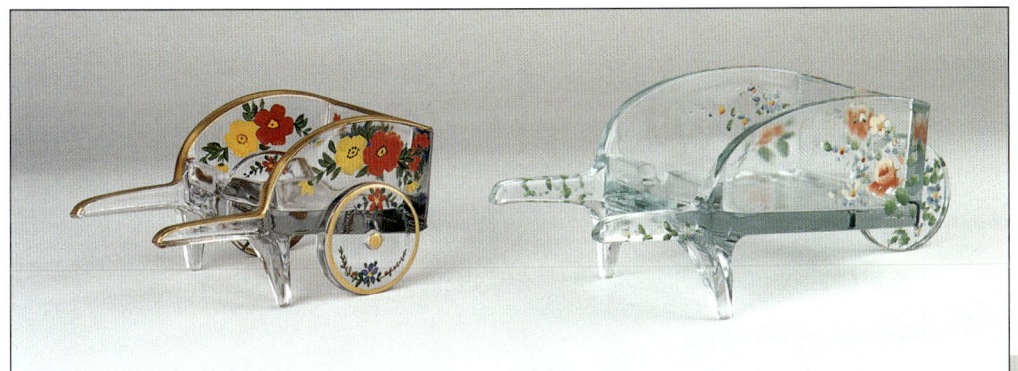

Cigarette Cart #508 decorated 5", 1940s-1950 crystal, $25-38; Wheel barrow #737 decorated 7" crystal, $30-46.

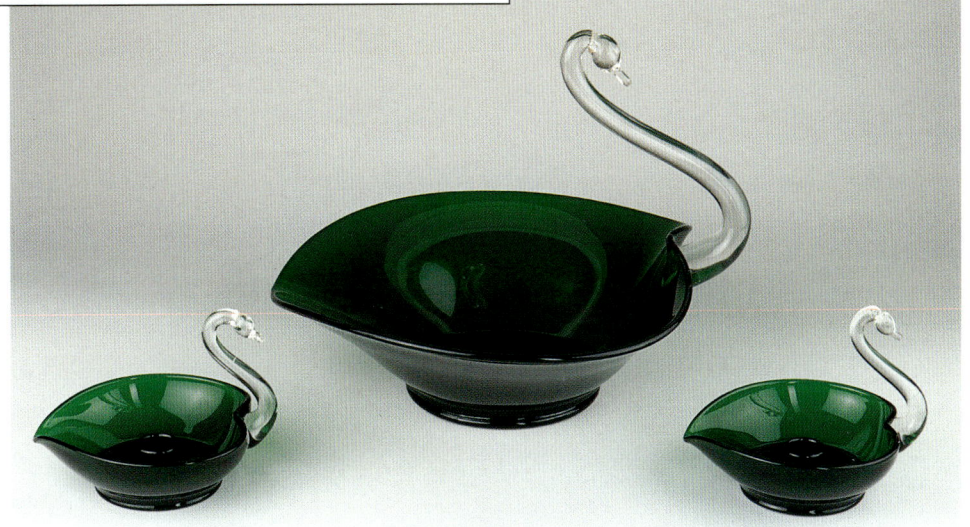

Swan handled candle bowl #993/1S evergreen, $35-48 each, appears in 1953 catalog in crystal, amber, and ebony. Centerpiece bowl with swan handles 10", #992/1S evergreen, $65-85, shown in 1953 price list.

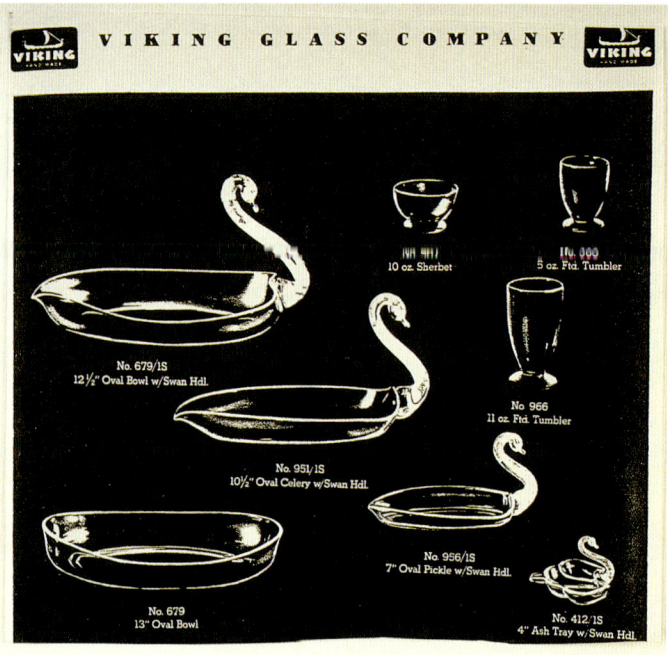

Viking Glass catalog illustration from 1948-49 catalog.

Viking Glass catalog illustration from 1950-51 catalog showing five forms of swan handles then in production.

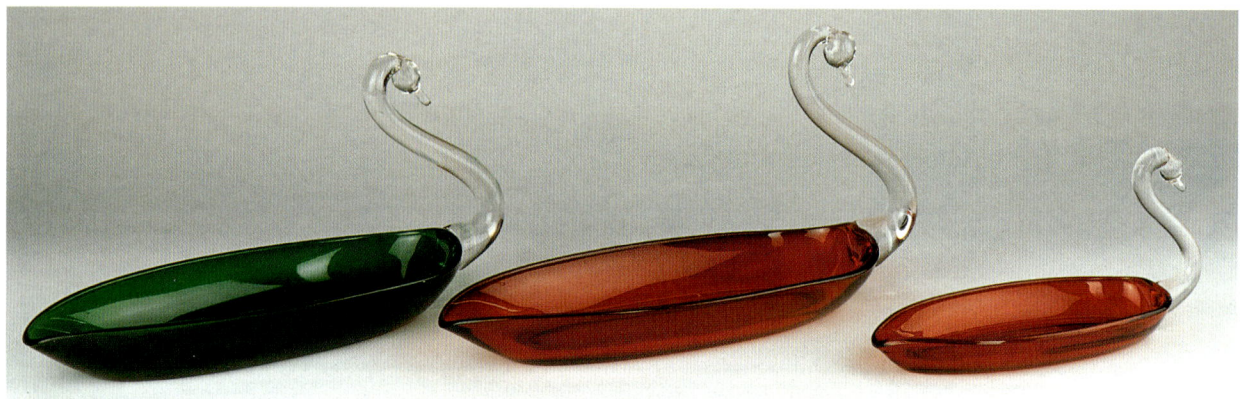

Swan handled oval celery ruby and evergreen 10-1/2", #951 evergreen, $38-48; ruby, $46-54; swan handled oval pickle 7", #956/1S ruby, $36-46.

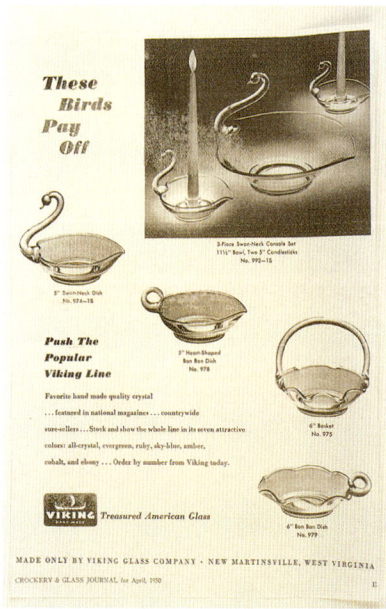

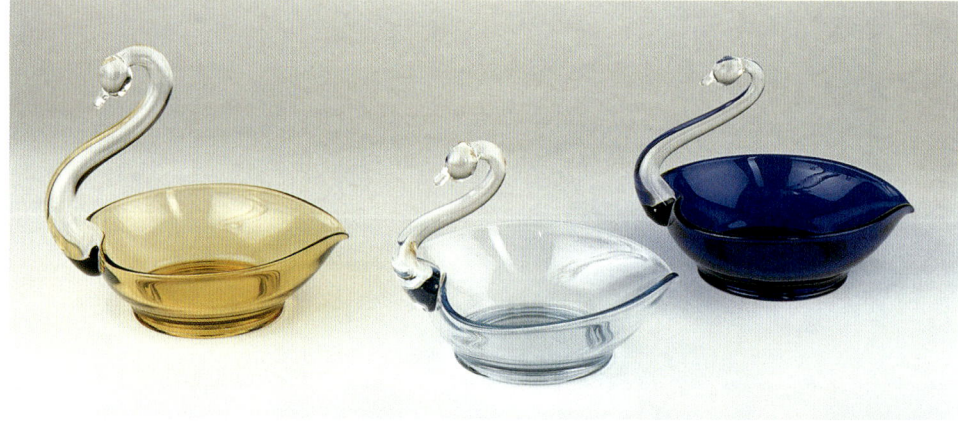

Various swan forms and the same bowls without swan handles. Viking Glass ad, *Crockery & Glass Journal*, April 1950.

Swan handled 5" dish in amber, $16-28; sky blue, $24-34; and cobalt, $32-38, all with crystal swan handles #974/1S.

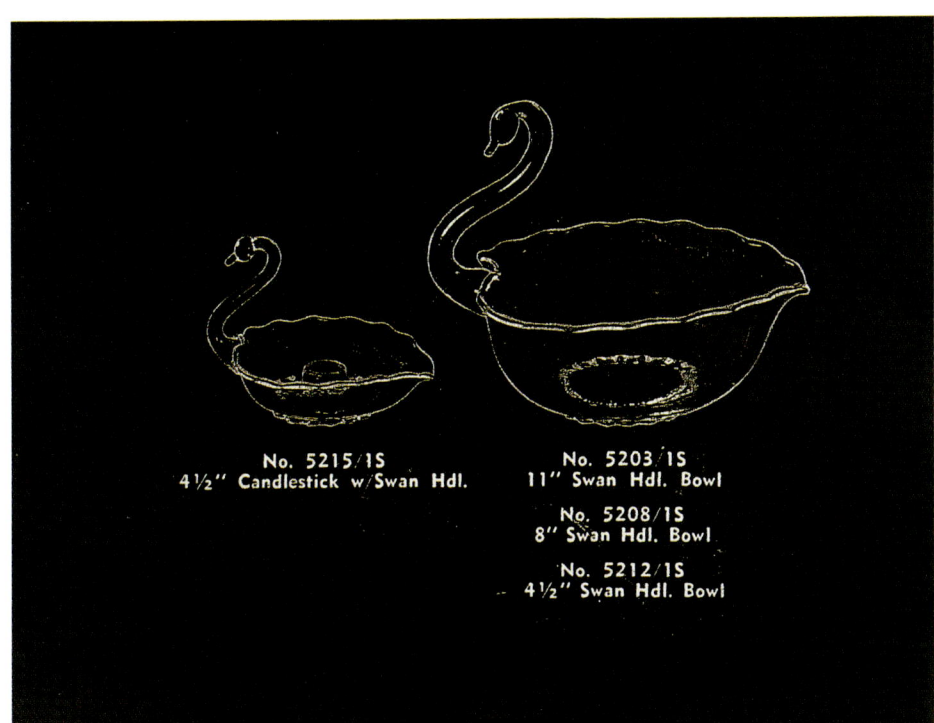

No. 5215/1S
4½" Candlestick w/Swan Hdl.

No. 5203/1S
11" Swan Hdl. Bowl

No. 5208/1S
8" Swan Hdl. Bowl

No. 5212/1S
4½" Swan Hdl. Bowl

Viking Glass catalog illustration from 1956 catalog showing Princess pattern base, swan handled candlestick, and bowl.

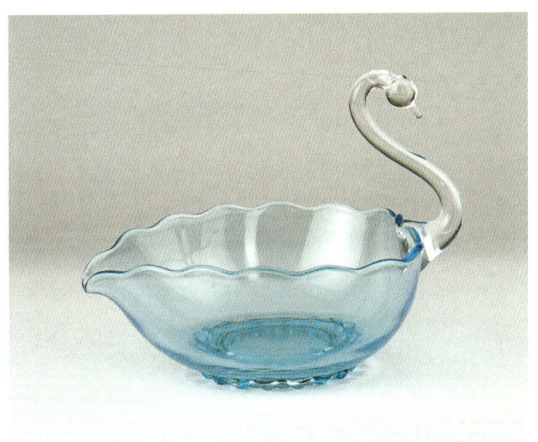

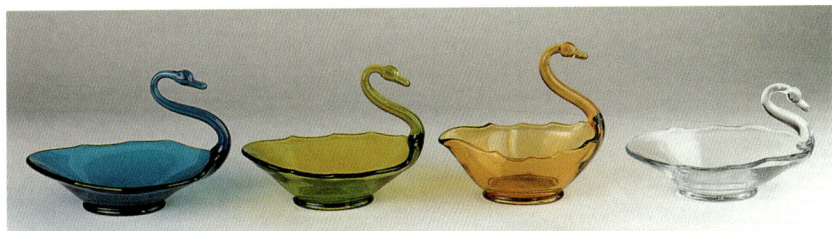

Epic swan #1324 bluenique, $22-32; avocado, $14-22; amber, $10-16; crystal, $12-18.

Swan handled dish, 8" in colonial blue with Princess pattern base #5208/1S, $24-38.

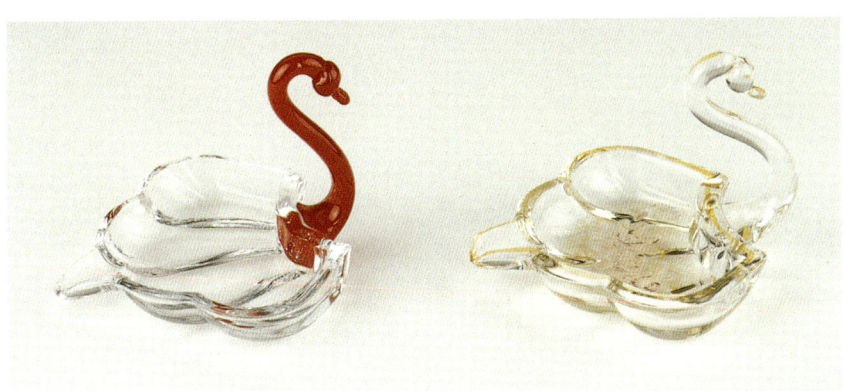

Swan handled ashtray #412/1S, 4" crystal decorated, $16-24; crystal with ruby neck, $22-32.

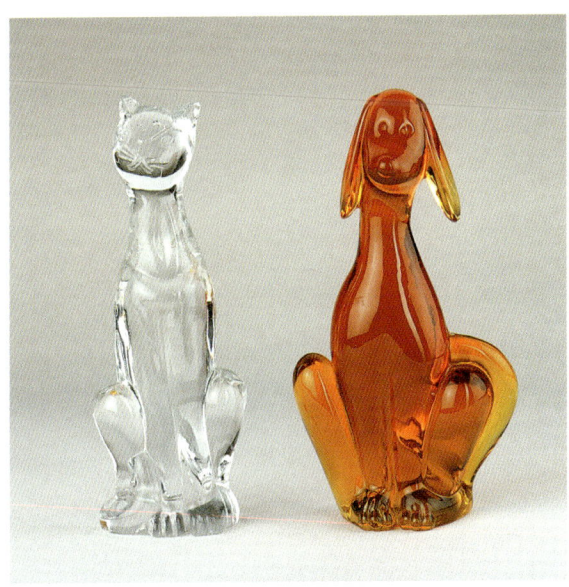

Epic cat #1322 crystal 8" (maybe produced after 1970), $35-50, Epic dog #1323 persimmon 8", $48-68.

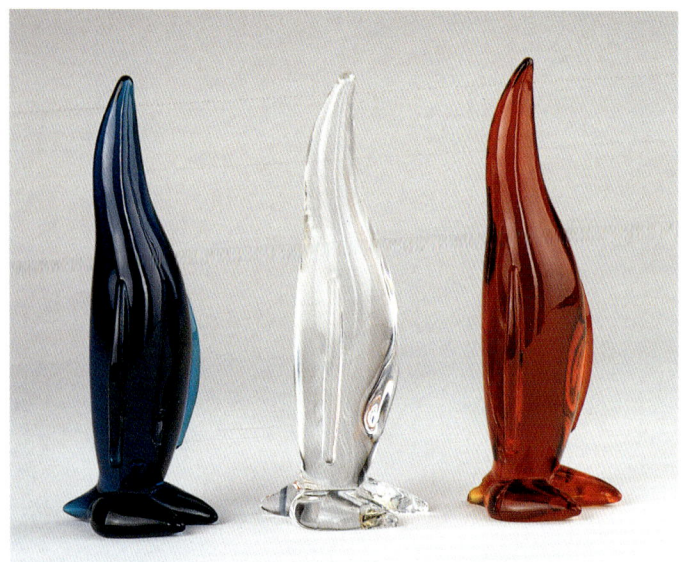

Epic penguin #1319, 7", bluenique, $58-78; crystal, $35-45; ruby, $68-88.

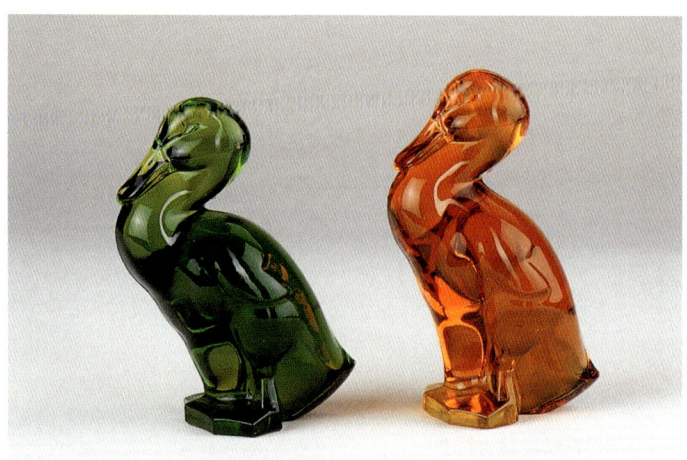

Epic duck collector dubbed "fighting ducks" #6712 originally sold as pair of upright and low forms. Upright shown in avocado, $30-45 and persimmon, $35-54.

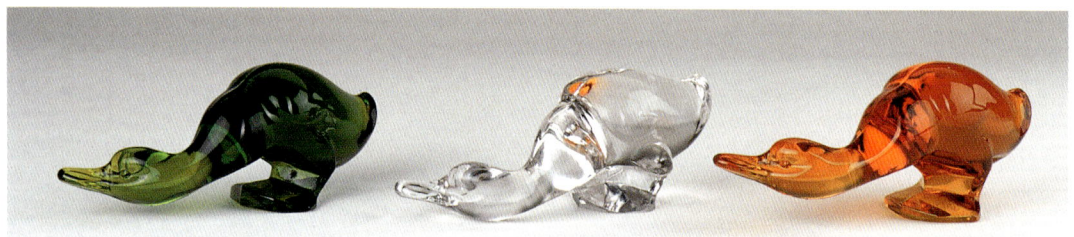

Epic duck collector dubbed "fighting ducks" #6712 sold as a pair with tall form. Shown here is the low form. Avocado, $30-38; crystal, $22-34; persimmon, $32-50.

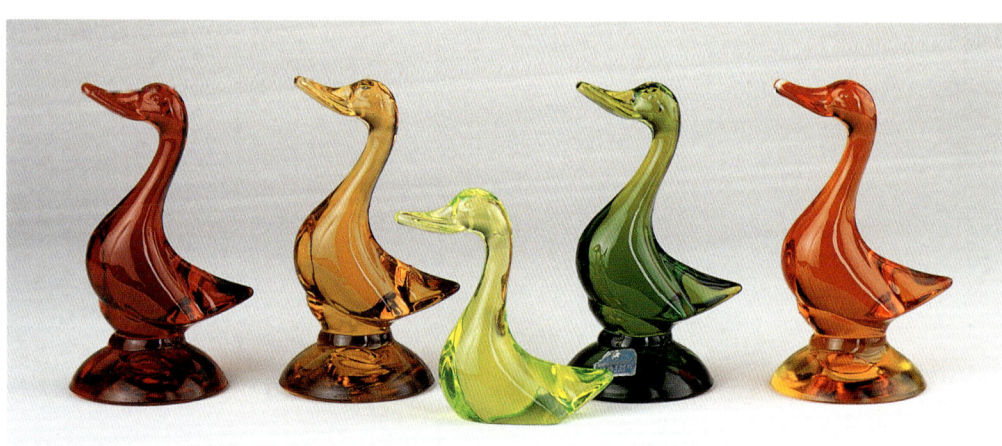

Small Epic duck #1316, 5" on base, ruby, $32-48; amber, $20-32; ground flat base in lime, $40-58; and on base bluenique, $28-42; and persimmon, $28-46.

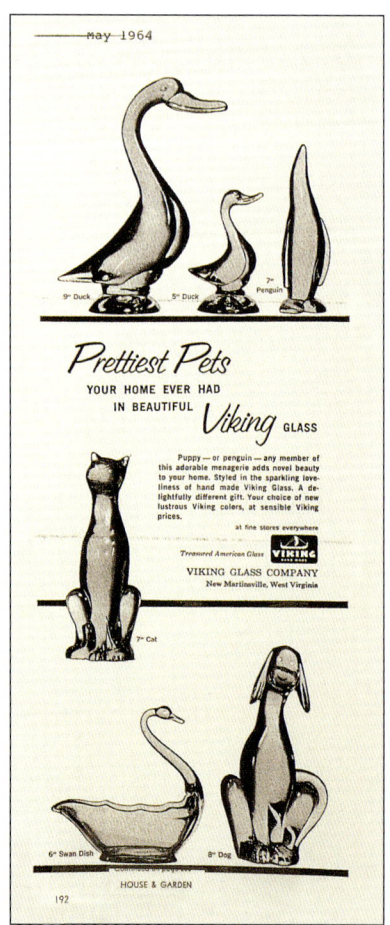

Prettiest Pets in Epic line illustrated in ad. *House and Garden*, May 1964.

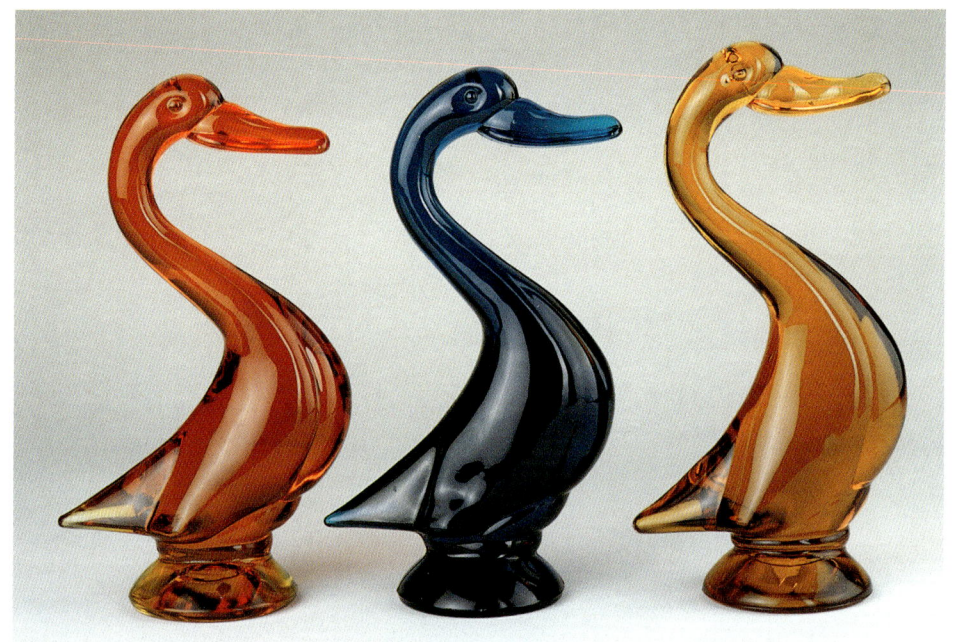

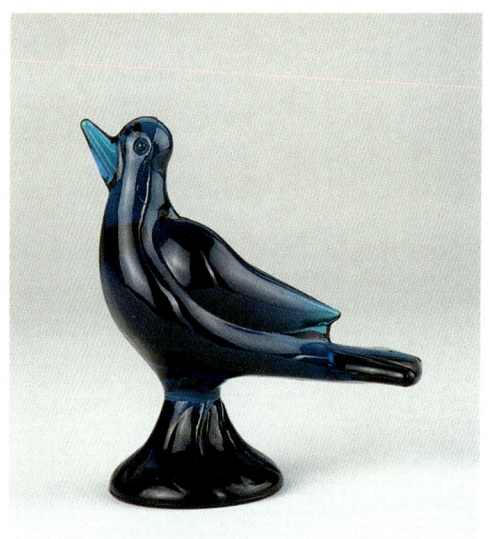

Bird on base #6807 bluenique, $28-44.

Large Epic duck 9", #1317 ruby, $65-85; bluenique, $50-75; and amber, $36-48.

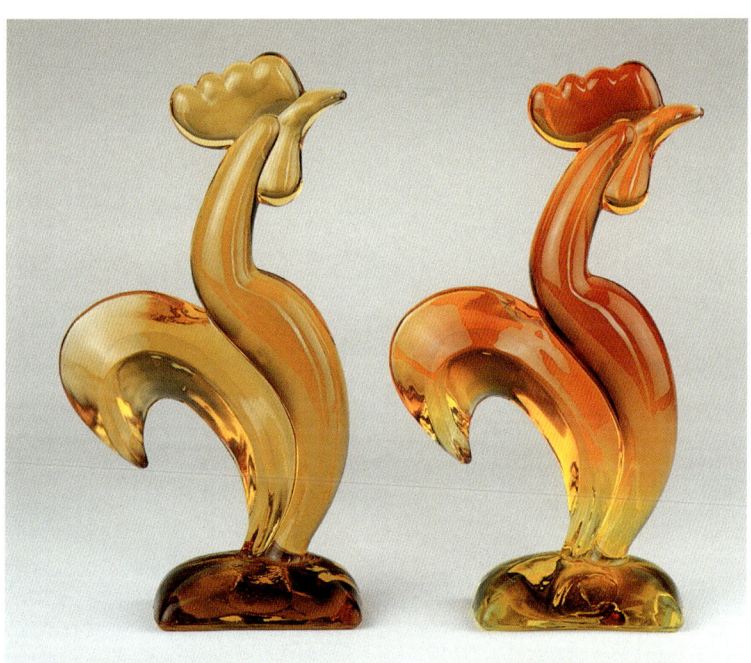

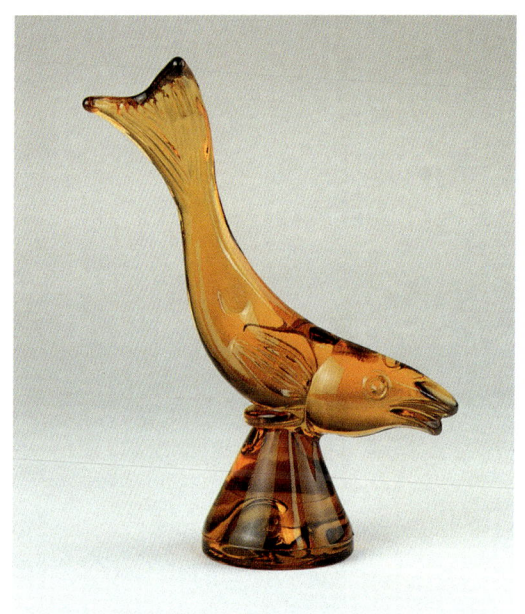

Epic rooster #1321, 9-1/2" amber, $32-52 and amberina, $50-75.

Epic fish #1320, 10" amber, $30-42.

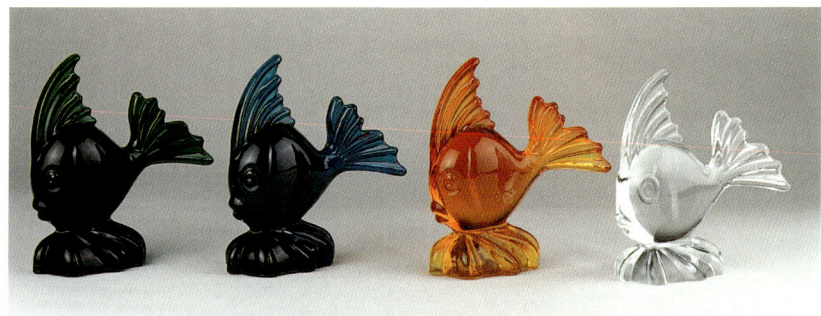

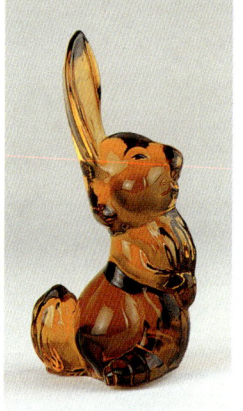

Angel fish #1301 evergreen, $48-68; bluenique, $45-65; persimmon, $48-68; and crystal, $45-65. Reissued by Dalzell-Viking in several colors.

Rabbit, collector dubbed "Thumper," #6808 amber, $28-40.

Those long-tailed birds

"The 1311 bird was the best seller Viking ever had. We kept one shop making them almost continually. They were $1.25 when we first sold them."

Franklin "Bud" Smith
VP Viking Glass,
with over thirty-three
years' work at Viking Glass

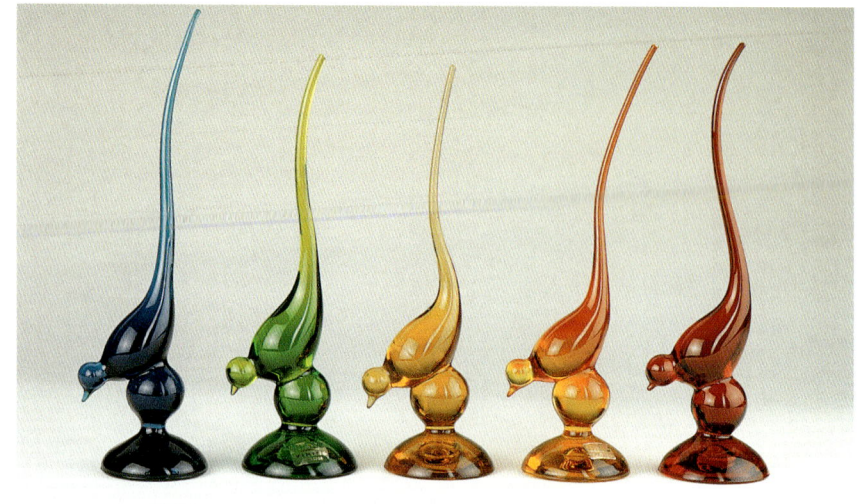

Epic long tailed bird #1311, the most popular, smaller size of this form shown in bluenique, green, amber, persimmon, and ruby. See text for pricing on all colors.

Long tail birds first appear as #1311 in the 1962 catalog. They were also on the cover of that year's catalog. They first seem to have appeared in late 1961. Ads in *The Gift and Art Buyer* of October 1961 show full-page advertisements that were going to appear in national consumer magazines. The bird is there.

In 1968, the catalog features #1310 long tail, #1311 shorter tail, and #1315 egret in ruby, amber, clear, amberina, bluenique, and amethyst.

Colors in which we document the long tail birds were made in the period between 1961 and 1970:

Amber, $20-28
Amberina, $24-38
Amethyst, $50-75
Avocado, $20-28
Bluenique, $26-36
Crystal, $35-60
Evergreen, $75-95
Honey, $18-24
Lime green, $55-70
Nile green, $35-48
Persimmon, $26-36
Teaberry, $100-120
Thistle, $80-95
Ruby, $30-45

Note for pricing that the difference between #1310 and #1311 is generally negligible. A long tail bird is a long tail bird to most collectors. The #1311 was widely produced while the #1310 is scarce and hard to find. The difference is not easily told by tail lengths, where there is great variety, but by the diameter of the round bases. The larger numbered #1311 bird is the shorter, smaller bird and its bases are always 2-1/2" or very, very near that. The number #1310 has a larger bodied bird but is best identified by the more consistent and measurable 3" in diameter base. See the chapter on Viking "confusables" for birds similar to these.

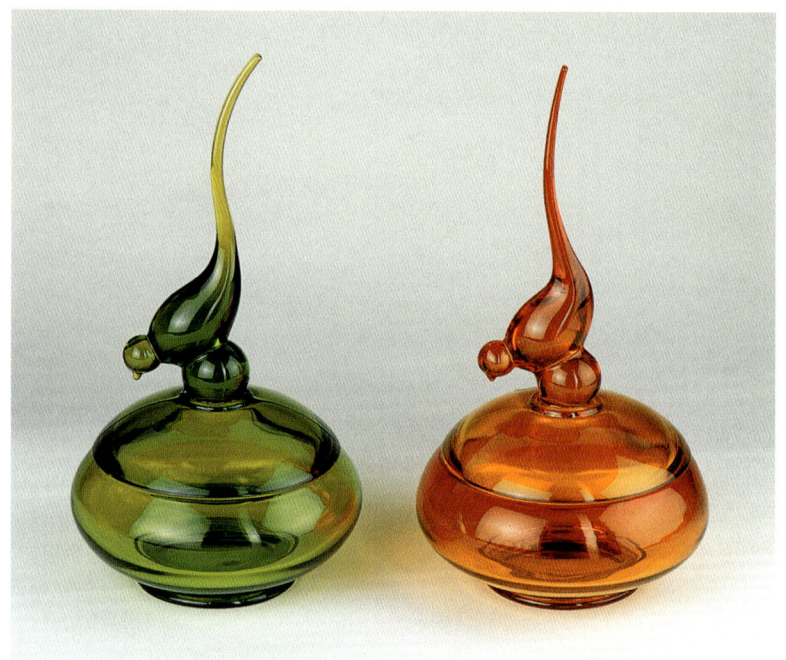

Epic long tail bird candy box with lid #1312 avocado, $30-48 and persimmon, $45-68.

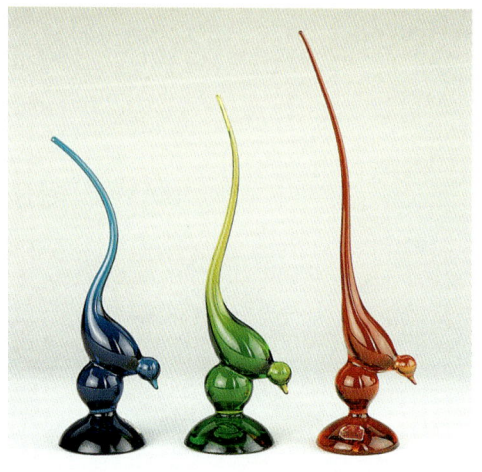

Variations in the length and form of the "long tailed birds". All shown are the same #1311. Be alert to broken and broken and repaired tails when buying!

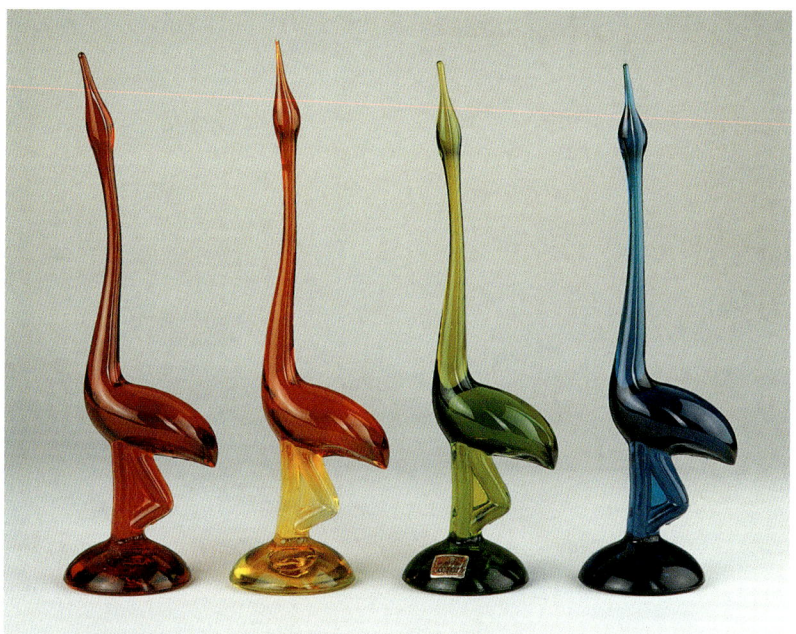

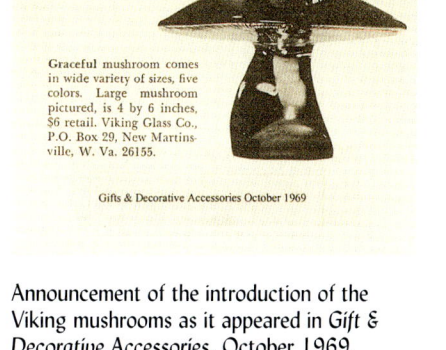

Graceful mushroom comes in wide variety of sizes, five colors. Large mushroom pictured, is 4 by 6 inches, $6 retail. Viking Glass Co., P.O. Box 29, New Martinsville, W. Va. 26155.

Gifts & Decorative Accessories October 1969

Announcement of the introduction of the Viking mushrooms as it appeared in *Gift & Decorative Accessories*, October 1969.

Epic egret #1315 ruby, persimmon, avocado green, and bluenique. At this time egret prices are not distinctly different from the long tailed bird prices. See those prices in the text for the same colors.

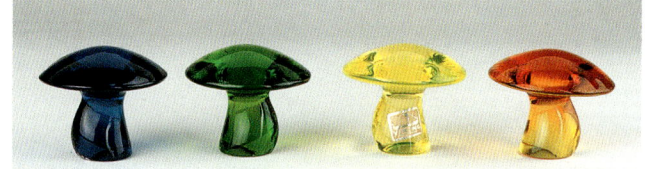

Mushrooms, small: bluenique, green, harvest gold, persimmon. Note the variances in the shape of the small and the other sizes shown elsewhere. While similar, each of the sizes has a distinctive shape.

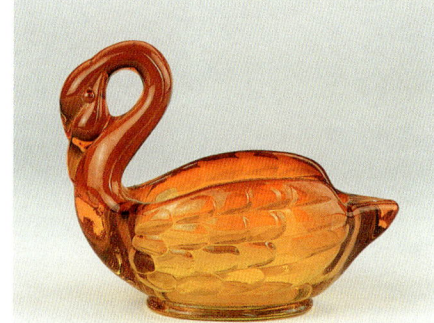

Epic open swan #69-46 shown in 1970 catalog, persimmon, $24-32.

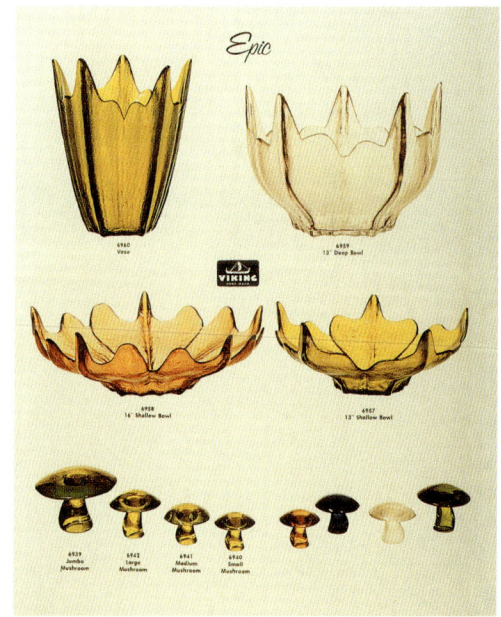

Viking Glass catalog showing mushrooms, 1970.

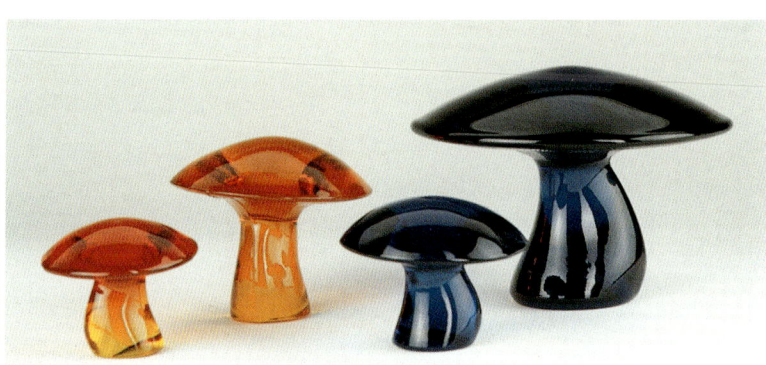

Mushrooms came in four sizes: small #6940, large #6942, medium #6941, and jumbo #6939. As shown here: small persimmon, $20-32; large persimmon, $26-38; medium bluenique, $22-36; and jumbo bluenique, $40-58.

Mushrooms, medium: bluenique, $22-36; green, $20-34; lime green, $24-36; harvest gold, $26-38; amber, $18-28.

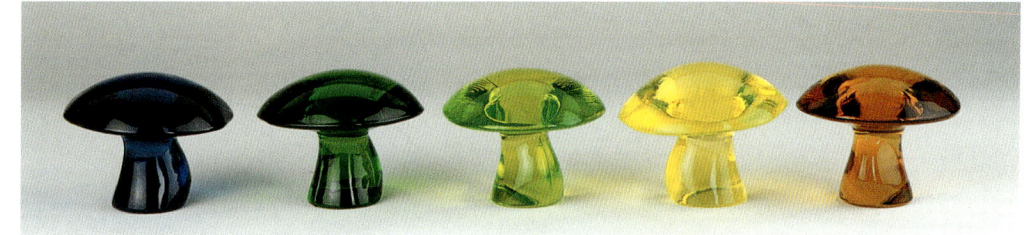

Baskets

Basket forms are found infrequently in the late New Martinsville Glass literature. By 1944, and with the arrival of Viking Glass, that is changing. The earliest Viking catalogs, dating from the late 1940s, have a number of basket forms. Four Janice shaped baskets, five Christina shaped baskets, and two crystal square baskets totaling eleven all crystal baskets are found in a single 1940s era catalog.

The 1962 catalog offers a single Epic line basket, the number 1179. A free-form basket, #6610, with two long, graceful, and not connected handles was produced in the 1960s until 1968. It was often called a vase, not a basket. To us it seems a basket. The 1968-1970 offering includes only the Epic #6711 basket. The variety in Epic line baskets offered over time is not necessarily in a variety of forms, but in variety of colors.

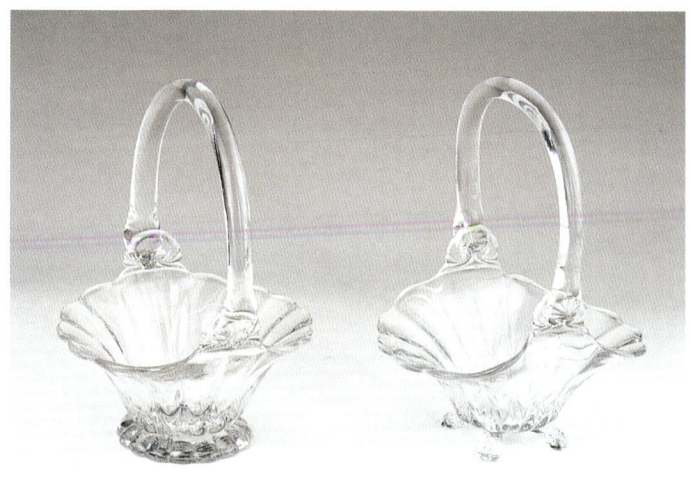

Janice pattern baskets, flat bottom, $45-66; crystal, $28-38; four toed crystal, $30-40.

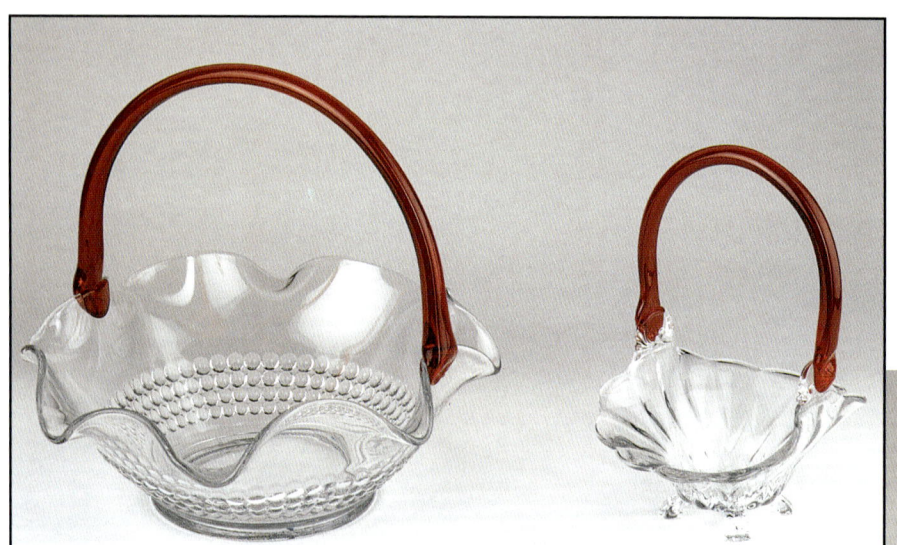

Ancestral pattern crystal basket with ruby handle #917 crimped 10", $58-78; Janice pattern basket four toed crystal with ruby handle, $48-65.

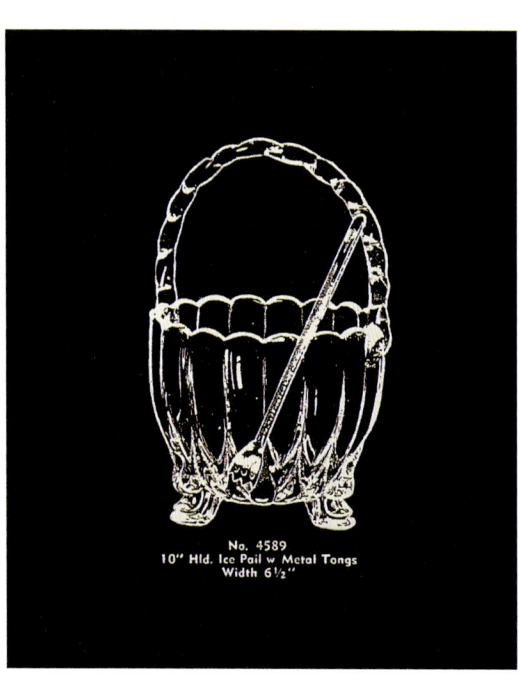

Viking Glass catalog illustration Janice crystal basket form ice bucket #4589, 10" tall.

No. 4589
10" Hld. Ice Pail w Metal Tongs
Width 6½"

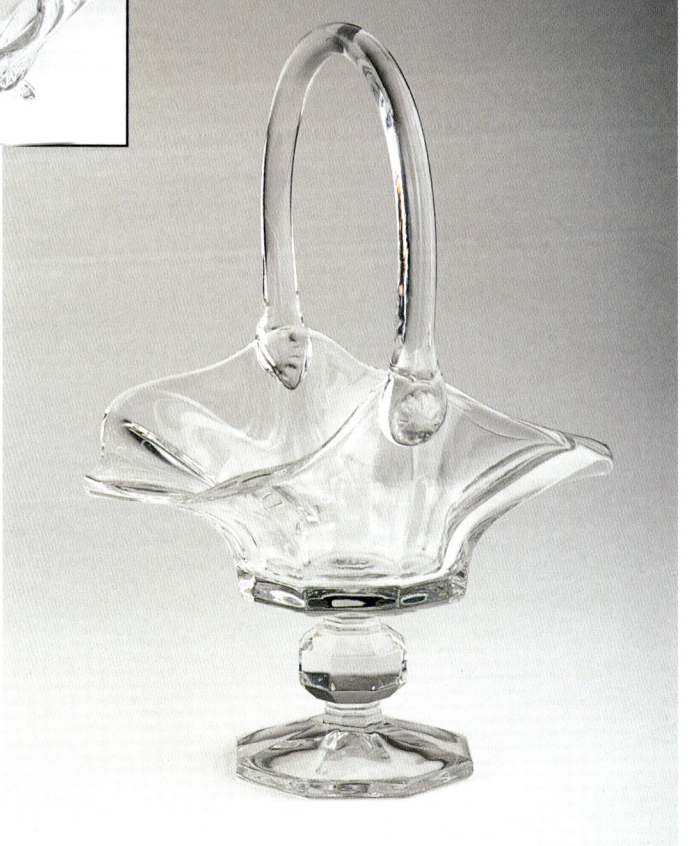

Christina pattern basket #801 crystal footed octagonal 12", $40-56.

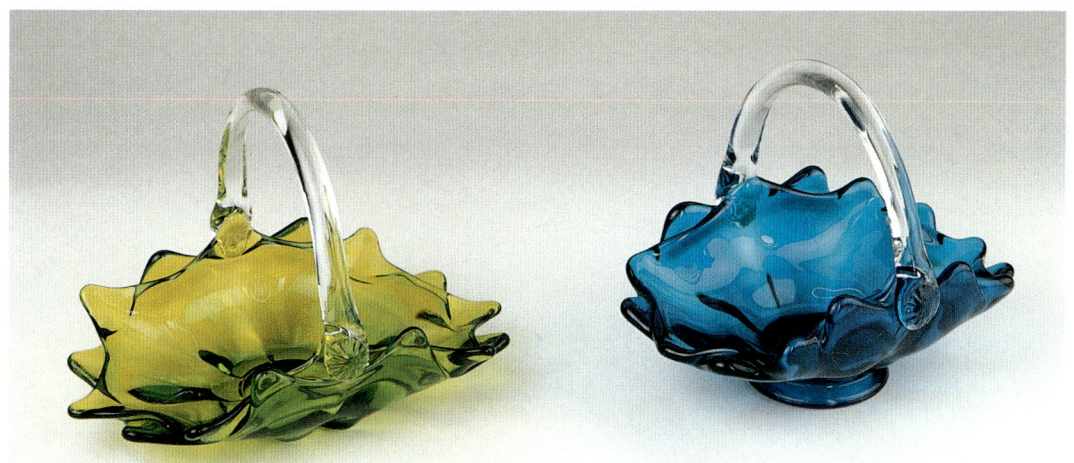

Epic basket #1510, 8-1/2", avocado, $16-24, and bluenique, $18-28, with crystal handles.

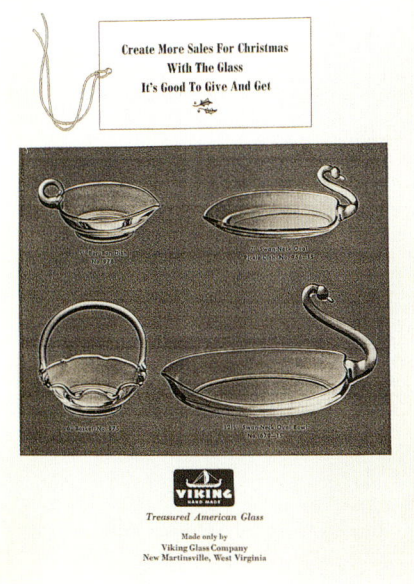

Basket #975 crystal crimped with bands around base shown in advertisement in *China, Glass & Decorative Accessories*, December 1949.

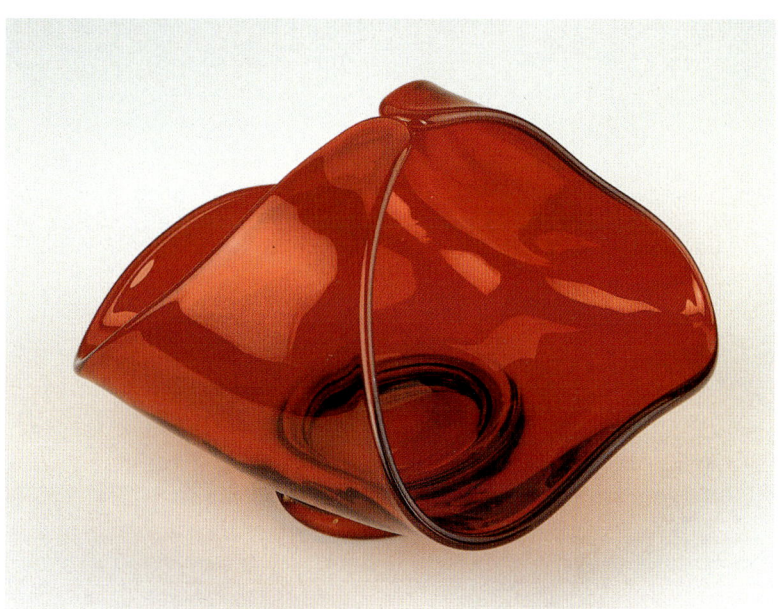

Ruby basket #1163, 6", discontinued January 1961, $28-38.

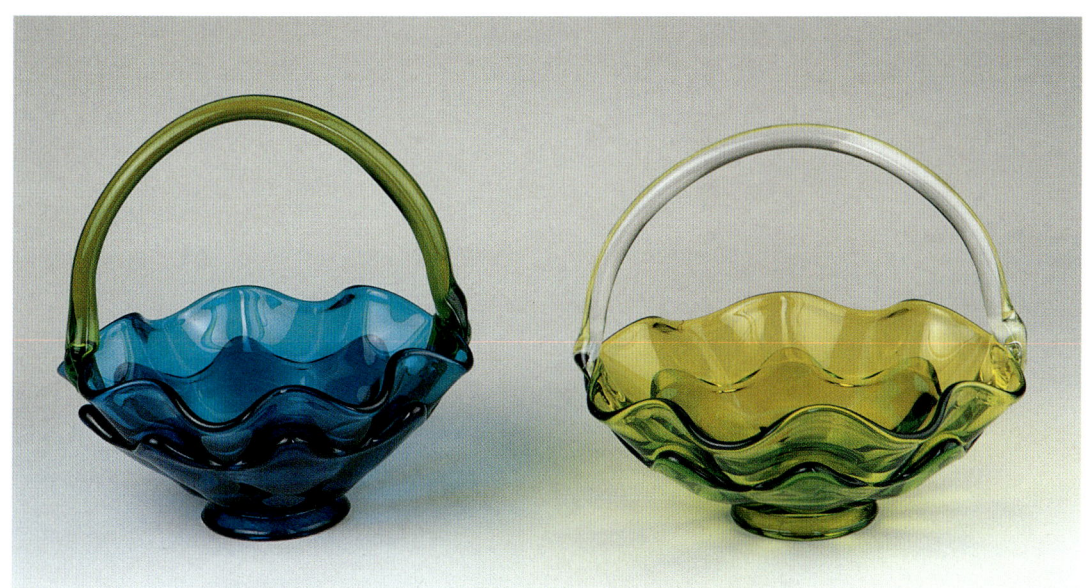

Epic basket #6711, 8-1/2" bluenique with avocado handle (believed to not be a line production item, possibly an experimental or for the gift shop?), $35-58; all avocado, $16-24.

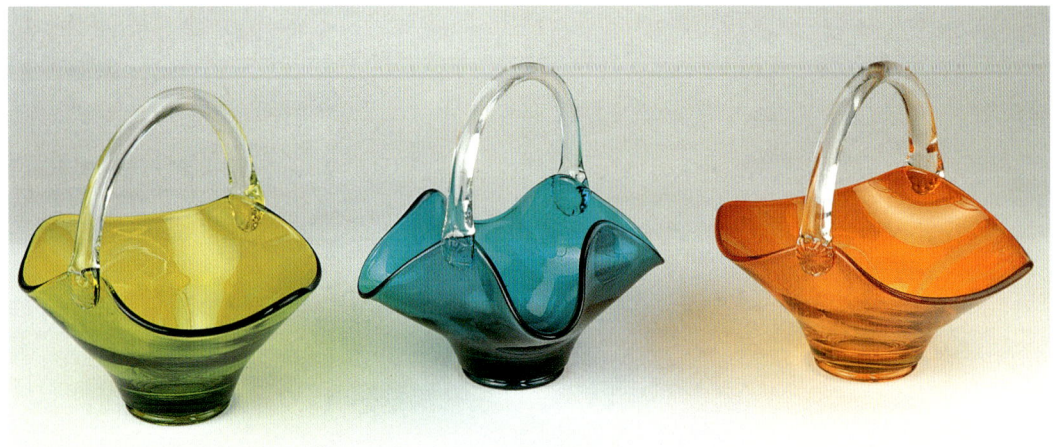

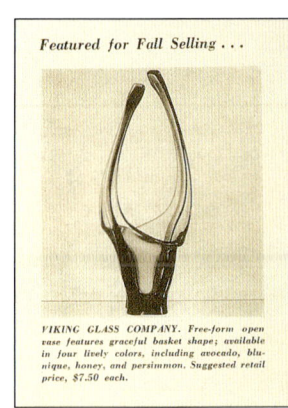

Trade journal announcement promoting Viking "free-form vase" as it appeared in *China, Glass & Tableware*, May 25, 1966.

Epic basket #1179, 6". Various hand crimped forms. Persimmon, $26-36; avocado, $18-28; bluenique, $28-36.

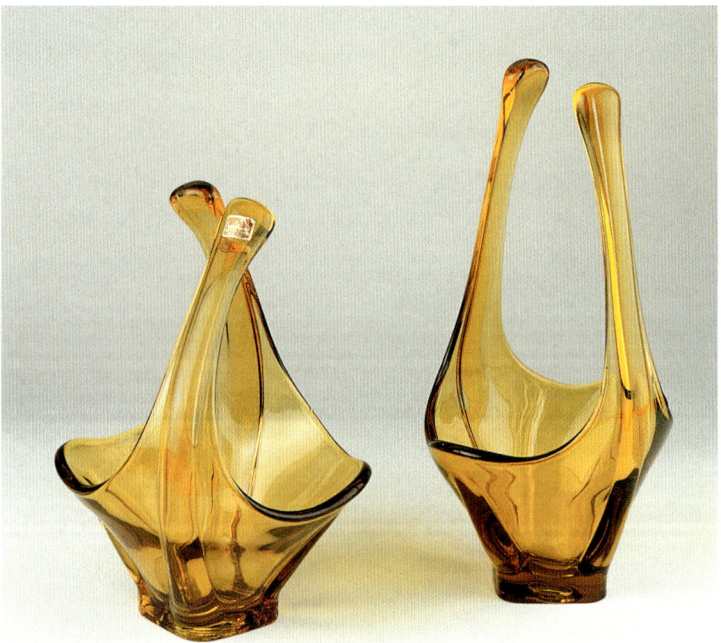

Epic basket #6610 called "open vase" in catalog, 16". Note extreme height variances shown here as a result of being individually hand formed. Amber, $40-54 each.

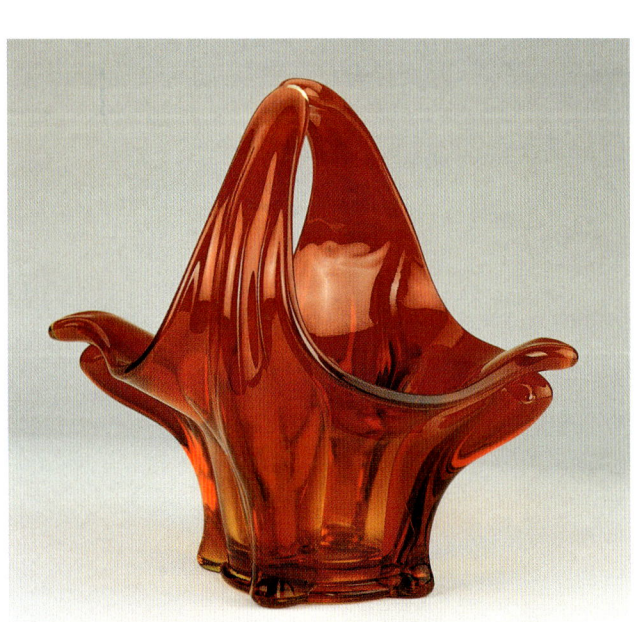

Epic basket #6610 called "open vase" in 1968 catalog. As shown, 14" allowing for variances due to hand forming of open handles. Persimmon, $55-68.

Bowls, Compotes and Candy Boxes: Covered and Open

These forms, bowl, compotes and candy boxes, were—from the beginning to the factory's closing—prevalent and important. However, trying to tell any significant story about such a diverse and unrelated mix of objects is perhaps impossible. The stories of many of the patterns and decorations shown here are found in the proper chapters. Please look there. This grouping is offered here only as a visual key to identifying an object with no attempt of weaving a story. This section is, by design, a loosely mixed lot without particular rhyme or reason. Many additional examples of these shapes and forms can be found within the individual pattern sections, please look there also.

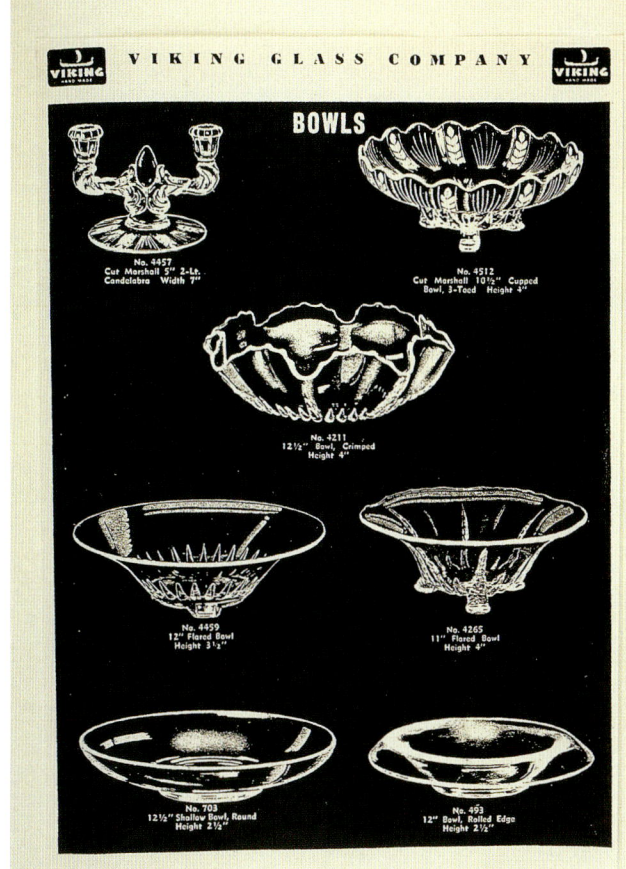

Viking glass catalog illustration for miscellaneous console bowls, one cut in Marshall pattern with matching candelabra, includes Radiance and Janice patterns. 1948-49 catalog.

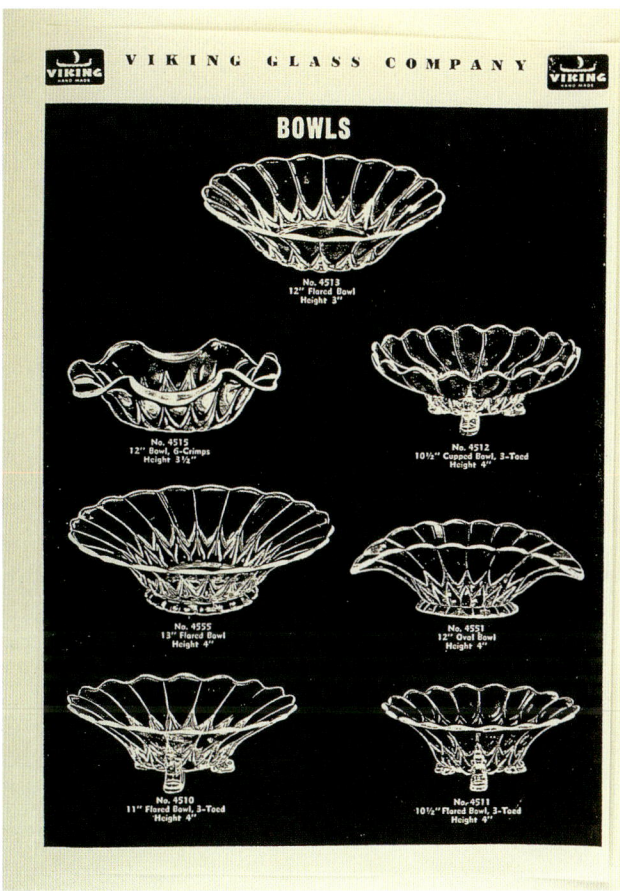

Viking glass catalog illustration for some of the Janice pattern bowls. 1948-49 catalog.

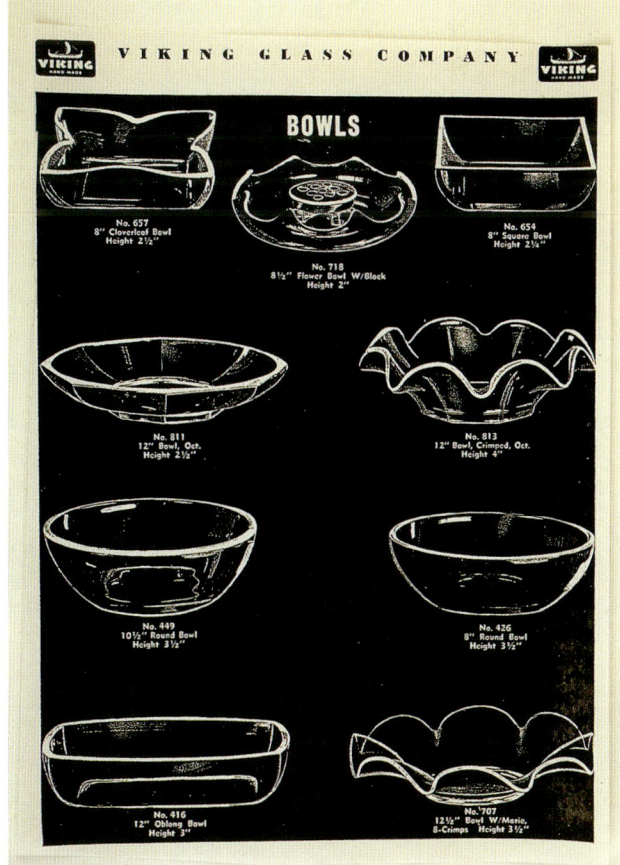

Viking glass catalog illustration for miscellaneous bowls for flowers and serving. Crystal. 1948-49 catalog.

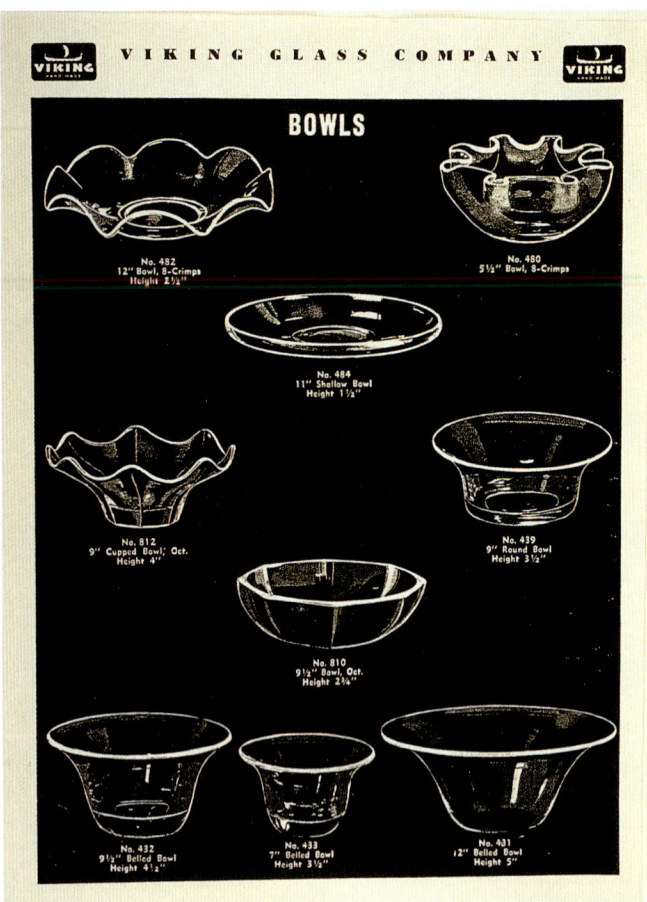

Viking glass catalog illustration for miscellaneous bowls. 1948-49 catalog.

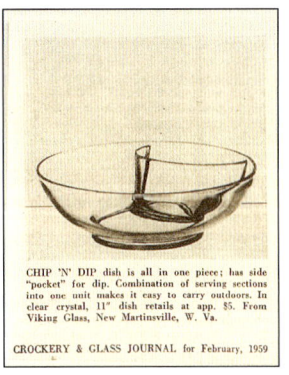

Divided Chip "N" Dip bowl, crystal. Illustration from *Crockery & Glass Journal*, February 1959.

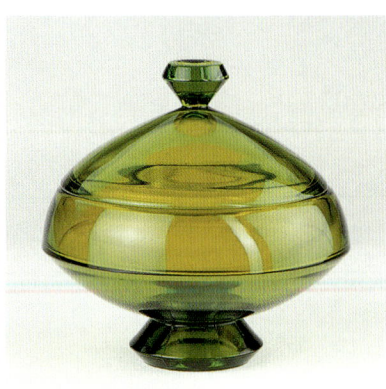

Right:
Epic candy with lid shown in *China, Glass & Tableware,* May 25, 1967, and noted as made in bluenique, avocado, honey, and persimmon. Shown in avocado, $18-28.

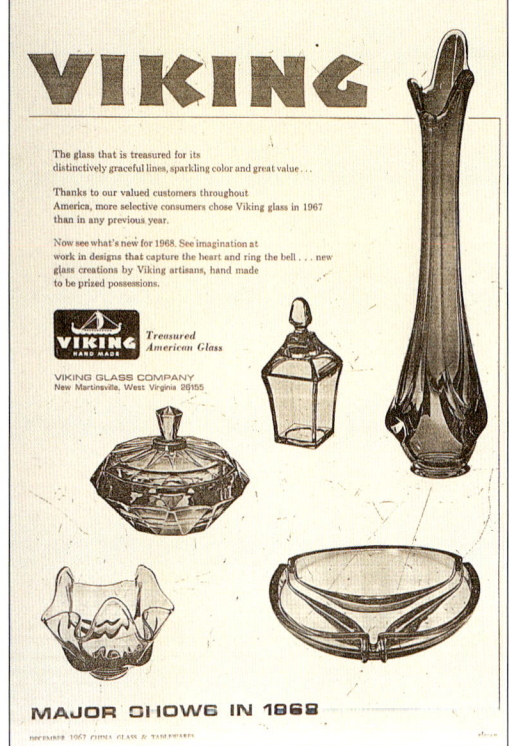

Advertisement illustrating, amidst other pieces, two covered candy boxes. *China, Glass & Tableware,* December 1967.

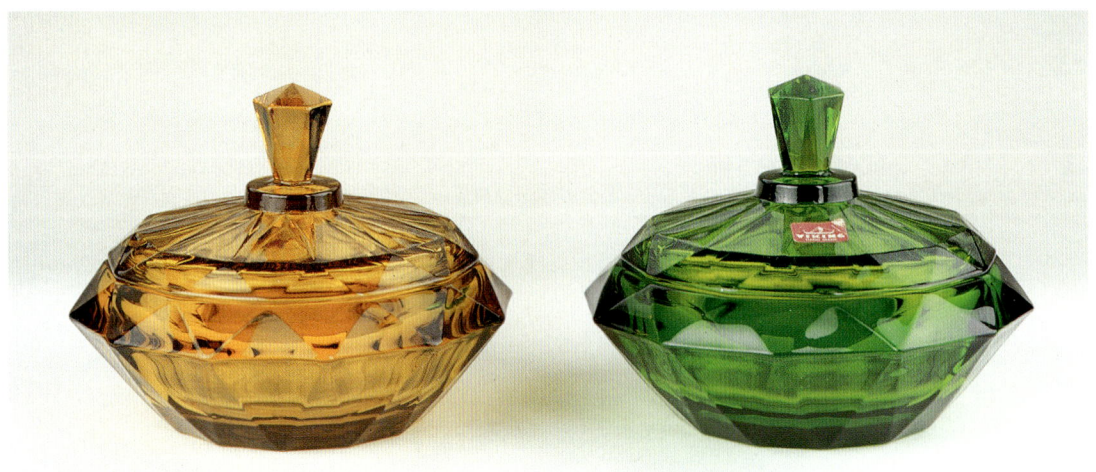

Epic covered candy #6816, 7-1/2" shown in the attached 1967 advertisement. Amber with lid, $12-20; green, $16-24.

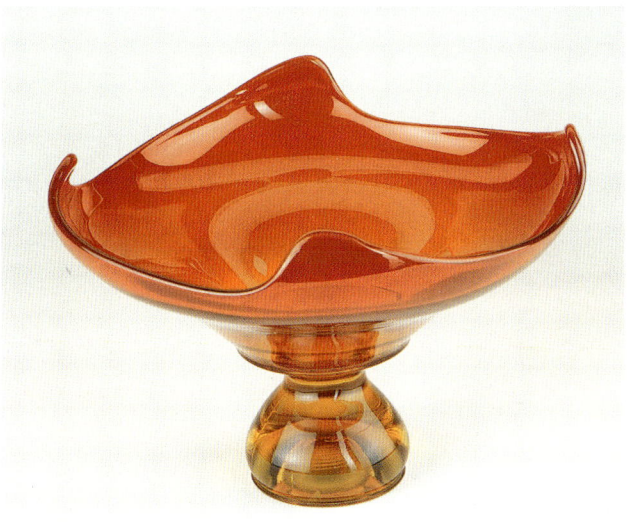

Epic "waves" footed bowl shown in 1960 catalog, 7-3/4". Persimmon, $25-38.

Right:
Advertisement illustrating Epic "twist" line covered candy shown in color elsewhere, also vase and Epic "twist" compote.

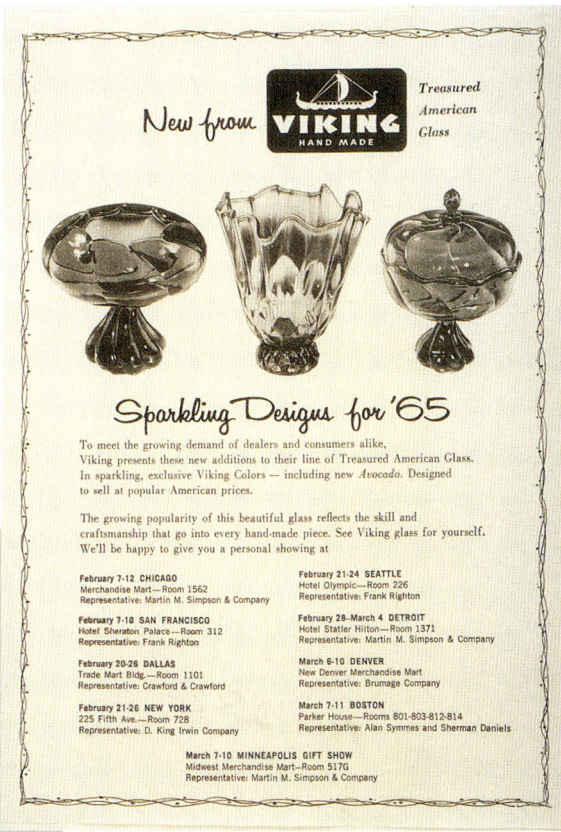

Left:
Epic "twist" line #1500. Candy with lid, 8", #1524 avocado, $16-22; small crimped vase, avocado, $10-16; compote, 9", #1522 avocado, $14-20.

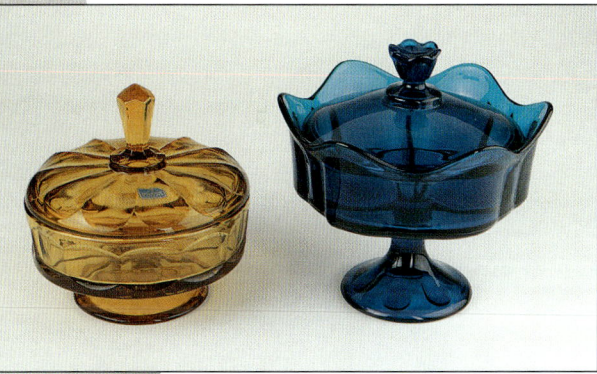

Epic line low candy with lid, amber, $12-18 and #1438 candy with divided three part interior and lid, 8", 1962 catalog bluenique, $22-28.

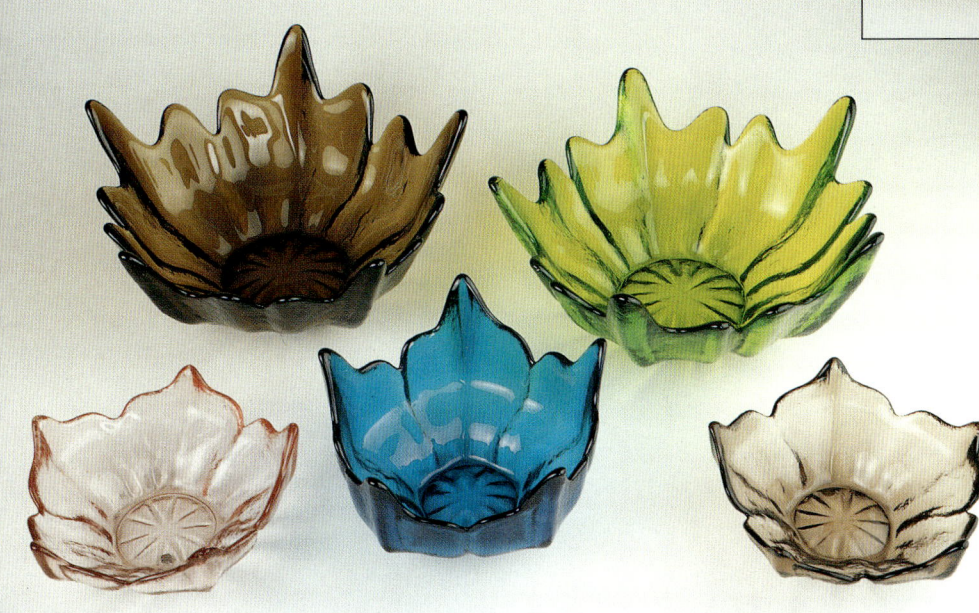

Epic line "spiked" bowls #6900 made in spin mold, introduced 1969. Small individual salad, pink, $6-12; brown, $6-12; bluenique, $8-12; and large serving size, brown, $12-20 and avocado, $8-16. Popular form and colors, circa 1970.g

Candlesticks, Glimmers, and Fairy Lights

Viking's lines of candle holding items are many. We will largely break them out to include candlesticks and candelabra and the later fairy lamps, or as Viking called theirs, Glimmers. Flowerlites, the flower blocks/frog with candle wells, are detailed in the Flower Bowl and Flowerlite chapter.

Viking, like New Martinsville Glass before it, was a major producer of elegant and traditional candlesticks capable of holding one candle and candelabras made to hold two or more candles. Many Viking sticks, in the 1940s and '50s particularly, were offered with or without a bobeche with dangling prisms. The prisms were certainly not Viking products but were most likely European imports.

When Viking emerges in 1944 there are a number of candlestick forms that are continued from the earlier New Martinsville molds. A New Martinsville Glass catalog page that also bears the Viking brand name, dating probably to 1941-44, includes elegant candelabra and a selection of elegant candlesticks.

With informal dining and living on the rise, elegant candleholders with dangling cut glass crystal teardrops gave way to more informal candle light devices.

In 1968 objects titled Glimmers by Viking first appear. In the initial offering only a diamond patterned #6700 is offered. It was made before 1970 in avocado, bluenique, honey, crystal, charcoal, ruby, lime green, and thistle. In 1969 the Owl Glimmer #6900 is introduced and is in the 1970 catalog in the colors of Avocado, bluenique, honey, crystal, charcoal, and ruby.

The year 1970 saw the addition of the short-lived Stove Glimmer #7000. It was produced that year in avocado, bluenique, honey, crystal, charcoal, and ruby. Other glimmer designs would follow at Viking and the idea of a two-part candle lamp was popular throughout the 1970s.

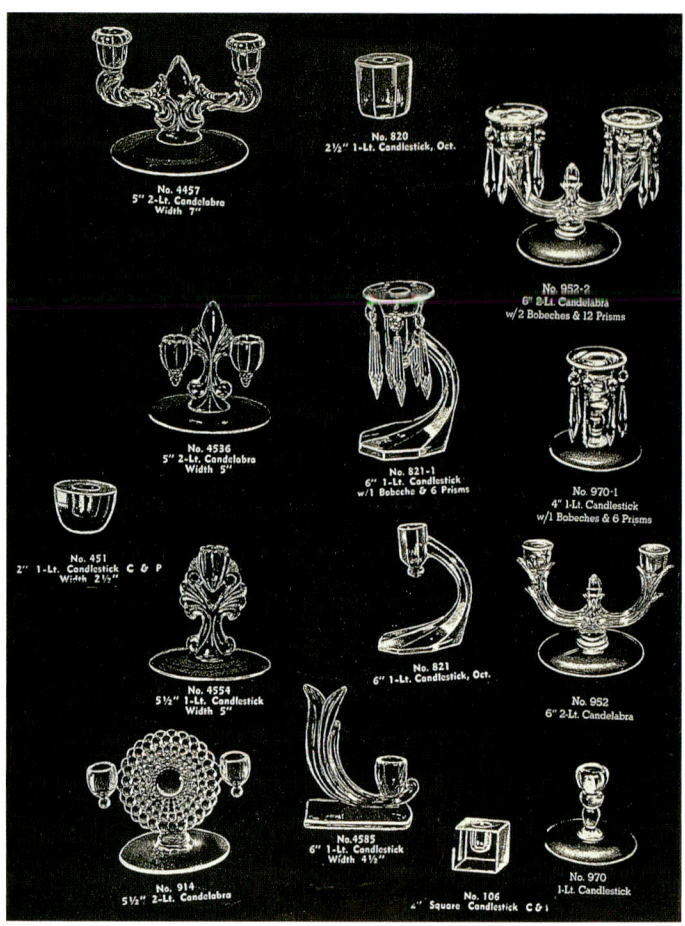

Author compiled page from original catalog illustrations, a selection of candlesticks from the 1948-49 catalog.

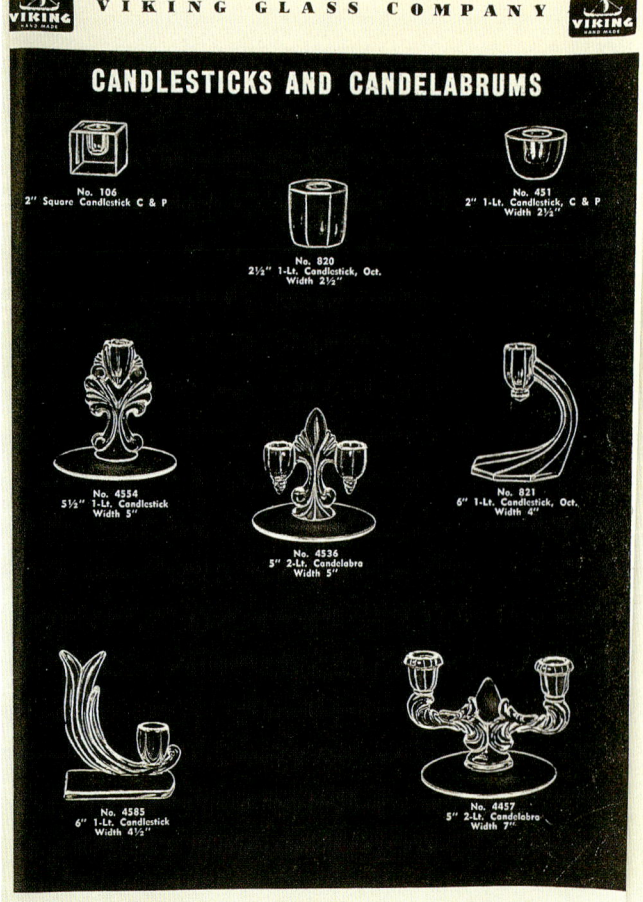

Viking Glass catalog page for candlesticks and candelabrums, 1950-51.

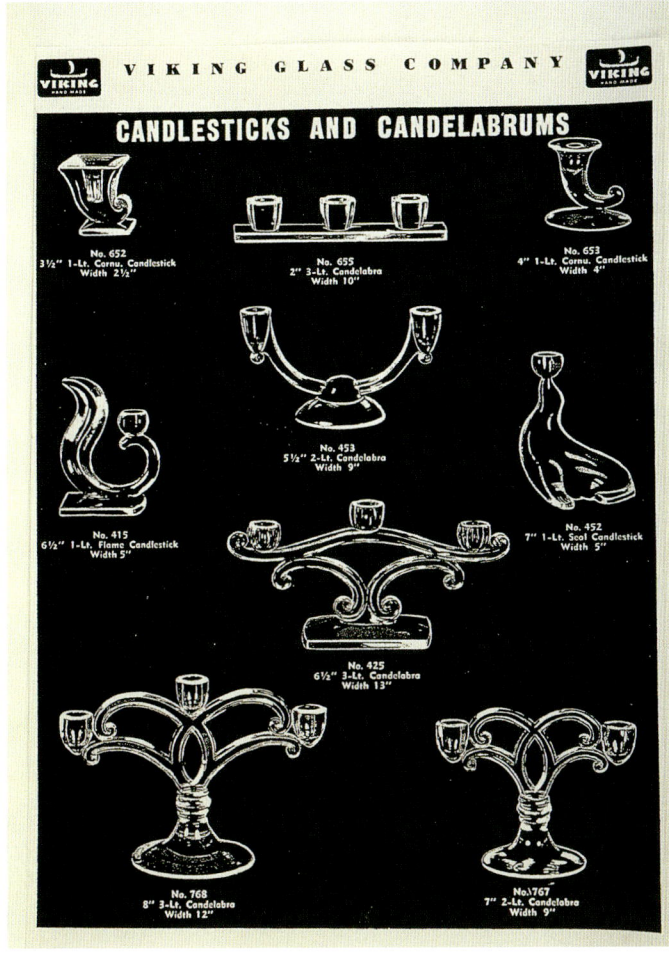

Viking Glass catalog page for candlesticks and candelabrums, 1948-49 catalog.

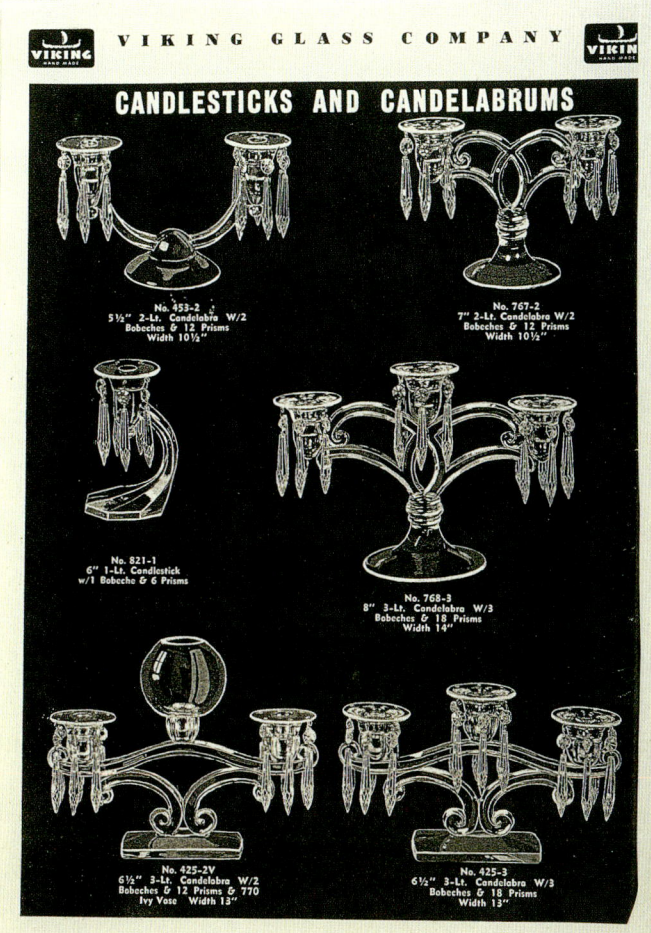

Viking Glass catalog page for candlesticks including prisms and one with pegged ivy vase. 1950-51 catalog.

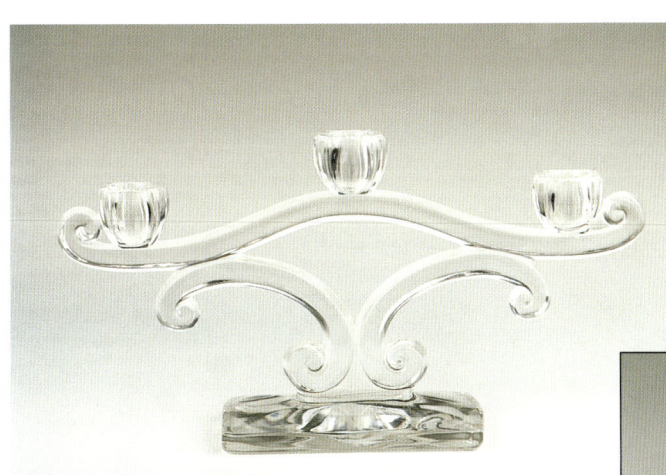

"Elegant arms" three light crystal #425 candelabra 13" wide, $65-78 each.

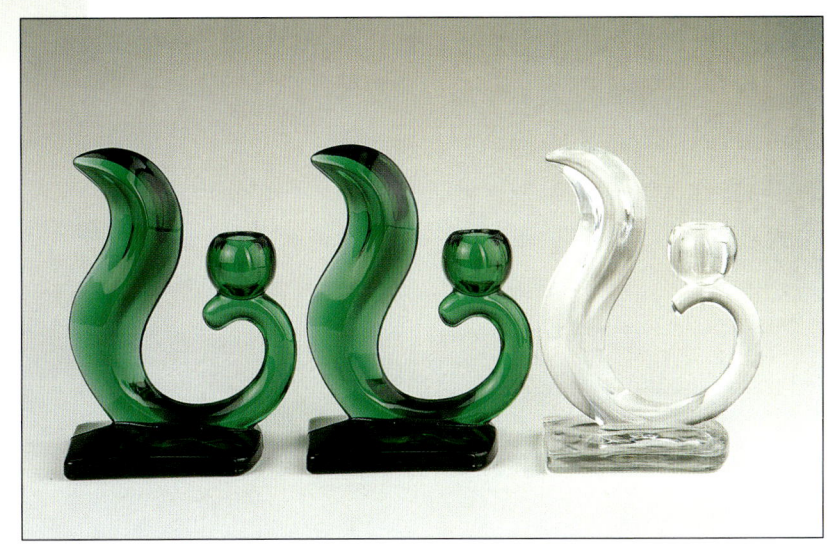

Flame candlestick, one light #7/40, circa 1953, crystal, $14-20 each; evergreen, $24-32 each.

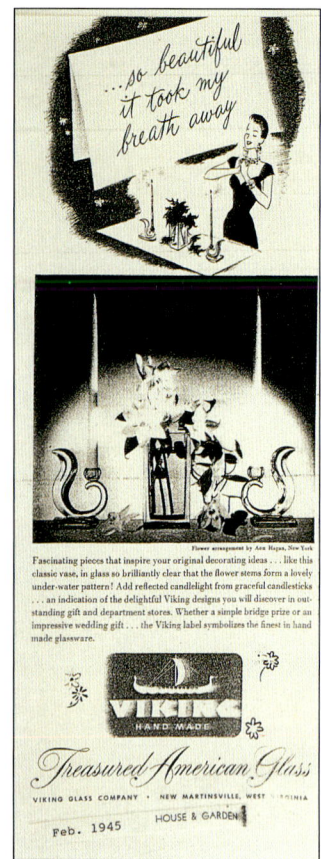

Viking ad for flame candlestick and square vase *House and Garden*, February 1945.

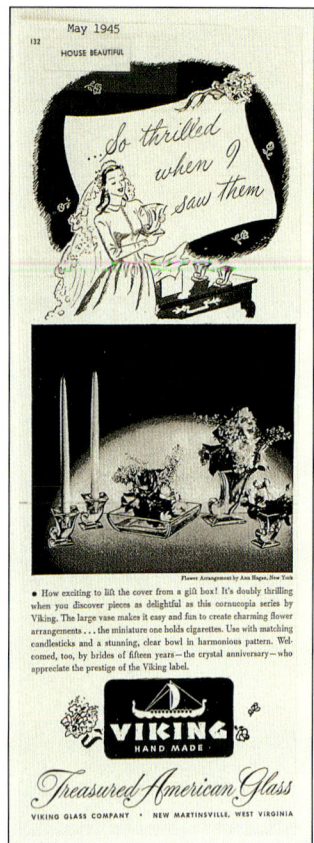

Viking ad for cornucopia candlesticks, vases, and square bowl, all in "Swedish crystal." *House Beautiful*, May 1945.

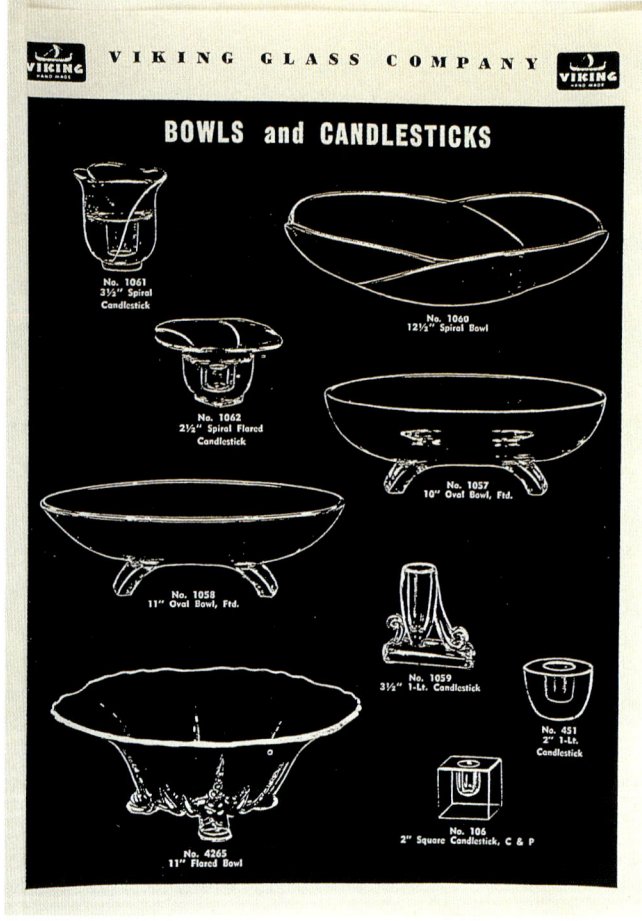

Viking bowls and candlesticks page from the 1956 catalog. Note one light scroll #1059 candlestick.

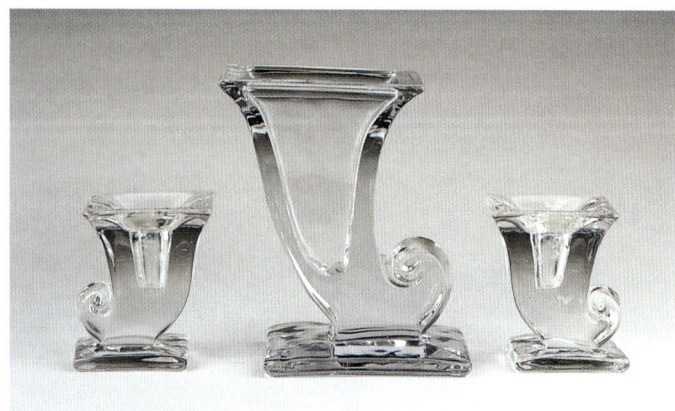

Cornucopia candleholder, square one light 3-1/2" tall crystal, 1940s-1952 crystal, $18-26 each; shown with exceptionally heavy crystal vase, 6-1/2" tall, $20-38. *Compliments Replacements, LTD.*

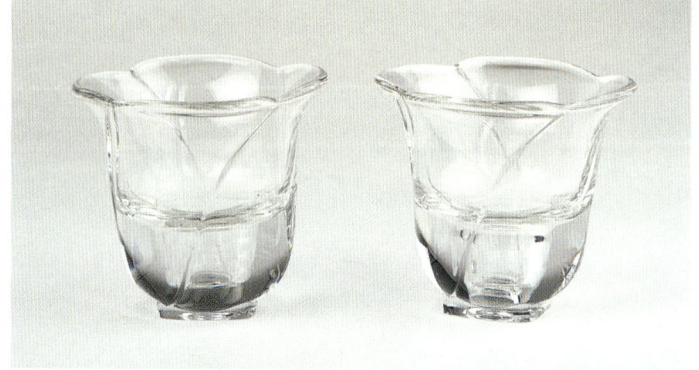

Spiral pattern #1061 crystal candlestick 3-1/2", $8-16 each. Shown in 1956 catalog.

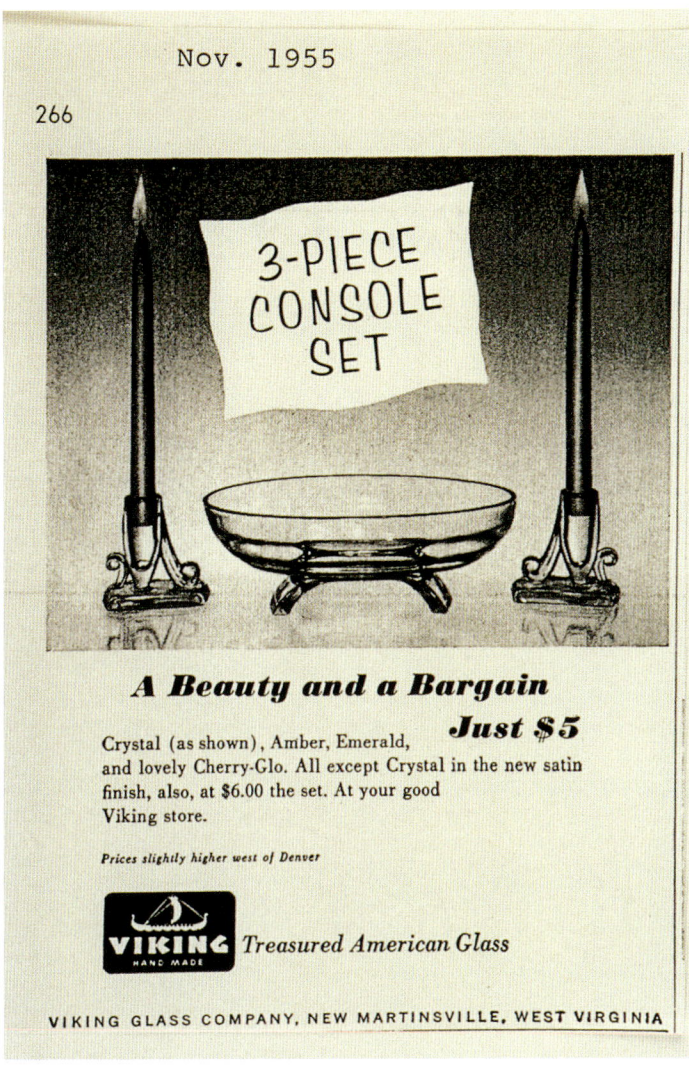

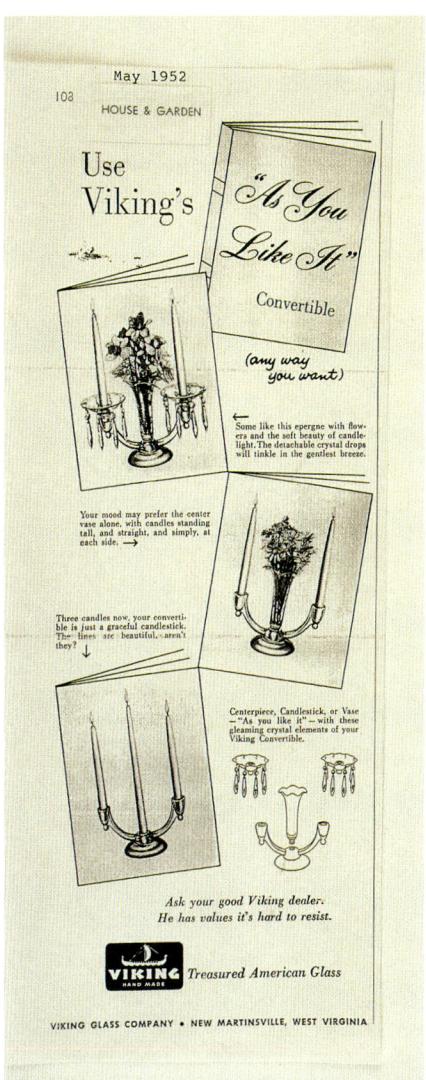

Left:
Advertisement for three piece console set in Scroll pattern. Noted as made in crystal, amber, emerald, cherry-glo. *House and Garden,* November 1955. *Image compliments of Tom Felt.* Note the form shown of open, single scroll candlestick and the other candlestick in a bowl form with two scroll foot, both Scroll pattern sticks.

Advertisement for Viking's "As You Like It" convertible candlestick-epergne-center vase components. *House & Garden,* May 1952. Cambridge, Fostoria, and other handmade glass companies had interchangeable component candle/flower bowls on the market in this same time period.

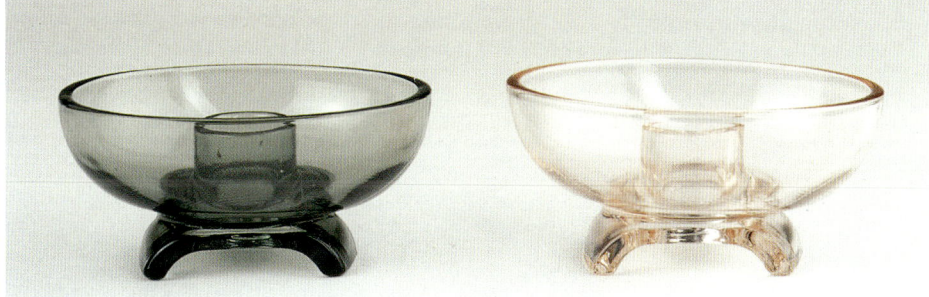

Scroll pattern bowl form, scroll foot candlestick. Charcoal or cherry glo, $18-26 each.

Cornucopia candleholder on light, round base (contrast to square cornucopia candlestick shown above) 3-1/2" crystal 1940s-1953, $8-16 each, and three light same as shown in the convertible component ad, $15-28 as shown.

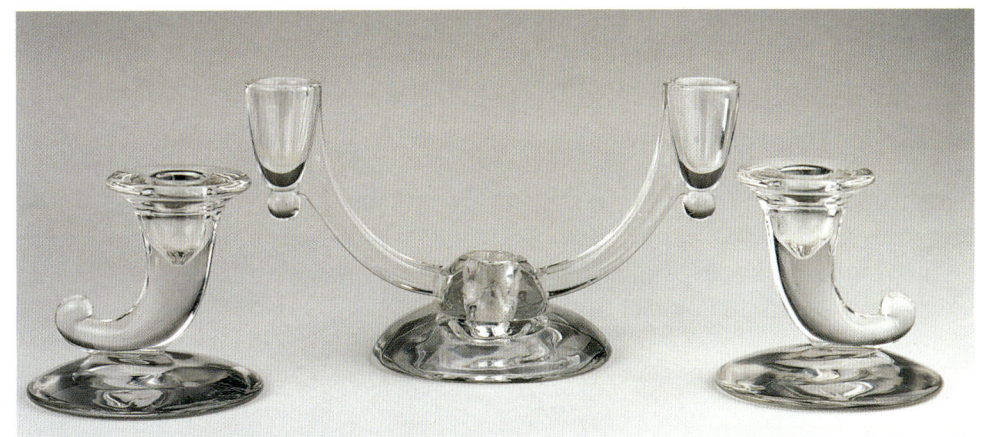

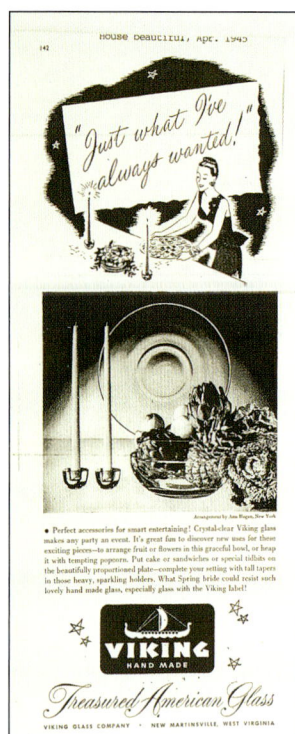

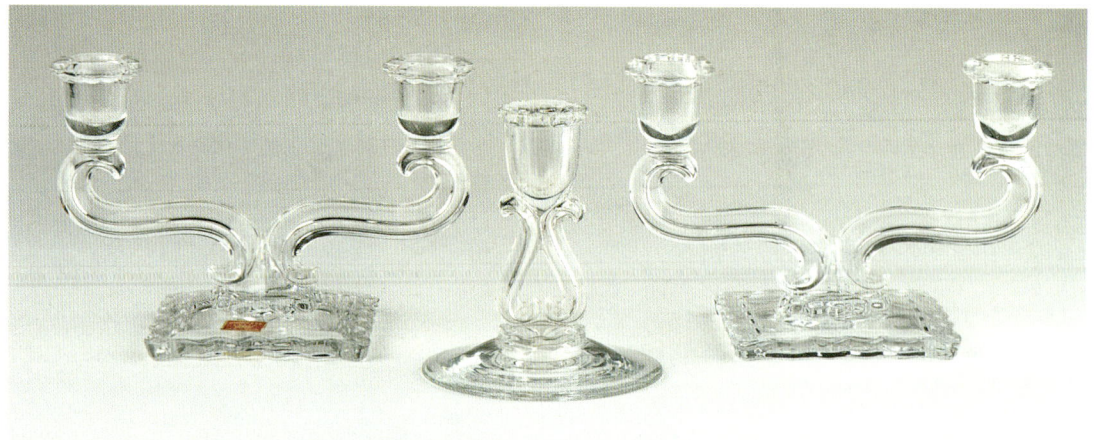

Princess Plaza (square base) pattern #5514 two light candelabras, crystal, $24-38 each and Princess (round base) single light #5213 crystal candlestick, $14-28 each.

Viking advertisement including #451, 2" one light candlestick, hand cut and polished with formal round serving pieces. *House Beautiful*, April 1945.

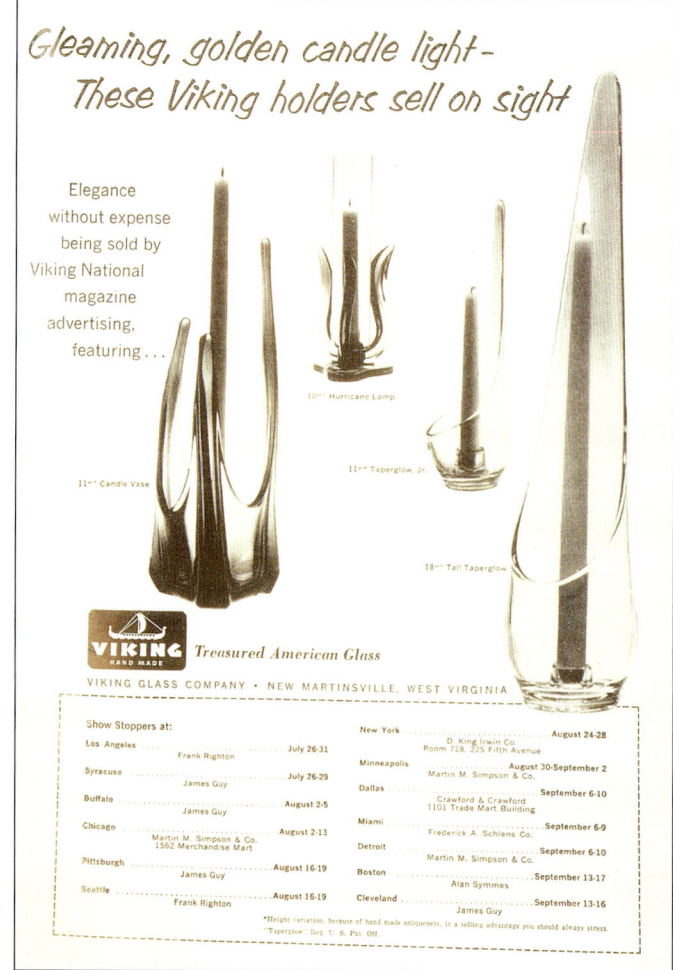

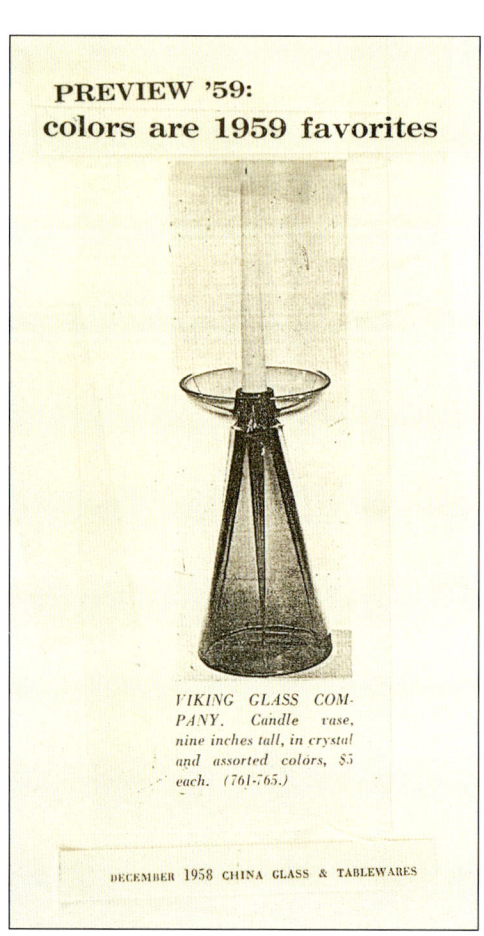

Ultra modern Viking candle forms: Candle vase, hurricane lamp with cylindrical crystal chimney and taperglow. As illustrated in *The Gift & Art Buyer*, August 1959.

Viking's illusive "candle vase," made in crystal and "assorted colors." The piece, as shown, is a candlestick and, when inverted, becomes a wide based vase. *China, Glass & Tableware*, December 1958.

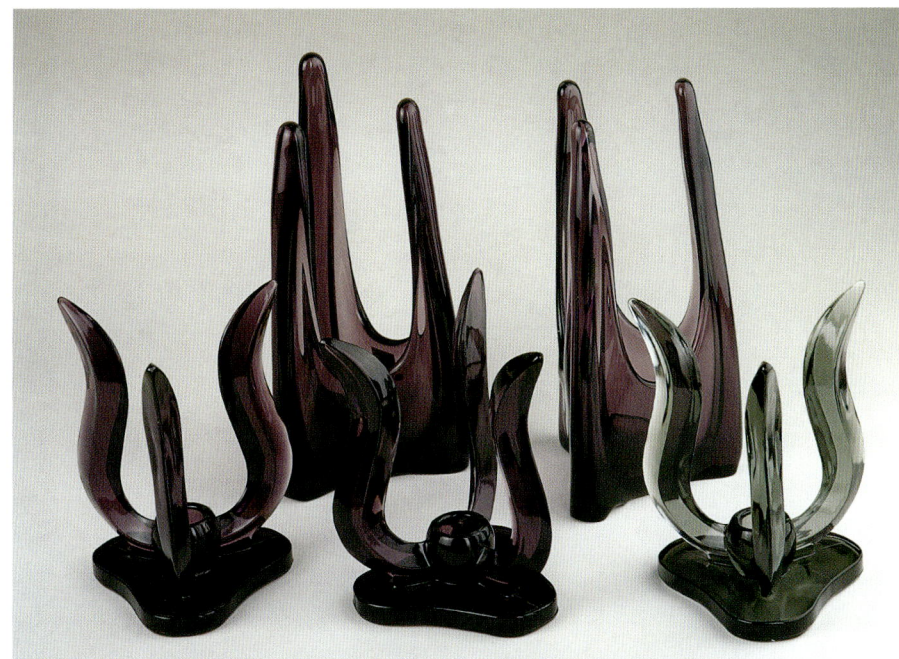

Hurricane lamp #1287 candleholder introduced circa 1957 and shown without crystal cylindrical chimney. Amethyst, $16-28 each as is, and charcoal, $14-24 each as is. Epic candle vase, back row, 11", #1222 amethyst, $18-30 each.

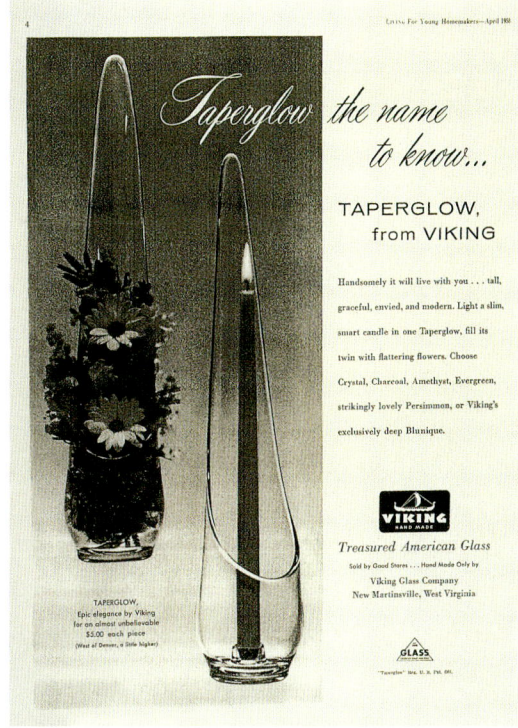

Advertisement stating "taperglow the name to know…Taperglow from Viking." Priced at $5 each and offered in crystal, charcoal, amethyst, evergreen, persimmon, and bluenique. *Living For Young Home-makers*, April 1958.

Advertisement for "Tall, tapered Epic Candleholder" in six colors. *The Gift & Art Buyer*, February 1958.

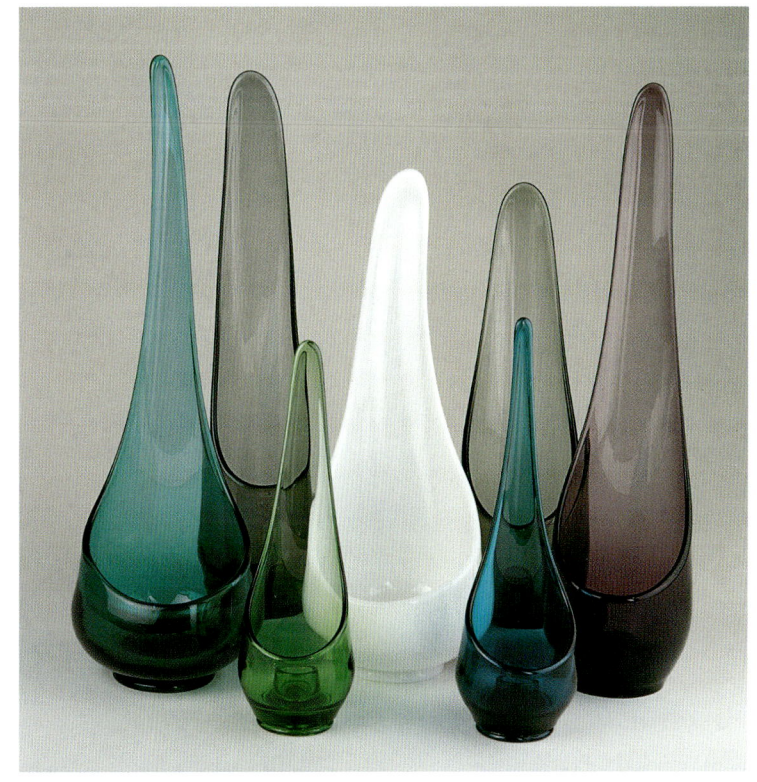

Epic taperglow candlesticks. #1192 "tall" in amethyst, $24-38; bluenique, $26-40; milk glass, $30-48; and charcoal, $24-38. #1194 "junior" in green, $20-34 and bluenique, $22-34.

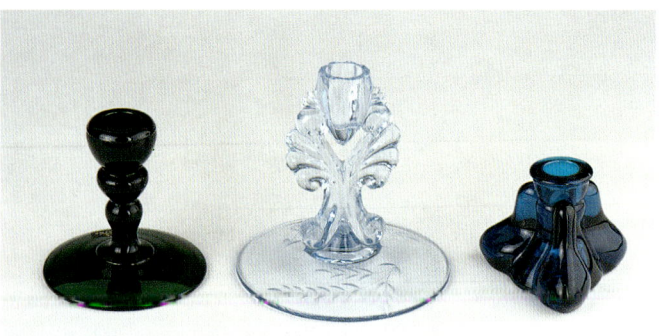

Candlestick #970 shown in *Crockery & Glass Journal*, January 1949, $22-28 each; Janice pattern single light candlestick #4554 colonial blue with gray hand cutting, $24-38 each; Epic three foil #1210 bluenique single light candlestick, $14-28 each.

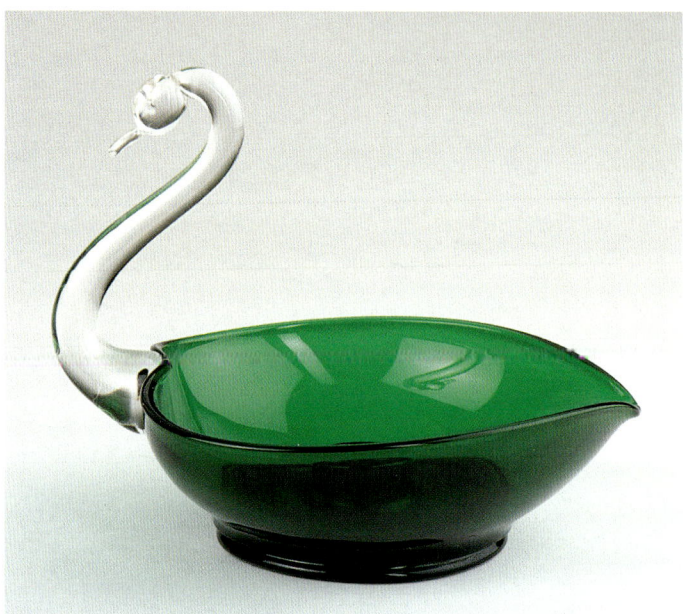

Swan handle candlestick evergreen #993/1S, $22-38 shown on the 1953 price list in crystal, amber, ebony, and evergreen.

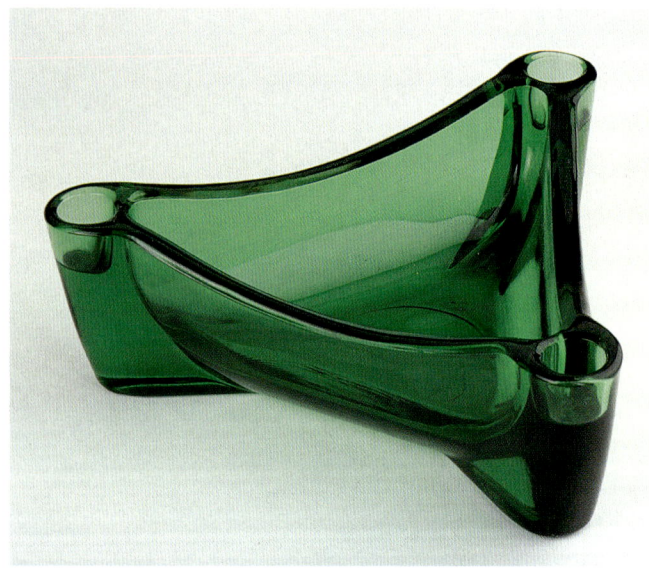

Candle bowl #1205 evergreen circa 1957 and in 1960 catalog, 9", $35-48.

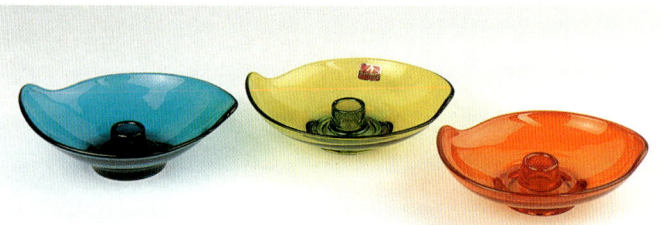

Epic "oblong" candlestick/candle bowl #1196, 7" bluenique, $14-28; avocado, $10-18; and persimmon, $14-28 each.

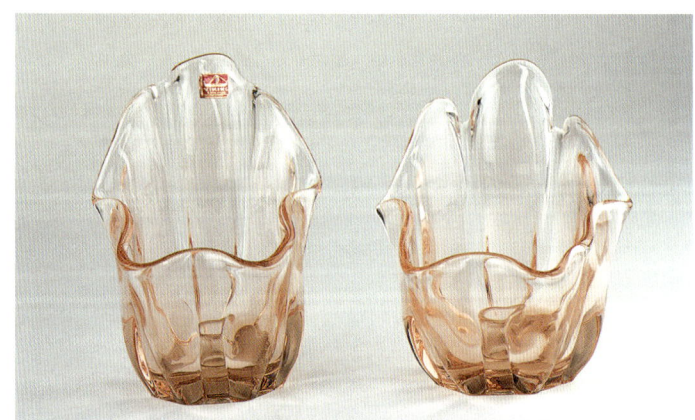

Epic "six petal" candleholders with original label on base "Viking New Martinsville 1416," Cherry glo, $20-38 each.

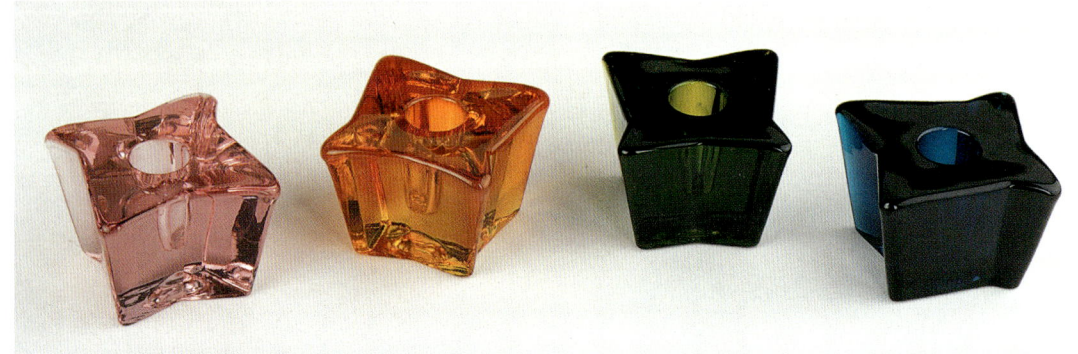

Astra pattern #6112 candlestick, 2-1/2". One of three styles of candle holders in this pattern. Teaberry, $22-34; Persimmon, $12-18; avocado green, $8-14; bluenique, $12-18 each.

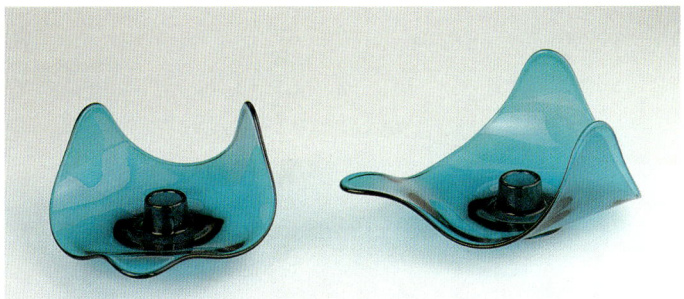

Epic "handkerchief" candlestick – candle bowl #1198, 6" bluenique, $16-28 each.

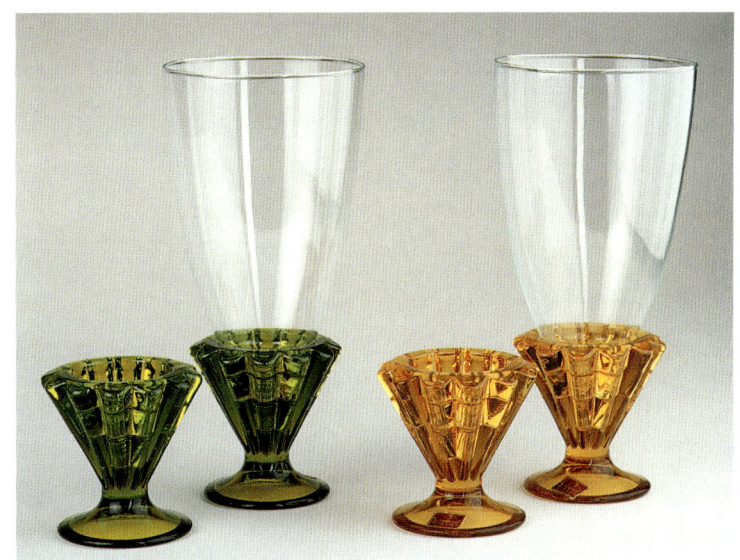

Epic candlestick #6803 sold with no shade, 3" amber, $5-9; avocado, $6-9 each; #6804 with crystal shade, 10" amber, $10-14; avocado, $12-15 each.

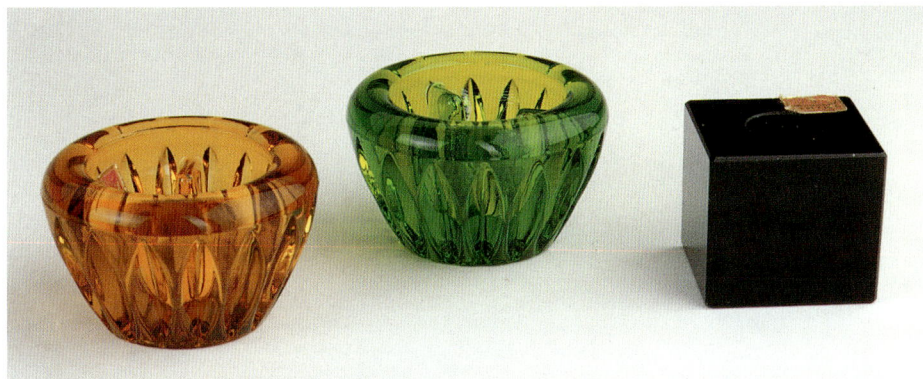

Epic single light #6801 candlestick 3" amber, $6-12; green, $8-14; ebony #3106 cut and polished square candlestick – exceptionally elegant, $20-32 each.

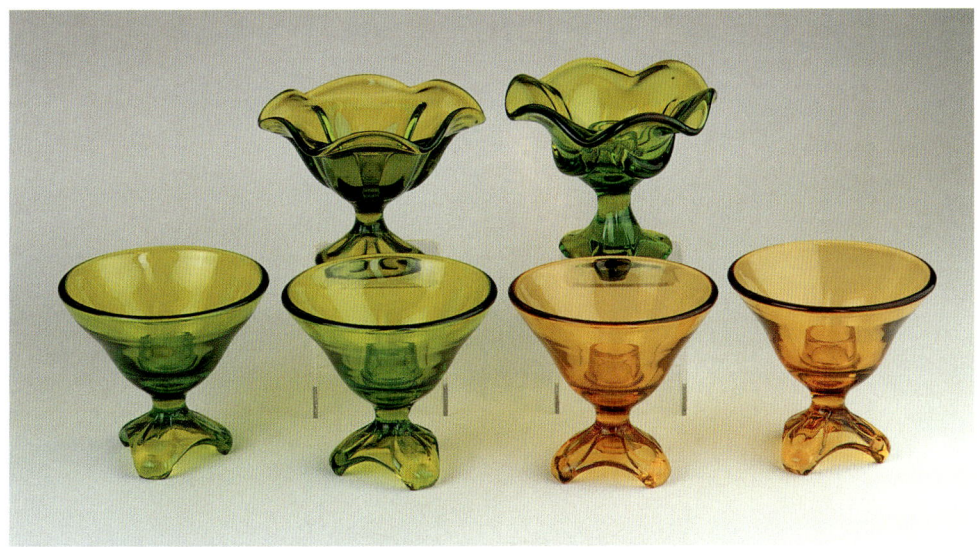

Epic candlestick #7003 flared candlestick 4-1/2" avocado green, $8-16; amber, $6-14 each. Epic drape fluted candlesticks, avocado green, $10-18 each.

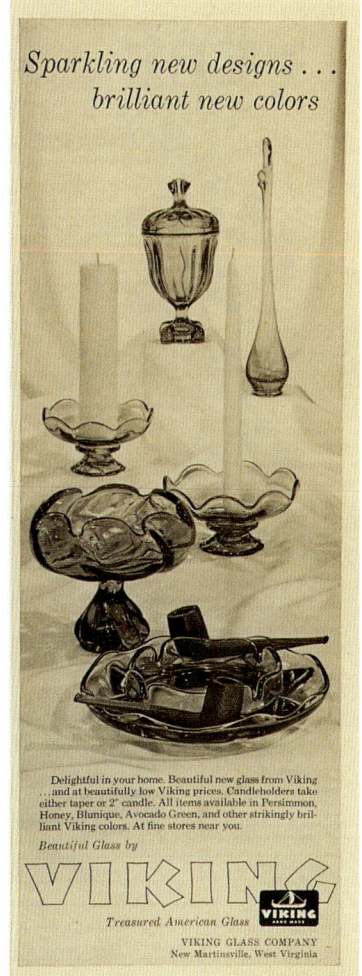

Ad for Viking showing Epic dual candlestick.

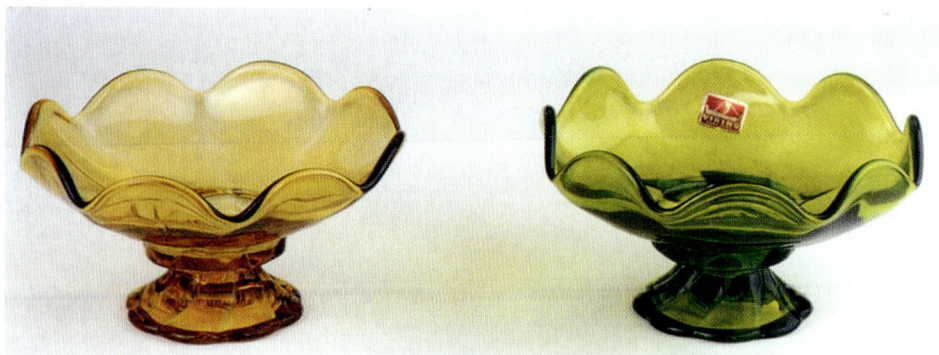

Epic dual candlestick (taper or pillar) #1411
amber, $10-16; avocado, $12-16 each.

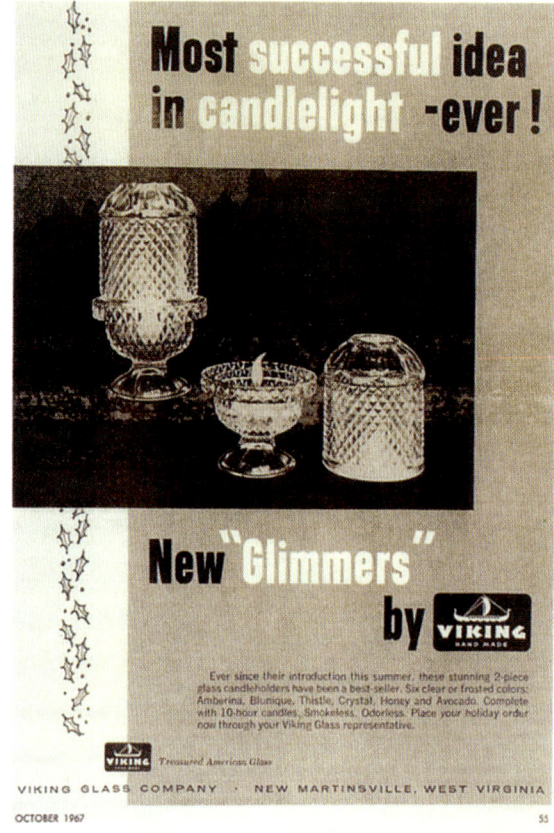

Advertisement for the "Most successful idea
in candlelight ever! New Glimmers by Viking."
Trade journal ad, October 1967.

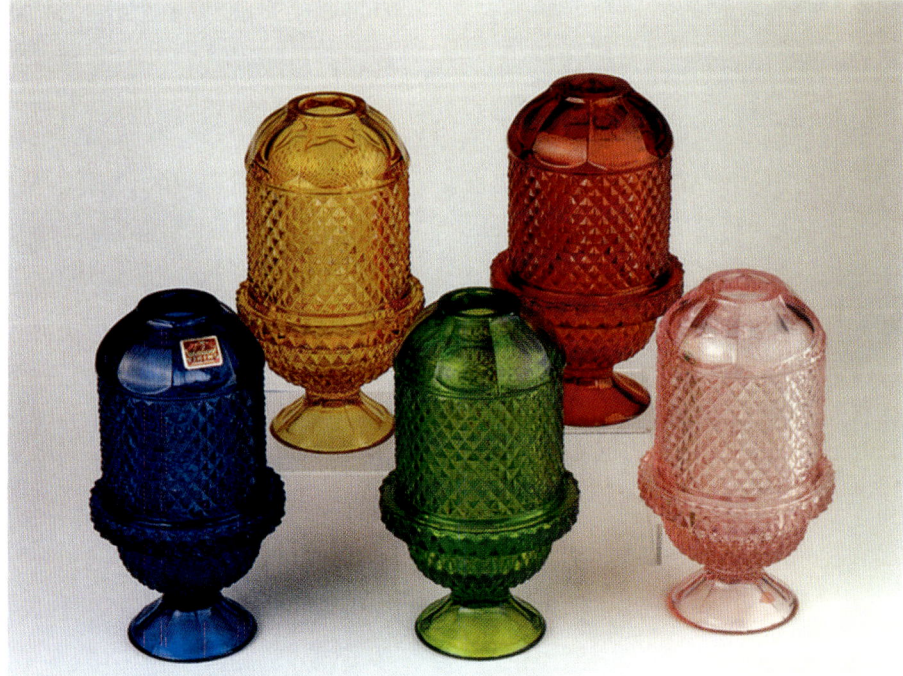

Glimmer #6700 two part candlelight.
Bluenique, $22-30; amber, $12-24; green,
$16-28; ruby, $25-38; thistle, $35-48.

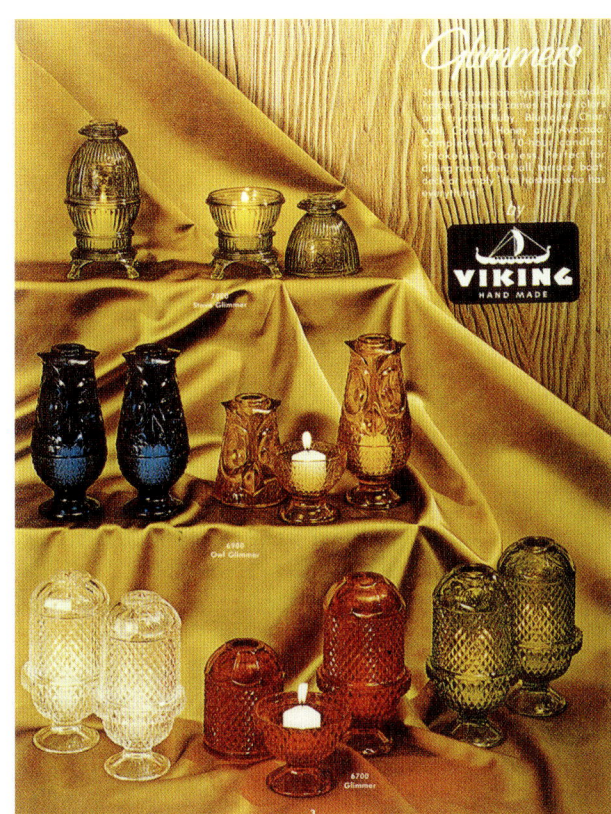

Viking Glass catalog page
showing the three Glimmer
patterns available in 1970.

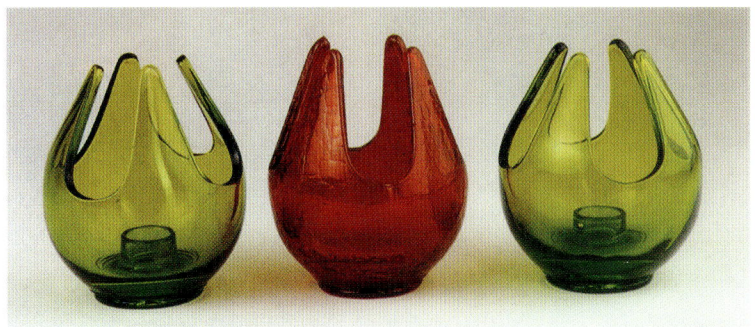

Owl two part Glimmer candlelight #6900 bluenique, $26-36; green, $18-30.

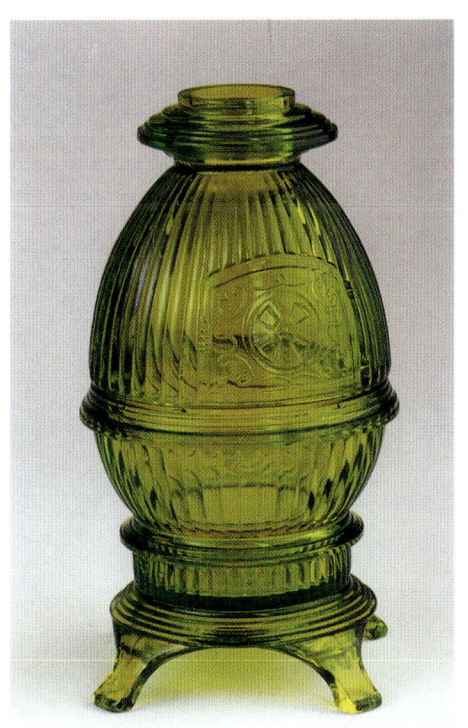

Epic Candle Cup, when with candle cup inside #7018, 4-1/2", and without
candle cup as Patio Lite #7019. Priced slightly higher for #7018 with candle
cup. As shown, avocado with candle cup, $8-14 each; ruby without candle cup,
$12-18 each.

Stove two part Glimmer candlelight, green,
$34-44.

Flower Bowls, Flowerlites, Frogs, and More

Viking produced a successful line for many years that included flower frogs, several forms of flower frogs in fact. Frogs are those glass inserts with perforations meant to have flower stems inserted through the hole in the glass and into water in the vase or bowl below. The frog served to hold the flowers in the arrangement and form desired. Viking was not the first or by any means the only producer of glass flower frogs, also known as flower blocks.

#718 one piece flower bowl with attached block/ frog:

The earliest connection with flower frogs and Viking would be the #718 one piece shown in a circa late 1940s Viking catalog. This object was made under a patent obtained originally by Ira Clark, the ex-plant manager of New Martinsville Glass. Although Mr. Clark was deceased by this time it would appear that the tools, process, and knowledge to make these one-piece objects remained at the Viking factory. It is 8-1/2" in diameter and a shallow 2" deep. Manufacturing it was a marvel as it required complex and hand skilled glass working to create. It disappeared from the Viking offerings early.

Another early mention of a flower frog is found in a June 1950 advertisement and features a #550 Flowerette and #549 Flowerlite three legged round bowl in "ebony, evergreen, amber, crystal, ruby, and cobalt. This illustrated ad shows a form collectors have come to distinguish as "tree trunk legs," indicating the textured, bark-like short legs on the piece. Beaumont Glass of Morgantown, West Virginia, made this form for many years. The mould used by Viking may have been the same as previously used at Beaumont. The frog marketed with this bowl is either a 3" flowerette with eleven stem holes, no candle well, and five raised "dots" of glass on the base or the 3" flowerlite frog with ten stem holes around a center hole that is larger and does not pass through, intended to hold a candle. These are the details that dedicated collectors of flower frogs and the matching bowls insist upon. Note also that Viking is only known to have made crystal flower frogs.

The use of frogs in Viking products after this earliest mention above can all be arranged by product number and what follows is organized by factory item number.

#1007 Flower bowl with Frog

Introduced circa 1950, this is the longest produced, most commonly found form for Viking flower containers. This little, 4-1/2", three toed fellow is an adaptation of the early tree trunk leg round bowl mentioned above. It may be the same mould reworked, or it may be an entirely new mould. The close resemblance and size similarities are not accidental. #1007 is intended to continue the form but replace the tree trunk legs that chipped so easily. This item remains in production at Viking from early introduction through the early 1970s. It is gone from the catalogs before 1975 but reappears later in the factory history. The feet and legs on these objects are the same as some found on items in the Janice line of shapes in the circa 1948 catalog. Perhaps the success of the Beaumont flowerlite led Viking to adapt an existing Janice molds? In any event, this is the most produced Viking frog and the line number is #1007 with the flowerlite frog (candle well in center) and #997 with the flowerette frog (all holes for flower, no candle well at all). While working on this book I have taken the egotistical, bold, and fun path of dubbing this shape "007" with the idea of easy and memorable reference. As an academically trained historian, this makes me grimace a little, but there are a few "author's prerogatives." We are in no way attempting to infringe on the James Bond trademark, 007 is just so easy to remember.

"007" is strikingly similar to a nearly identical form from Beaumont Glass of Morgantown, West Virginia. It has been suggested that an easy way to tell the Beaumont from the Viking tree-trunk footed bowls (beside some colors) is that Beaumont products have a seam down the middle of the underside of the feet. Viking reportedly removed this with fire polishing.

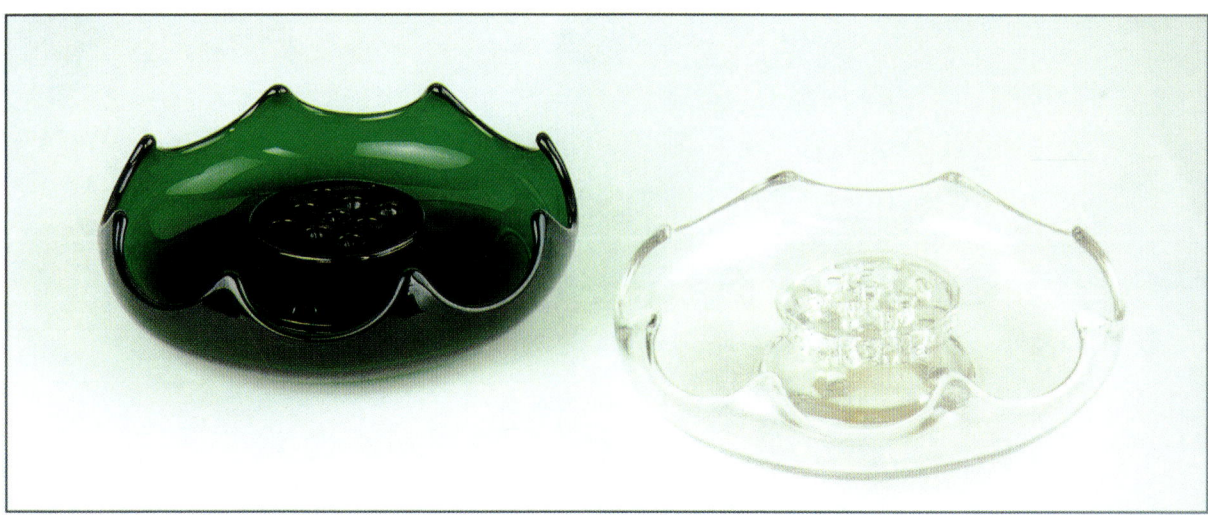

Flower bowl with block made in place, circa 1950, #718, 8-1/2". Only colors believed made by Viking are crystal, $42-48, and evergreen, $60-70.

#1014 flower bowl with frog

This is a very similar, slightly larger, 5-1/2" wide by 4-1/2" tall version of 1007. It appears in the late 1940s, circa 1950 catalog. Based on the colors in which this item is found, it dates into the early 1950s. This takes a 3-1/2" frog, not the 3" used on #1007. With the Flowerette frog, the line number is #999.

#1048 flower bowl with frog

Catalogs caption this the "1048 – 6-1/2" oval flowerlite." It is an oval bowl in the Scroll-shaped line made by Viking with a two-candle flowerlite frog in it. An ad showing this double candle, crystal frog insert with colored Scroll line bowl appears in September of 1954 as full-page ads in *Crockery & Glass Journal* and *China, Glass and Tableware*. The Scroll line included a 6-1/2" bowl as item #1975, without the flowerlite. This item is shown in the 1962 catalog several years after the other shapes in the Scroll line seem to have been discontinued.

#1049 flower bowl with frog

Captioned a "1049 – 12" oval flowerlite," this is an impressively large glass bowl that incorporates two extended candle holding arms on either end. The frog is the same as utilized for the #1048 above and incorporates two candle sockets itself, making this a four candle arrangement when in use. It is shown in the 1962 catalog. Note that it was sold as item #1050 without the frog. Indications are for a short production time as it has yet to be found in ads or catalogs other than the 1962 Viking catalog.

#5271 flower bowl with frog

This tall flower bowl is a shape from the Princess line of tableware. The base incorporates the crinkled ribbon design found on the base of Princess-shaped pieces. This open stemmed, tall bowl utilizes the 3" frog. It is shown in the 1955 and 1962 catalogs.

#1932 flower bowl with frog

Another Viking adaptation to a flower bowl with frog from a larger existing line is the #1932 flowerlite. A low, three-legged bowl with a hobnail pattern reminiscent of Viking Ancestral pattern is included in the Yesteryear line. The form may be either crimped or flattened to form a shallow bowl, both objects then being sold as bonbons. When it is cupped upward the same mold forms a 5" flower bowl ready to accept a crystal frog or flowerlite. This forming to make multiple objects is true of many Viking flower bowls that accept frogs, as they are made from moulds also used for bonbon dishes, lemon dishes, and other forms. #1932 was sold as a part of the Yesteryear line as well as shown in the 1962 catalog with the other "flower containers." It has disappeared from the line prior to the 1968 catalog.

#1815 flower bowl with frog

This pattern is both a part of the Yesteryear line and also properly the Yesteryear Pattern. Collectors have taken to calling it the "Yesteryear Bull's-eye" pattern. This low bowl is not in the 1968 catalog but appears in 1970. By 1975 it is gone from the catalog. This requires the less common 3-1/2" flower frog, a size used only on this and the #1014 bowls.

#1931 flower bowl with frog

Appearing in the 1960 Viking catalog is a milk glass pineapple formed bowl with a crystal flower frog where a lid might otherwise be. Noteworthy is that the copy of the catalog used has a note stapled inside the front cover which reads, in part, discontinued as of January 1, 1961, page 7, 1931 6" Pineapple flowerlite. Item #1930, the Pineapple cover jar, featuring a lid that resembles a true pineapple top with leaves, is shown in ads in 1957. In major ads appearing in *The Gift & Art Buyer* March 1958 and other trade journals is a two-page advertisement for Viking showing both the Pineapple flowerlite and Pineapple jar & cover.

#1507 flower bowl with frog

The 1964 price list Epic line section includes item #1507, a flowerlite. It is not in the 1962 catalog or 1963 catalog supplement. This flower blossom-like form appears to have petals as its design motif. It is shown in the 1968 catalog but not in 1970.

The actual glass "frog," the inserted object for holding floral stems, made at Viking in this era are few in number. Six forms are known and all in crystal only. One additional Viking size at least was produced in the years after this book. It is 4-3/8" in diameter. Of interest is that a few years before Viking, in the "depression era," these forms were called flower blocks but are today's frogs!

3" flowerlite- with no dots or feet on the bottom and have the candle well in center.

3" flowerette- has five "dot feet" on the bottom and no candle well.

3.5" flowerlite- with no dots or feet on the bottom and has the candle well in the center.

3.5" flowerette- in the 1953 price list, not found in any of the available catalogs.

3.5" frog #1005 shown in a 1962 catalog and appears to be a "mounded" style but further information is needed.

6" oval double flowerlite- no dots or feet on bottom and two candle wells.

Note: all sizes are diameter at the base.

The creation of candle holding glass continued to the end at Viking; however, the forms made changed. While candlelight frog and flower bowls were obviously popular for two decades, they had disappeared completely sometime between 1970 and 1975. Taking their place as popular candleholders would be votive holders and two part fairy lights, called Glimmers at Viking.

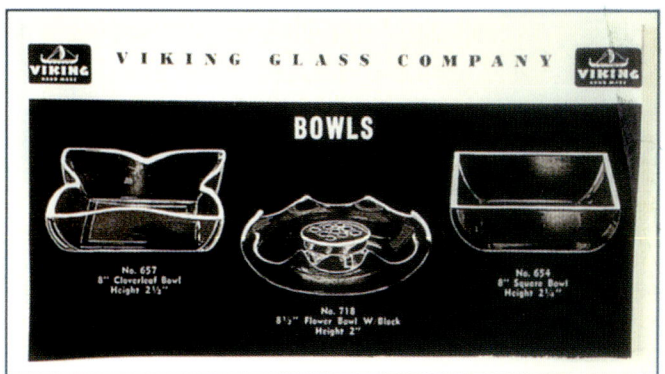

Viking Glass catalog illustration, circa 1950.

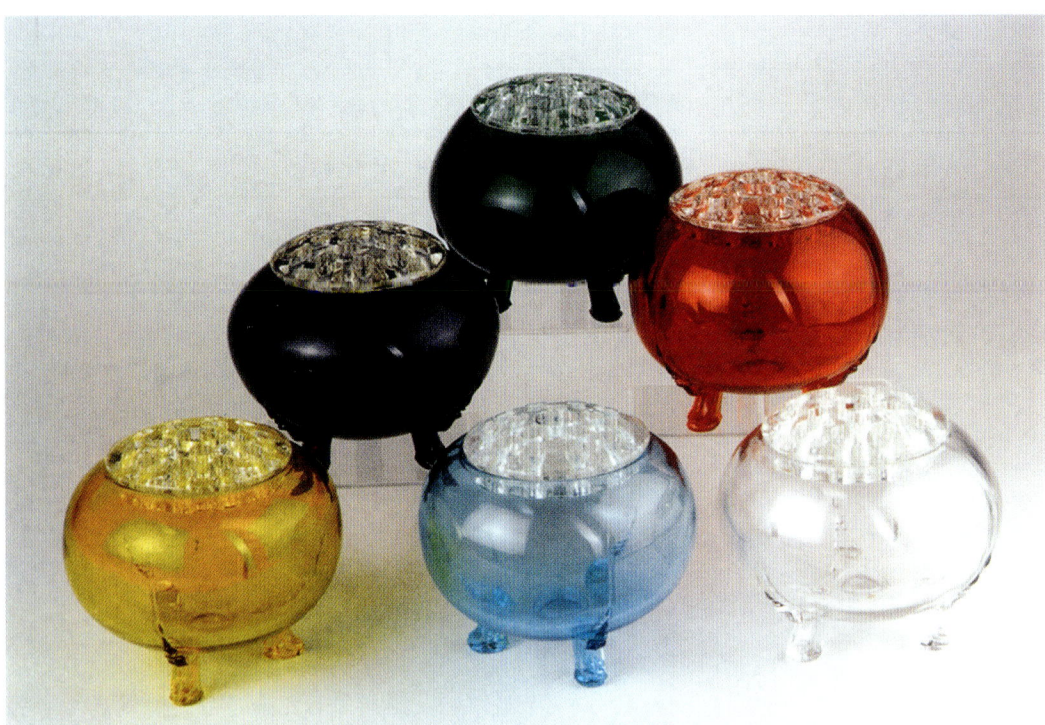

Flowerlite #1014 harvest gold, $77-87; ebony, $55-65; evergreen, $75-85; colonial blue, $75-85; ruby, $75-85; and crystal,
$45-55. Includes proper crystal frog.

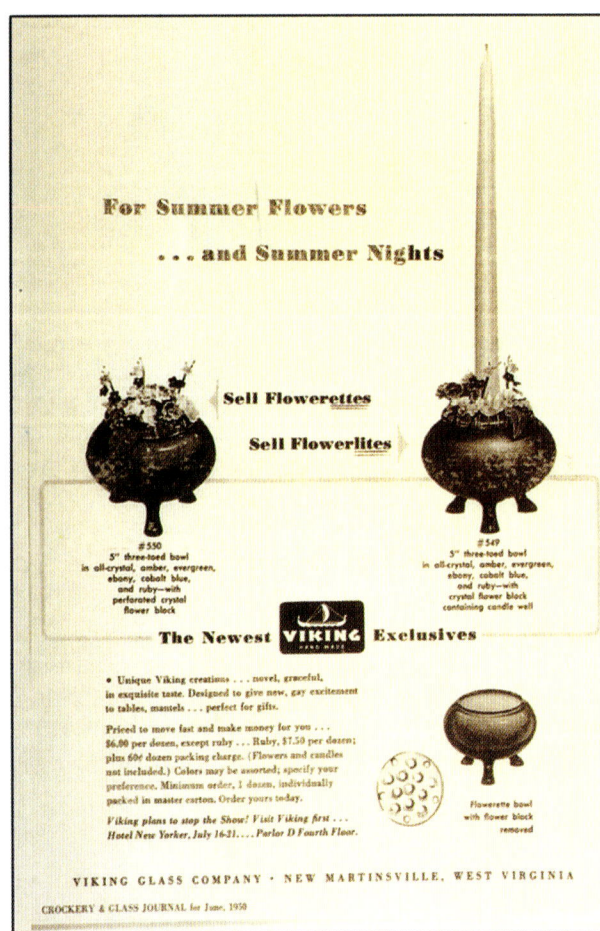

Flowerettes and Flowerlites, advertised by Viking as "the newest
Viking exclusives" in *Crockery and Glass Journal*, June 1950.

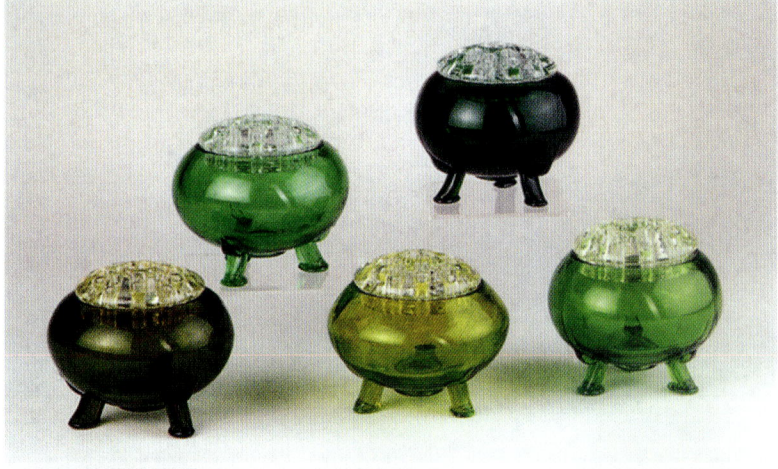

Flowerettes and Flowerlites, advertised by Viking as "the newest Viking exclusives"
in *Crockery and Glass Journal*, June 1950.

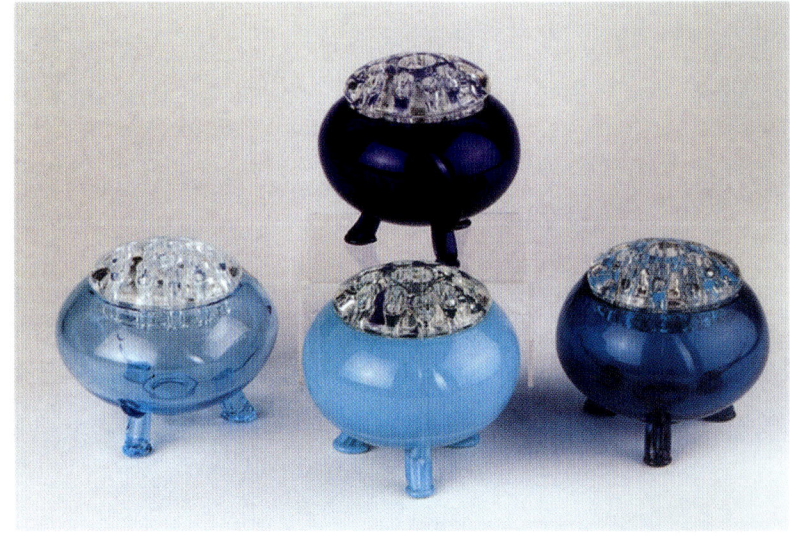

"007" bowl with crystal frog: colonial blue, cobalt blue, blue milk glass, bluenique.

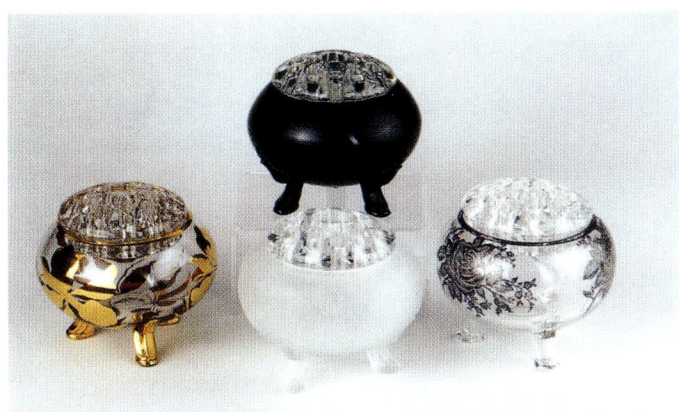

"007" bowl with crystal frog: crystal with gold decoration, ebony, crystal frosted, crystal with silver decoration.

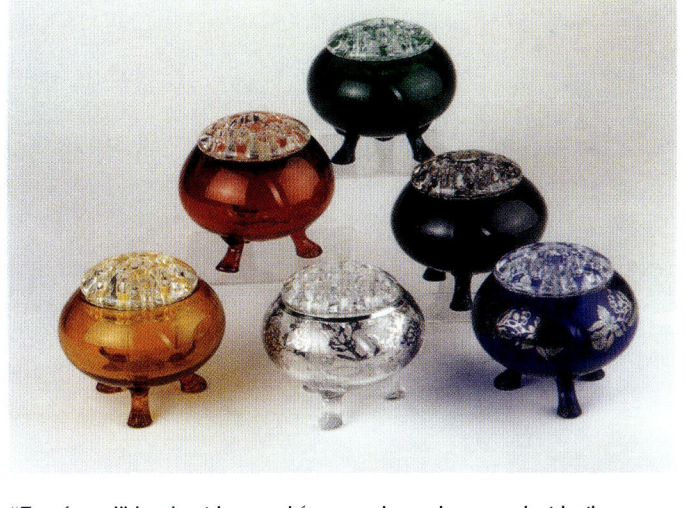

"Tree footed" bowls with crystal frogs: amber, ruby, crystal with silver decoration, ebony, and cobalt with silver decoration. This form was restyled around 1951 to add pads on the feet and remove the "tree bark" texture on the legs. It is likely this is the bowl shown in the 1950 Viking ad above.

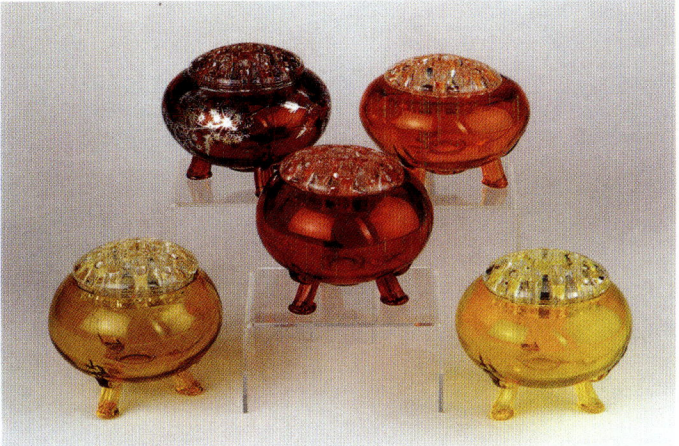

"007" bowl with crystal frog: amber, ruby with silver decoration, ruby, persimmon, harvest gold.

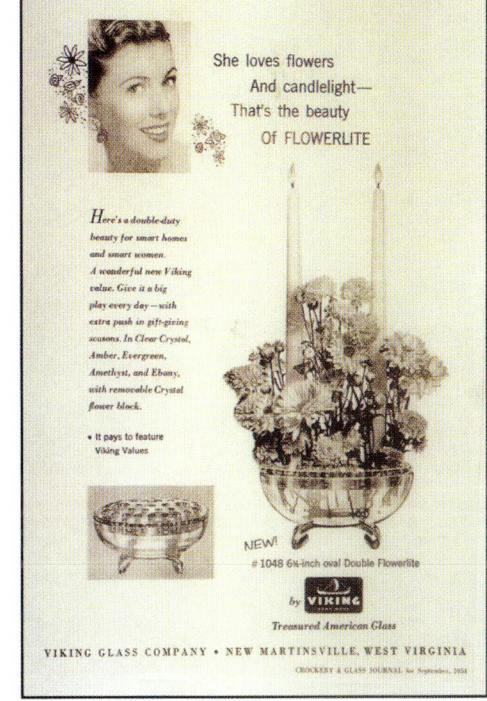

"She loves flowers and candlelight – that's the beauty of Flowerlite" says this 1954 ad for the "New #1048 double flowerlite." The Scroll pattern bowl as shown in *Crockery & Glass Journal*, September 1954.

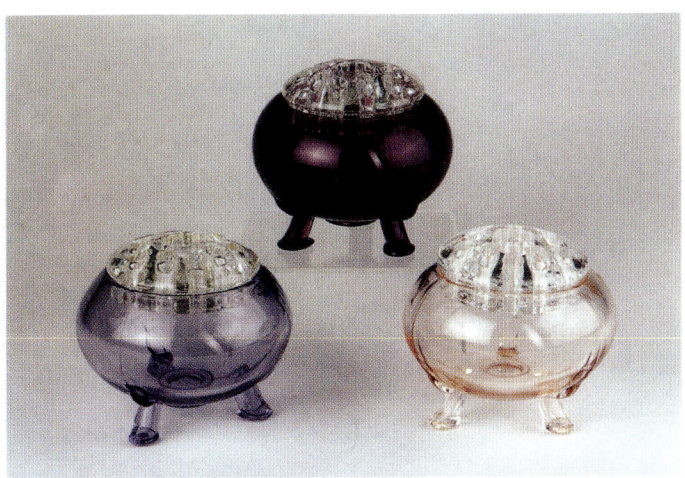

"007" bowl with crystal frog: teaberry, amethyst, and cherry glow.

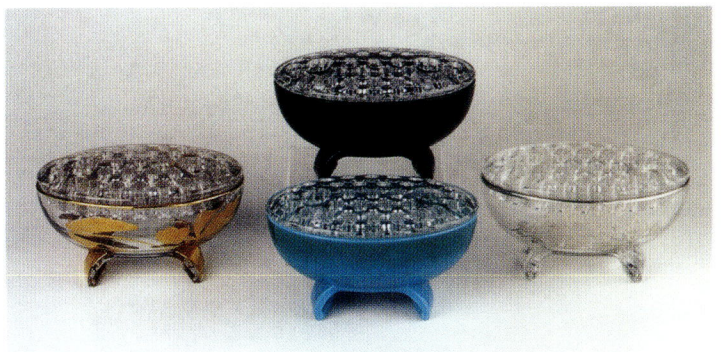

Scroll oval flowerlite #1048 with crystal frog: crystal with gold decoration, $55-65; ebony, $80-90; blue milk glass, $125-150; crystal with silver decoration, $55-65.

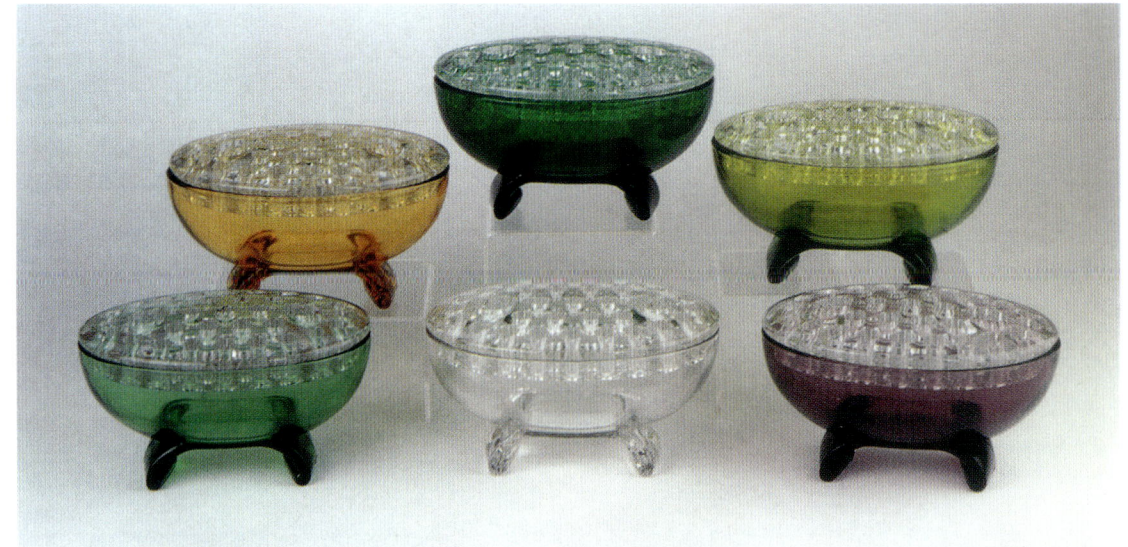

Scroll oval flowerlite #1048 with crystal frog: emerald green, $70-80; amber, $55-65; evergreen, $80-90; crystal, $50-56; avocado, $68-78; amethyst, $72-82.

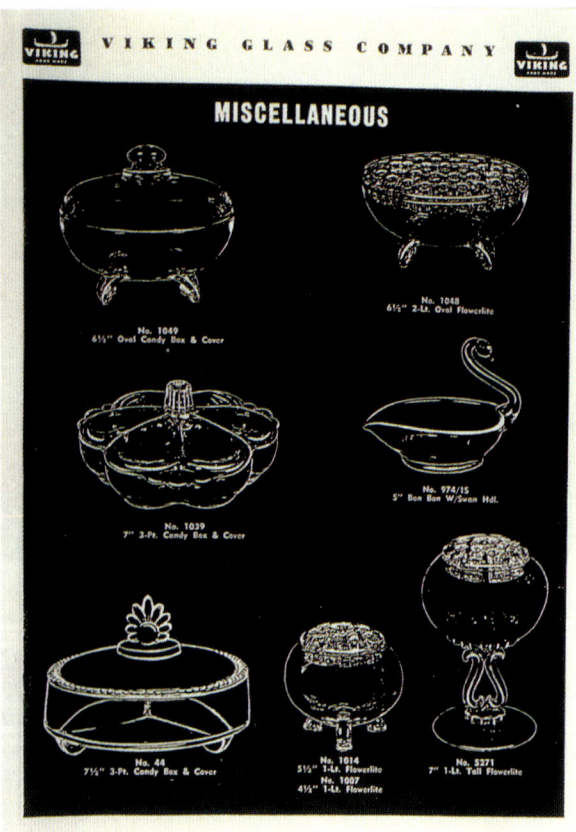

Viking Glass catalog showing Scroll #007/1014 and Princess flowerlites 1956.

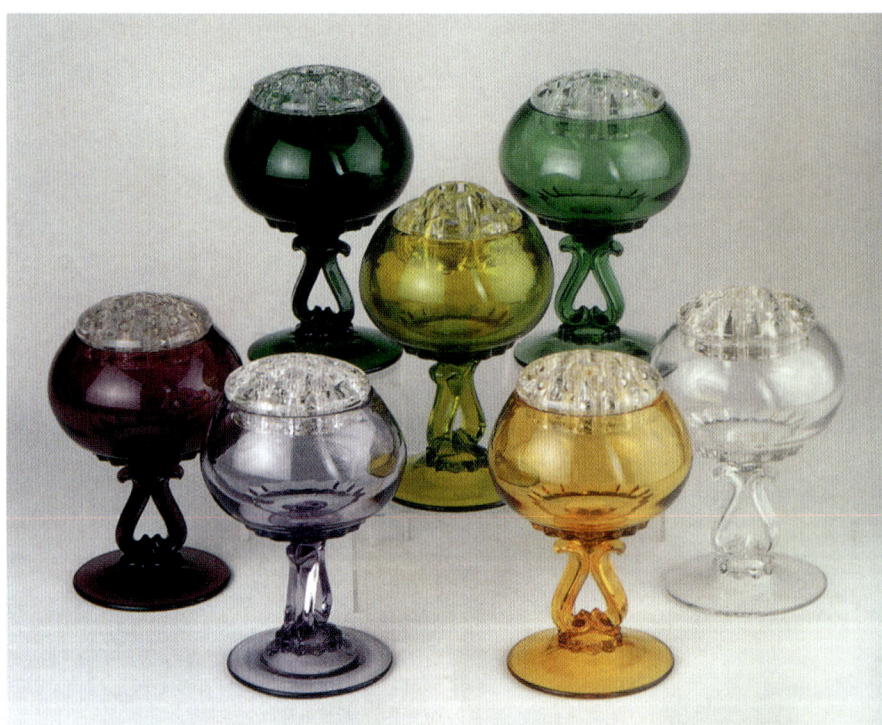

Princess pattern 7" "tall flowerlite" #5271 with crystal frog: amethyst, $75-82; teaberry, $85-94; evergreen, $80-90; avocado, $70-76; emerald green, $74-78; amber, $55-68; and crystal, $55-68.

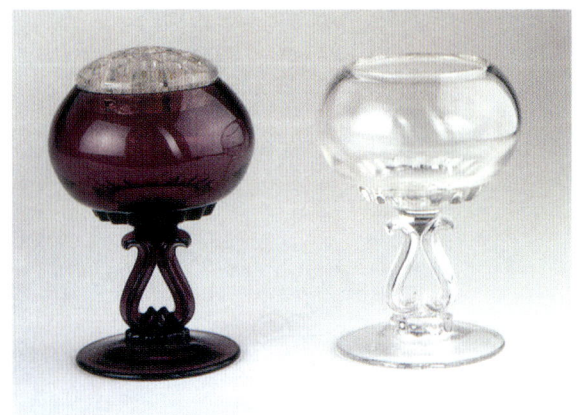

Princess pattern tall flowerlite #5271 amethyst bowl with crystal frog in place, $75-82, crystal bowl shown with no frog, $40-48.

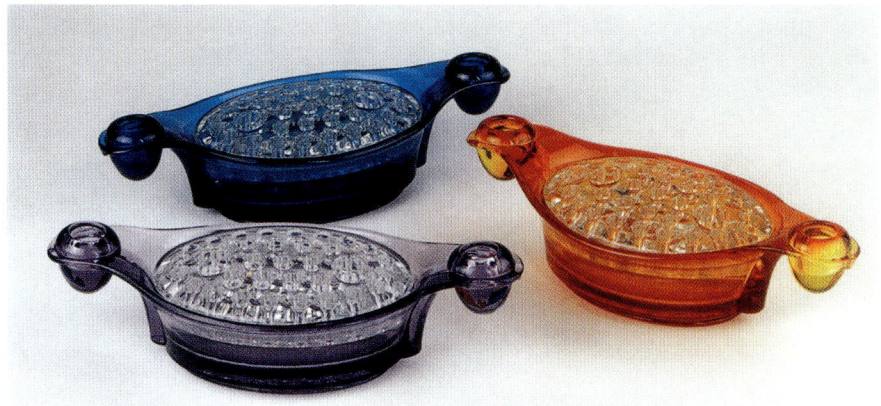

Candle bowl #1050, 12" oval with crystal frog, amethyst, $40-55; bluenique, $50-60; and amberina, $60-68. Shown in 1962 catalog.

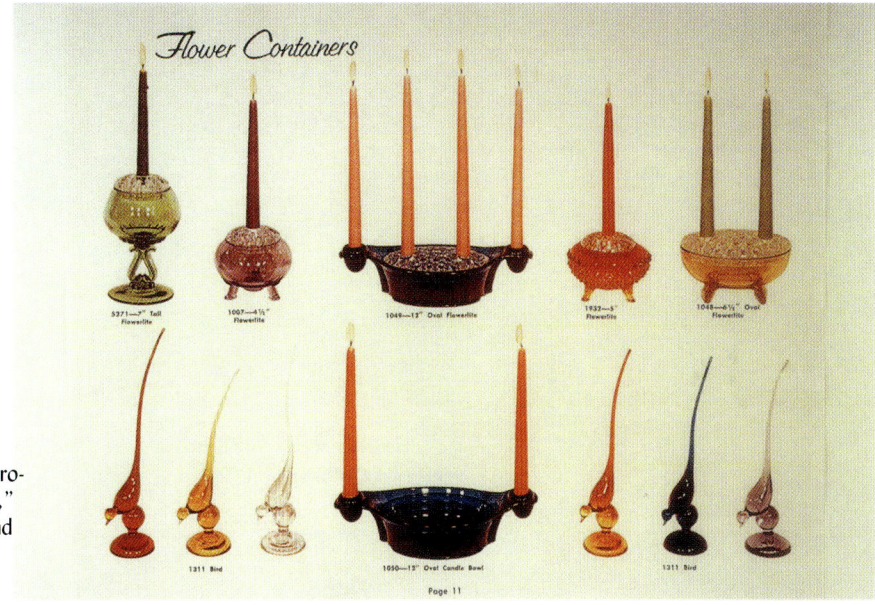

Viking Glass 1962 catalog showing five then in production flowerlites. Princess "tall" #5271, "007," oval bowl #1049, Yesteryear hobnail #1932, and oval Scroll #1048.

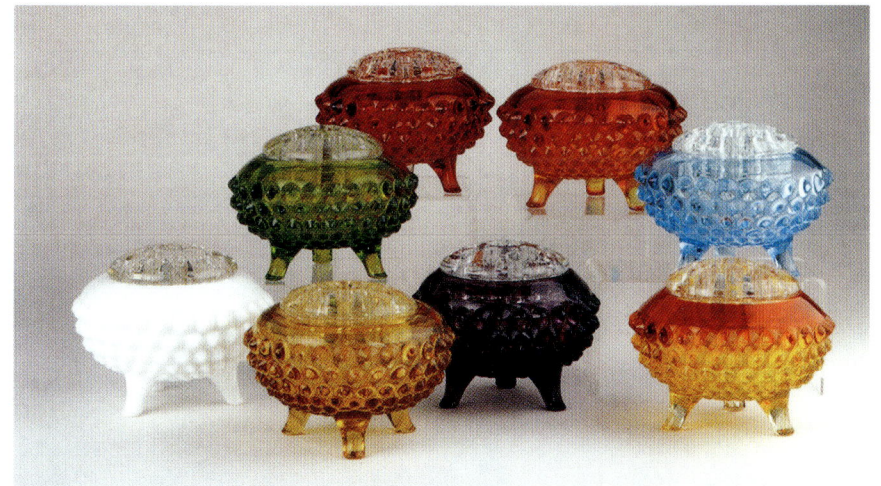

Yesteryear line hobnail flowerlite #1932 with crystal frog: milk glass, $48-58; avocado, $35-48; amber, $35-45; ruby, $48-58; amethyst, $45-52; persimmon, $46-54; colonial blue, $45-54; and amberina, $45-55.

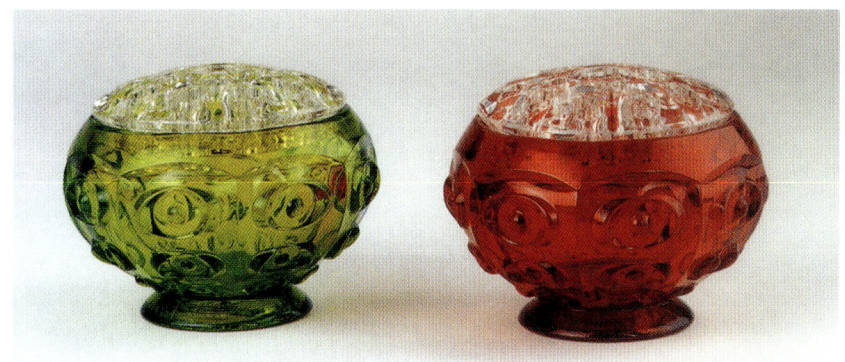

Yesteryear line "bull's-eye" flowerlite with crystal frog, ruby, $60-65, and avocado, $52-58.

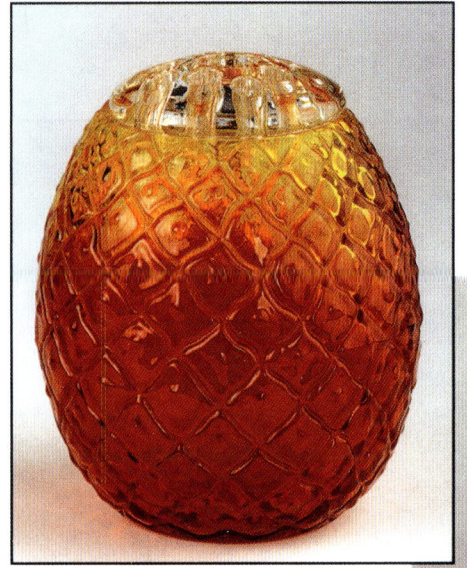

Yesteryear line "Pineapple" flowerlite amberina with crystal frog, $55-68.

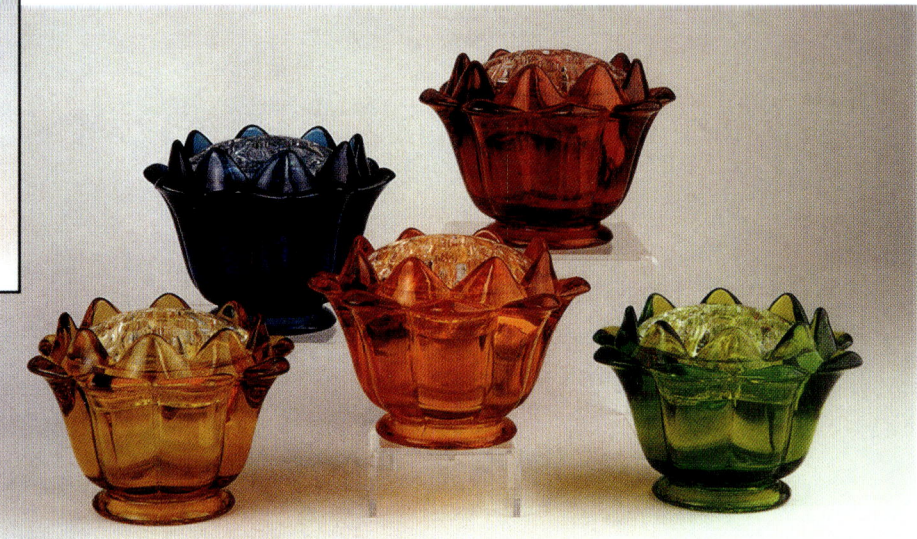

Epic flowerlite #1507 with crystal frog: amber, $40-45; bluenique, $48-58; persimmon, $50-60; ruby, $52-62; and avocado, $45-55.

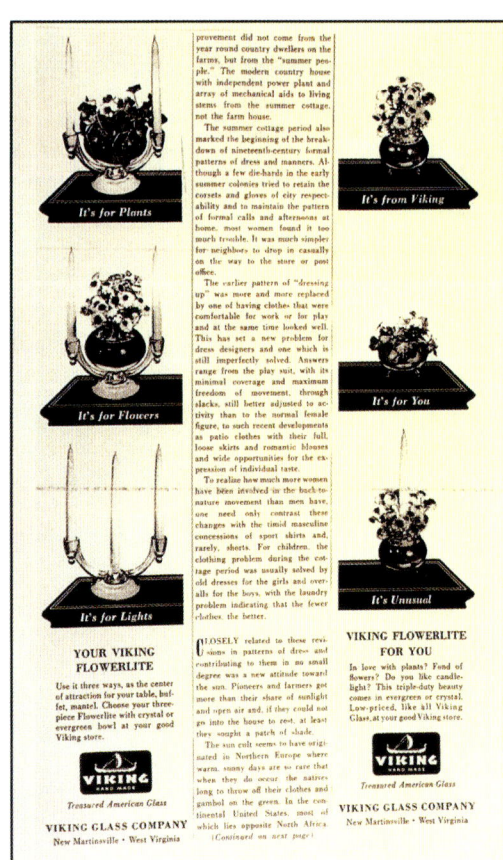

Advertisement showing adaptive combinations of bowl, candlesticks, pegged round bowls, and flower frogs. *House Beautiful*, November 1951.

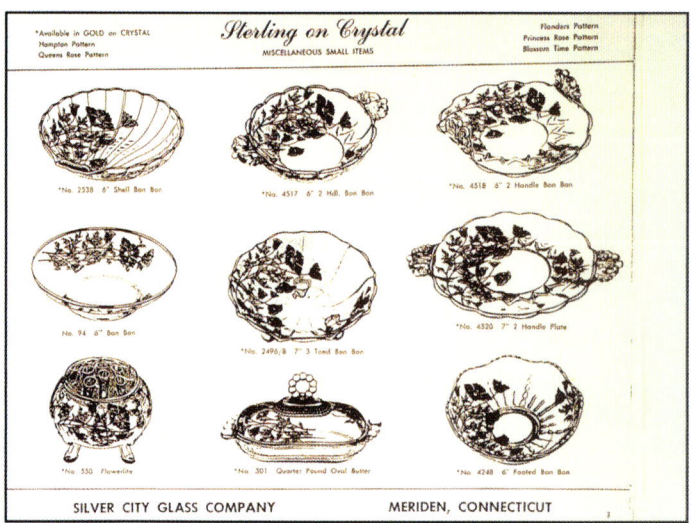

Silver City Glass Company catalog page with several Viking forms (Janice, Radiance, and flower frog bowl). Silver City is one of the major decorators using Viking glass. Noted in the history section of this book is the connection between the two companies.

Novelties and Miscellany

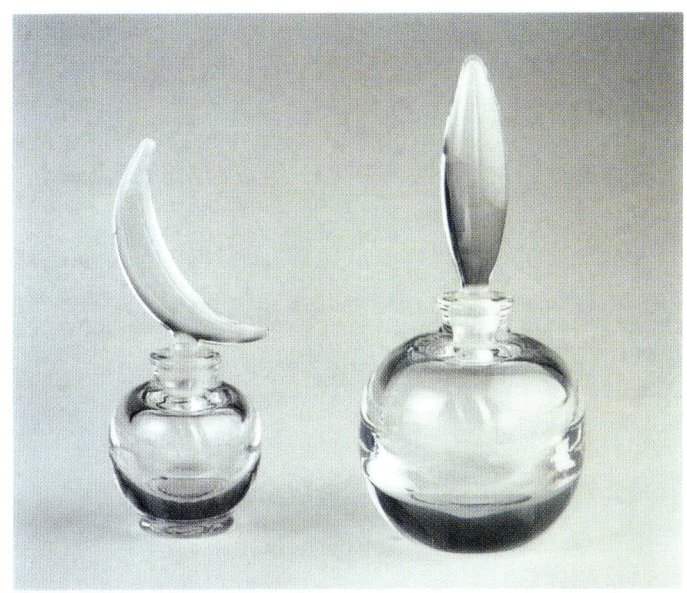

Perfume #675, 3/8 oz. with crescent stopper, 5", crystal, $35-40; perfume #677, 1-1/4 oz. with stopper, 6", crystal, $30-35.

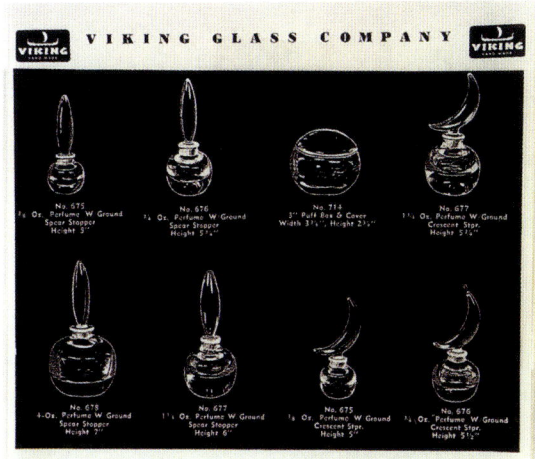

Bedroom and boudoir items were much more plentiful in New Martinsville Glass Co. lines than in Viking. Shown here is the selection from the 1948-49 catalog.

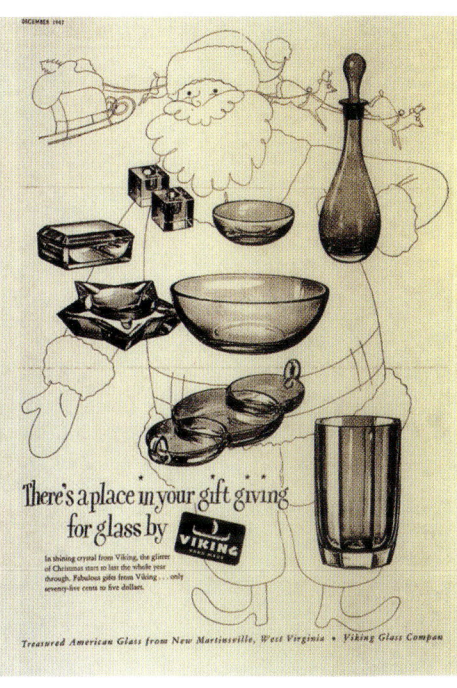

Viking advertisement showing diverse crystal products. Note the novel five part, "three ring" divided relish made with ring handles and without the decanter with stopper.

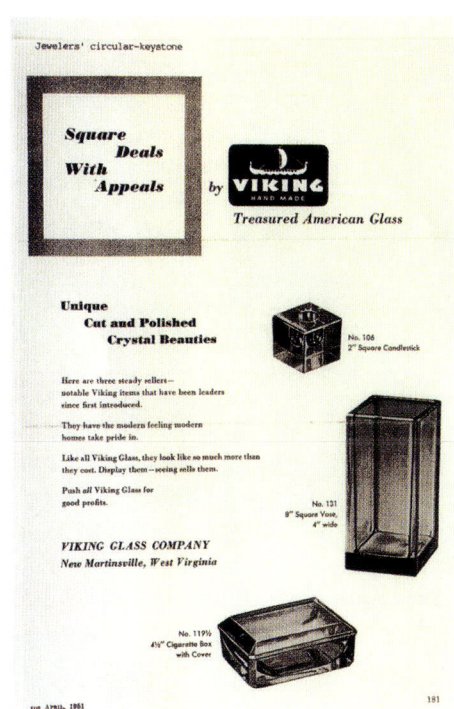

Viking advertisement showing a widely used line of square shapes that were adapted for cutting and decorations.

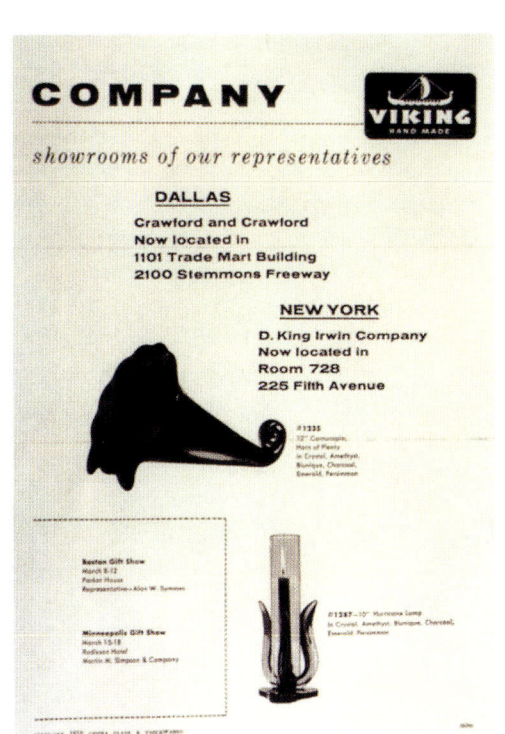

Viking advertisement showing hurricane candlestick and cornucopia.

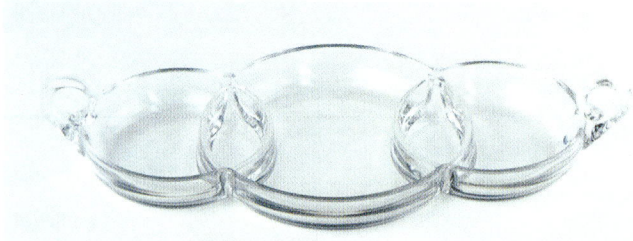

Relish, five part, "three ring" divided relish in crystal #659, $20-28.

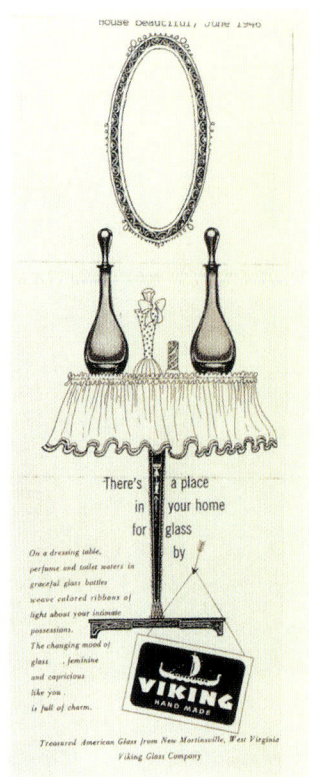

Viking advertisement showing the crystal decanter with ground stopper.

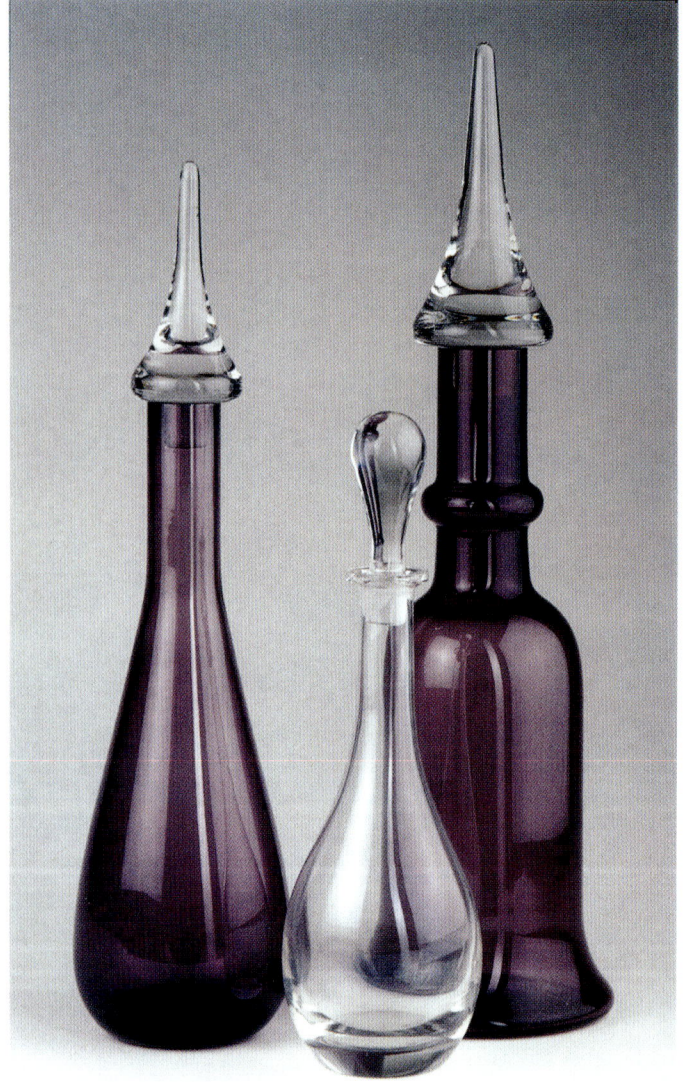

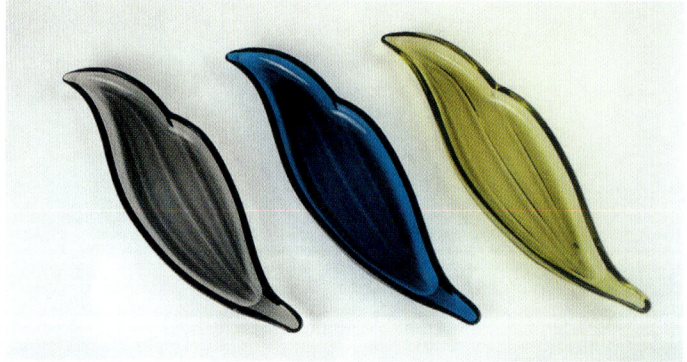

Leaf relish #760, 12-1/2" charcoal, $18-26; bluenique, $20-28; and avocado, $12-16. Made divided and undivided.

Decanters: Epic amethyst with crystal ground stopper #1255, 16", shown in 1959 catalog, $40-55; crystal with ground stopper #711, 20 oz., 12 /14", $20-32; Epic amethyst with crystal ground stopper #1257, 18", shown in 1959 catalog, $58-72.

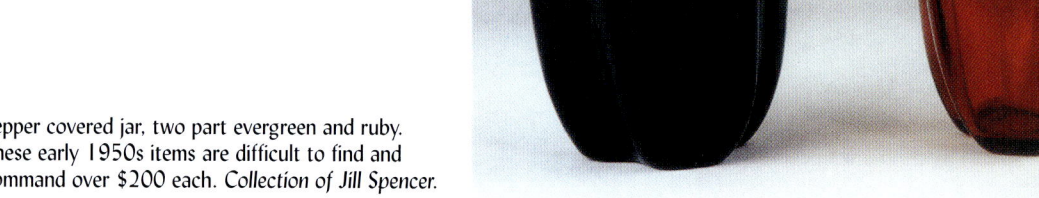

Pepper covered jar, two part evergreen and ruby. These early 1950s items are difficult to find and command over $200 each. *Collection of Jill Spencer.*

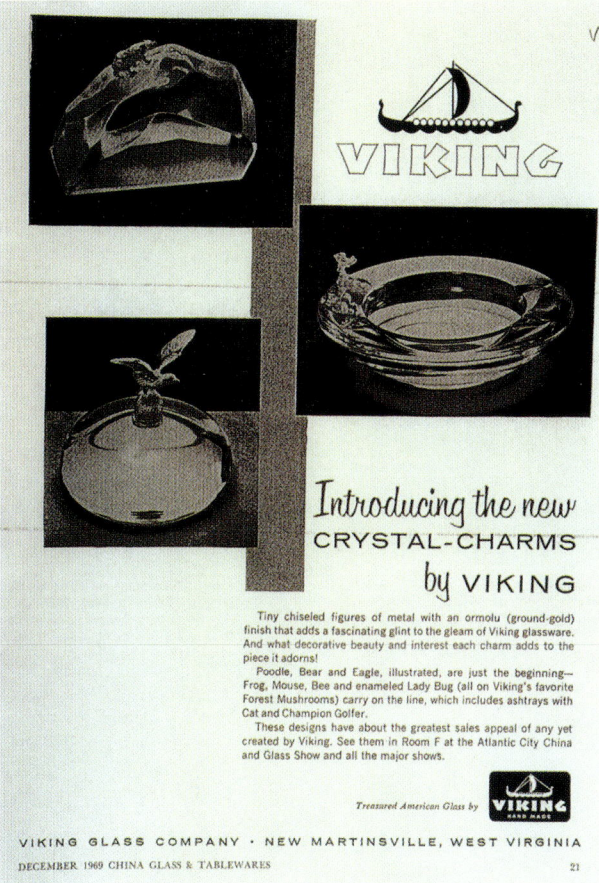

Epic Jewelry Tree #7020 was produced a short time, 8",
bluenique, $40-58.

Viking introduced a line of glass in 1970 with metal figurines
affixed to the glass. It was a short-lived line. Trade journal ad.

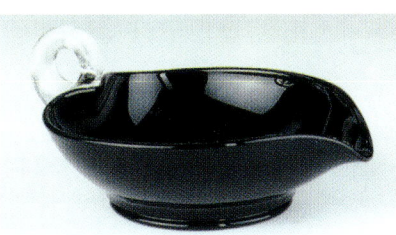

Heart-shaped bonbon
#978 ebony with
crystal handle, 5".
Late 1940s-early
1950s, $22-32.

Smoking Items

In the earliest Viking catalogs found, "Smoker Items" are there, labeled as such at the page header, and constituting at least two full pages in each catalog and as many as thirty-six items. This format and a very similar commitment to the smoking item product line remains unchanged over time. In 1968, thirty-four items appear on two pages with the heading Smoker Items. Here is one seeming constant over time. Amazingly a few items from the later 1940s remain in the late 1960s, spanning at lest twenty year of production. The small "horseshoe ashtray" is one of these long-lived items. It originally appears as #413 and later as a set of four as #996. It appears largely unchanged over time. The other survivor is a round, cupped in 7" ashtray. It was #27 and available in ebony only in some early catalogs. It was little changed in form and was still the #27 in 1968, but now was available as one of a selection of crackled ashtrays.

The wonderfully designed Pilot ashtrays, invoking the pilot's steering wheel on a riverboat, and numbered 773, 774, and 775 depending on size, were in production for some time. Pilot ashtrays appear in the late 1940s catalogs and are still in the line in 1962, but are gone before 1968. These were popular as one of the forms etched and dated as an annual New Martinsville, West Virginia, Magnolia Yacht Club souvenir.

Some inquiry taught us that the Magnolia Yacht Club was a bar and boat docking facility on the Ohio River, very near the Viking factory. "You couldn't work at Viking and not know a lot about the Magnolia Yacht Club" one employee told us. The Magnolia part of the name is taken from the local high school. The Yacht Club sponsored annual boat races on the Ohio River that were well attended and respected. Numerous employees reminded us that the famous Guy Lombardo, being one of the most remembered, returned to participate in the races year after year. Magnolia Yacht Club ashtrays are generally dated and a series of colorful and collectible Viking.

Ashtray and cigarette lighters are a collectible field unto themselves. Viking was a major producer of these and the distinctive forms and color make Viking products particularly attractive to collectors. Ashtrays are included in some of the extended patterns; there is a massive 11" ashtray in the Astra line looking very much like it was borrowed from the George Jetson™ home.

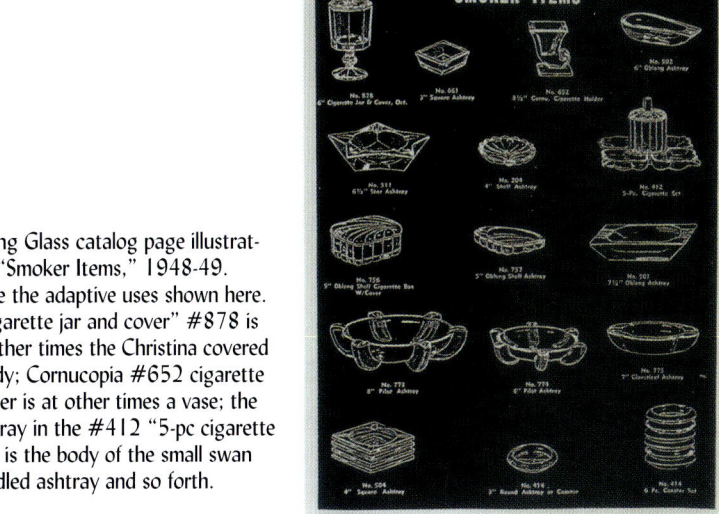

Viking Glass catalog page illustrating "Smoker Items," 1948-49.
Note the adaptive uses shown here. "Cigarette jar and cover" #878 is at other times the Christina covered candy; Cornucopia #652 cigarette holder is at other times a vase; the ashtray in the #412 "5-pc cigarette set" is the body of the small swan handled ashtray and so forth.

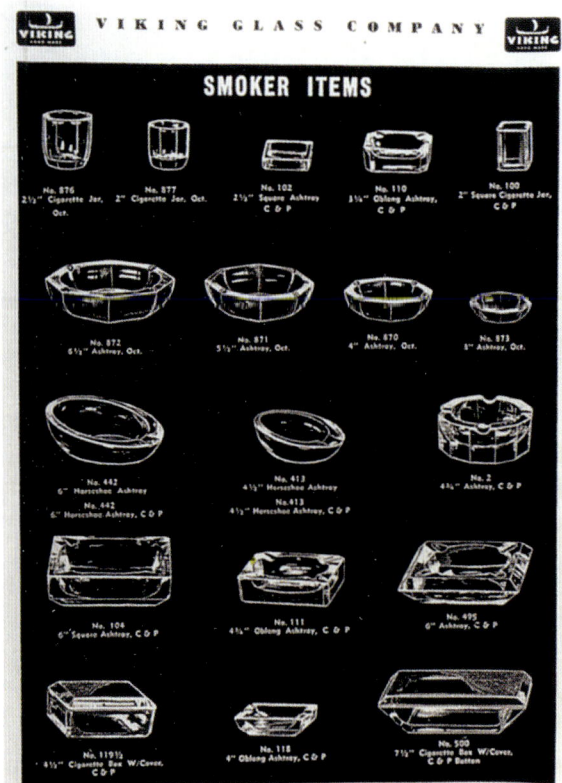

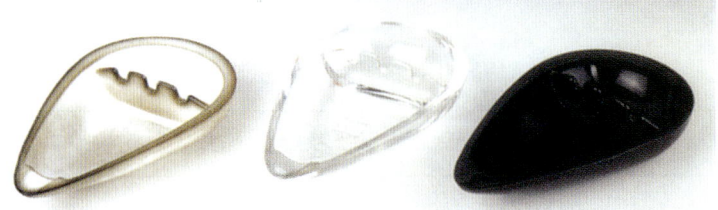

Ashtray #1044 driftwood, $45-58; crystal etched "Magnolia Yacht Club 1954," $20-24; ebony, $18-28. This shape appears from 1948 until well into the 1970s and possibly beyond.

Viking Glass catalog "Smoker Items," 1948-49. These early forms are crystal and exceedingly geometric compared to the late 1950s-1960s use of color and form that was to follow.

Viking Glass catalog "Smoker Items," 1956. The cigarette boxes, the #27 form that would later be used for crackle glass ashtrays, the three sizes of Pilot Ashtrays, and the wonderfully shaped #1044 are by this time integral parts of the line. Line #1044, like others show here, remained in the line so long that a collection of just a single shape could be built with varying colors, etc.

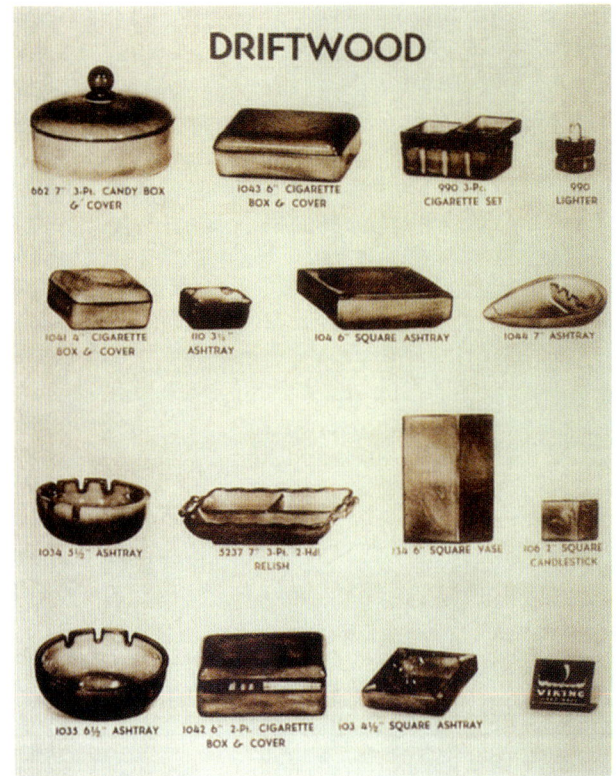

Viking Glass catalog images featuring driftwood colored objects. This mid-late 1950s line was produced for only a short time. Shown here are a number of smoking items and other shapes.

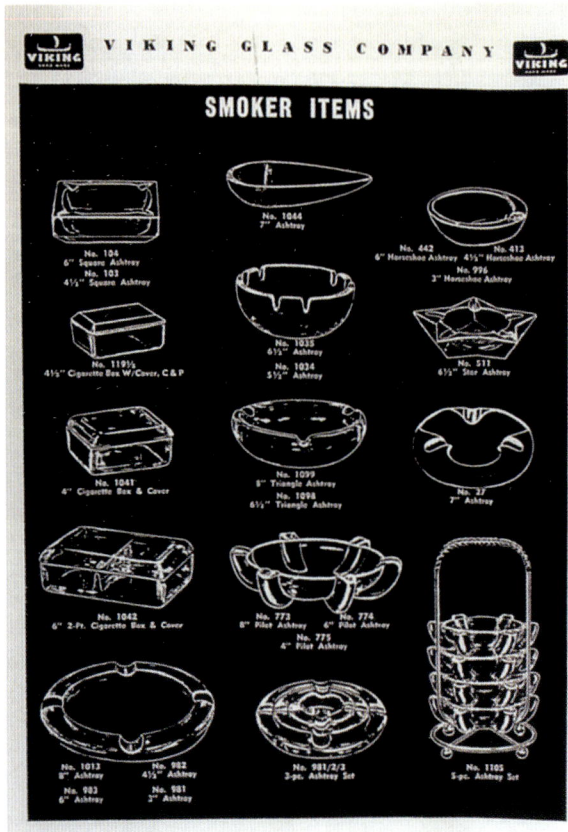

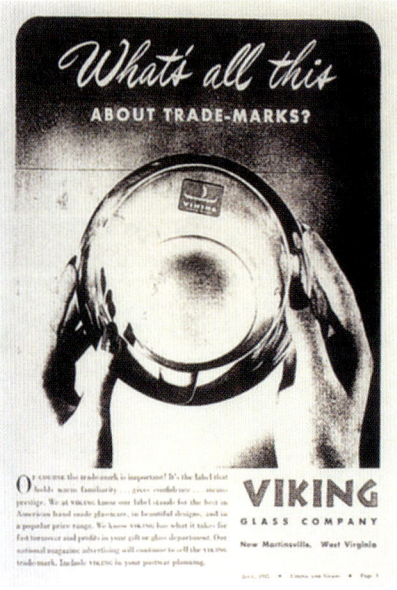

Viking advertisement posing the question "What's all this about trade-marks?" and featuring a trademark etched #400 line horseshow ashtray. These company marked ashtrays are much sought after.

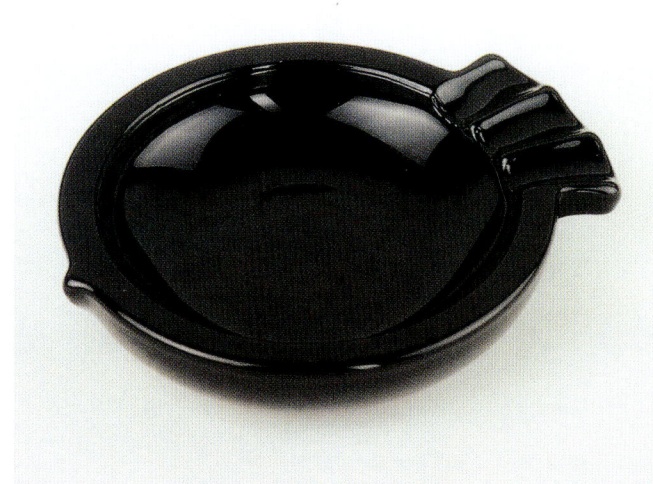

"Fish ashtray" #436, 4", circa 1954, ebony, $14-24.

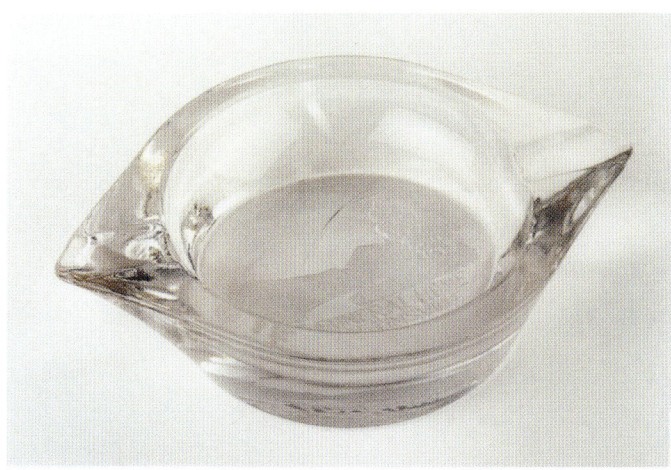

Ashtray #503 etched "Iams Funeral Home New Martinsville, W.Va.": form shown in 1945 catalog. 5-1/2" crystal, $12-22.

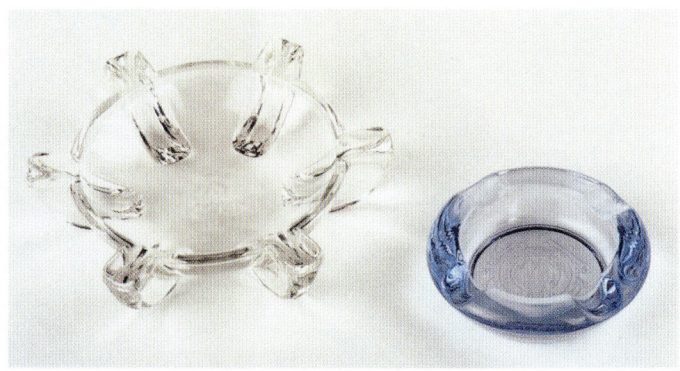

Pilot ashtray #774 etched "Tri-County Shriners 1953" crystal, $15-20; Horseshoe ashtray #996 colonial blue etched "Member A.P.B.A 1950," $18-28.

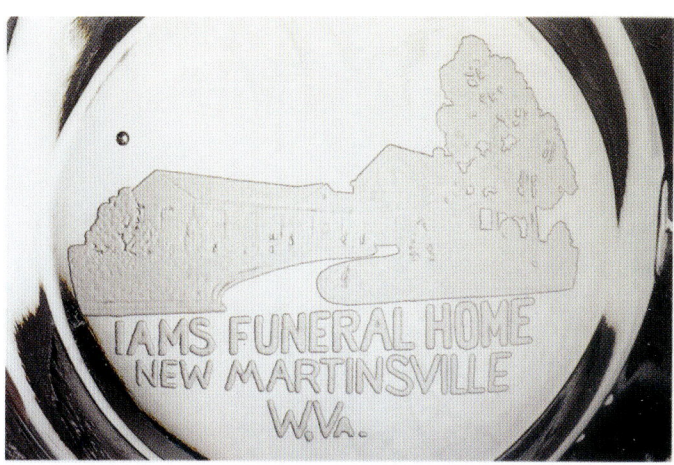

Detail of etching on Iams #503 ashtray: note the detail attained in this particularly deep acid etched specialty item.

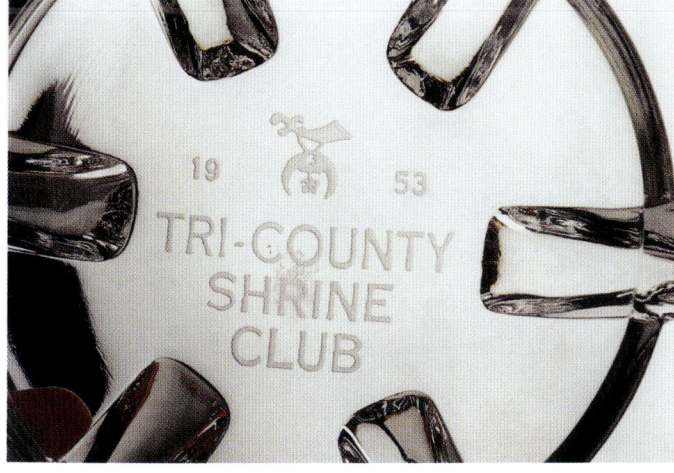

Detail of #774 shown above.

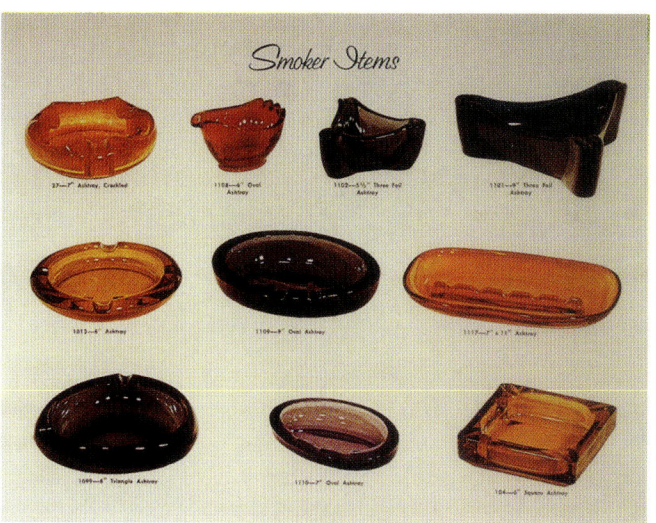

Viking Glass catalog page of "Smoker Items," 1962.

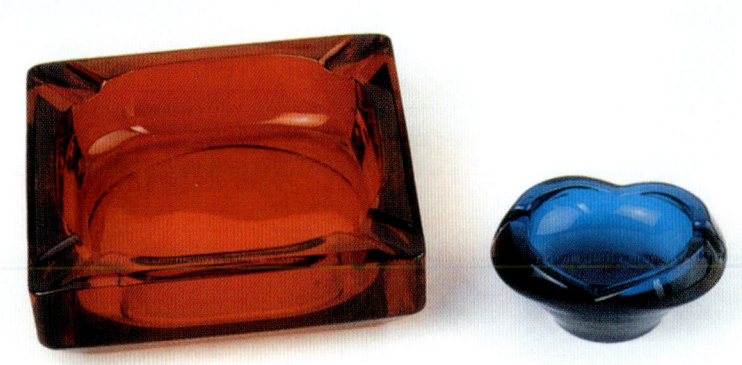

Square 6" ashtray #104 ruby, $12-18. This form appears from 1962 into the 1970s, ashtray #6720 introduced in 1967, bluenique, $8-16.

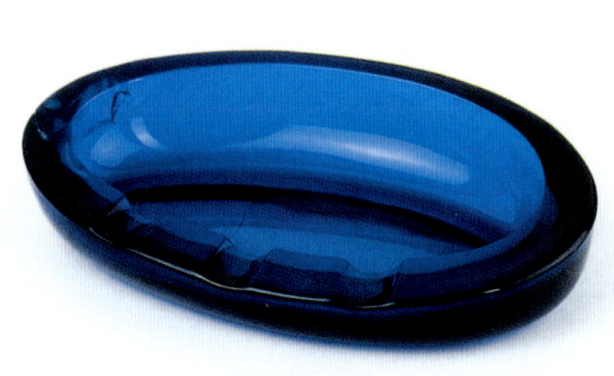

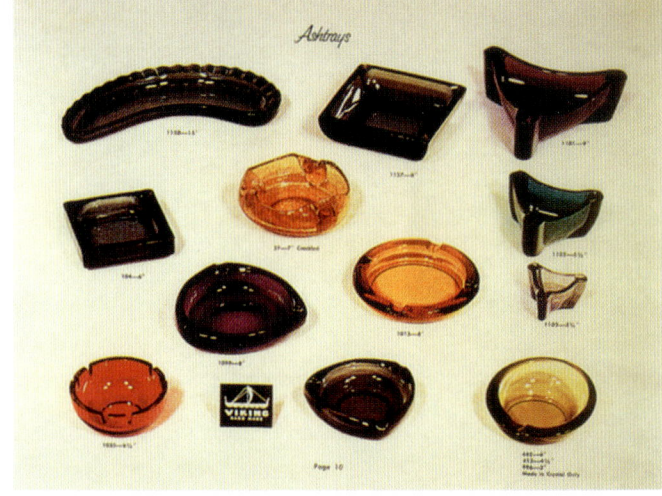

Ashtray, oval #1110 appears in the 1962 catalog in this 7" size and a larger 9". Bluenique shown here, $10-16.

Viking Glass catalog 1960 "Ashtrays:" noteworthy here are the #27 crackle glass ashtray, the three sizes of the triangle-shaped #1100 line, and the predominance of charcoal colored items shown.

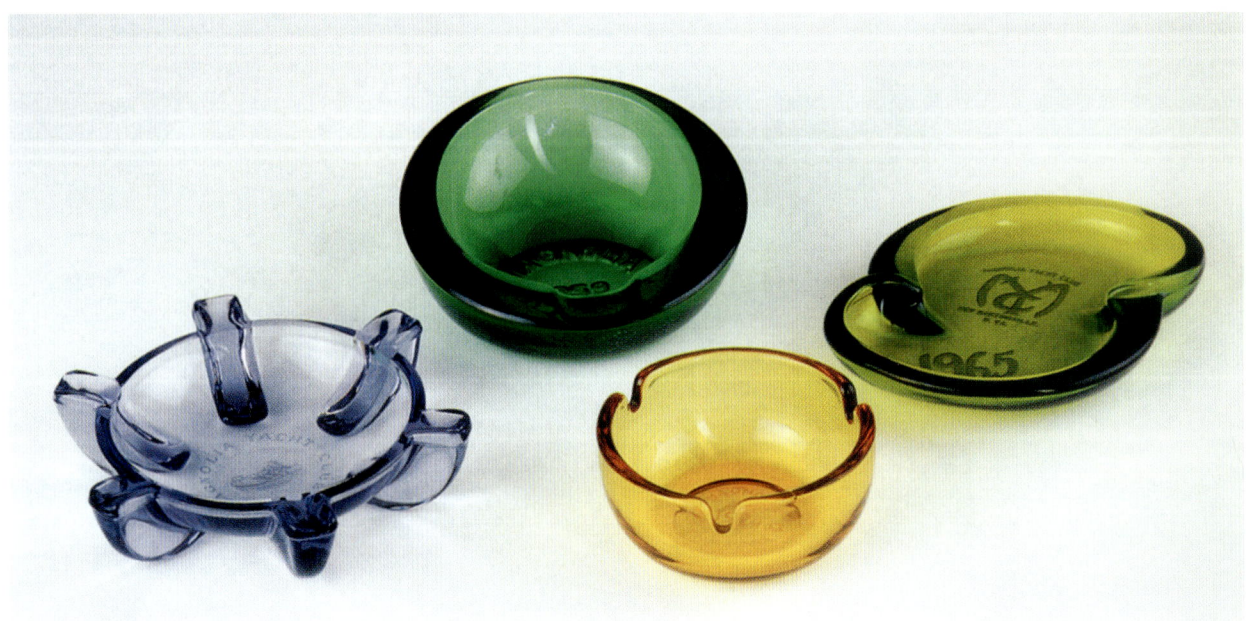

A selection of the annually produced "Magnolia Yacht Club" ashtrays. Pilot #775, $26-32; horseshoe emerald green #413, $20-28; #1036 amber 3-1/2", 1961, $14-20; avocado swirl 5" etched "Magnolia Yacht Club MYC (monogram) New Martinsville W.VA. 1965 on the Beautiful Ohio", $14-18.

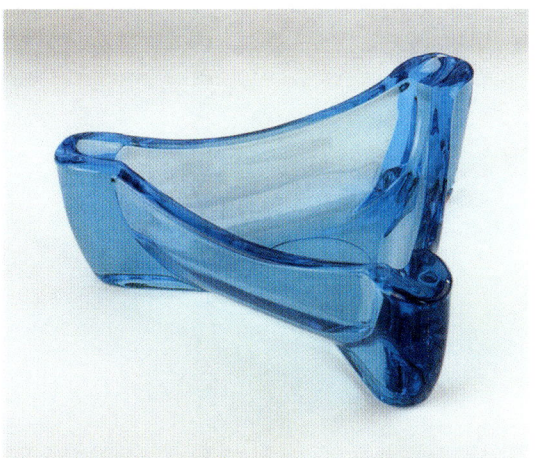

"Triangle" ashtray #1101 colonial blue 9", the largest of the three sizes made. Shown in the 1960 catalog in 9", 5-1/2", and 3-1/4" sizes. Note also that the identical mold and form was used to create the triangular candle bowl where candle wells replace the cigarette rests. As shown here, $20-26.

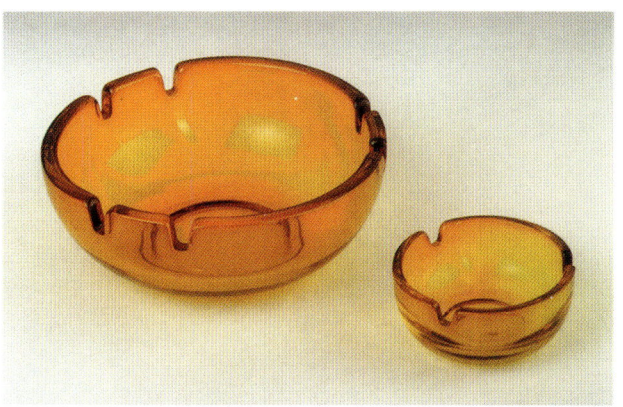

Ashtray #1035 persimmon 6-1/2", $12-20; #1036 persimmon 3-1/2", $6-12.

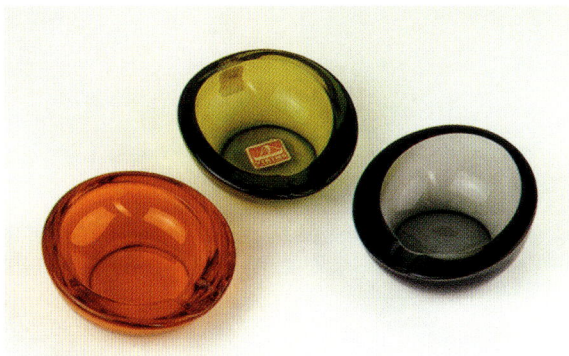

Horseshow ashtray #996, 3", persimmon, $8-14; avocado, $4-8; charcoal, $6-12. With label, add $2-4 to price.

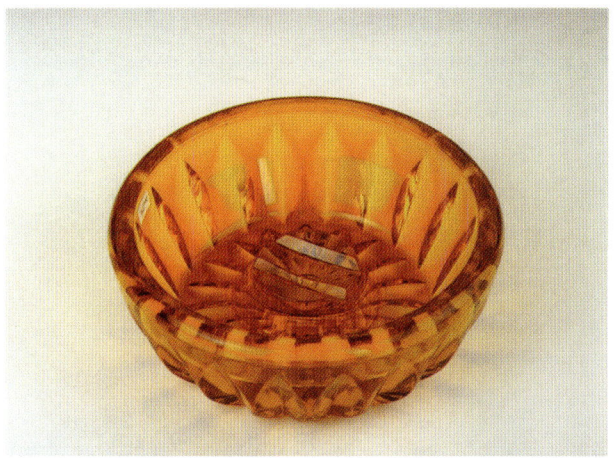

Bowl ashtray 7-1/2" persimmon, $18-24. Same form made as serving bowl without cigarette/cigar rest in center. *Collection of Jill Spencer.*

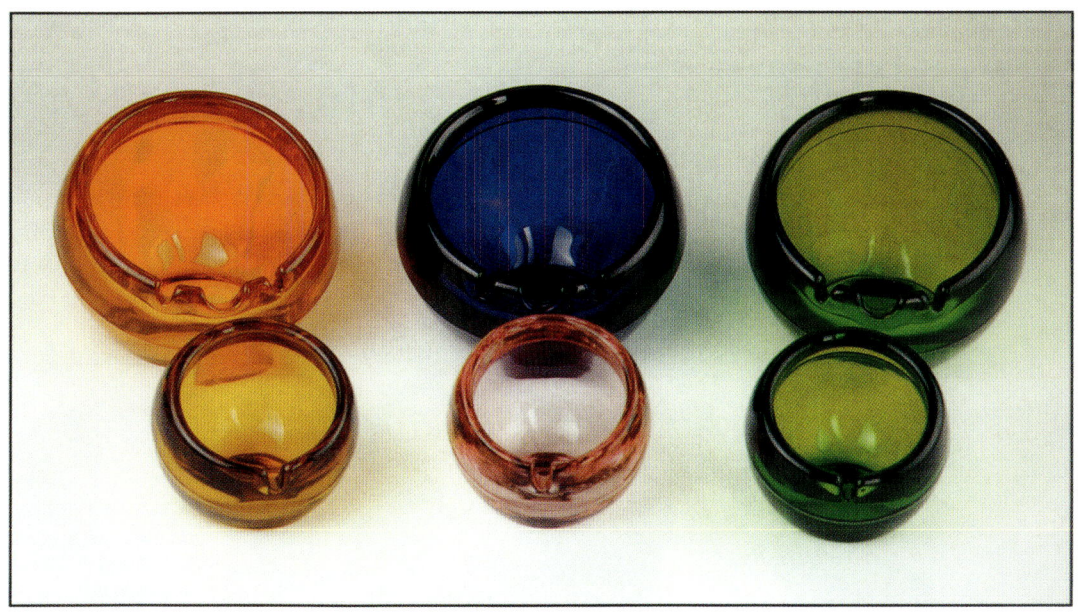

Sphere ashtray: front row: #6625, 4" amber, $6-10; thistle, #328-36; avocado, $8-16; back row: #6827, 6" persimmon, $25-38; bluenique, $20-26; avocado, $14-22.

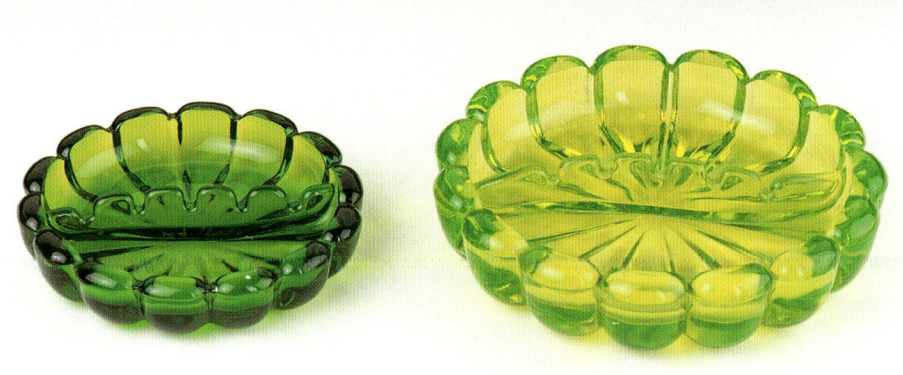

Ribbed ashtray 6-1/2" emerald green, $8-14; #1134, 8" lime, $26-42.

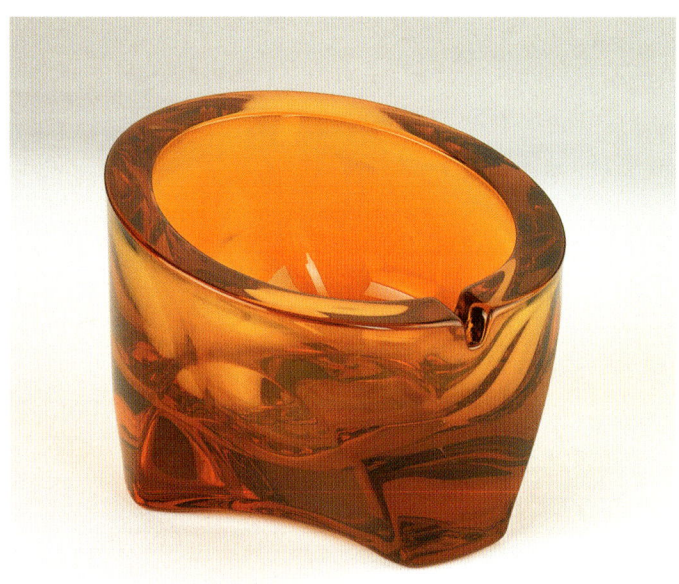

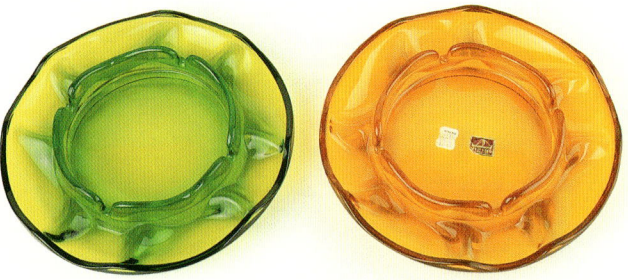

Ashtray, round #1135, 8" avocado, $8-14; persimmon, $12-18. Original labels add $2-4. Original factory price and line sticker states original retail price to be $4.00.

Ashtray #7034, 5-1/2" persimmon, $20-32. Introduced in the 1970 catalog.

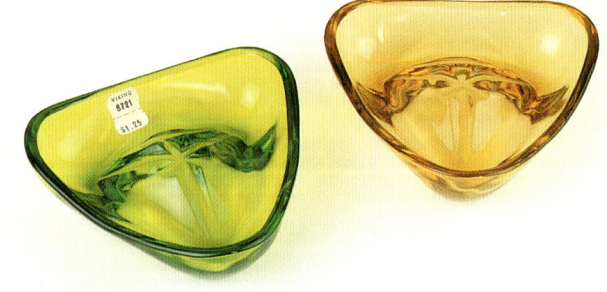

Ashtray #6721, 4-1/2" avocado, $4-6; amber, $3-5.

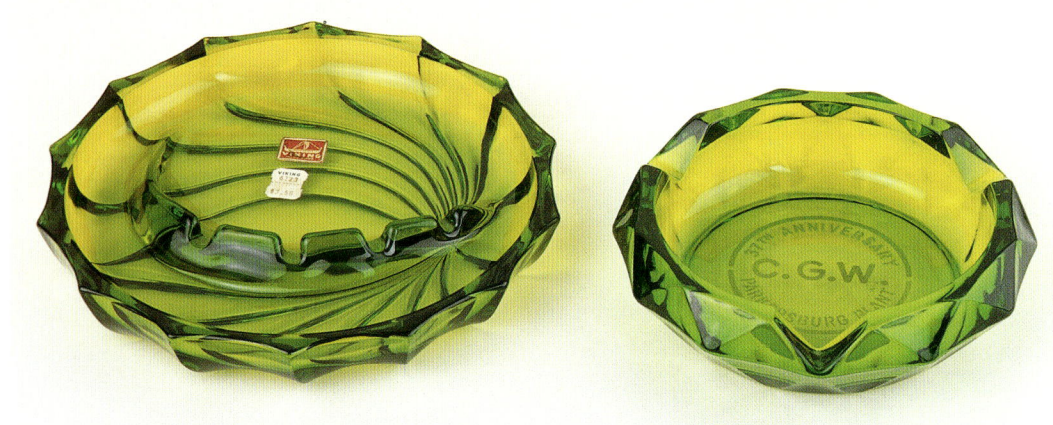

Ashtray #6723 avocado, 8", $10-14; #6724 avocado, $8-14. Both introduced in 1967. #6724 on right is shown with the etching "37th Anniversary C.G.W. Parkersburg Plant," a commemorative for the Corning Glass Works. Add $10 to the price if so decorated.

Right:
Ashtray #7031 square 7-1/4" persimmon, $12-18; ashtray #7032, 7-1/4" avocado, $6-10. Both introduced in the 1970 catalog.

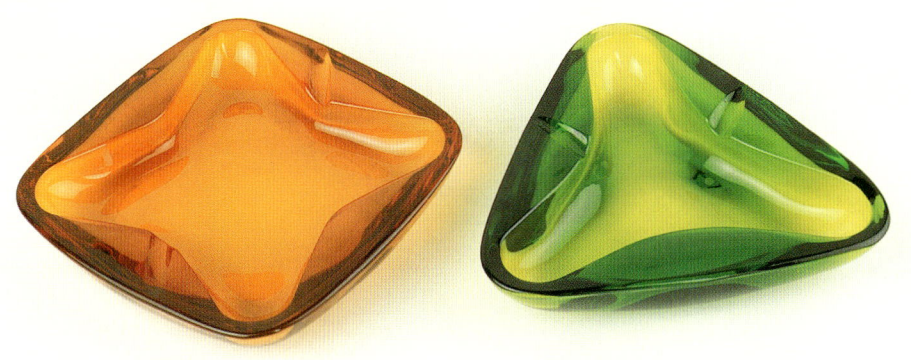

Below:
Epic "drape" ashtray #6810, 8-1/2" amber, $8-14. Introduced 1968 as per line number.

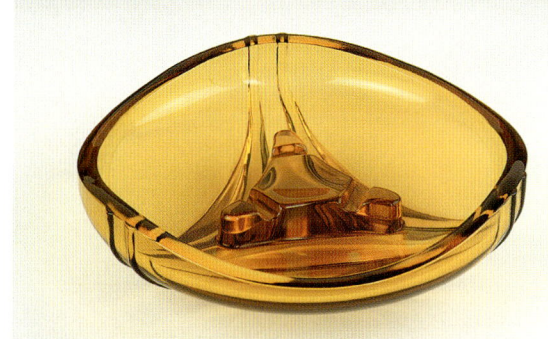

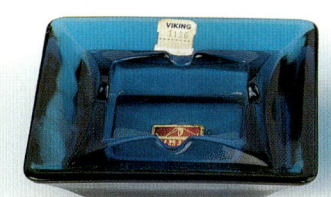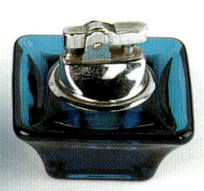

Ashtray square #1126, 4" bluenique, $6-12 and matching lighter bluenique, $20-32. Commonly sold as a four piece set #1126-30 with three sizes of the same form stackable ashtray and matching lighter that stacked on top of the ashtrays.

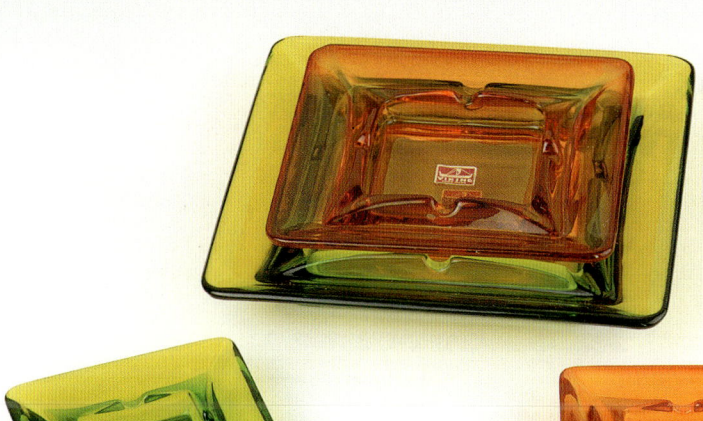

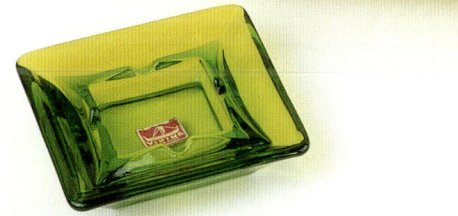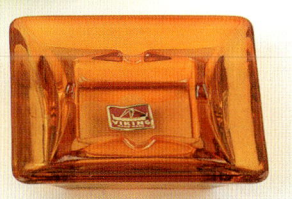

Left:
Square ashtray in all four sizes, 4", 6", and 8". #1128 bottom of stack in back: square 8" avocado, $9-16; top of stack in back: 6" persimmon, $8-14; #1126 front left: avocado, $4-8; and front right: persimmon, $8-12.

Lighters: square #1130, 2-1/2" persimmon, $22-36; bluenique, $20-32; and persimmon from the same mold as the candlestick, $20-28.

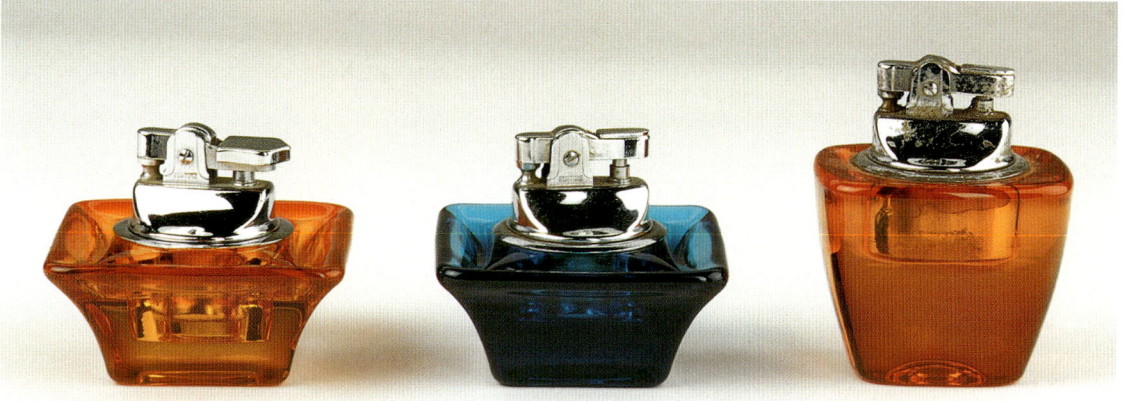

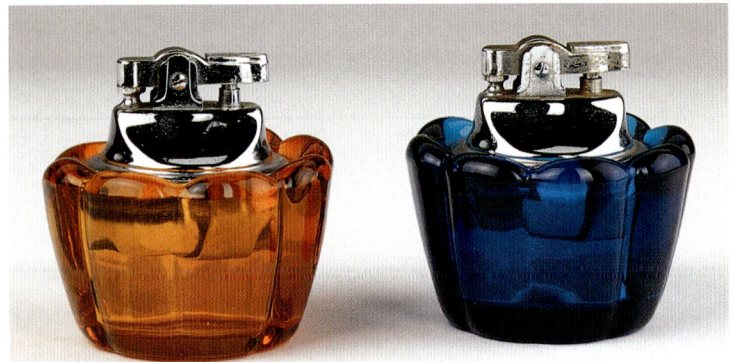

Lighters: rounded rib amber, $12-20; bluenique, $22-28.

Lighters: the column ribbed Epic lighter was introduced after 1970 emerald green, $20-28. The green is similar to #1125, but ever so slightly varying in shape. Note also the brass versus chrome lighter insert. This appears to be a Viking product but has not been confirmed. See the proper shape for #1125 lighter below.

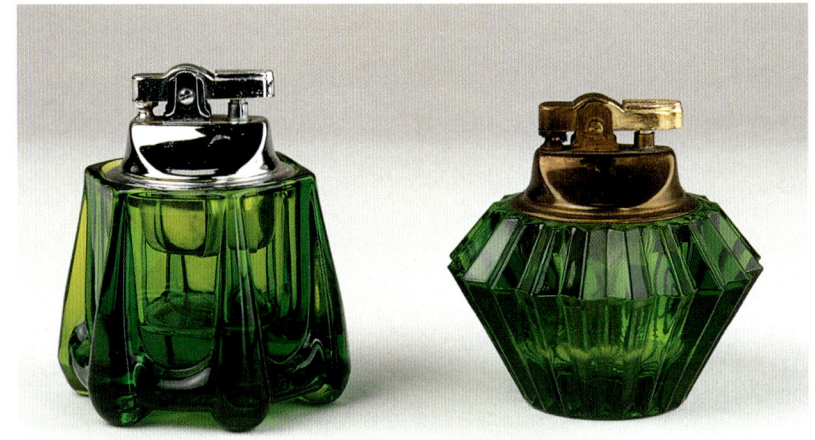

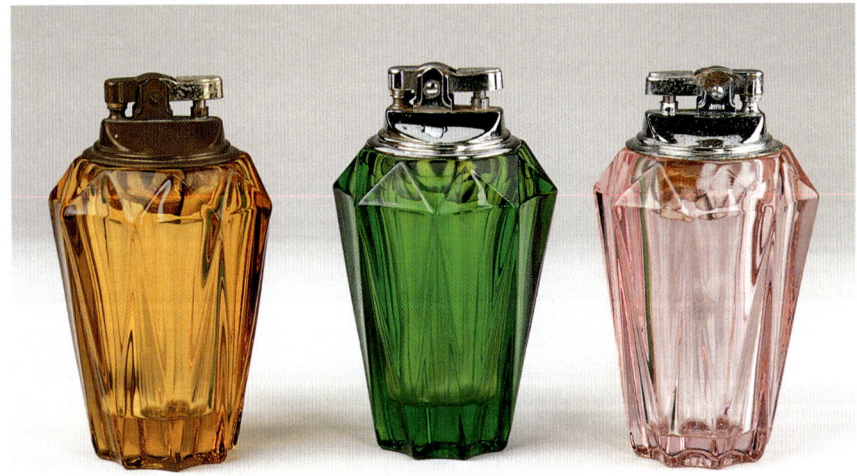

Lighter #6823, 4-1/2" amber, $14-26; emerald green, $18-28; thistle, $38-55.

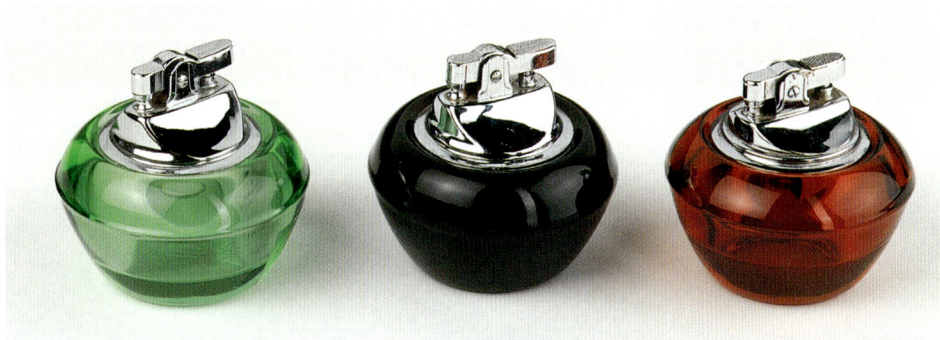

Lighter #1125 green, $18-28; ebony, $24-32; ruby, $28-38.

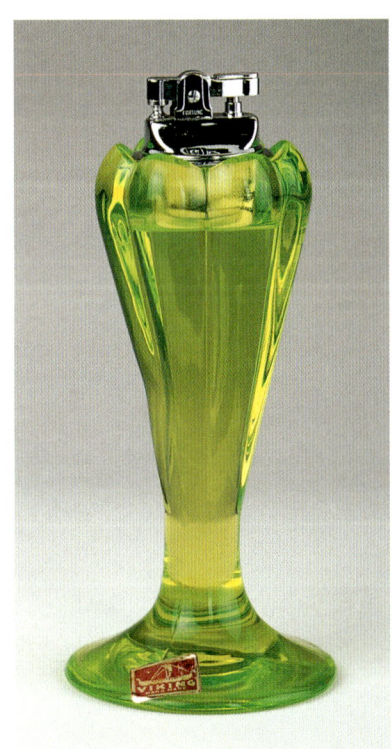

Lighter #6628, 6-1/2" lime, $35-55. Shown with the original factory labels and retail price of $6.00. Quite expensive for its day. With labels add $4-6 to value.

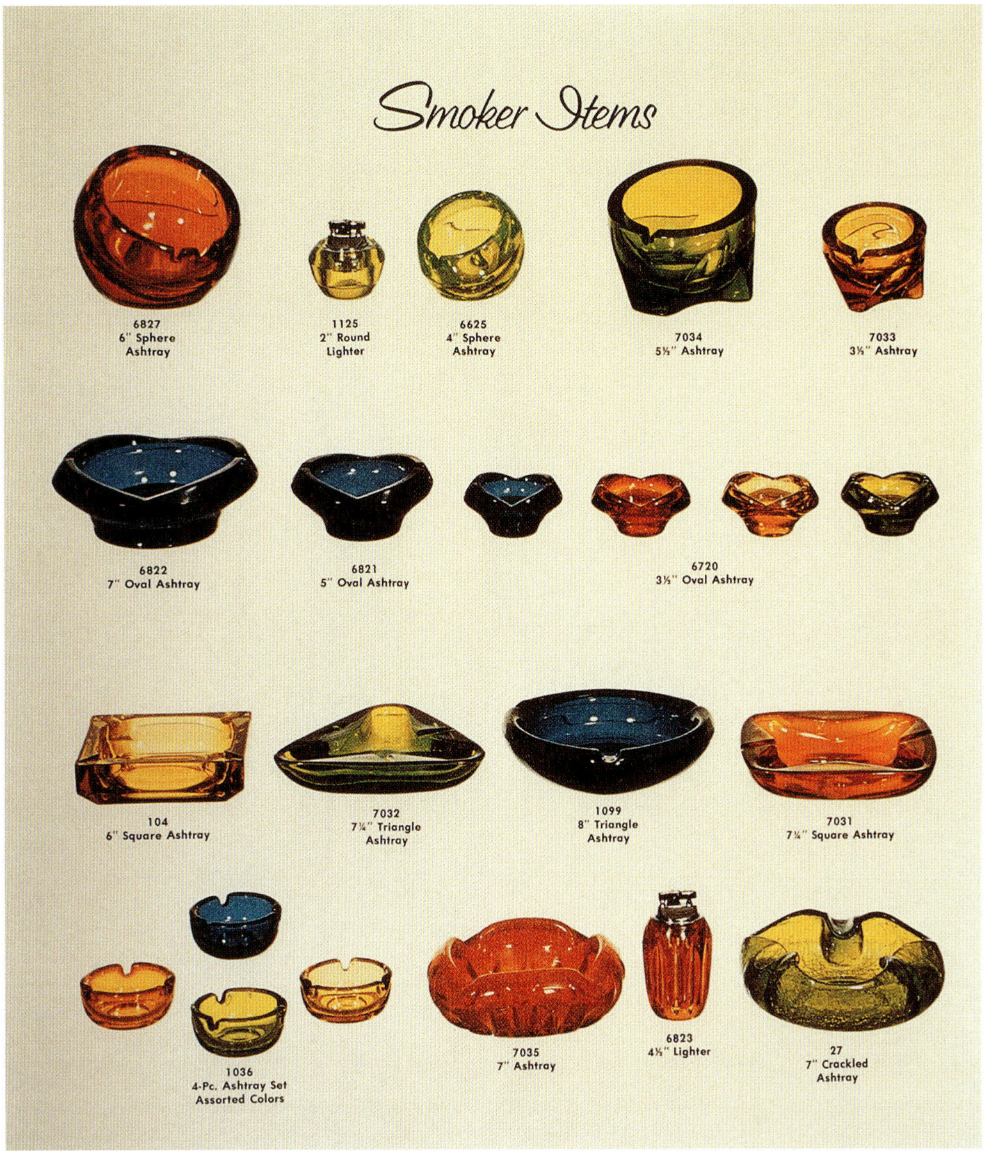

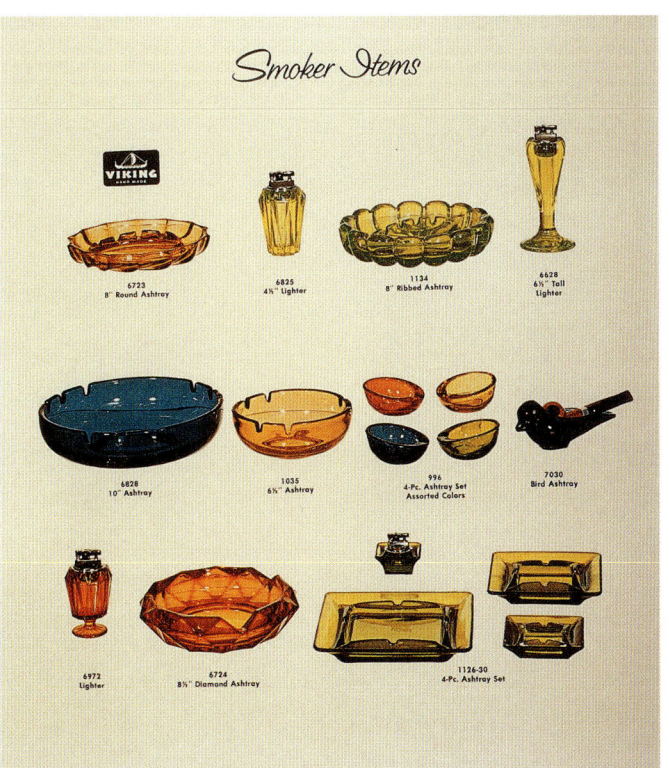

Smoker Items

6827
6" Sphere
Ashtray

1125
2" Round
Lighter

6625
4" Sphere
Ashtray

7034
5½" Ashtray

7033
3½" Ashtray

6822
7" Oval Ashtray

6821
5" Oval Ashtray

6720
3½" Oval Ashtray

104
6" Square Ashtray

7032
7¼" Triangle
Ashtray

1099
8" Triangle
Ashtray

7031
7¼" Square Ashtray

1036
4-Pc. Ashtray Set
Assorted Colors

7035
7" Ashtray

6823
4½" Lighter

27
7" Crackled
Ashtray

Viking Glass catalog page of
"Smoker Items," 1970.

Smoker Items

6723
8" Round Ashtray

6825
4½" Lighter

1134
8" Ribbed Ashtray

6628
6½" Tall
Lighter

6828
10" Ashtray

1035
6½" Ashtray

996
4-Pc. Ashtray Set
Assorted Colors

7030
Bird Ashtray

6972
Lighter

6724
8½" Diamond Ashtray

1126-30
4-Pc. Ashtray Set

Viking Glass catalog page of
"Smokers Items," 1970.

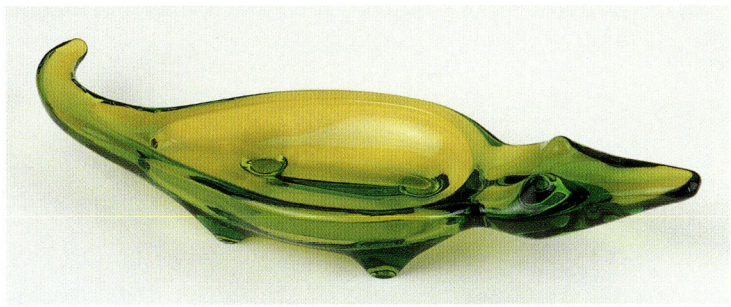

Alligator ashtray #6948. Illustrated in *House and Garden*, September 1969
and introduced in 1969. This ashtray is not in the 1970 catalog. 10-1/2"
avocado, $30-42.

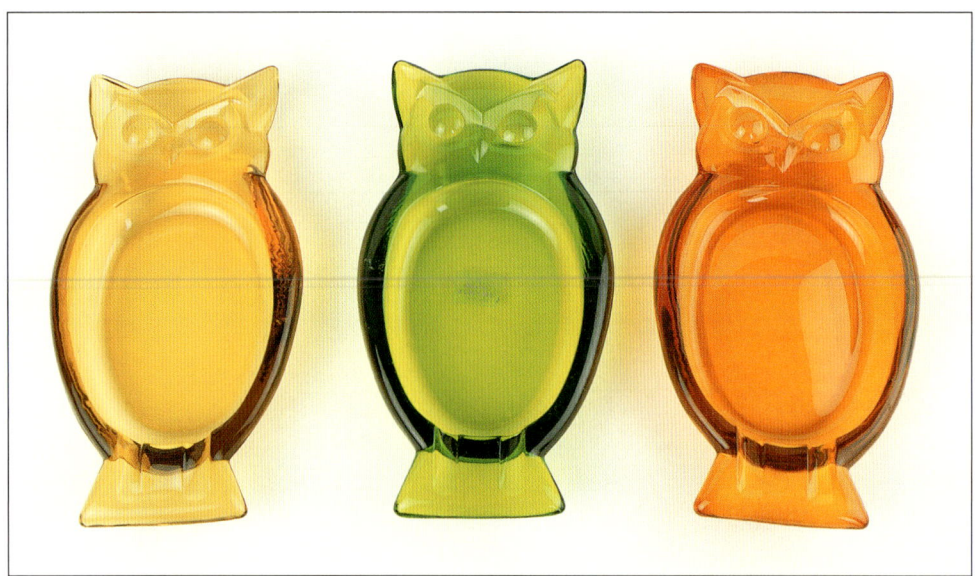

Owl ashtray #6944 amber, $12-18; avocado, $14-22; persimmon, $18-28.

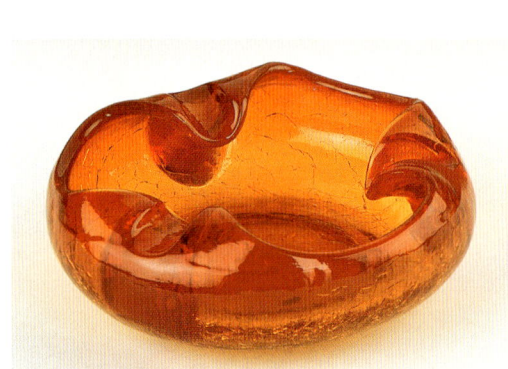

Ashtray #27, 7" crackle persimmon, $22-38.

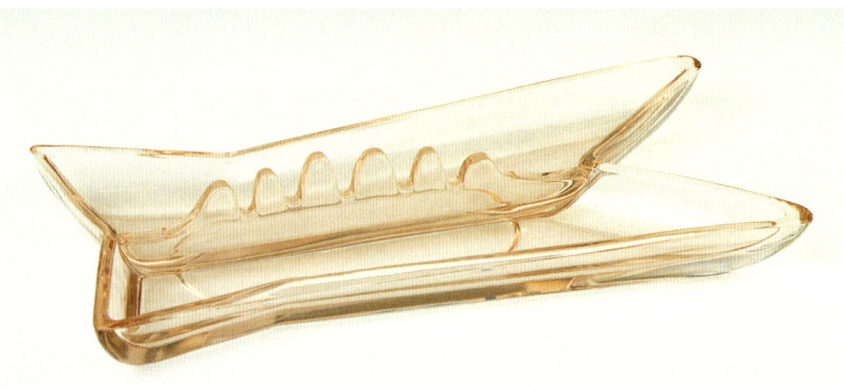

Astra pattern ashtray #6188, 11" cherry glo, $22-32.

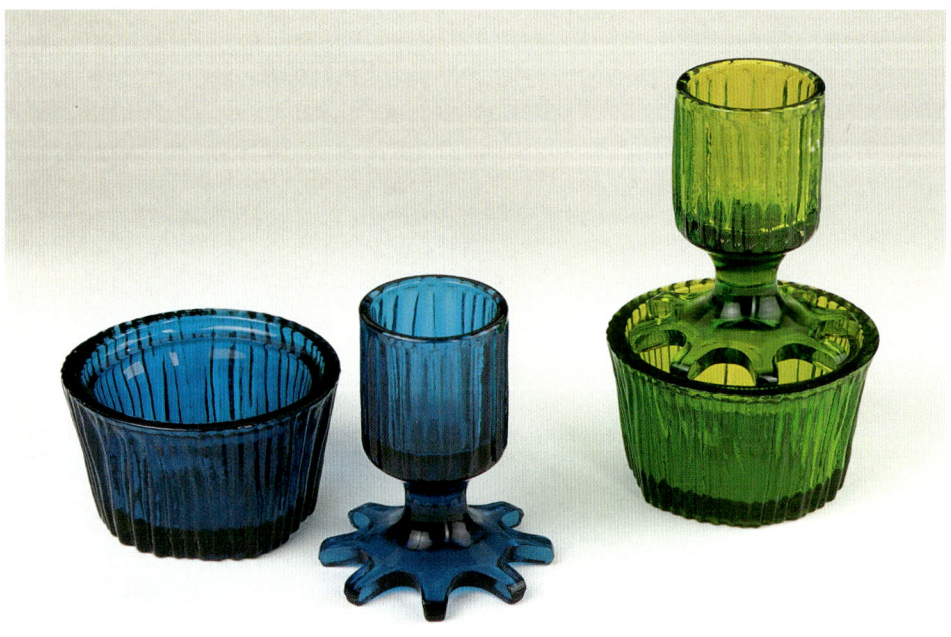

Ashtray with cigarette urn lid, two part. One example has the original
Viking label. Bluenique, $24-38; avocado, $18-32.

Tableware

Some glass factories, like nearby Fostoria Glass, in Moundsville, West Virginia, were predominately dedicated to glass tableware. Others, like nearby Fenton Art Glass in Williamstown, West Virginia, have made tableware but been more dependent on giftware. Viking's product line has always been a mixture of both tableware and giftware. The relative proportions in the mix of tableware and giftware vary over time. At the beginning of our period one could argue production was predominately tableware. By the end of 1970 and the era covered in this book, tableware was indeed a small part of the production. Giftware constituted the bulk of sales for Viking by 1970. Thus, tableware lines are predominately earlier in time. Each is covered in their respective sections in the Pattern section of this book. Look there to see more detailed text on:

Ancestral: 1947-1949 as a line, some miscellaneous pieces before and after

Astra: 1961-1962, some pieces remain later as part of miscellaneous production

Georgian: 1953-to the end, some pieces in production at factory closing

Janice: 1940 and earlier for miscellaneous pieces – in production at factory closing

Mount Vernon: 1962-mid-1960s, some pieces remain later and until closing

Princess: 1951-beyond 1970

Princess Plaza: 1955-early 1960s

Vases

Early Viking vases, circa 1940-50s, were classic and continental in their effort to look "Viking," a term generally meant to mean to look Scandinavian/Swedish modern: crystal, heavy, bold. The early years of Viking Glass were heavily dependent on using and adapting the earlier products of New Martinsville Glass. The earliest Viking offerings are shown in this section in a cut and paste compilation from various late 1940s-1950s catalogs. One of these all crystal catalogs offered eighteen diverse shapes for vases.

In the late 1940s-1950s era catalogs, vases were offered in expected forms and patterns. Janice patterned vases, Christina patterned vases, Radiance (the large 10"-12" flared vases and 9" ball) vases, square Swedish-looking vases including those with Rock Crystal engraving, heavy rounded modern forms, and a line of "crown shape" vases with heavy crimping to impart the "crown."

The dominant vase lines of the 1944-1970 period are those made for the wildly eclectic Epic line. The text below and images will help provide some language and identification for discussing the Epic Vase and lines. However, there are no consistent line numbers or names given by the factory. It is with no small hesitancy that the attached naming of Epic vases is created for this book. Some lines, like Trefoil, come from company literature, other are simply self-descriptive. Notice that several shapes within Epic evolve over the years and have redesigned feet or bases, complicating this Epic business even more. We need to remain mindful that at the time of production this was a business for Viking and not developed to make easy cataloging for collectors decades in the future. Selling products dictated the shapes and only ease of production was likely to otherwise alter a shape. Please refer to the Epic list for identifying lines within the line.

In 1960 the catalog shows fifteen Epic line vases, two Yesteryear, and one "miscellaneous" 800 line of very free-form vases. By 1962 Epic had arrived in full force and modernistic free-form tall swung shapes that had been around since circa 1956 were the dominant forms. These free-formed and brightly colored wares would dominate until after 1970 for vases. Shown in 1962 are eighteen different Epic vases, five in Astra, and two in the traditional Yesteryear line.

Epic Vases in the line in 1962:

Vase, crimped #890, 13-1/2" (from old Christina line molds)

Vase, bud #1208 Trefoil 11"

Vase, #1215 Trefoil 22"

Vase, #1218 Trefoil 17"

Vase, tall #1220

Vase, tall #1221 Trefoil

Vase, tall bud #1283

Vase, #1405, 8"

Vase, #1408, 6"

Vase, #1415, 15"

Vase, tall flared #1425

Vase, tall bud #1427

Vase, tall footed #1432

Vase, footed #1433, 9-1/2"

Vase, tall bud footed #1435

Vase, footed #1436, 8-1/2"

Vase, tall #1452

Jumping forward to 1968, the vases produced remain tall, free-formed, and of the "swung" type with flowing tops. What would appear to be a glass basket, form #6610, in the catalog was called an open vase; but, you will find it in the basket section of this book. There are seventeen Epic vases and one Yesteryear vase.

Epic Vases in the line in 1968:

Vase, bud #1140, 11"

Vase, tall #1220

Vase, tall #1221

Vase, tall footed #1432

Vase, tall bud footed #1435

Vase, footed #1436, 8-1/2"

Vase, bud footed #1465, 10"

Vase, tall footed #1474

Vase, open #6610, 16"

Vase, bud #6703

Vase, bud #6704

Vase, footed #6707, 12"

Vase, #6805, 8"

Vase, #6813, 17"

Vase, tall #6817

As the 1960s end Vikings vases are larger, more colorful, and almost exclusively of the free-form swung type.

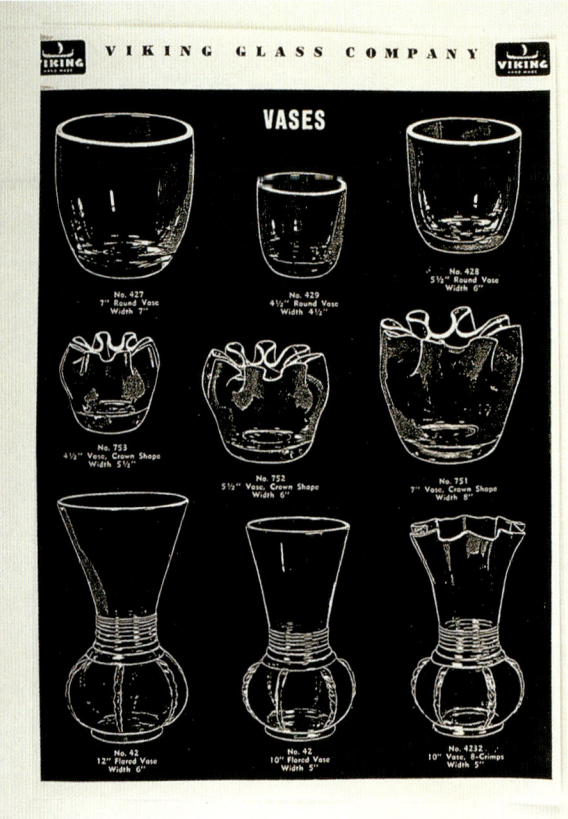

Viking Glass catalog page "Vases," 1948-49. Note that the Radiance No. 42 larger crimped vases at the bottom is a long used pattern by New Martinsville Glass continued by Viking.

Right:
Viking Glass catalog page "Vases," 1950-51. Janice flared three toed vase, the Cornucopia bookend vase, and larger #650 with #800 line Christina vases, the Radiance Ball vase/punch bowl, and the #130 line square vases – all important forms to recognize as Viking.

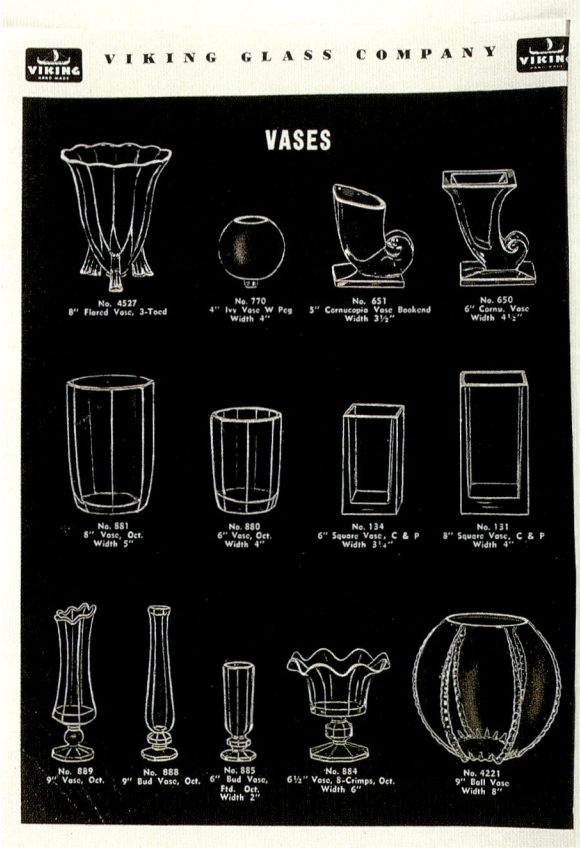

Viking Glass catalog "Vases," 1948-49. Note the flower cart shown in the animal and figural part of this book. The Cornucopia line was in full use at the end of the 1940s in heavy "Swedish styled crystal" and is represented here in two forms.

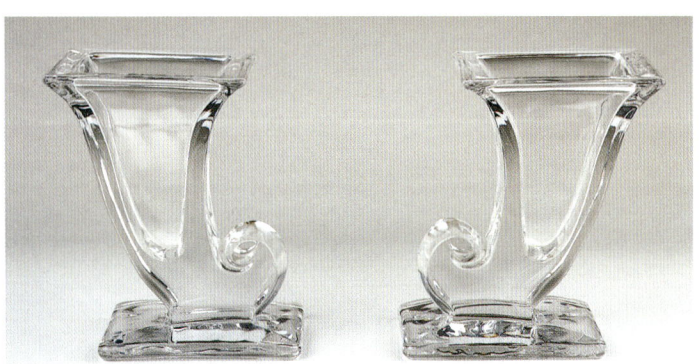

Large cornucopia vases in heavy crystal, 6", 1940s-50s, $25-38 each. *Compliments of Replacements, LTD.*

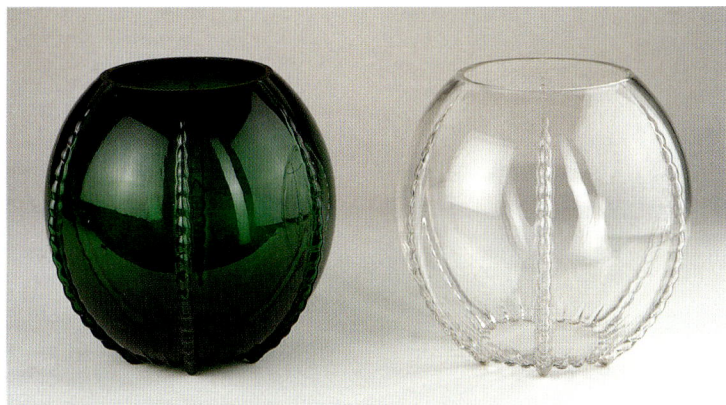

Radiance pattern ball vase or punch bowl #4221, 9" evergreen, $75-90; crystal, $55-68.

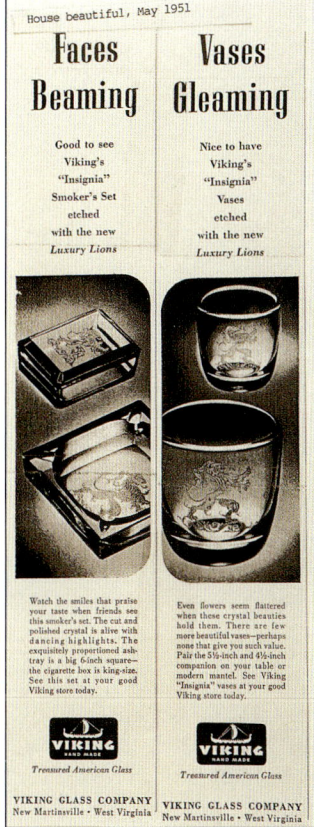

"Faces Beaming Vases Gleaming" two part advertisement appearing in *House Beautiful*, May 1951. The crystal covered cigarette box, ashtray, and vases are etched with the lion decoration "Insignia." These pieces look very un-American and were actually turned away a few years back by one of the authors as "clearly European." The efforts at Viking at this time to emulate Swedish glass worked.

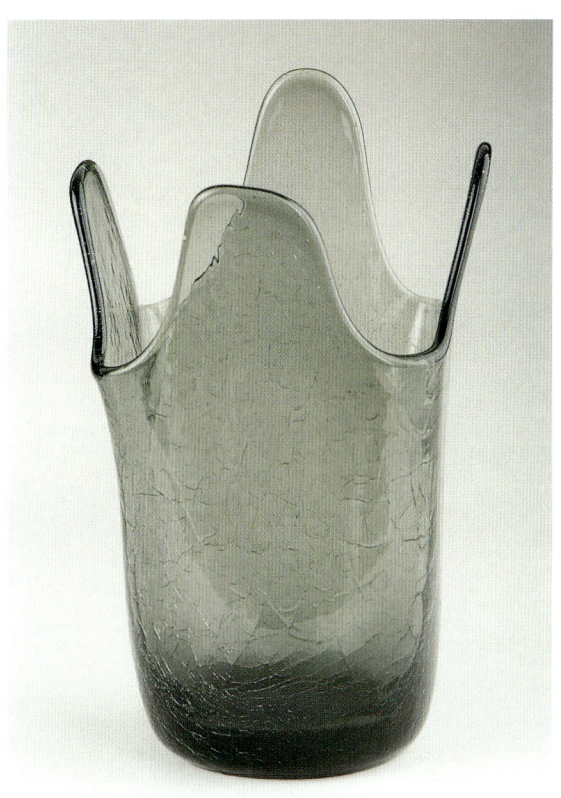

Epic crackle vase, 9-1/2", shown in November 1956 *Crockery & Glass Journal* ad (ad shown in Epic chapter), $35-45.

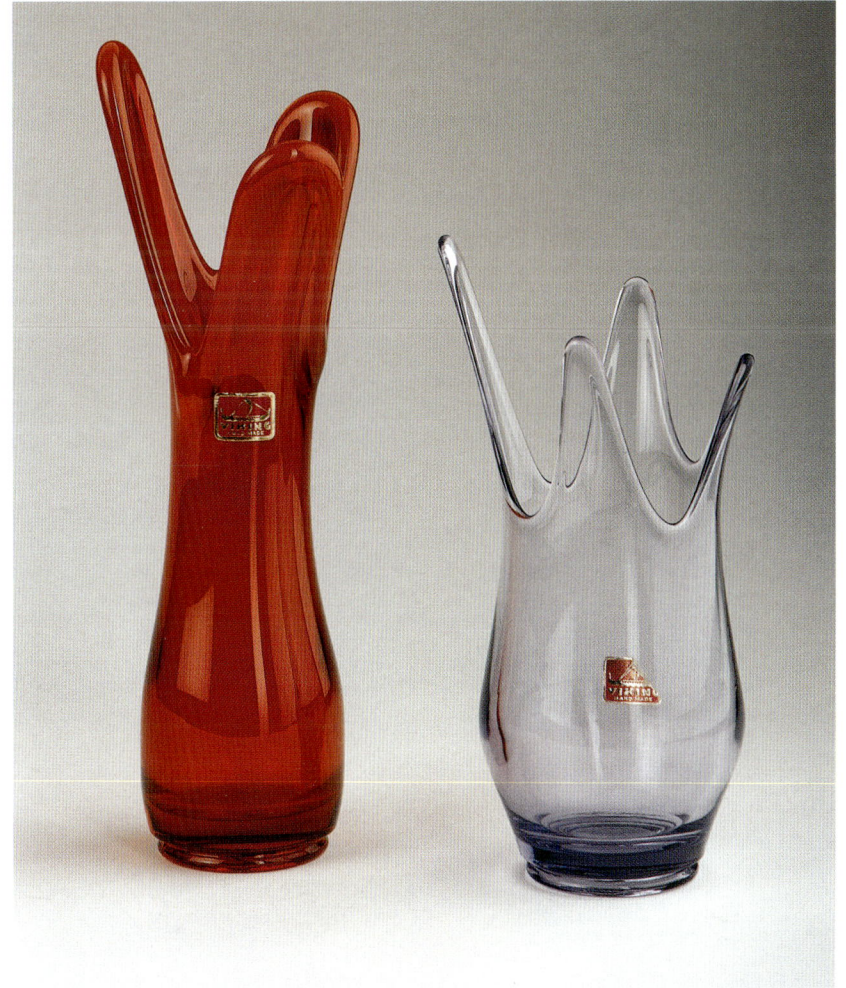

Epic vase reported in trade journal in June 1940, ruby, $22-35; Epic vase #1405, 8" teaberry, circa 1960, $28-38.

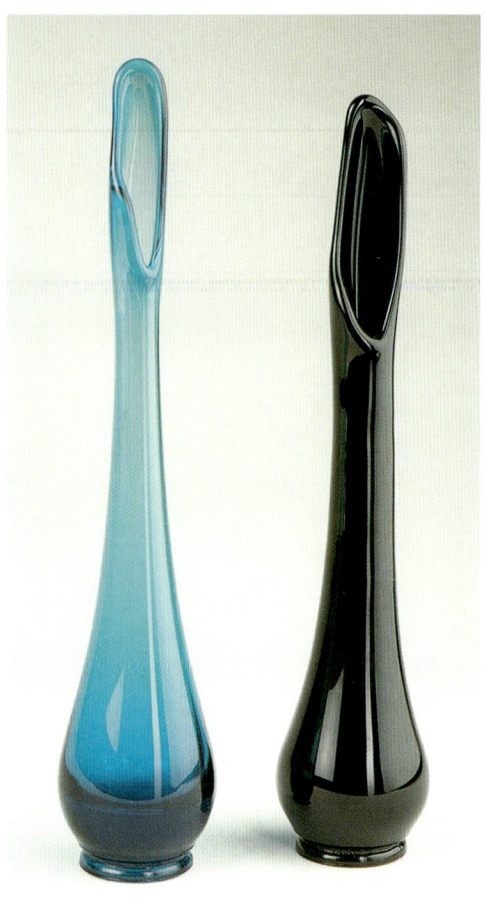

Epic bud vase
#1140, 11" ebony,
$12-20; bluenique,
$12-20.

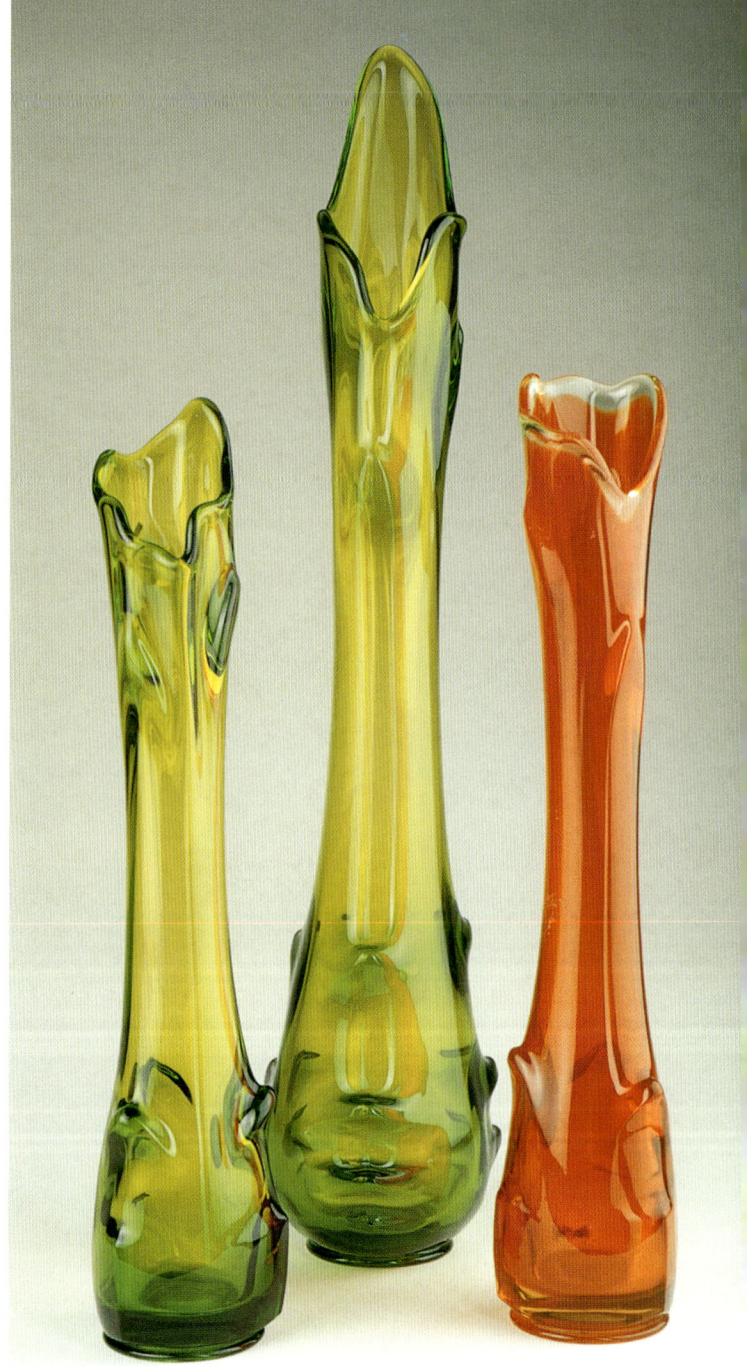

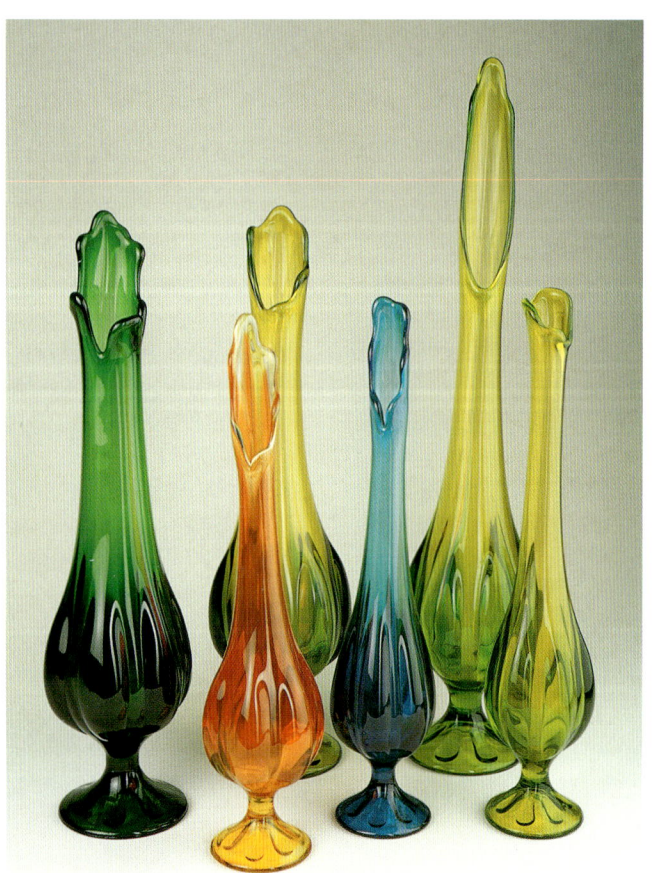

Selection of Epic "six petal" swung vases.
See Epic chapter for pricing and details.

Tundra line vases. Swung vase #6652, 13" avocado, $24-32; "tall"
#6655, 23" avocado, $32-46; swung vase #6652, 13" persimmon,
$28-38.

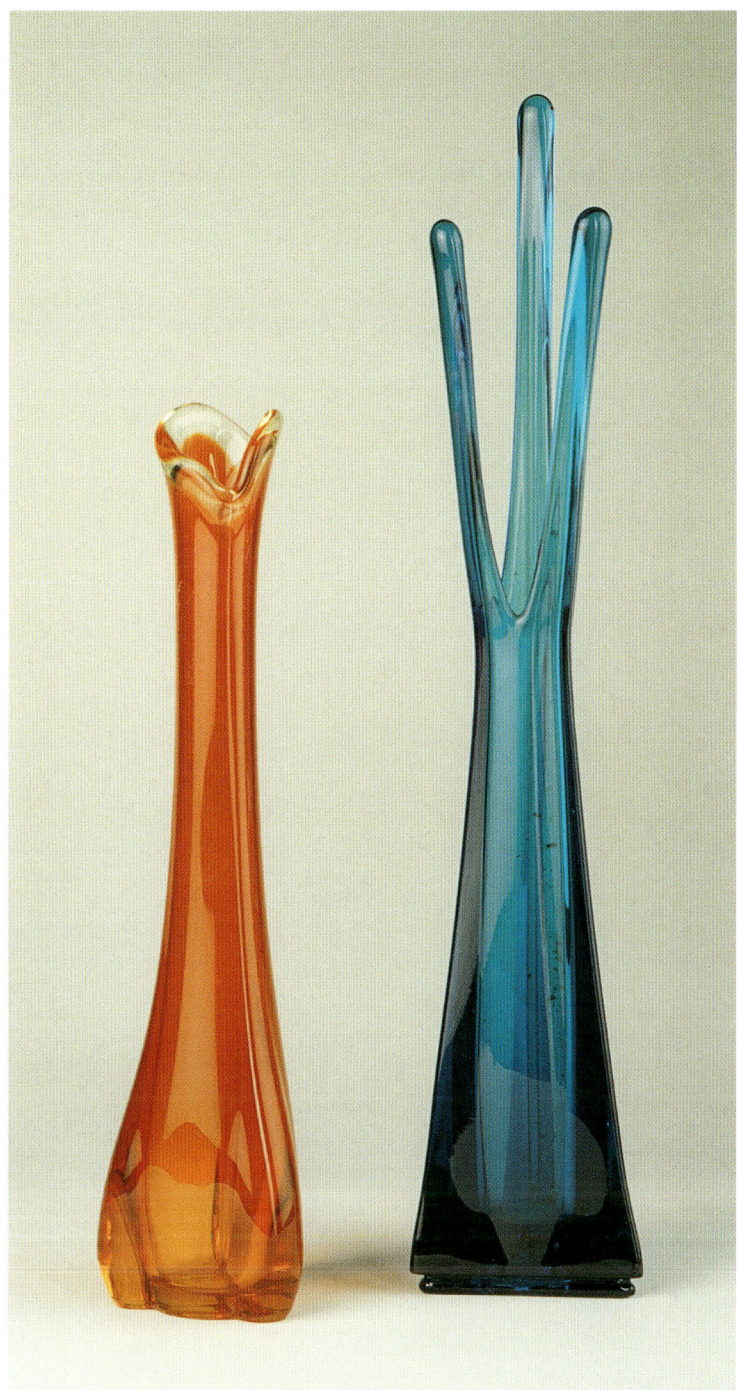

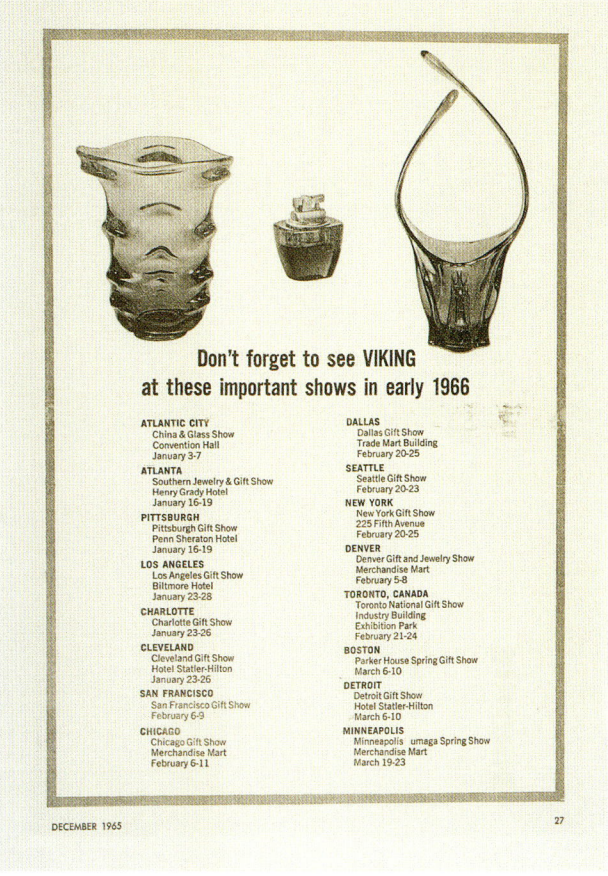

December 1965 Viking trade journal advertisement stating "Don't forget to See Viking ...in early 1965." Shown is a Tundra vase and the vase/open basket surrounding one of the cigarette lighters.

Epic Three Foil #1208 bud vase 11" persimmon, $14-22, shown in 1962 catalog; Epic swung vase featured on front of a later Viking promotional brochure, bluenique, $10-18.

Undated Viking Factory Tours brochure, circa 1972, as it mentions both the New Martinsville and then acquired "Rainbow" glass factory in Huntington. Note the bluenique vase shown above appears prominently on the cover.

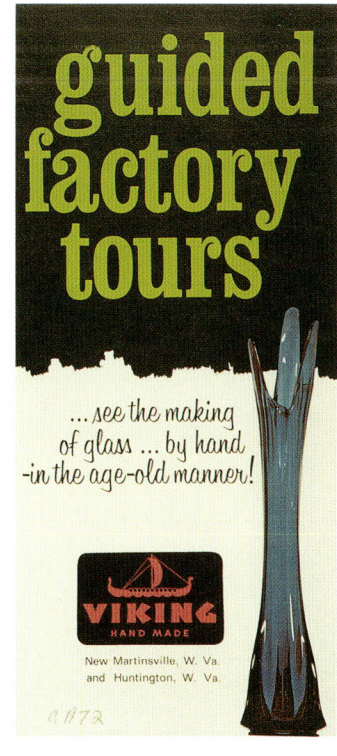

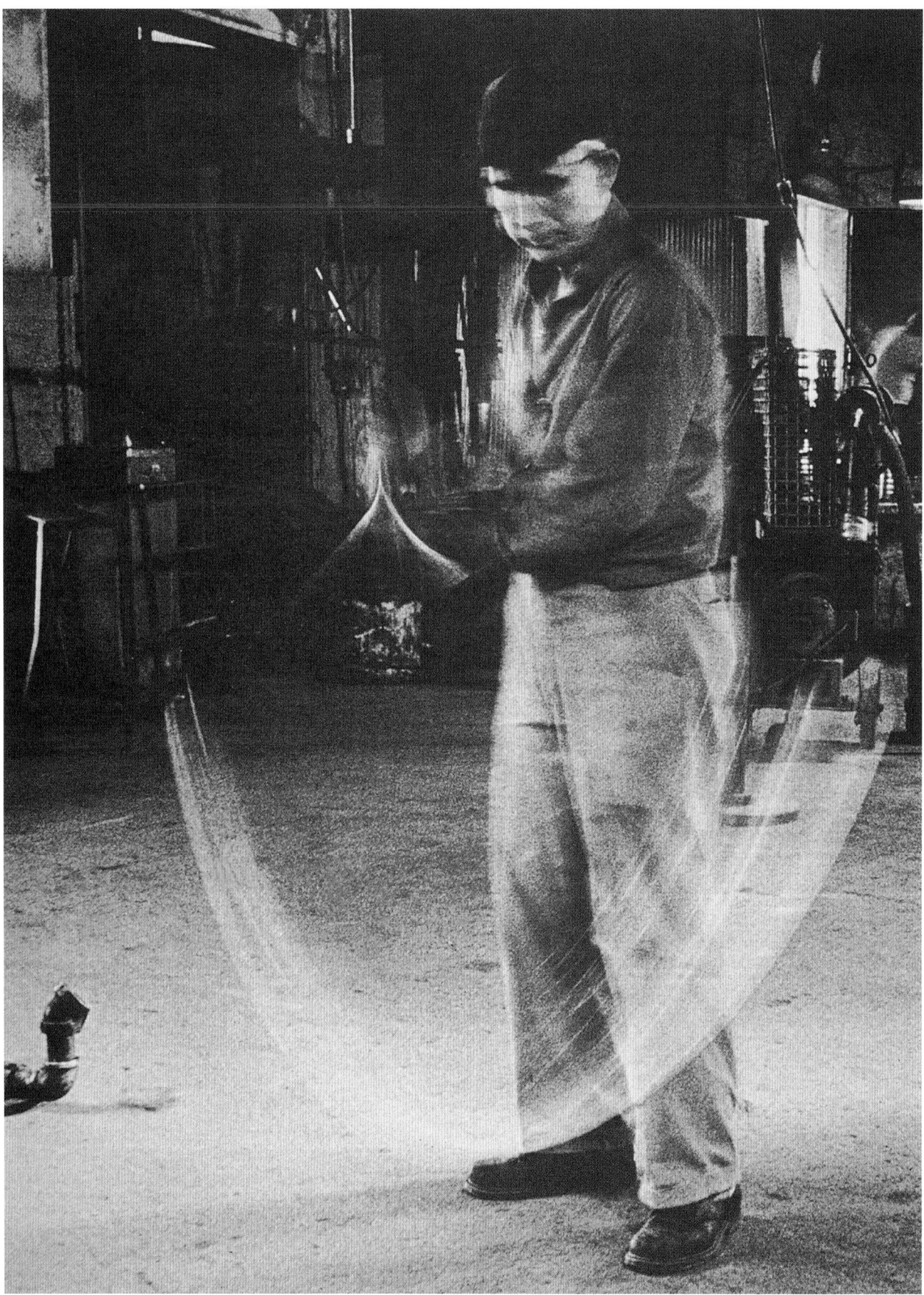

From period Viking Glass factory photos, these are steps in making the famous swung vases that were prominent in Epic and other lines. Shown is the actual swinging of a "swung vase." A swung vase is literally that, swung while the glass is still molten hot. The gravity pulls and forms the top of each vase into a unique finish. This accounts for the inability to create consistency in vase heights. The twirling hot glass vases are still attached to the snap in this step. The snap grasps the base by a ring of extra glass called a "marie," which allows holding and manipulation of the fiery hot, semi-liquid glass.

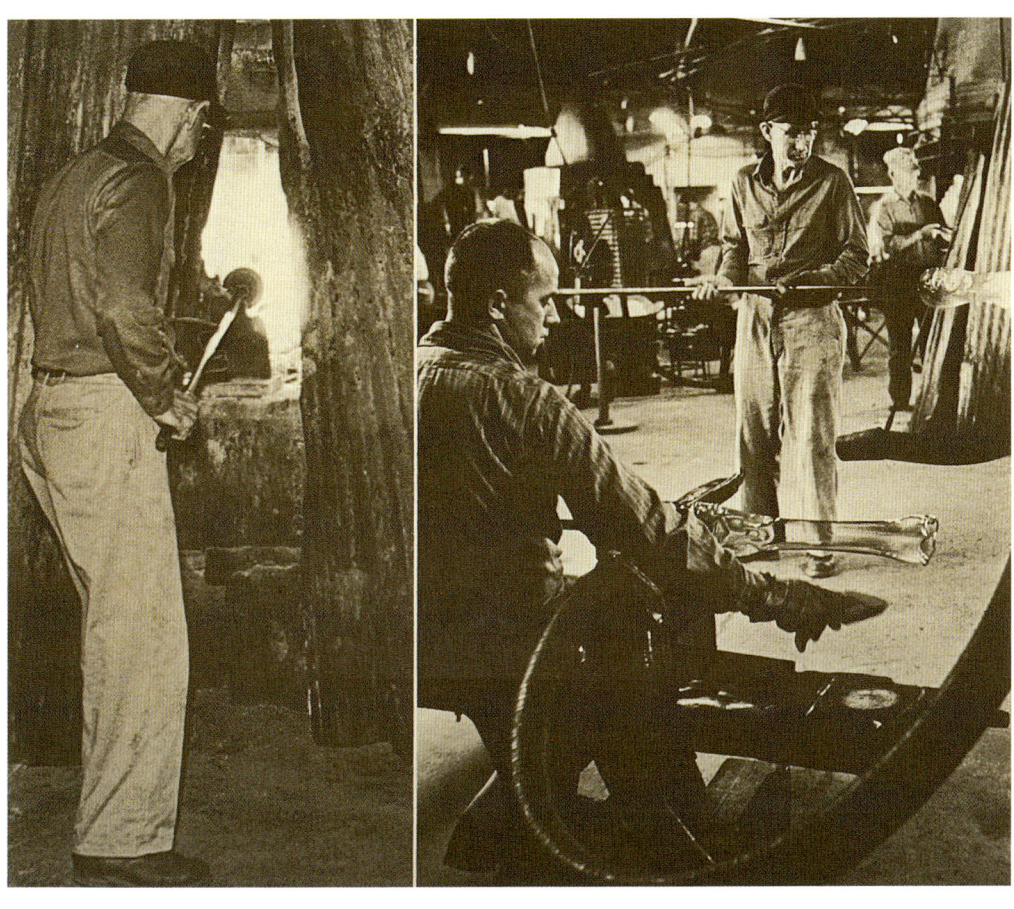

Further steps in creating swung vases include this left image showing the already pressed and then swung vase being reheated at a glory hole (a side furnace just for this reheating step) to make the glass again malleable and ready to be further shaped. The right image shows a "warming in boy" holding a hot vase on the snap (a rod for holding the 2,000 plus degree hot glass) awaiting the attention of the "finisher's" touches to the vase.

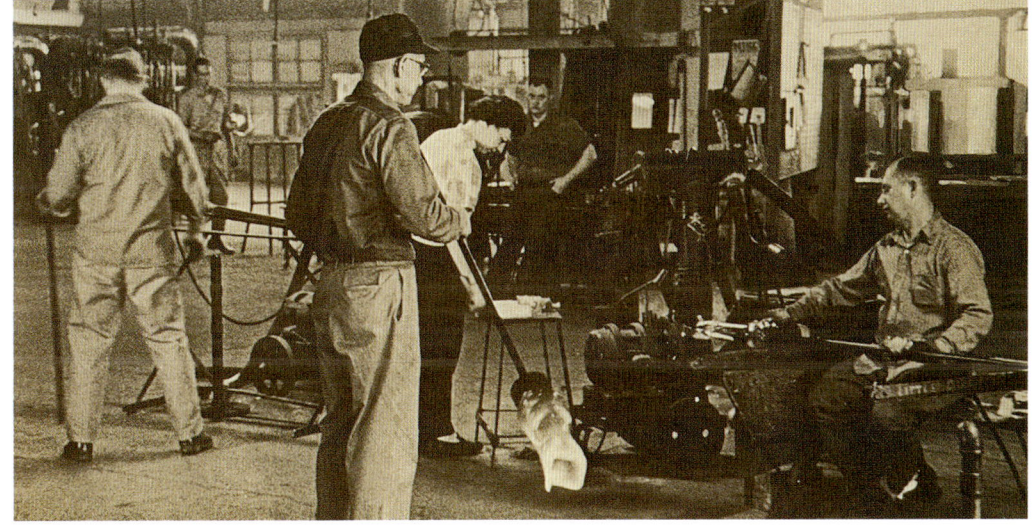

This view of the still glowing hot swung vase shows the vase held on a snap by a "warming in boy" as he waits to pass the nearly complete vase to a finisher.

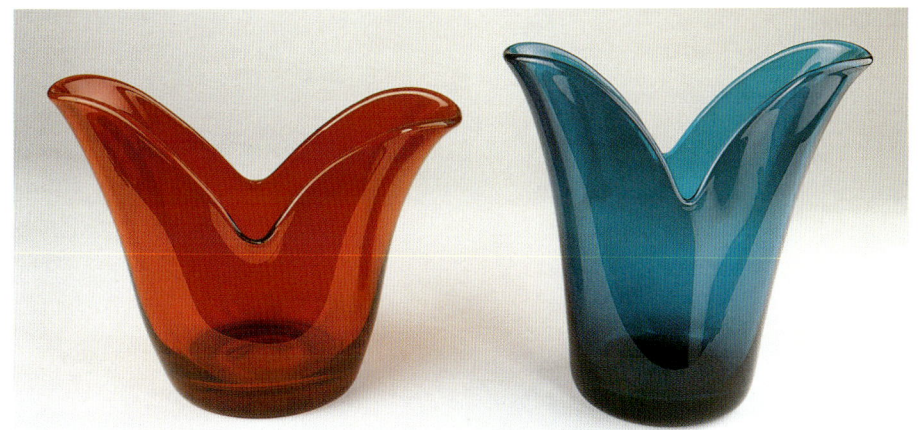

Split Vase #1187, 10", circa 1957, ruby, $65-85; bluenique, $55-75.

The Patterns of Viking 1944-1970

These relate to the forms and shapes created as hot glass.

ANCESTRAL Line #900: A Viking Glass advertisement in the trade magazine *China, Glass and Decorative Accessories* of December 1947 tells us of a "complete new stemware line and full service just introduced." *Crockery Glass and Decorative Accessories* ran an ad in February 1948 showing a stork carrying in pieces of Ancestral captioned, "this is the birth announcement of your new best seller - Viking Ancestral Stemware." One might suggest that the Ancestral line was introduced at the turn of the year 1947-48. It was not to be found in the production of the several years prior. However, if one looked back further to Viking's predecessor, New Martinsville Glass, and examined Line #14 in trade journal notices, the new line of Viking seems less new. New Martinsville Glass had called their line #14 Raindrops. Introduced in May of 1942, the New Martinsville line of hobnailed-like bumps was short-lived as the Raindrops line. But this pattern has an even longer, more complex history. Raindrops was made in the older molds of New Martinsville's earlier Line #38, "Repeal" or "Hostmaster." In an April 1945 letter from Viking Glass stating what was available for sale in the last half of that year, it is listed as Viking's Antique. Few lines anywhere underwent so many attempts at revival and with so little success.

This "new" Viking Ancestral pattern appears to have continued use of the stemware from Line 14 but clearly includes differently shaped cream, sugar, and perhaps other pieces. However, a crimped bowl shown with New Martinsville's No. 14 in 1942 appears to be the identical mold, but with different crimps and treatments, when it appears as tort plate, flared bowl, and crimped bowl in a 1940s Viking catalog. The two patterns, No. 14 Raindrops and #900 line Ancestral, appear to have common forms as well as unique shapes.

While looking for sources for Ancestral, it merits comment that the form of the two light candlestick, two candle cups on either side of a flattened circle, has some striking resemblance to the New Martinsville Glass Radiance pattern two light candlestick. It appears that Viking did not make the Radiance stick. The question is whether the Ancestral candlestick was the reworked Radiance stick.

Of the early Viking catalogs, discussed at length at several other places in this book, only one of those includes Ancestral. The 1948, supplemented to 1949, catalog has three pages of Ancestral. By the issuance of the next catalog, believed to be 1951, Ancestral is no longer included as a line. The exact length of the period of production is unknown. An ad for Ancestral is found in *House and Garden* in May of 1948, *House Beautiful*, April 1948, *China, Glass and Decorative Accessories* in February and April of 1948. The last sighting for this briefly reincarnated pattern is in *House & Garden* of May 1949. The circa 1951 price list has no items listed as Ancestral and no item numbers that match the Ancestral designations.

This is a line reminiscent of hobnail pressed patterns manufactured by numerous other manufacturers for over a century. It was marketed for traditional appeal. Crystal only is reported from the field or found in the literature to date. The exception is the stemmed ivy ball, which is found in several colors and is featured as a part of the Yesteryear line as item #1927 as early as 1960.

Items shown in the one catalog reviewed include:
Basket, handled and crimped #917, 10" (found with colored handles)
Bowl, belled #911, 11-1/2"
Bowl, crimped #912, 12"
Bowl, flared #910, 12"
Bowl, oval crimped #913, 12-1/2"
Candelabra, 2-light #914, 5-1/2"
Cocktail #903, 3-1/2 oz.
Compote, flat #915, 6-1/2"
Compote, crimped #916, 6"
Cordial #920, 1 oz.
Cup and saucer #926
Goblet, water #901, 10 oz.
Oil bottle with ground stopper #923, 6 oz.
Plate, salad #907, 8"
Salt and pepper #924
Sherbet, tall #902, 5 oz.
Sherbet, low #918, 5 oz.
Sugar & creamer #925
Torte Plate with rimmed edge #909, 13-1/2"
Torte plate #908, 14"
Tumbler, footed #904, 12 oz.
Tumbler, flat #921, 10 oz.
Tumbler #905, 7 oz.
Tumbler, juice #906, 5 oz.
Tumbler, whiskey #922, 2 oz.
Wine #919, 3-1/2 oz.

Items listed by Viking in 1945 and called the Antique line but not appearing as Ancestral include:
Bonbon, six crimps #14/8, 7-1/2"
Compote, eight crimps #14/10, 5" wide and 3-1/2" tall
Tumbler, 12 oz., #14
Tumbler, Old Fashioned 5 oz., #14
Vase, flared, six crimps #14/2, 5"

Any of these interchangeable Antique, Raindrops, Ancestral or Yesteryear pieces could be used or collected together as they are indistinguishable in design and appear to have been often from the exact same mold.

Collector's note: Ancestral hobnails are stacked in straight, vertical, one directly above another, rows and are not offset as many other hobnailed patterns are. This may help identify Ancestral amidst a sea of similar hobnail patterns.

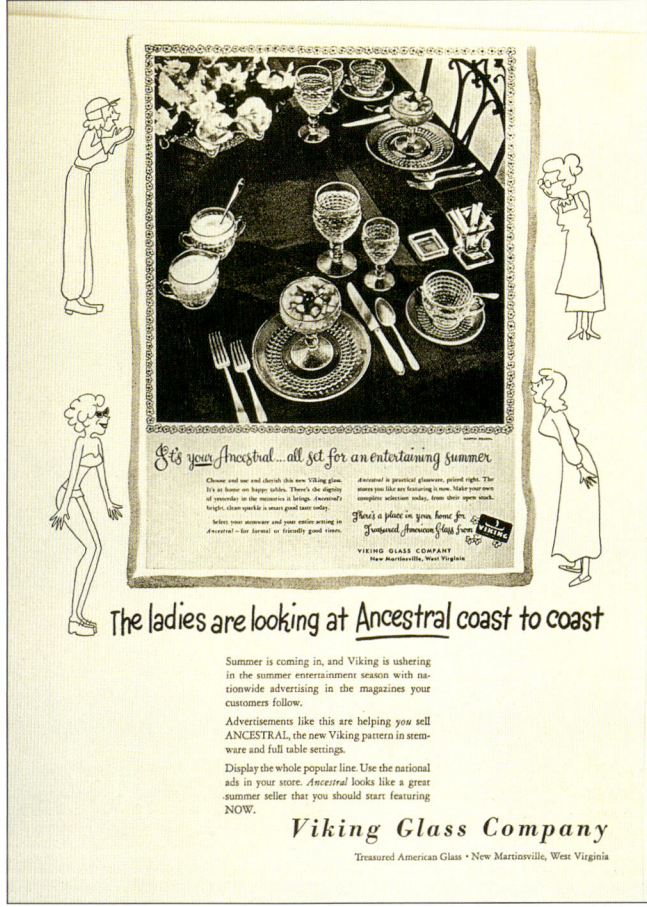

Viking advertisement in trade journal announcing a 1948 national ad campaign for the pattern Ancestral. *China, Glass & Decorative Accessories*, April 1948.

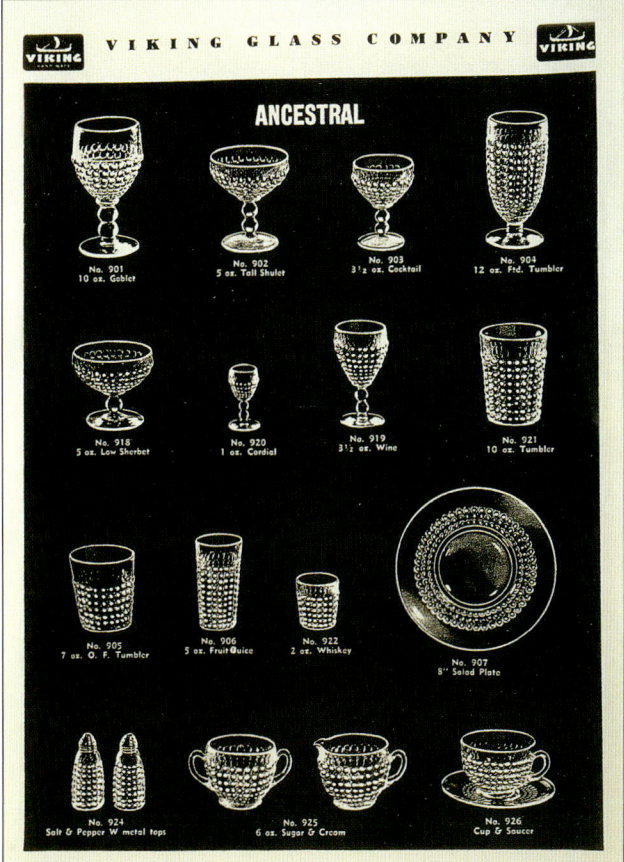

Viking Glass catalog page, 1948-49, featuring Ancestral pattern tableware.

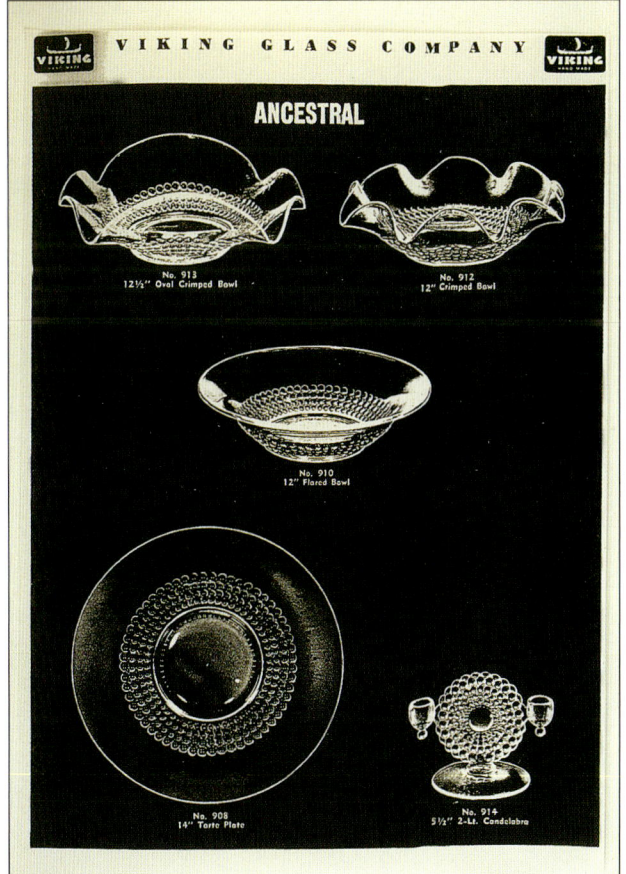

Viking Glass catalog page, 1948-49, featuring Ancestral pattern bowls, torte plate, and the illusive two light candelabra.

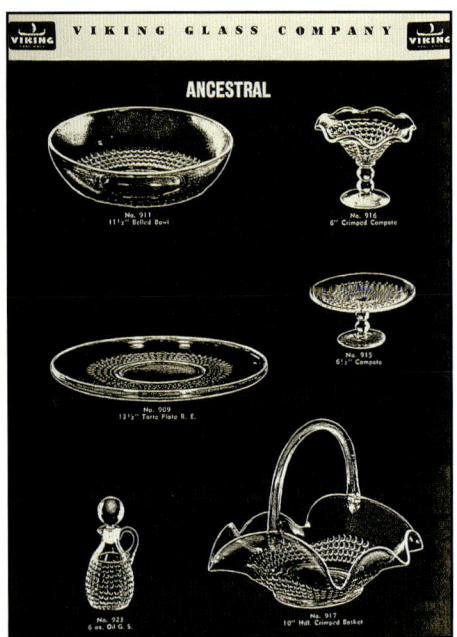

Viking Glass catalog page, 1948-49, featuring the Ancestral pattern.

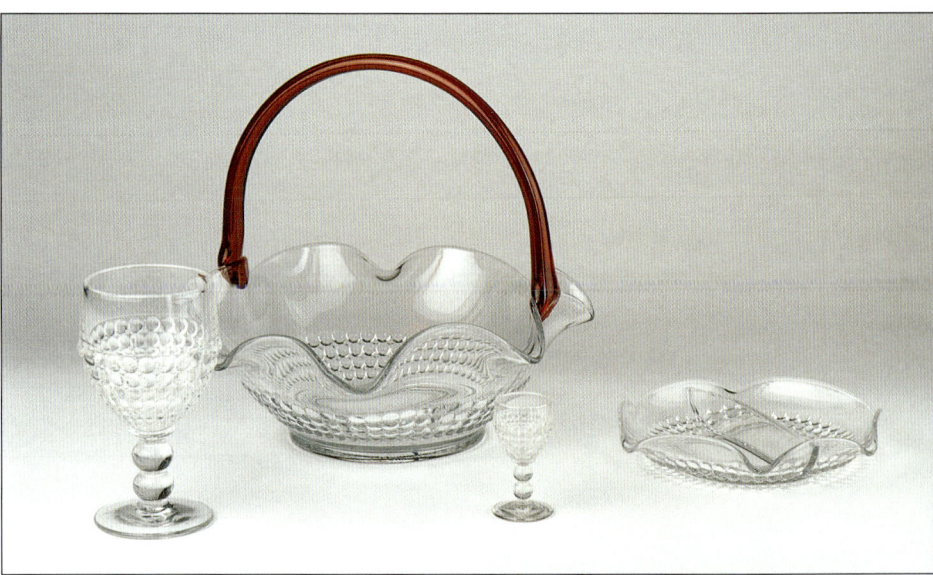

Ancestral pattern 10 oz. goblet #907 crystal, $14-18; divided relish (maybe made only by New Martinsville Glass?), $12-18; 1 oz. cordial #920, $16-24; and 10", #917 basket with ruby handle, $45-58.

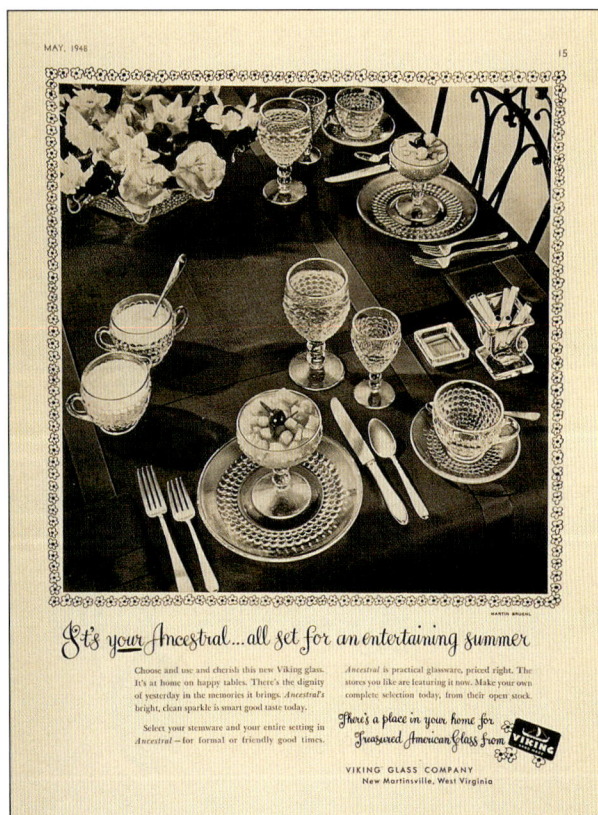

Viking advertisement for Ancestral proclaiming "It's your Ancestral...all set for an entertaining summer." Full page ad appearing in May 1948 House & Garden. Note the edge of the large Ancestral bowl peeping from under the flowers and the Viking cornucopia cigarette urn.

ASTRA Line #6100 is a line of shapes with a "star motif in base of each" (*Crockery & Glass*, Feb 1961). Astra was announced as a "new article to make first appearance at Atlantic City...full assortment of table accessories, ashtrays and vases." in *Crockery & Glass*, December 1960. At the same time an illustration of a free-form console bowl and two candlestick blocks appeared. The 1962 catalog features twenty-five shapes in Astra. A four-page catalog supplement, featuring just Astra, announced the line and shows:

Ashtray, 11", #6188
Ashtray, 6", #6187
Ashtray, 3-1/2", #6186
Bonbon, square 6", #6181
Bowl, shallow 13", #6101
Bowl, oblong 12", #6103
Candelabra, two light 5", #6114
Candlestick, one light 4", #6113
Candlestick, one light block 2-1/2", #6112
Cake salver, "footed bowl" 10", #6169
Cake salver, 11", #6126
Celery, 11", #6149
Cheese and cracker, two part 14", #6132
Chip and dip, two piece 13", #6195
Compote, cheese flat top 6-1/2", #6133
Compote, flared 6", #6128
Cream, #6147
Mayonnaise, three pieces includes ladle #6136
Plate, torte, rolled edge 14", #6117
Relish, three part, two handles 11", #6138
Sugar, #6147
Vase, bud swung tall #6171
Vase, 8" swung #6172
Vase, footed swung 15", #6173
Vase, flared swung 13", #6174
Vase, swung tall 20", #6175

In nationally placed magazines ads in April 1967, the Astra single light candle block appears promoted as a part of the Epic line! Additional catalogs from that era were not found, so the extent of the continued use of Astra in this time is unknown.

Astra pattern "The Heavenly New Crystal by Viking" full page ad appearing in *House & Garden*, April 1961. The ad copy cites the designer, New Martinsville resident Dick Schnacke, an uncommon Viking action.

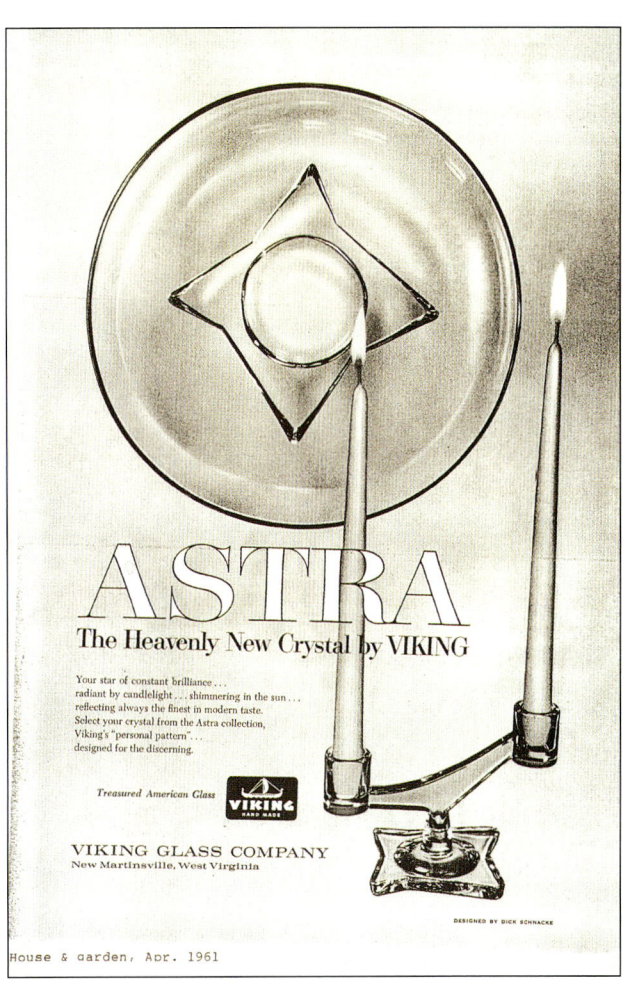

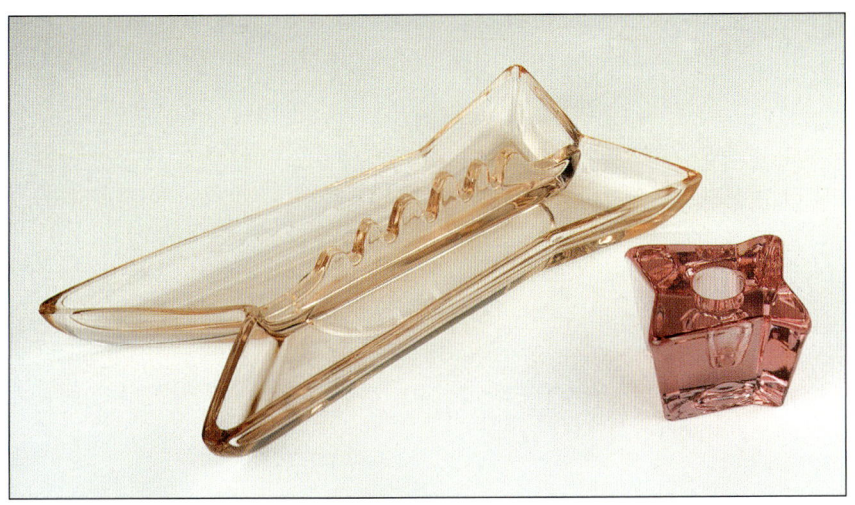

Astra pattern #6188, 11" ashtray cherry glo, $22-32; #6112, 2-1/2" one light candlestick thistle, $22-28 each.

Astra pattern #6147, two piece cream & sugar crystal with corporate logo. Set without logo, $22-32. *West Virginia Museum of American Glass collection. Gift of Jaime Robinson.*

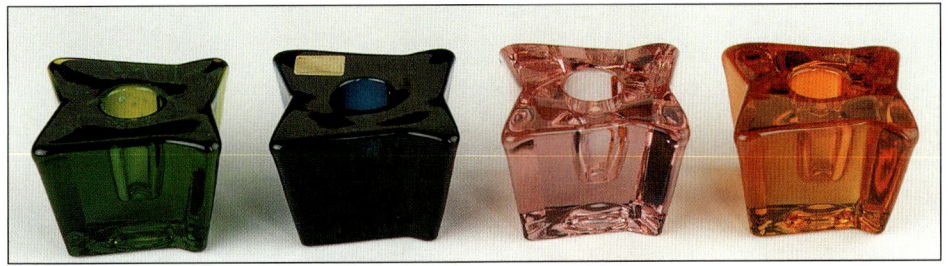

Astra pattern #6112, 2-1/2" one light candlestick green, $10-14; bluenique, $14-20; thistle, $22-28; persimmon, $16-22 each.

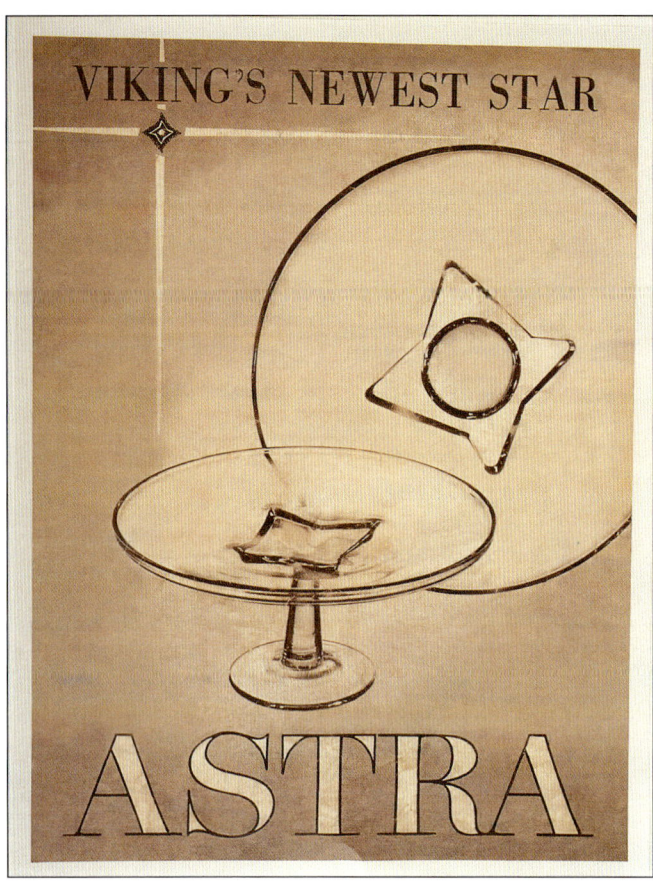

Astra catalog cover to four page Viking Glass special catalog.

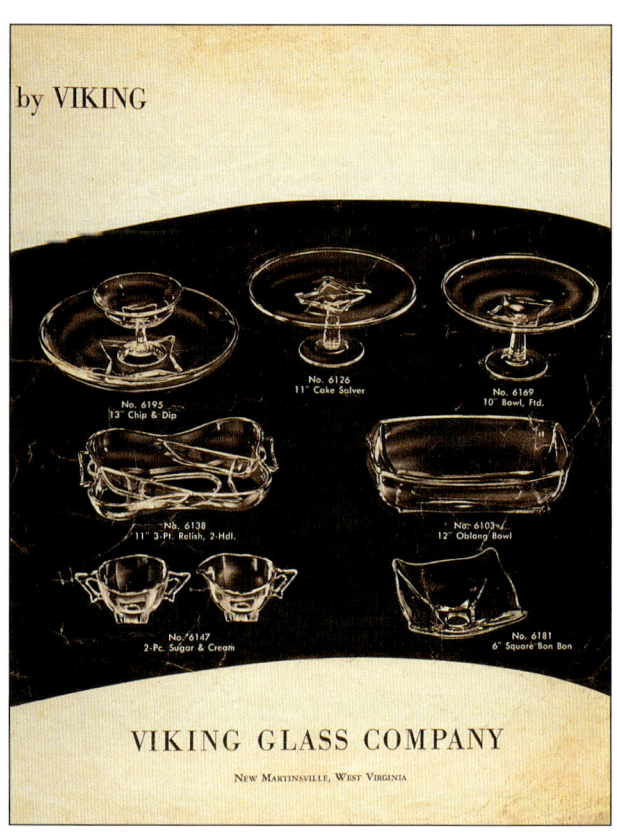

Astra catalog Viking Glass.

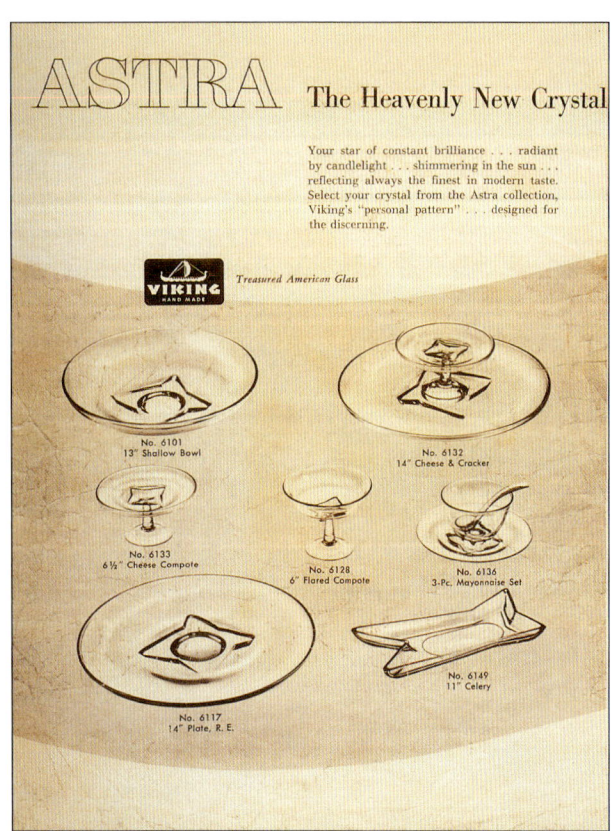

Astra catalog Viking Glass.

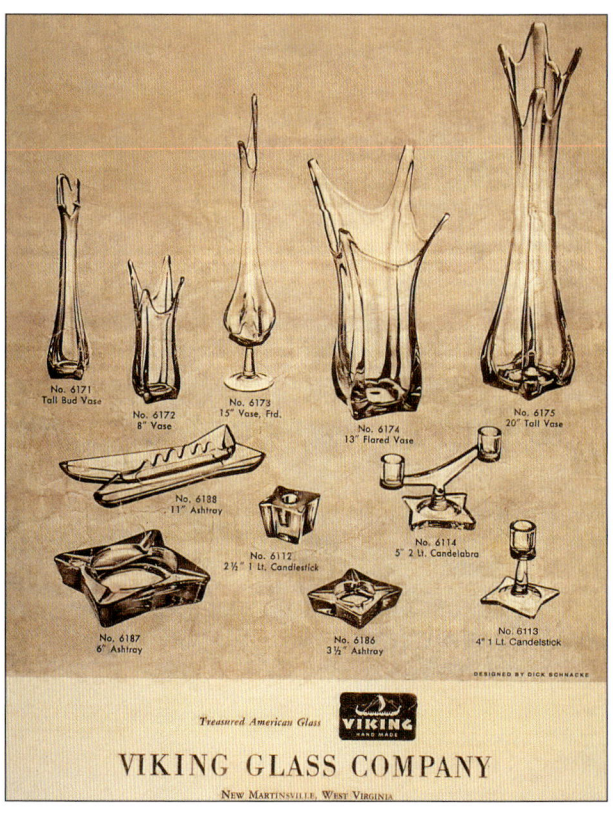

Astra catalog Viking Glass.

BURLAP: "Burlap plate gets name from textured back. New glassware line comes in amber, crystal, green." we were told in *Crockery & Glass*, December 1953. A plate is illustrated.

CHRISTINA Line #800 is a part of a line of colorless glass marketed as Krystal Klear. Christina is a set of shapes and pieces with octagonal stems and often octagonal bodies within the Krystal Klear line and is assigned product numbers in the #800s. These shapes are heavy, crystal, and an effort to advance the perceived Swedish or modern look the then new Viking line was seeking to invoke. Later, in 1950-51, a few Christina shapes appeared in colored glass as noted below.

The first in print reference showing the Christina pattern appears in *Crockery & Glass* in July 1944 and describes the covered candy only as "octagonal." It is indeed Christina but the ad is still for New Martinsville Glass. An ad in *China, Glass and Decorative Accessories* in December 1946 illustrates pieces in Christina but does not mention the pattern name. In an ad in the McClure's catalog of Chicago titled "Gifts for 1948" an illustrated ad promotes "Viking handmade crystal glass… Christina and Janice patterns sold open stock."

There were four pages of Christina in the Viking 1948-49 catalog:

Ashtray, octagonal 6-1/2", #872
Ashtray, octagonal 5-1/2", #871
Ashtray, octagonal 4", #870
Ashtray, octagonal 3", #873
Basket, octagonal flat 10" tall, 10-1/2" wide, #8001
Basket, octagonal footed 12" tall, 9" wide, #801
Basket, octagonal flat 7" tall, 8-1/2" wide, #803
Basket, octagonal flat divided two part 7" tall, 8-1/2" wide, #804
Basket, octagonal, footed 9" tall, 6" wide, #805
Bowl, octagonal 2-3/4" tall, 9-1/2" wide, #810
Bowl, octagonal cupped 3" tall, 9" wide, #812
Bowl, octagonal low flat 2-1/2" tall, 12" wide, #812
Bowl, octagonal crimped 4" tall, 12" wide, #813
Cake salver, octagonal 2" tall, 7" wide, #856
Cake salver, octagonal 3" tall, 10" wide, #855
Candlestick, octagonal 2-1/2" tall one light #820
Candlestick, octagonal 6" tall one light #821
Candy box, octagonal with lid, 4" tall, 7" wide, #831
Candy box, octagonal with lid, two compartment, 4" tall, 7" wide, #832
Candy jar, octagonal with lid, 9" tall, 4" wide, #830
Compote, octagonal 5" tall, 8" wide, #840
Compote, octagonal 4" tall, 5" wide, #841
Compote, octagonal 4" tall, 6" wide, #842
Cream & Sugar with lid, octagonal, footed, 7 oz., #865
Jug, octagonal 24 oz., 6" tall, 4" wide, #850
Marmalade, octagonal with lid, footed, 6" tall, 3" wide, #852
(Note: identical item is offered as cigarette jar with lid as item #878.)
Plate, octagonal 14", #854
Relish, divided octagonal two part, two handles, 2" tall, 7" wide, #860
Relish, divided octagonal two part, eight crimps, 2" tall, 8" wide, #861
Relish, divided octagonal two part, two crimps, 2" tall, 7" wide, #862
Urn, cigarette, octagonal 2-1/2" tall, 2" wide, #876
Urn, cigarette, octagonal 2" tall, 2" wide, #877
Vase, octagonal 6" high, 4" wide, #880
Vase, octagonal flat 8" high, 5" wide, #881
Vase, octagonal flat eight crimps flared, 4-1/2" high, 8" wide, #882
Vase, octagonal flat four crimp, 6" high, 6" wide, #883
Vase/compote, octagonal footed crimped, 6-1/2" high, 6" wide, #884
Vase, octagonal footed 6" high, 2" wide, #885
Vase, octagonal footed flared 5" high, 4" wide, #886
Vase, octagonal footed crimped 5" high, 4" wide, #887

By 1950, twelve pieces of Christina remain in the line. The name Christina was no longer used and they are listed as "oct" meaning the octagonal line. Six pieces were produced then in ebony and three in evergreen.

There are no Christina shaped items in the 1955 catalog, but in 1962 there is a #890 crimped vase as a part of the Epic line that still bears the Christina line number (800s) and has the octagonal form. Again in 1970 Christina shapes seem to appear in the catalog where we find a twelve-ounce highball #814 with the Zodiac decoration.

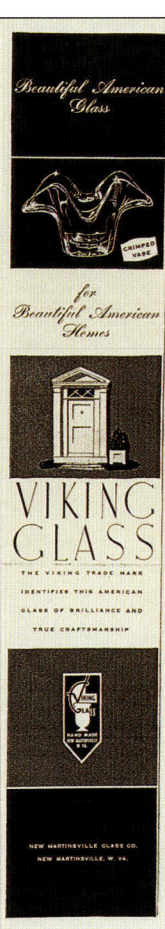

Octagonal shaped line items by New Martinsville Glass Co. marketed under the emerging Viking glass trademark. These identical shapes would become the Christina line of shapes. *House Beautiful*, October 1944.

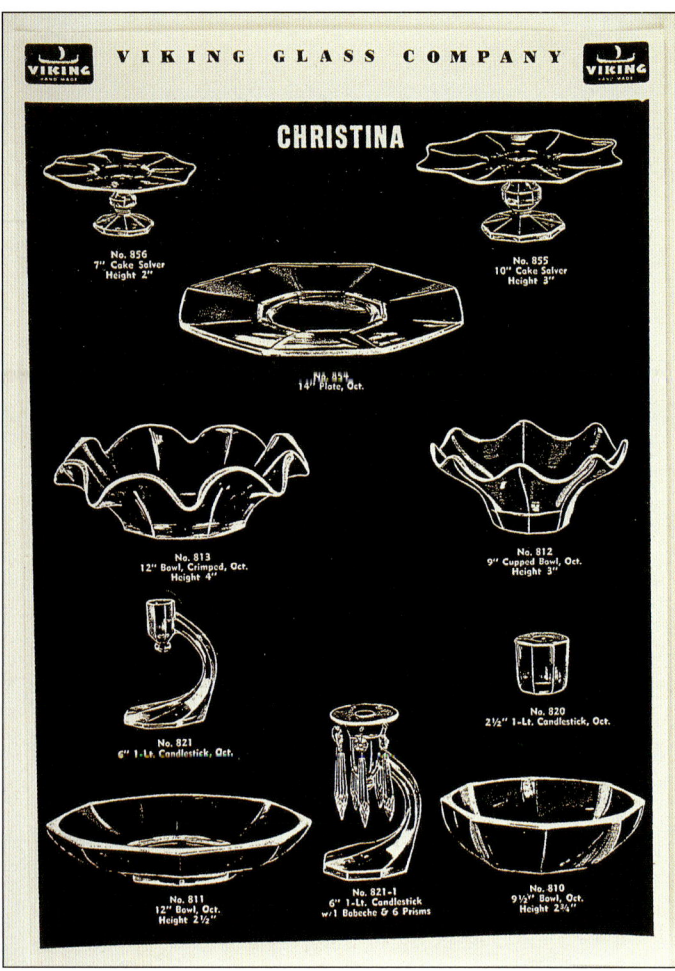

Viking Glass catalog page for "Christina" pattern 1948-49. The arched candlestick #821 is difficult to find.

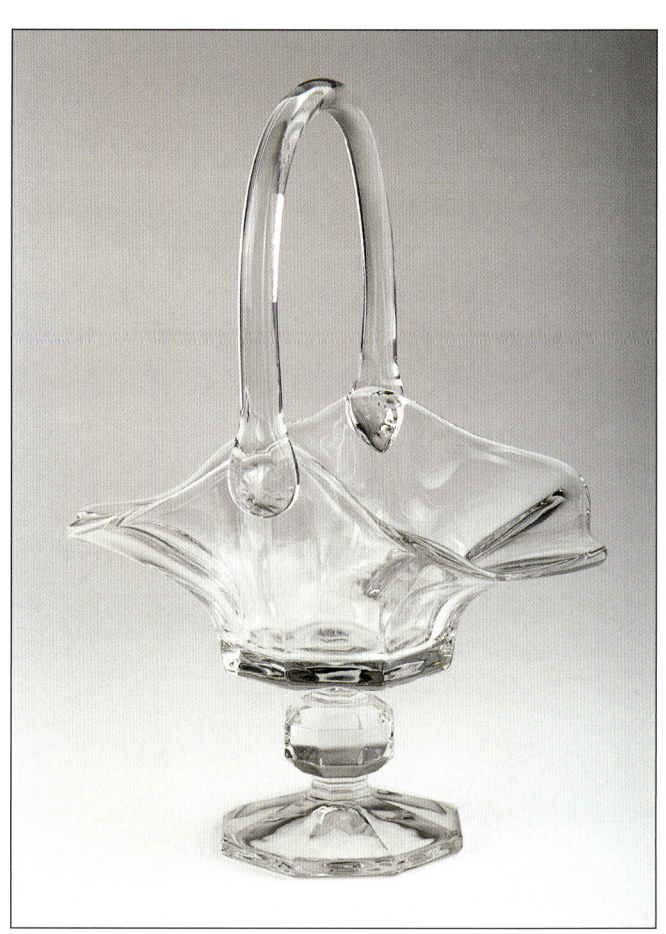

Christina pattern #801 octagonal basket with hand applied handle, crystal, $30-38.

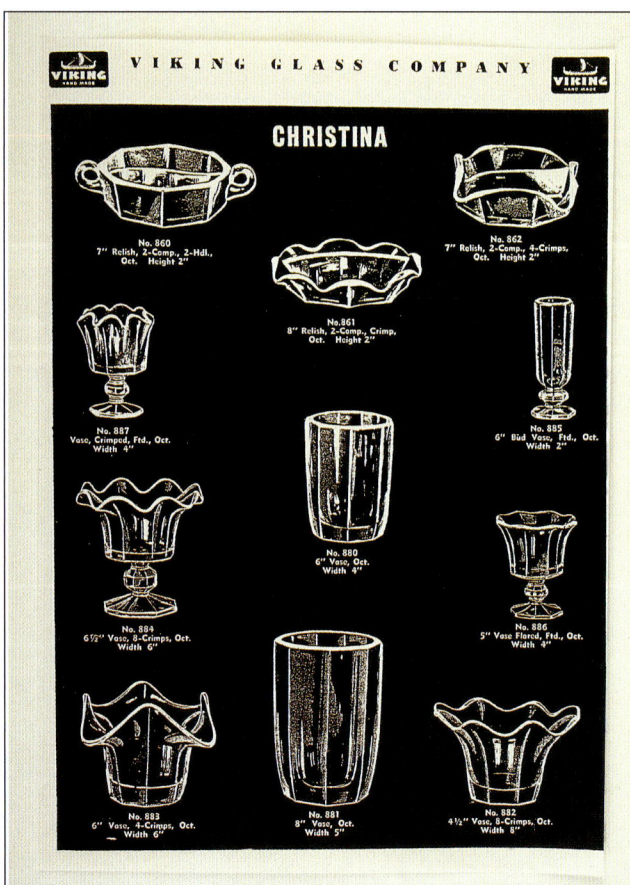

Viking Glass catalog page for "Christina" pattern 1948-49.

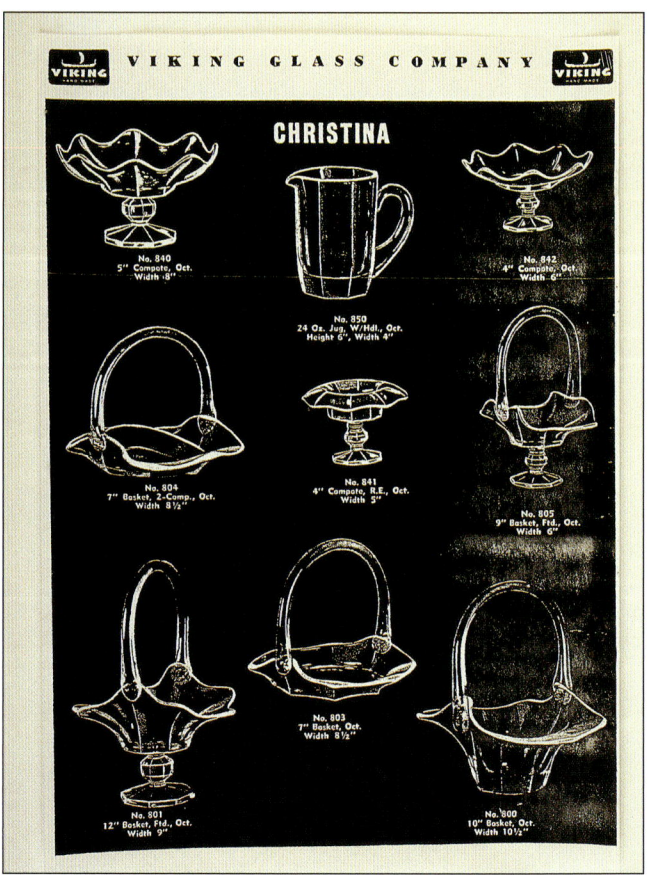

Viking Glass catalog page for "Christina" pattern 1948-49. Note the variety of baskets.

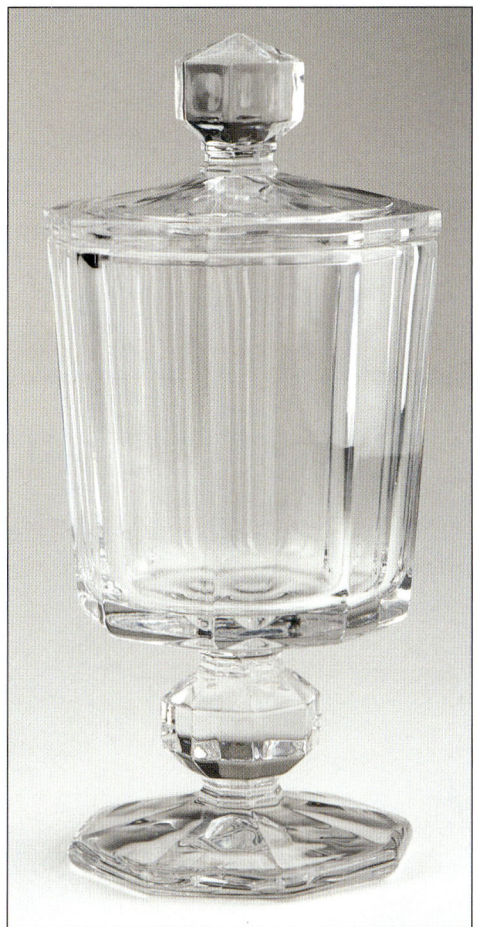

Christina pattern candy with lid #803 octagonal crystal footed 9", $24-32.

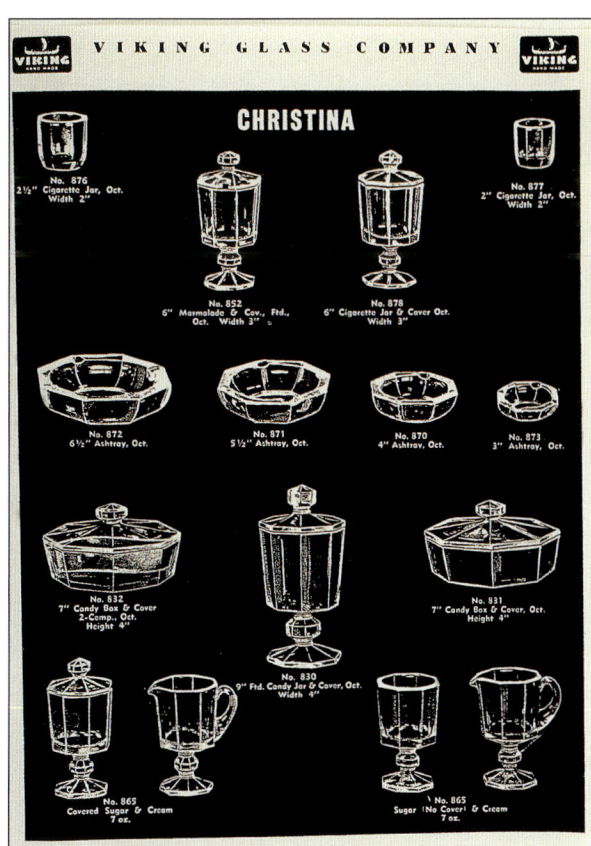

Viking Glass catalog page for "Christina" pattern 1948-49.

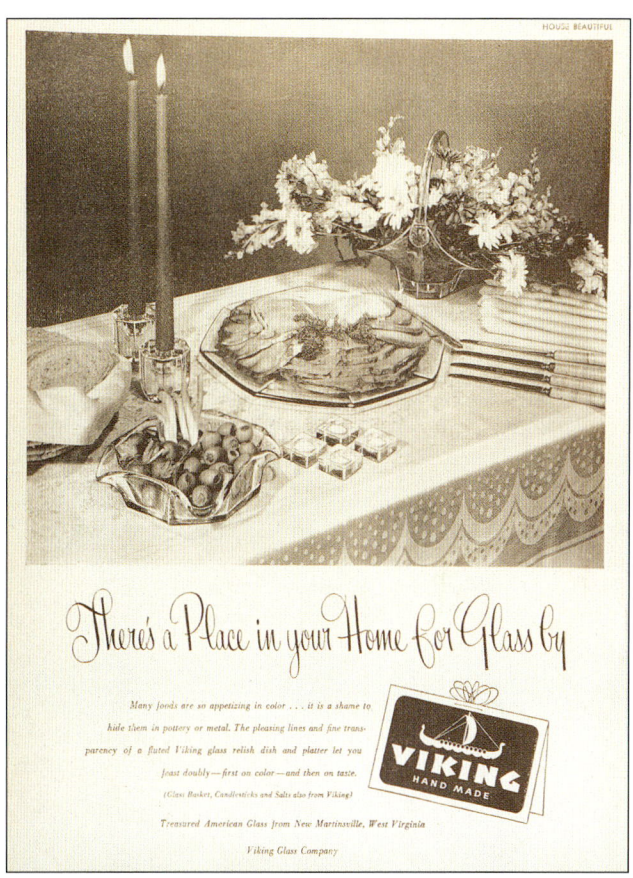

Viking Glass full page advertisement featuring Christina patterned items in crystal. *House Beautiful*, November 1946.

CRACKLE: *Crockery & Glass*, September 1952, "beautiful crackle glass salad bowl in new subtle shade of olive green or crystal, individual bowls to match from Viking." The January 1, 1953 price list has section titled "Crackled Items." Listed are several sizes of salad plates and bowls and an ashtray. Also listed in 1953 are 10, 18, 32, and 64 oz. Crackle jugs with crystal or evergreen handles. Crackle glass today has a collecting following and Viking is rarely attributed with making the ware. However, we found Viking crackle on the market, in literature, and later period Viking catalogs in numbers that far exceeded our expectations. Viking made a noticeable amount of crackle over time.

The 1955 price list cites the Scroll line as being produced in crackleware. Pieces of the Princess shape in ruby have been found crackled and an example is shown in this book. The period of Crackle Princess is not yet known. Years later, in the mid-1970s, after Viking acquired the Rainbow glass factory in Huntington, West Virginia, and operated it as Viking II, crackle again played a role in the Viking line. The products from Viking II were not similar to those of this pre-1970s period and should not easily be confused in shape or form. It did, however, have paper labels identifying it as Viking.

EPIC: This is the singularly most eclectic mix of shapes and patterns within the expansive Viking glass production. For collectors it might be deemed a mess. There are no common characteristics, style or discernable elements making any piece Epic. It was a marketing term used for many, many styles. Epic was "new" when mentioned in the *China & Glass Journal* of August 1956. It appears then as a free-form line. A large, swirl-ended bowl was making appearances in the glass press. This piece was noted as being 16" and then available in crystal, amber, charcoal, olive green, and amethyst. This long, low, graceful bowl is one of the signature forms for Viking and a 1950s icon that was continued in production into the 1970s.

By December 1956 Viking was adding to the Epic line. New was a vase in 8", 10", and 12" sizes and in crystal, amber, amethyst, olive green, and charcoal. (*Crockery & Glass Journal*). Note both Epic pieces mentioned cite the same five colors, likely the popular colors for Epic at that time. It is noteworthy that the 1956 Viking catalog contained the single largest color offering from Viking found at any time, sixteen colors available in that year, but not all were used for the growing Epic line.

In 1959 Viking Glass had filed suit in Federal Court to refrain L.E. Smith Glass Co. of Mt. Pleasant, Pennsylvania, from selling a line of glass that Viking claimed was an imitation of Viking's "swungout" items in the Epic line. Swung out denotes those items that were swung from the end of a glass workers snap or tool while still hot, thus allowing centrifical force to shape the abstract and fluid form of their tops.

The case was not without some detrimental wisecracking. The plaintiff C.T. Swartling, president of Viking, noted that Viking used only "pot" glass with no visible parting line (assumed to mean mold lines) and with no defects and that Smith used "tank" glass cast in sectional molds and with visible parting lines and defects. Smith was charged with making an imitation of Viking's taperglow candlestick, a 10" and 16" pitcher, and an 11" vase. Smith, in defense, alleged that the "swungout" design is a well-known process in the glass industry. Smith further asserted it had produced swungout items for over thirty years and denied having ever advertised nationally and of course asserts it makes glass that is clear and free from defects. (*Home Furnishings Daily*, March 2, 1959) Smith was not refrained from producing swung items by the court and it is some of these very contested objects that constitute some of the most confusing items found resembling Epic-like objects.

Epic and the use of that name by Viking were perhaps described best in a two page advertisement spread in *Gifts & Decorative Accessories*, December 1966. "The Norsemen of old were famed for their Epics – legends of great deeds of valor. Today, Viking creates a new and exciting Epic in this brightly beautiful line of handmade glass. Epic... as beautiful as a Scandinavian fjord, will capture and captivate your customers with its dramatic coloring...and its striking design." It was in this way that Viking pitched its namesake and the romanticism of legends and Epics. It worked well for many years for Viking.

Epic remains strong and prevalent in the 1962 line with fif-

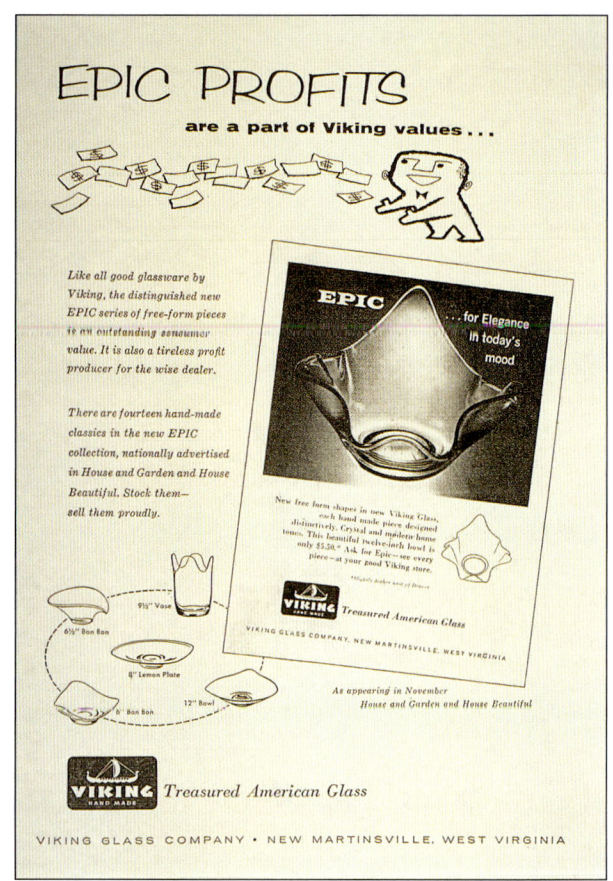

"Epic profits" begins this full page Viking Glass advertisement. One of the earliest mentions found of the Epic line, this ad copy cites "There are fourteen hand-made classics in the new EPIC collection..." Five of these earliest forms are shown in the ad. *China & Glass Journal*, November 1956.

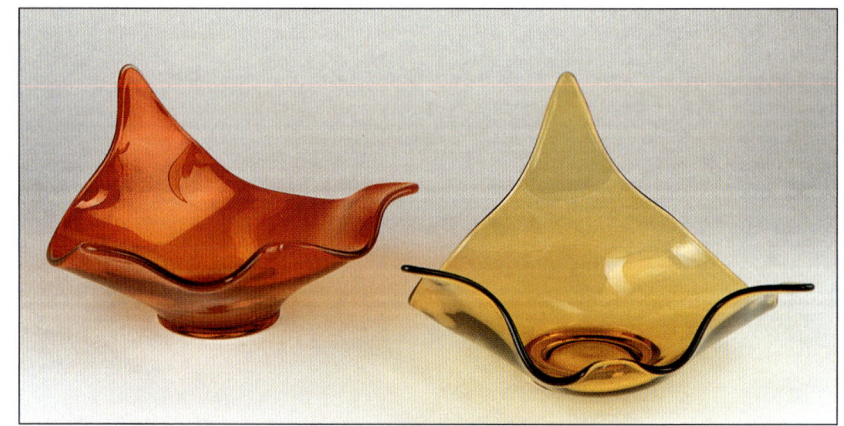

Epic handkerchief bowl #1160, 10". Shown in *House & Garden*, November 1956 and *China & Glass Journal*, November 1956 as well as the 1962 catalog. Persimmon, $18-32; amber, $12-20.

ty-one pieces included on a July price list. In 1970 almost eighty items appear in the Viking catalog on pages boldly captioned and titled as "Epic." The product mix is wild: figural mushroom to patio lights, from traditional cup and saucer to massive free-form vases. While the 1970 Viking catalog retained ten colors, Epic pieces were available only in five of those: avocado, bluenique, honey, persimmon, and ruby. Remember that Epic in 1970 and throughout time seldom had meaning other than to identify a product as a part of the Viking product line and did not denote specific related shapes or patterns.

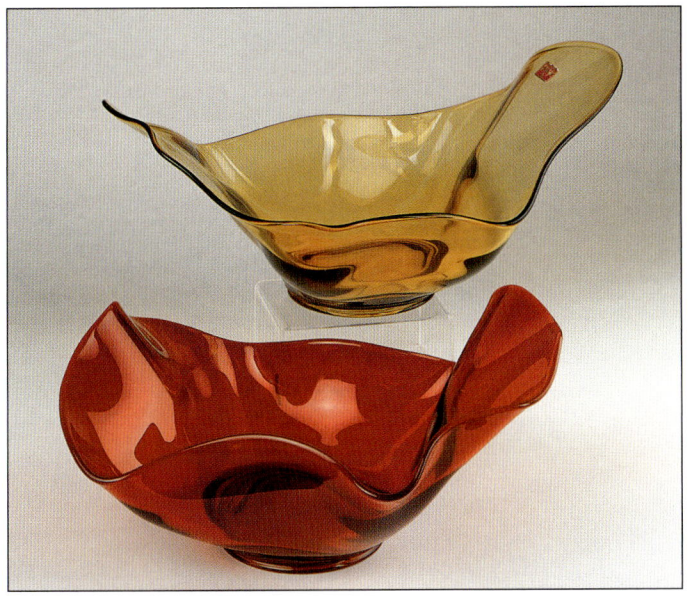

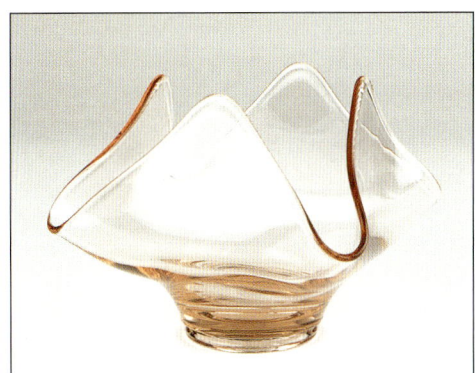

Epic crimped bonbon #1147, 6" cherry glo, $18-26, shown in the 1959 catalog.

Epic large handkerchief bowl #7017, 12". Introduced in 1970. Ruby, $40-52; amber, $18-28.

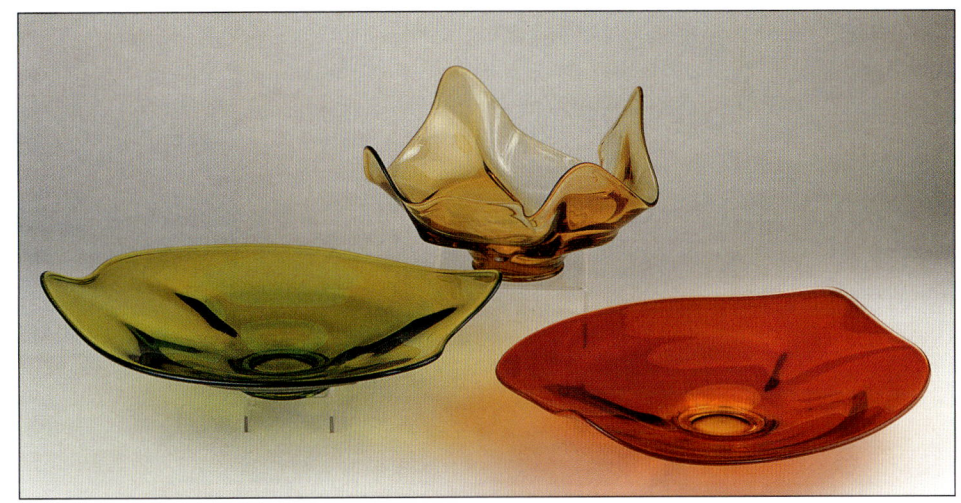

Epic large free-form bowls, all beginning from the same mold. Note this mold has two large blocks extending out from opposite sides on the base and along the free-form, avocado, 15", $18-26; amber, 10", $12-18; persimmon, $20-28.

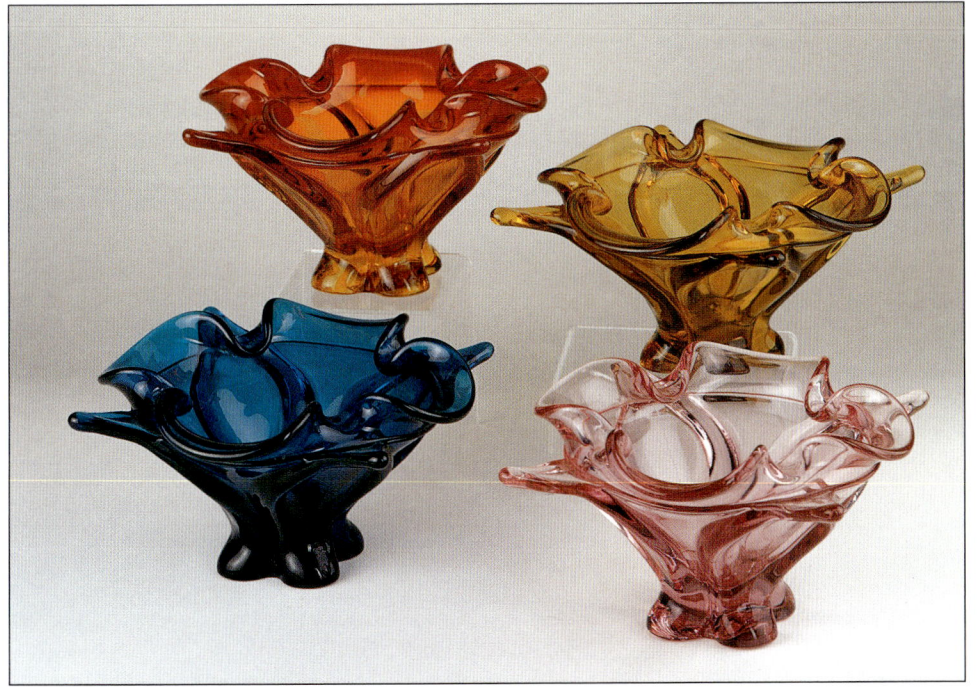

Epic crimped bowl #6718, 8" bluenique, $32-42; amber, $24-32; persimmon, $45-58; and thistle, $48-65. This form, one of the four toed Epic pieces, gives rise to falsely attributing endless Italian and other forms to being Viking. In the Viking offerings, it stands alone in style and form. Beginning as a pressed piece of glass, always apparent from looking at the base, the #6718 varies very little from one piece to the next, unlike many other Epic forms—see the picture.

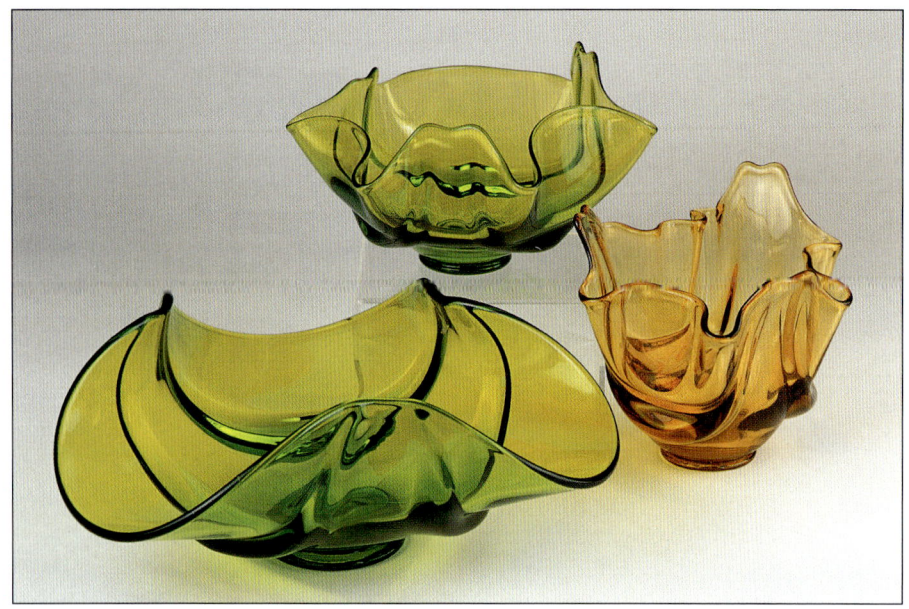

Epic bowl #6814, 10" avocado, $16-24; Epic bowl #6806 avocado, $10-16; Epic bowl #6806, 5" amber, $6-10.

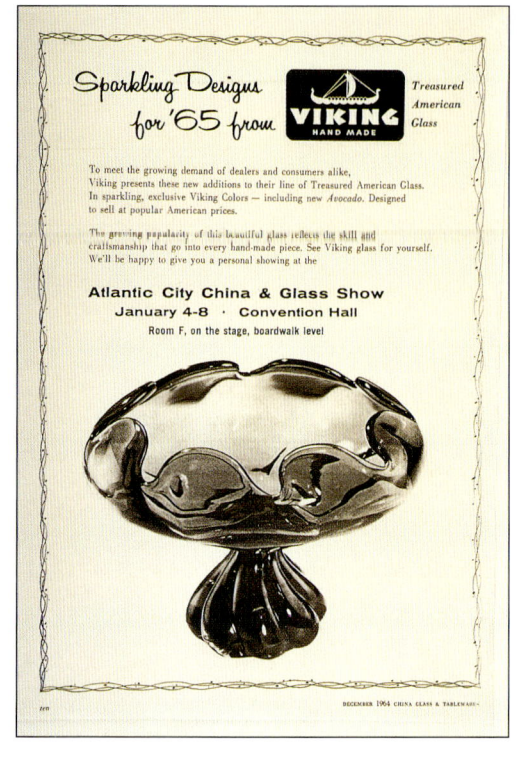

"Sparkling Designs for '65 From Viking…including new avocado." This line #1500 in Epic has been dubbed "Twist" to distinguish it by the radically twisted cone shaped base. This pressed foot emulates the ribbing imparted by hand dipping hot glass into a ribbed optic mold on then popular Italian glass.

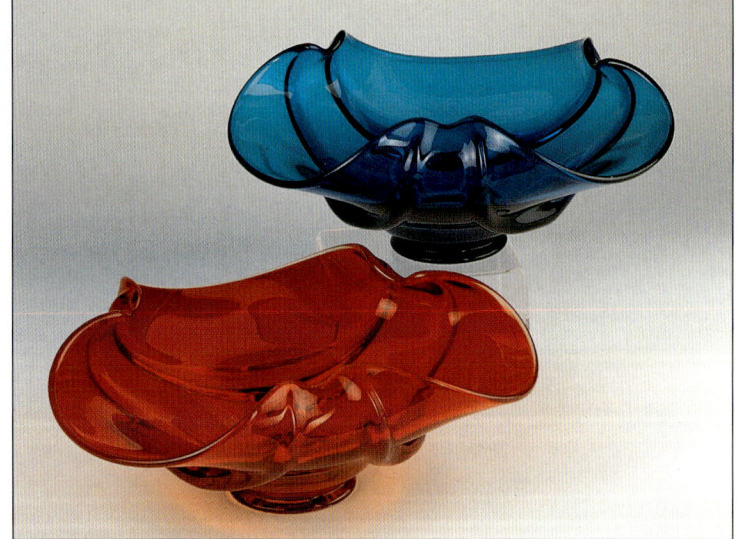

Epic bowl #6818, 12" three folded sides, persimmon, $28-38; bluenique, $24-32.

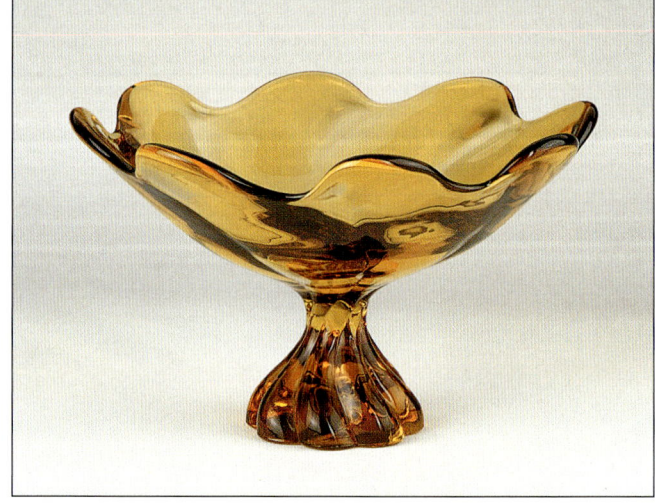

Epic "twist" #1500 line compote, #1522 amber, 9", $12-18. Other examples of Epic twist are found in the bowl chapter.

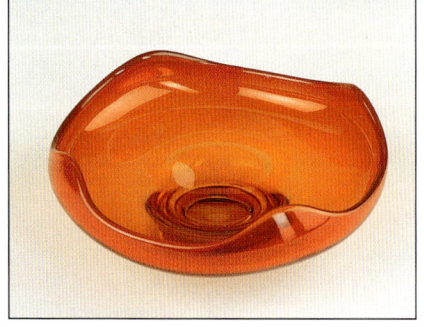

Epic bonbon #6602, 7" persimmon, $14-20.

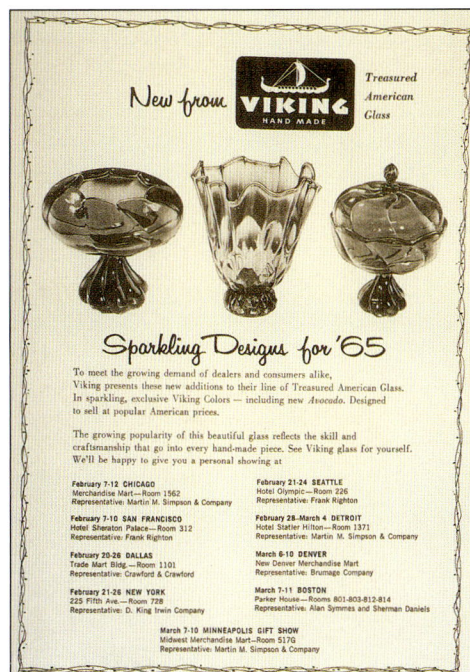

Viking advertisement for "Sparkling Designs for
'65" includes two pieces in the #1500 line "twist."
China, Glass & Tableware, February 1965.

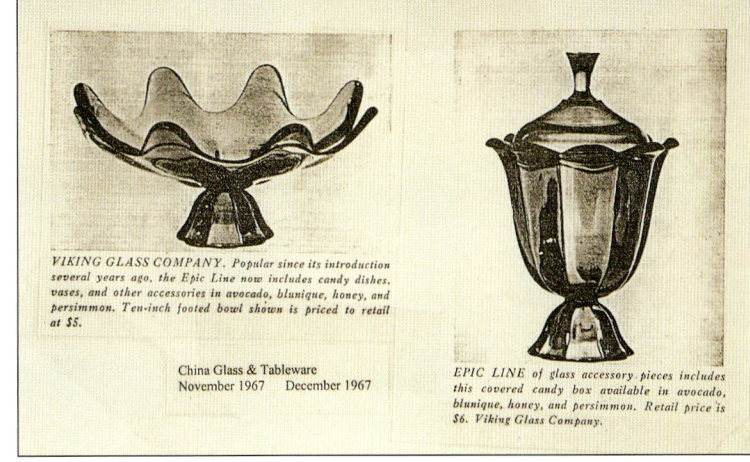

Viking advertisements for the Epic line with "petal foot" introduced in 1967. Left:
open compote shown in *China Glass & Tableware,* November 1967; right: covered
candy featured in December 1967.

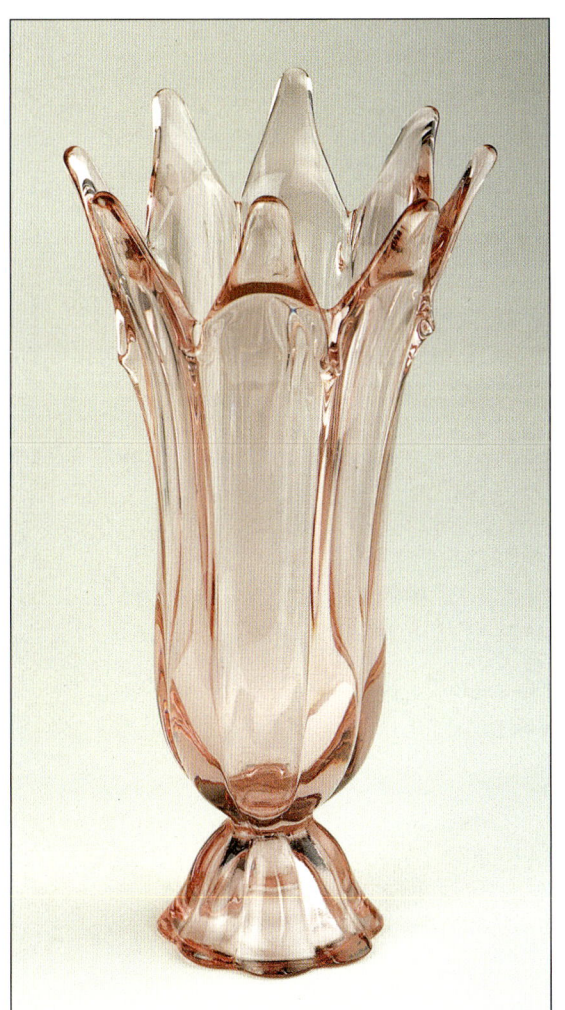

Epic #6707 footed vase, 12", thistle, $38-48.

Viking Glass catalog page for "Epic," 1960. See candle chapter for more on many of
these objects. The punch bowl is uncommon.

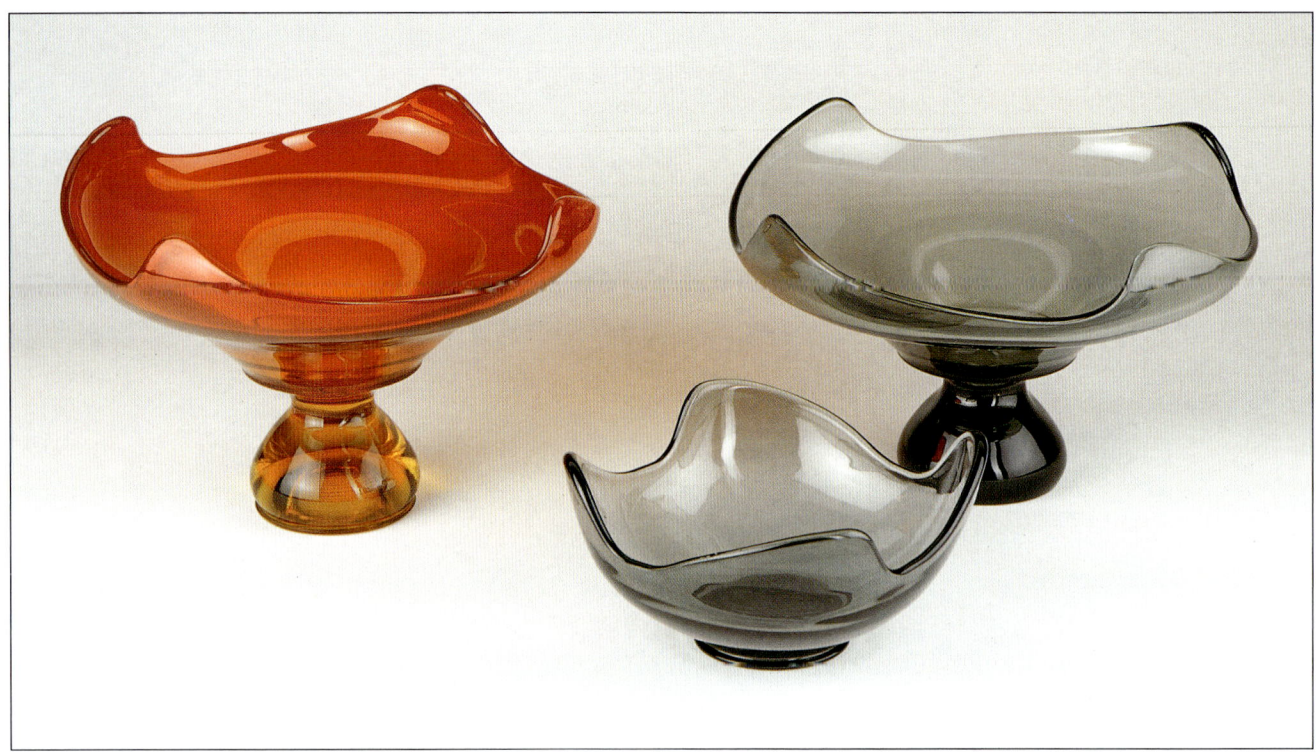

Epic "waves" #1100 line, footed bowl #1190, 9" persimmon, $26-38; low charcoal 7-3/4" bowl, $16-22; footed bowl #1190 charcoal, $24-36. #1190 shown in 1960 catalog page nearby.

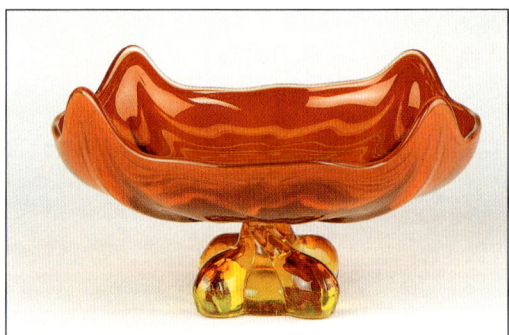

Epic "four square" #1475 footed bowl, persimmon, $22-38.

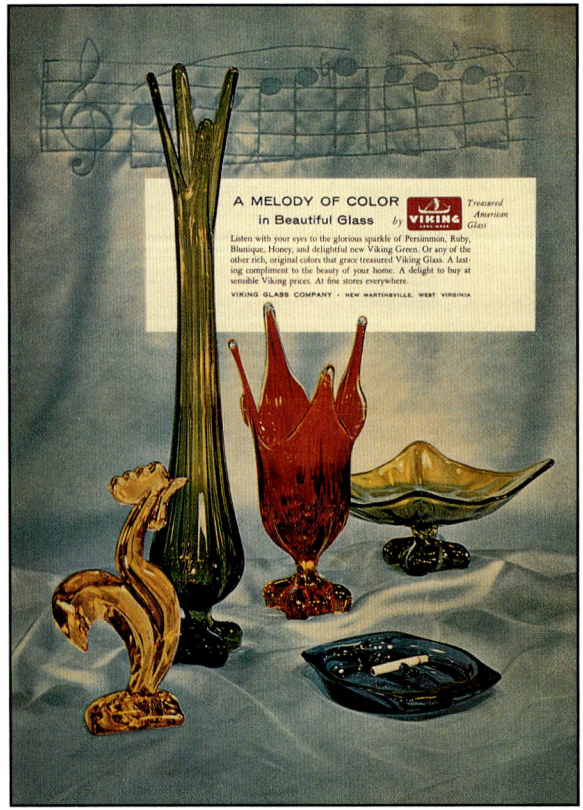

Viking full page, full color advertisement appearing in *House Beautiful*, April 1964, Epic "four square" vases and bowl as well as ashtray and Epic Rooster. See animal chapter for more on Epic animals.

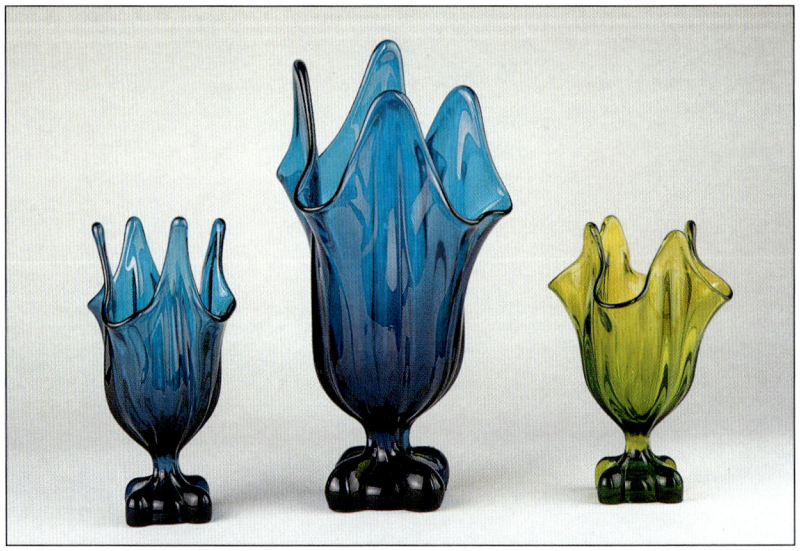

Epic "four square" #1400 line footed vase, 7-1/2", bluenique, $14-20; tall footed vase, 12", bluenique, $20-28; footed vase, 7-1/2", avocado, $10-16.

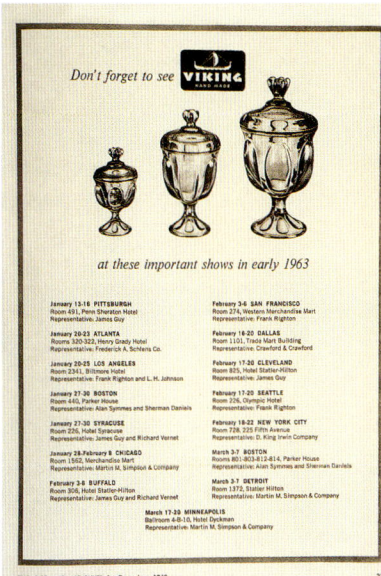

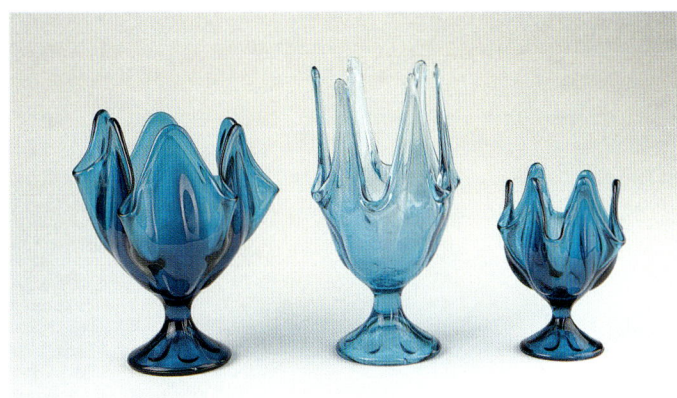

Viking advertisement for 1963 trade show is illustrated by Epic "six petal" covered candy in the three sizes produced. *The Gift & Art Buyer*, December 1962.

Epic "six petal" #1436 vase 8" bluenique, $14-18; center vase is NOT Viking, form in imitation of Viking includes crude six petal motif on base, etc. Noted are seedy glass, sharp tool marks appear where points were pulled to form petals, value, $1. Epic six petal #1466 vase 5" bluenique, $22-28. Note that it is from same mold as the small Epic six petal mint jar #1492.

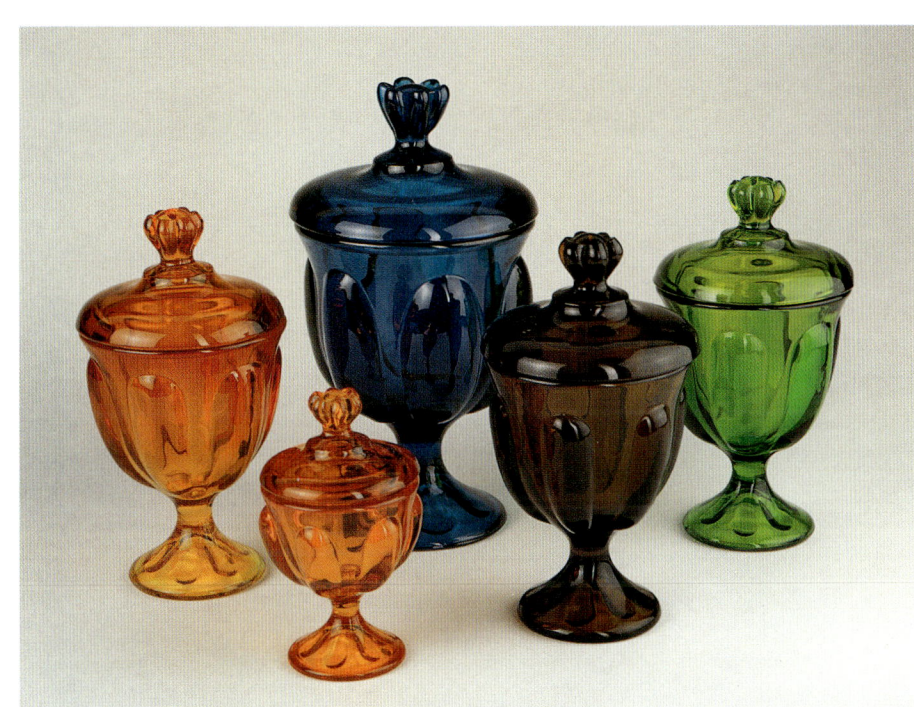

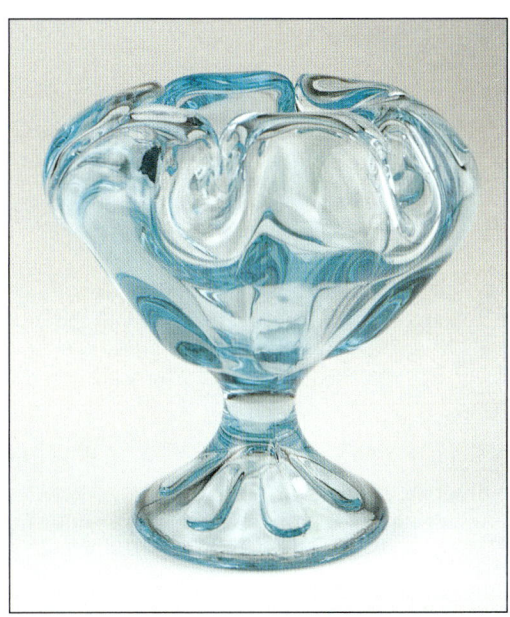

Epic "six petal" elaborately crimped colonial blue vase. Factory whimsy? Factory gift shop special? Unconfirmed details, $35-48.

Epic "six petal" covered candy with lid, medium #6812, 8" jar and lid persimmon, $20-32; mint jar #1492 with lid 5" persimmon, $30-38; large jar and lid bluenique, $20-32; medium jar #6812 with lid 8" brown, $20-28 and green, $16-24.

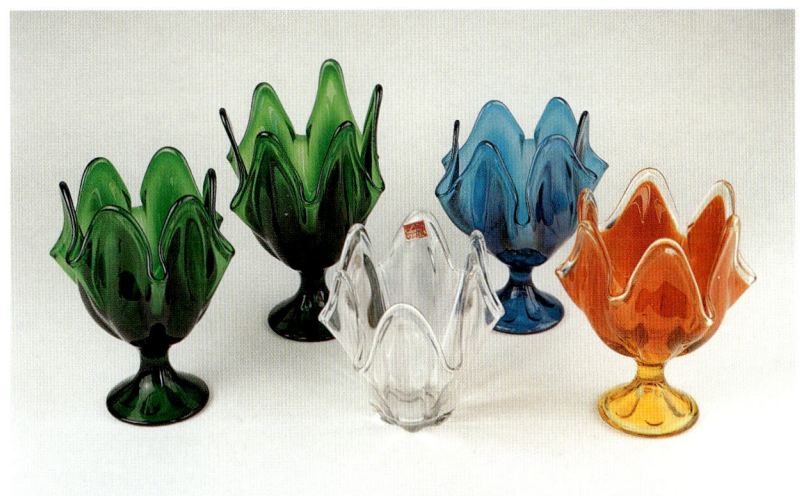

Epic "six petal" footed vase #1436 evergreen (two shown to illustrate variances in hand finishing of tops), $16-28; crystal same form but ground to remove foot, $6-12; bluenique, $14-18; and persimmon, $16-20, average height 7"-8". Note this open vase is made from the same mold as the medium sized #6812 candy jar!

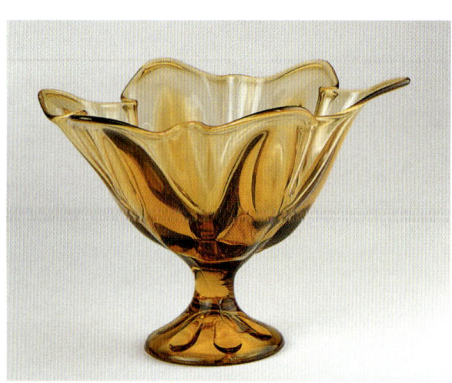

Epic "six petal" #6815 footed bowl 10" amber, $14-20. Circa 1968.

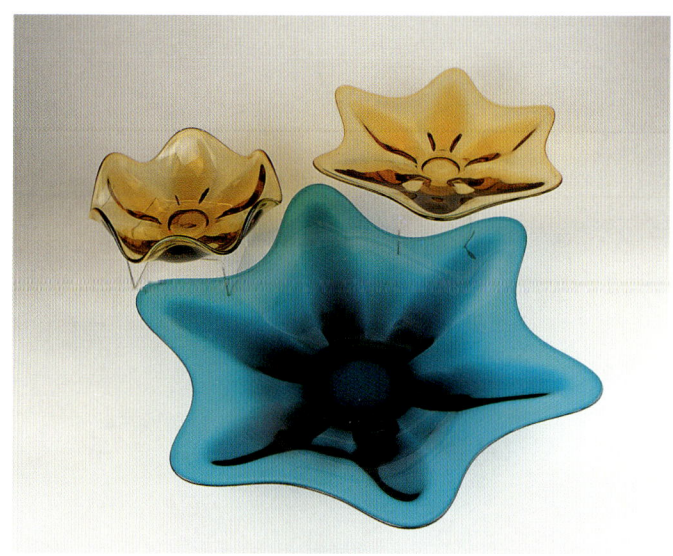

Epic "six petal" shallow bowl #1421, 14" amber, $14-22; cupped bowl amber 10", $8-14; shallow bowl #1311, 22" bluenique, $52-74. See attached 1962 catalog page.

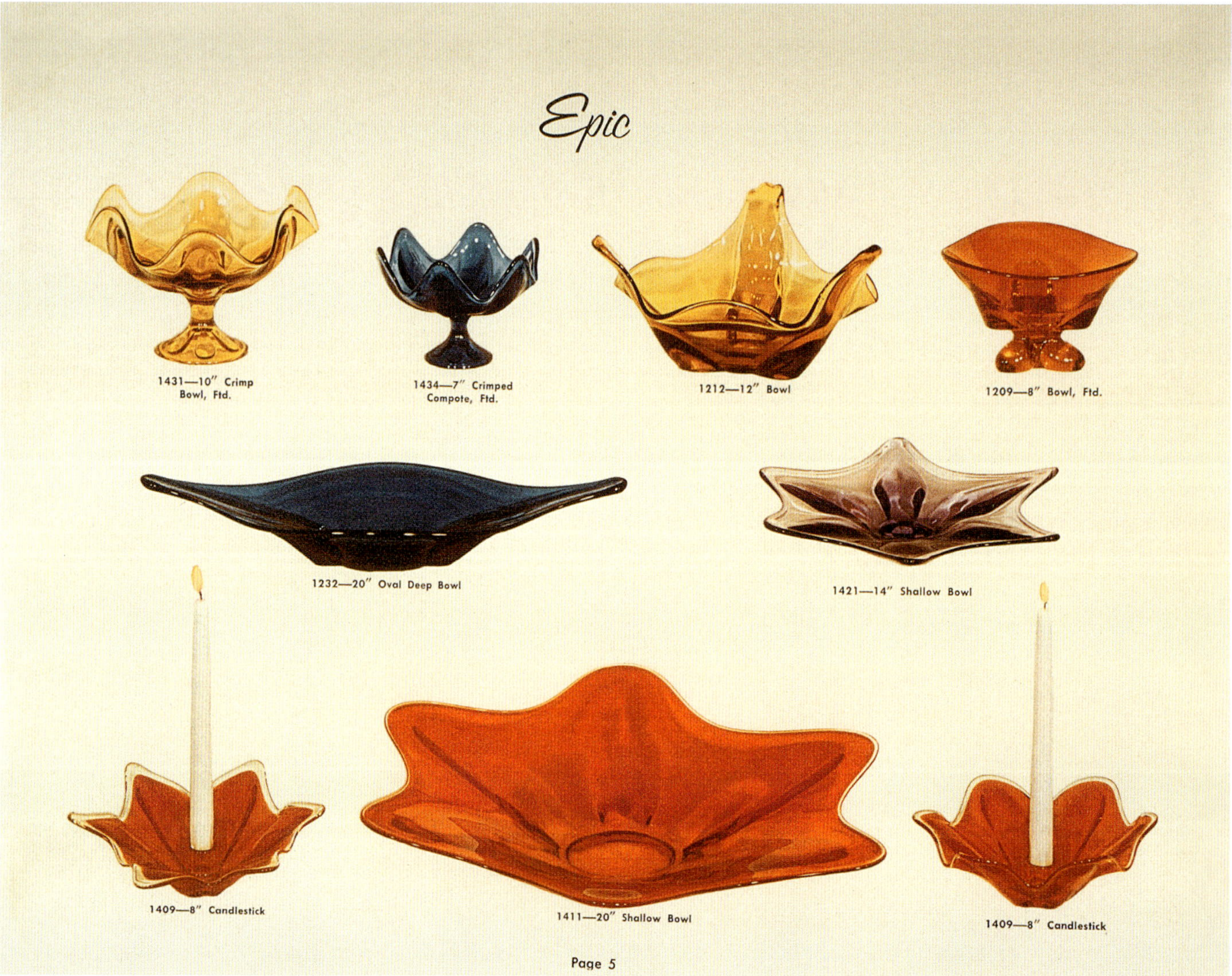

Epic

1431—10" Crimp Bowl, Ftd.

1434—7" Crimped Compote, Ftd.

1212—12" Bowl

1209—8" Bowl, Ftd.

1232—20" Oval Deep Bowl

1421—14" Shallow Bowl

1409—8" Candlestick

1411—20" Shallow Bowl

1409—8" Candlestick

Page 5

Viking Glass catalog page "Epic" 1962. Note how on some pieces the use of crystal to case the persimmon (and make the more expensive orange glass) goes further and there is a crystal edge showing. The incidental "crest" of crystal was not intentionally part of the design. This is a desirable trait in early 1960s Viking, although it at present impacts the pricing little or none.

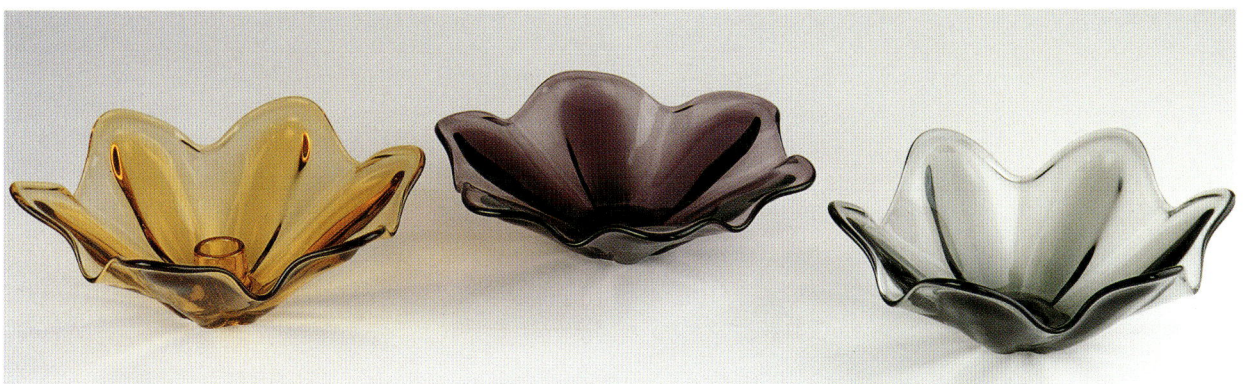

Epic "six petal" candle holder #1409, 8" amber, $12-16 each; Epic "six petal" bowl #1407, 8" amethyst, $12-20; and charcoal, $10-18. Again, note the use of the same mold with a different plunger to impart either a smooth interior or a candle cup.

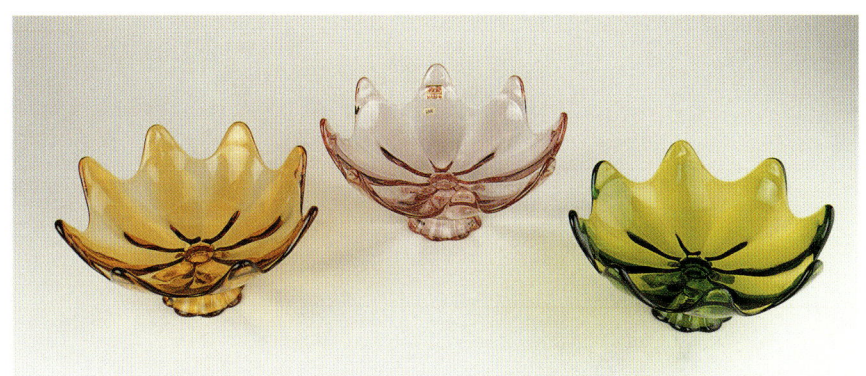

Epic footed bowl #6708, 10" thistle, $32-48; amber, $12-18; avocado, $14-20.

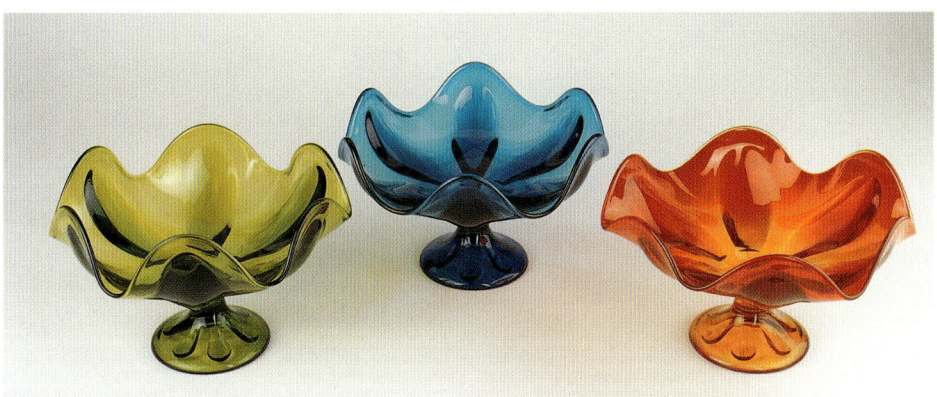

Epic "six petal" compote or "Footed fruit bowl" in Viking literature. #1431, 10" avocado, $12-18; bluenique, $16-22; persimmon, $18-26.

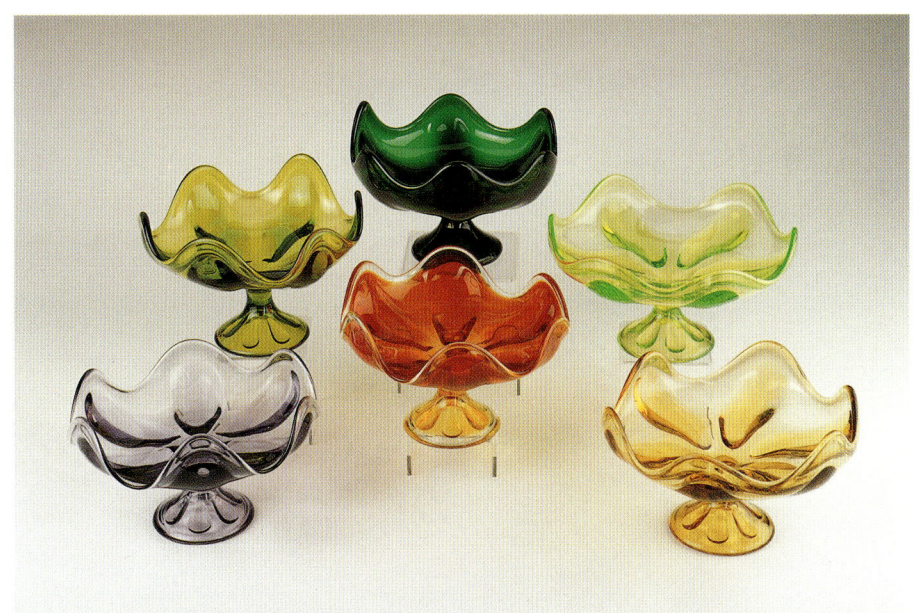

Epic "six petal" crimped compote #1434, 7", one of the most popular and widely sold Epic forms and sizes. Teaberry, $30-42; avocado, $12-18; persimmon, $18-28; evergreen, $20-32; lime, $28-38; amber, $10-16. Shown in the 1962 catalog.

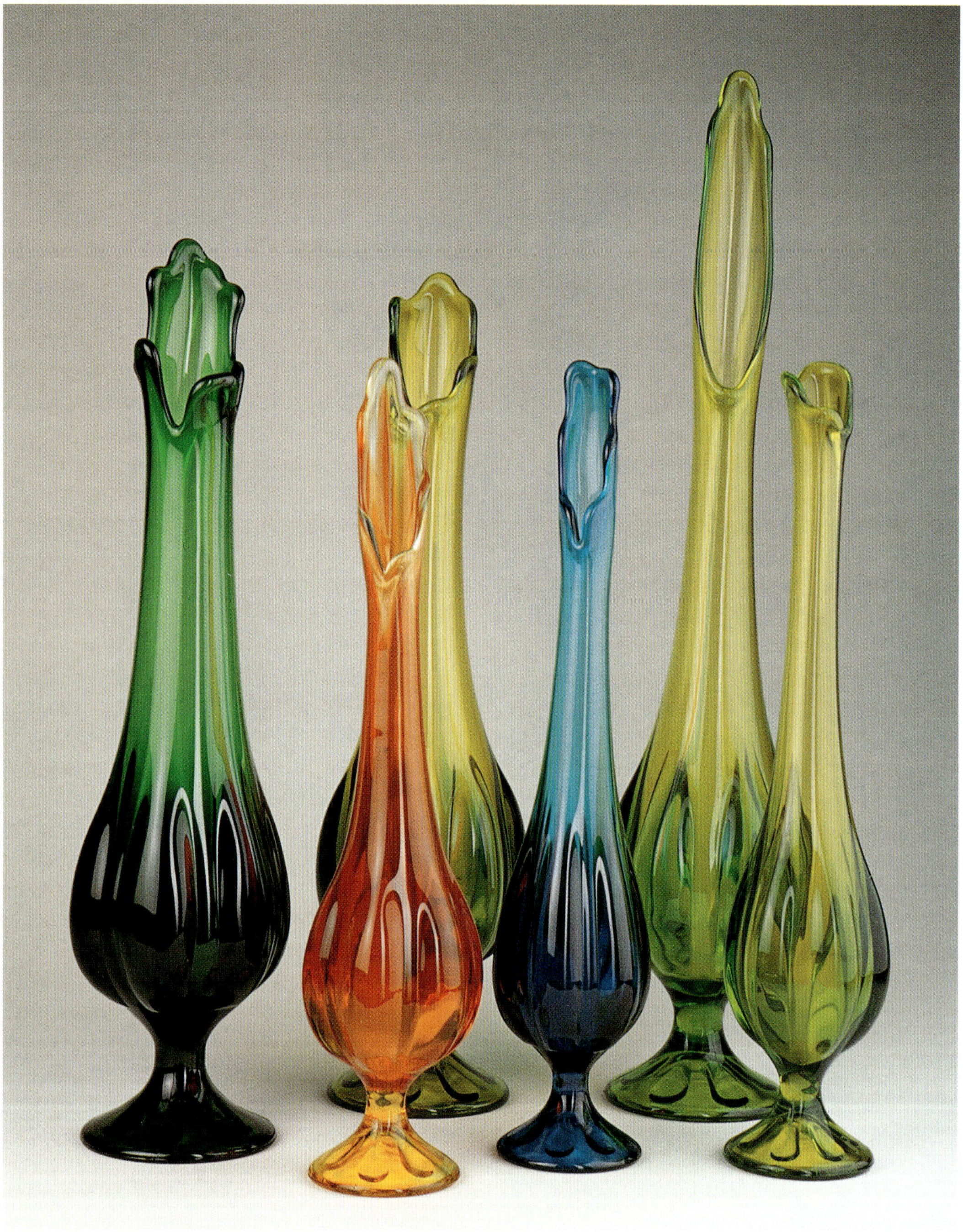

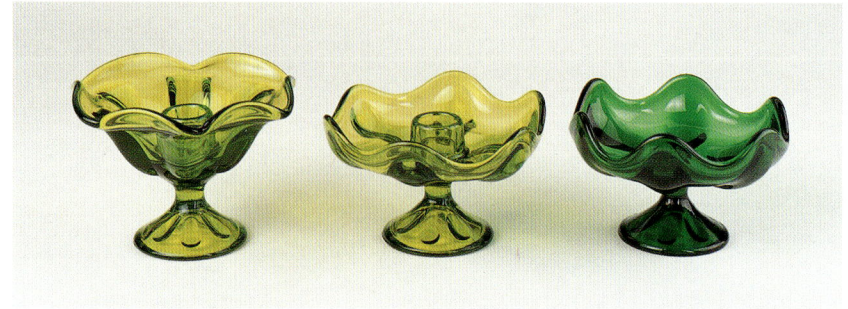

Epic "six petal" swung vases. #1432 "tall" 22" show in avocado (second from right and in back—note variances in actual height and top finishing), $16-24; and #1432 evergreen, $22-38; all others #1435, 15"-18" persimmon, $18-28; bluenique, $16-26; and avocado, $12-18.

Epic "six petal" #1422 candlestick crimped avocado, $10-16 each; flared avocado, $10-16 each; and evergreen from the same mold, as small compote with no candle cup, $14-22. Variations on a theme again.

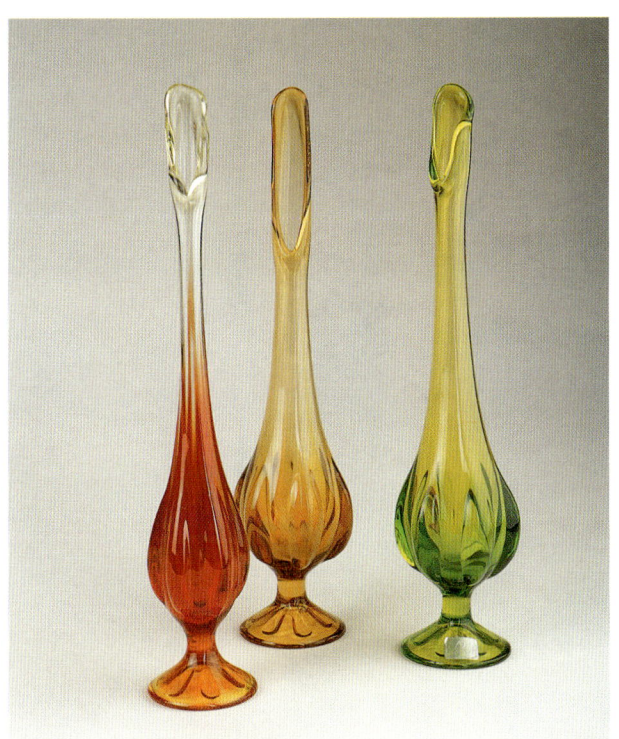

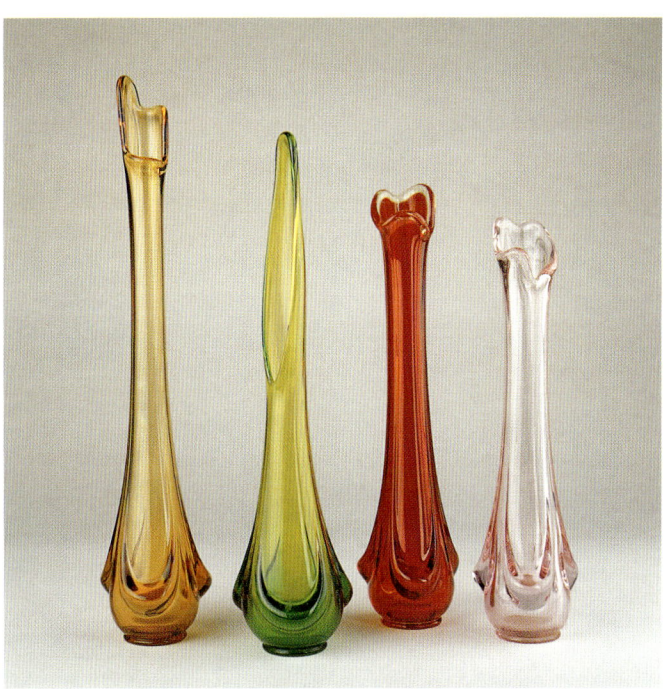

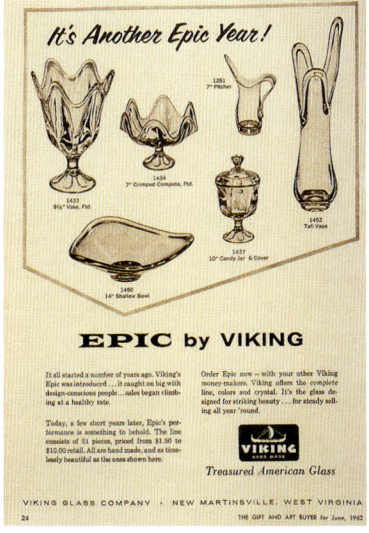

Epic "six petal" bud vase #1465, 12-1/2" persimmon, $12-20; amber, $6-12; avocado, $8-15.

Epic Drape swung bud vase, "tall" #6713 avocado, $12-16; amber, $10-14; #6704, 12-1/2" ruby, $26-36; thistle, $30-40.

Left:
Viking advertisement for "Another Epic Year" includes a number of the challenging to find rolled edge pieces (#1452 vase and #1450 bowl).
The text says there are now fifty-one pieces in the Epic line. *The Gift and Art Buyer,* June 1962.

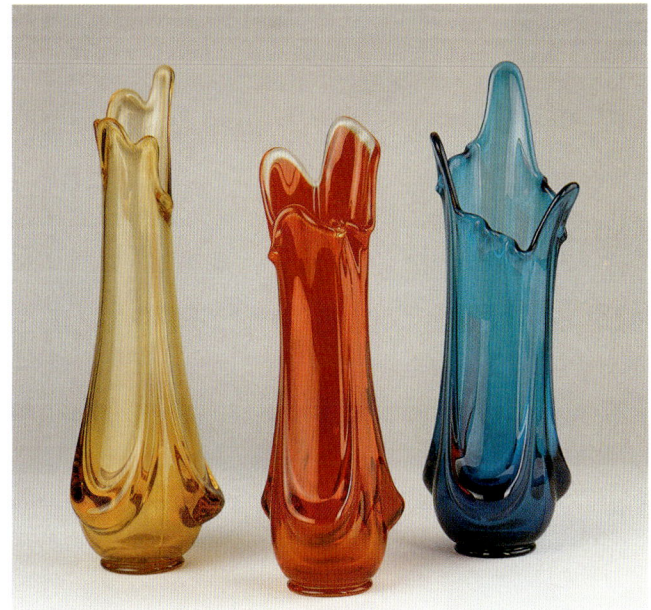

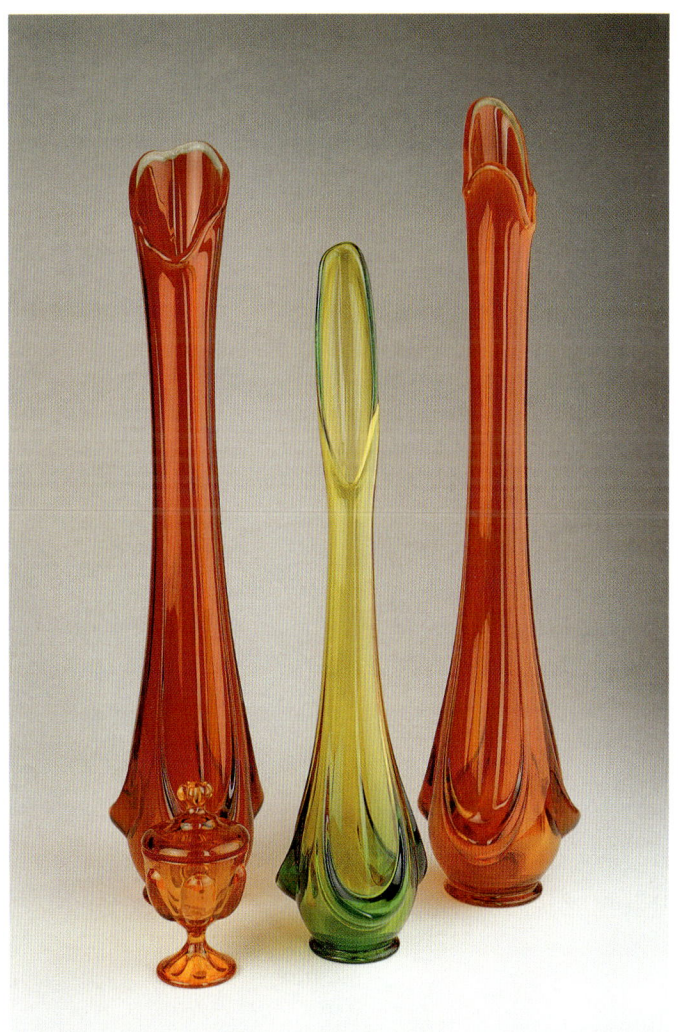

Epic Drape vase #6805, 8-1/2" amber, $8-14; ruby persimmon, $14-20; bluenique, $12-18.

Epic Drape "tall" swung vases, 23"-25", #6817. Persimmon (two shown), $28-42; avocado, $24-36. Covered Epic six petal candy shown in front for scale.

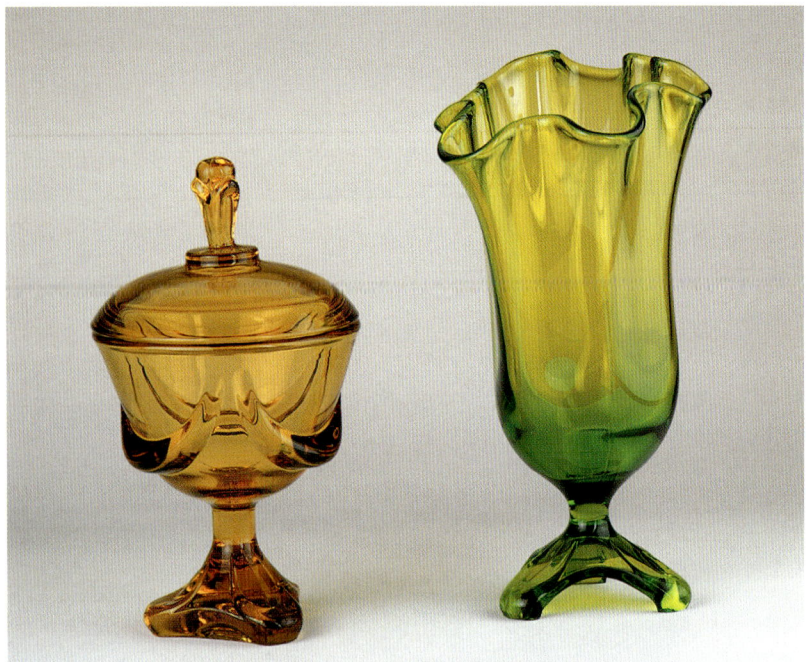

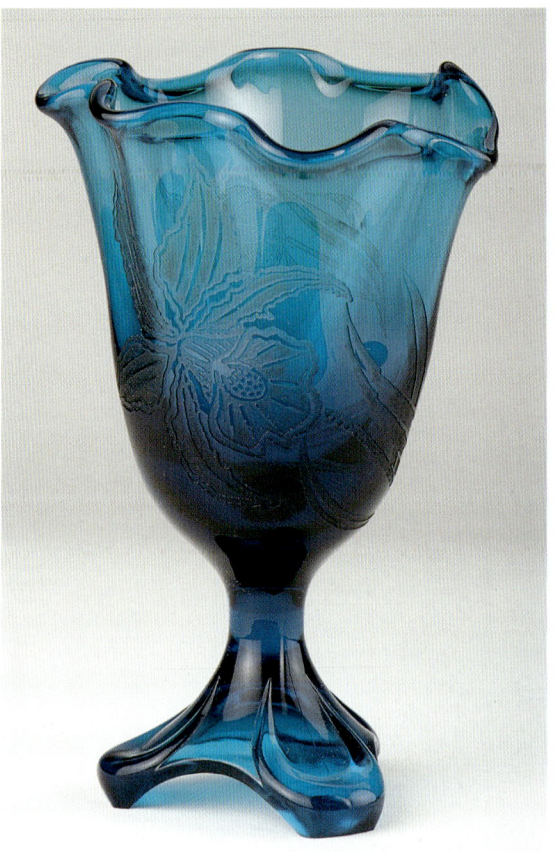

Epic Drape candy with lid amber, $12-20; #7010 crimped vase avocado, $12-18. Note how the foot on the amber candy has been made flat and solid across the bottom and the vases remains gracefully raised on the three-toes. The amber dish is after 1970 when the foot was redesigned. Note that Epic flat-based pieces as shown are post 1970.

Epic Drape "Headache" vase. Bluenique vase with plate etched Paden City Orchid on the side. This complex object combines a depression era plate etching from one company (Paden City Glass) on a 1960s era form and color from a distinctly different company (Viking), proving the traveling nature of glasshouse machinery and assets and the ever-exploratory nature of product development. A wonderfully neat object that represents a historian's or author's worst possible discovery, and a possible headache to explain, $60-85.

Epic Drape bowl, #7019, 9" flared avocado, $12-22; candlestick #7003, 4-1/2", $10-18 each. Both of the bowl and candlesticks forms are found with smooth sides and draped foot and later with the drape added to the body as well as the foot.

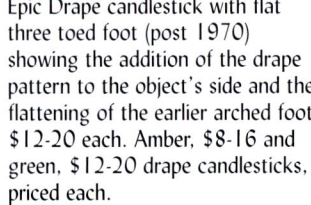

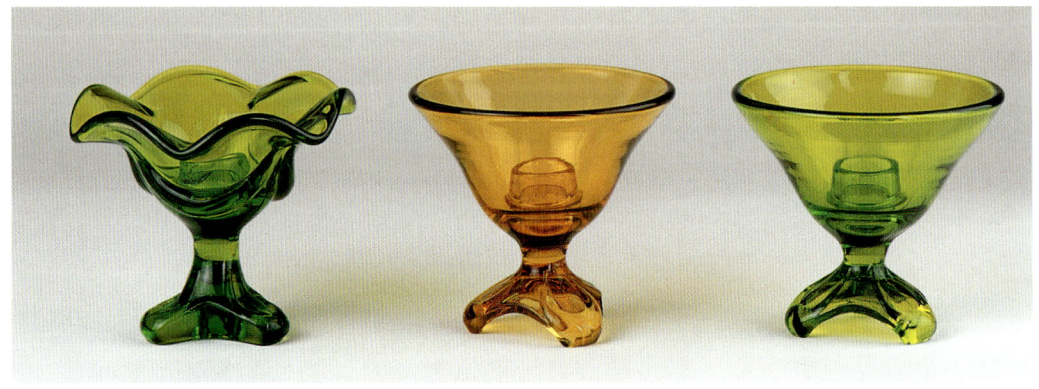

Epic Drape candlestick with flat three toed foot (post 1970) showing the addition of the drape pattern to the object's side and the flattening of the earlier arched foot, $12-20 each. Amber, $8-16 and green, $12-20 drape candlesticks, priced each.

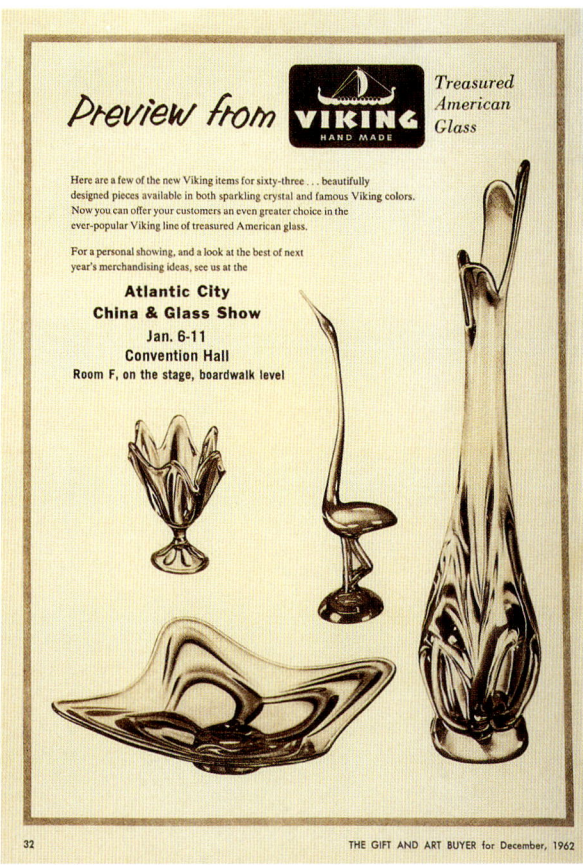

Left:
Viking advertisement showing a flat bowl and swung vase in the shortly produced Epic Loop. *The Art & Gift Buyer,* December 1962. Also shown are an Epic "six petal" vase and the egret.

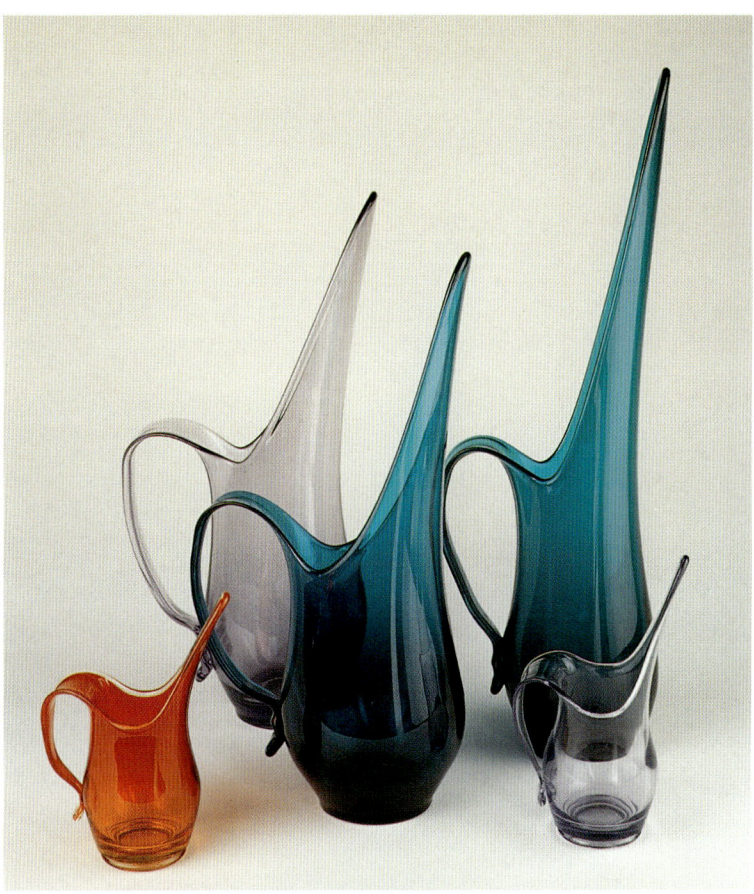

Epic swung pitcher. Left: small #1251 persimmon, $18-28; right: teaberry, $28-38; large pitchers, teaberry, $45-58; bluenique, $30-40. This form was once the only piece of Viking shown at the Corning Museum of Glass and one of the few pieces of American twentieth century factory glass. The large form was an award winning and highly acclaimed design in the 1950s.

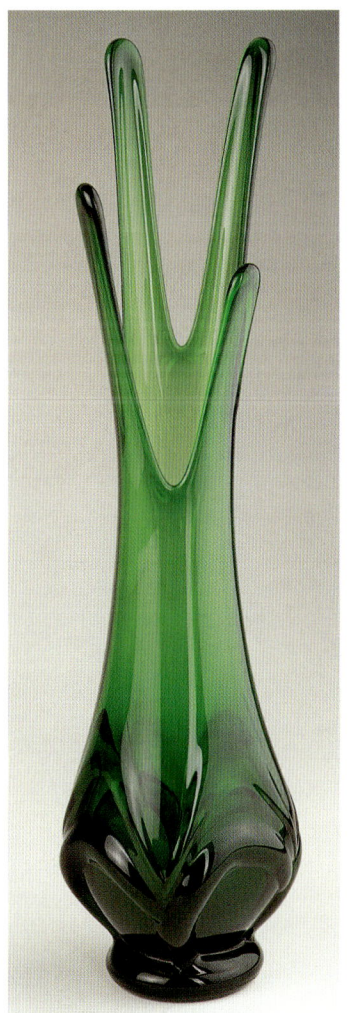

Epic Loop swung vase #1472 evergreen 17-1/2", $35-48. Shown on the cover to the 1963 Viking catalog, Loop is a difficult line to find.

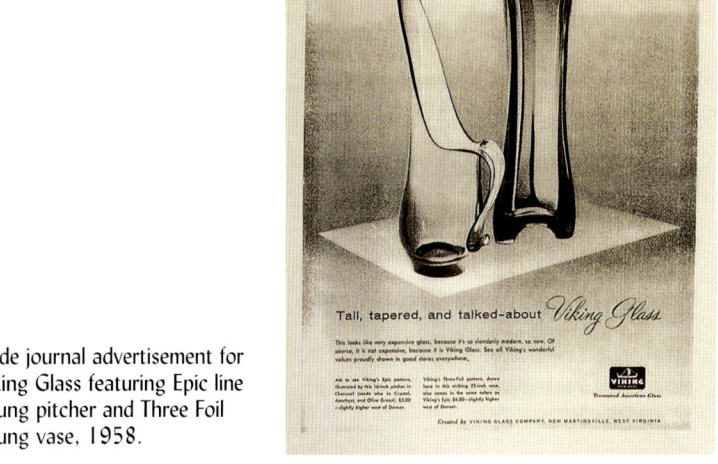

Trade journal advertisement for Viking Glass featuring Epic line swung pitcher and Three Foil swung vase, 1958.

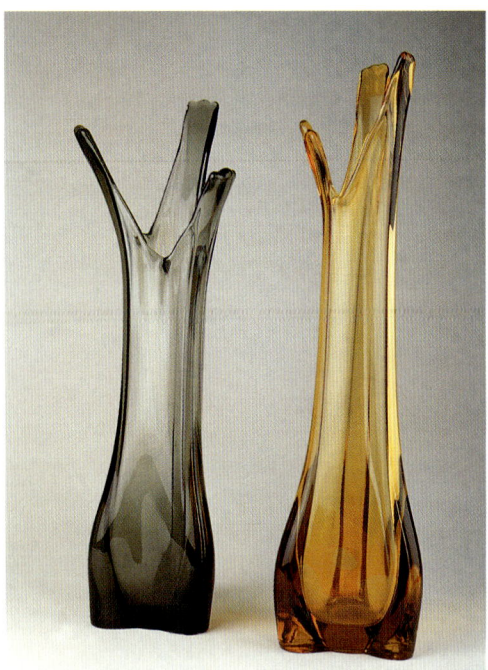

Epic Three Foil swung vase #1215, 20"-22". Note the charcoal uses the earlier "splayed out" finishing form, $28-28 and the amber uses the later more vertical finishing, $18-26.

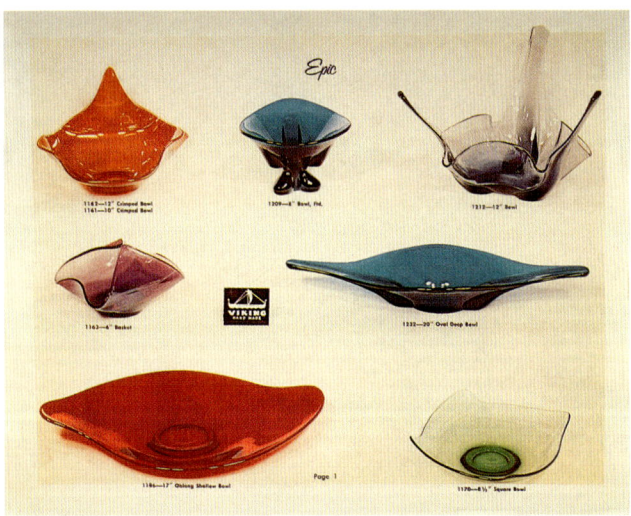

Viking Glass catalog page "Epic," 1960. Note that each object on this page is shown elsewhere in this book as photographed from actual objects. The colors of the catalog page and the actual objects illustrated and priced vary.

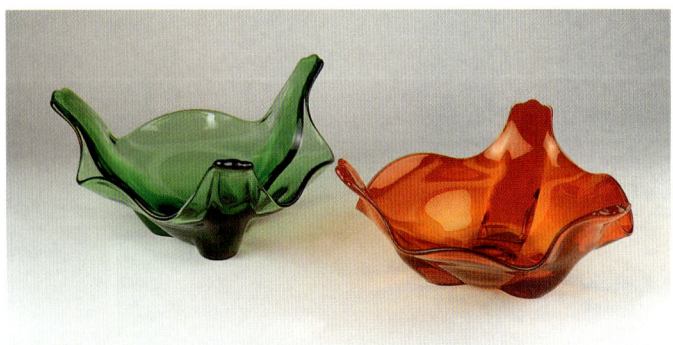

Epic Three Foil #1212 bowl, 12", persimmon, $28-42; green, $24-36. Shown in the 1960 catalog.

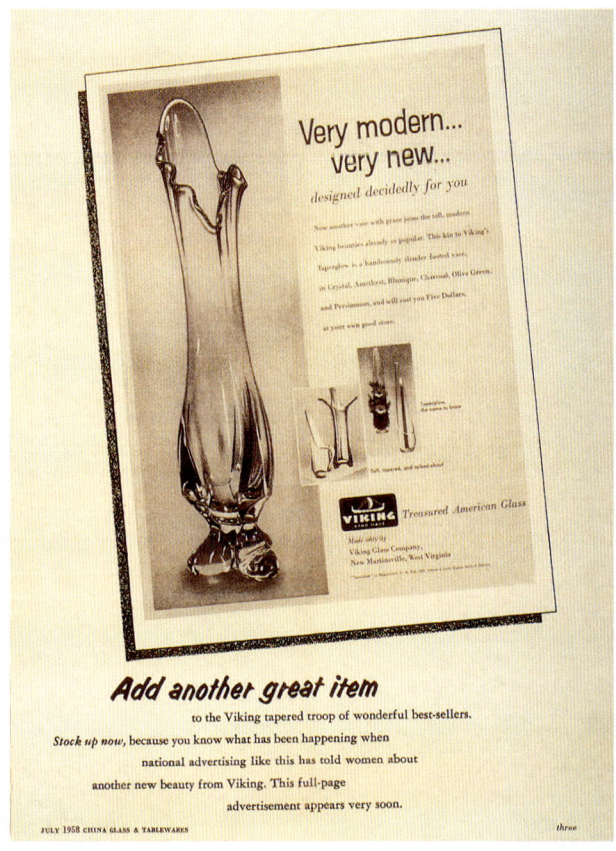

"Very Modern...Very new..." reads the copy in the Viking Glass advertisement for Epic "three toe." The pitch of this trade journal ad is that full pages showing various Viking designs would shortly run in national magazines. *China, Glass & Tablewares,* July 1958.

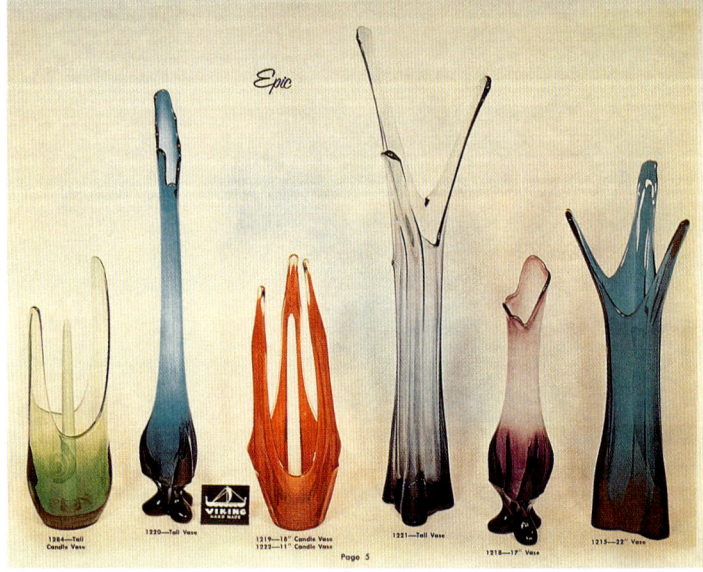

Viking Glass catalog page "Epic," 1960. Note the three toed vases and the "splayed out" treatment of the top of the swung vases. This was not the finishing treatment used only a few years later on the same forms.

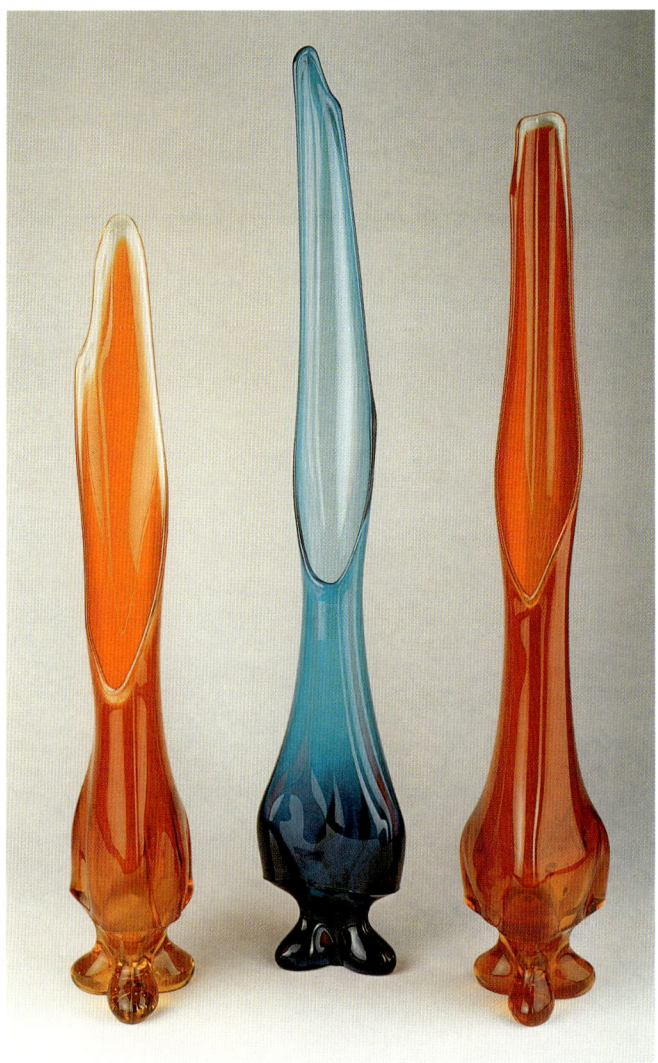

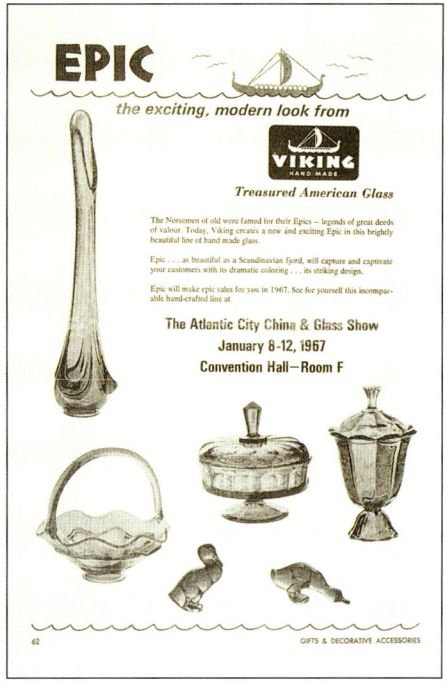

"Epic, the exciting, modern look from Viking" proclaims this ad featuring a number of different Epic forms and lines. *Gift & Decorative Accessories*, December 1966.

Epic Three Foil swung vases #1220, 19"-22", persimmon, $24-36; bluenique, $20-32. Featured in *House Beautiful*, October 1958.

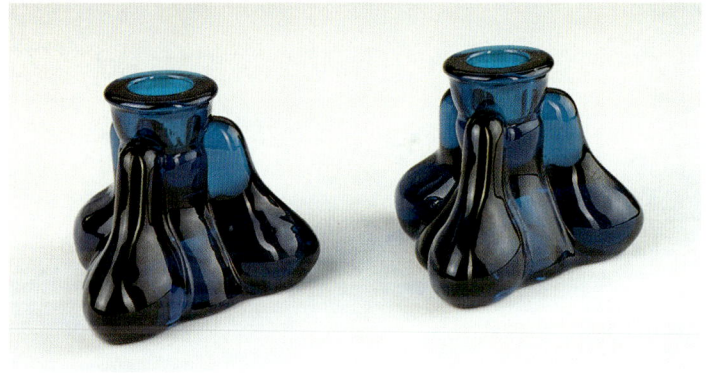

Epic Three Foil #1210 candlesticks, 3-1/2" tall, bluenique, $24-34 each. Shown in 1963 Viking Glass catalog supplement.

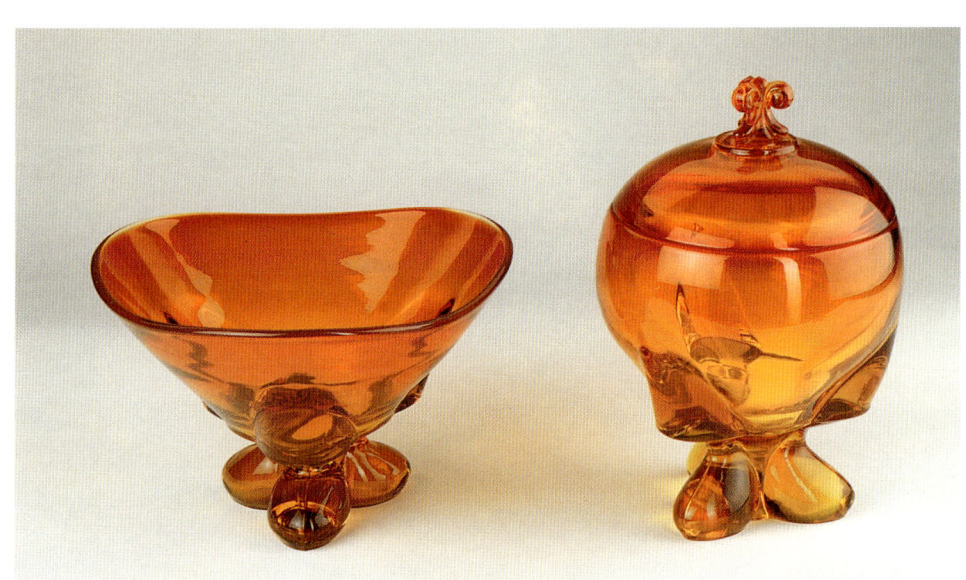

Epic Three Foil #1209 flared bowl, persimmon, $28-34; #12207 candy bowl with cover, 6", persimmon, $30-40. Note that both are created from the identical mold.

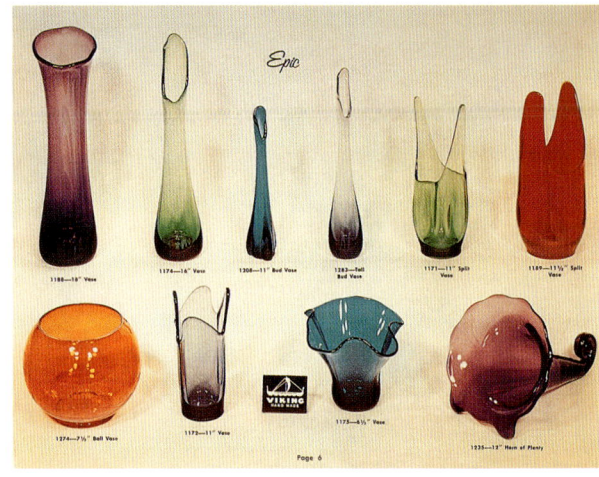

Viking Glass catalog page "Epic," 1960. Note the illusive cornucopia, the #1172 charcoal vase in the "waves" form and the "split" vases.

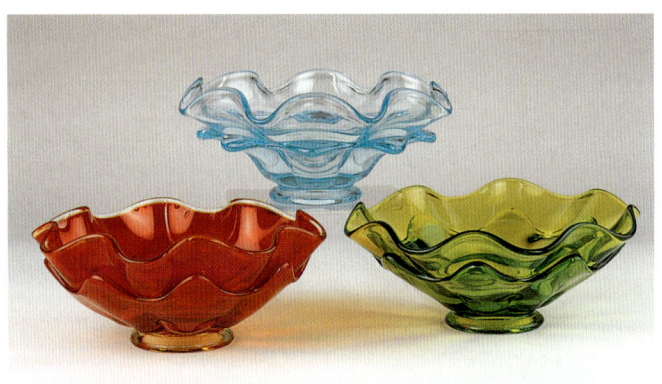

Epic crimped bowl #6604, 8", persimmon, $12-20; colonial blue, $18-24; avocado, $8-14. Shown in 1968 catalog, line number suggests 1966 introduction.

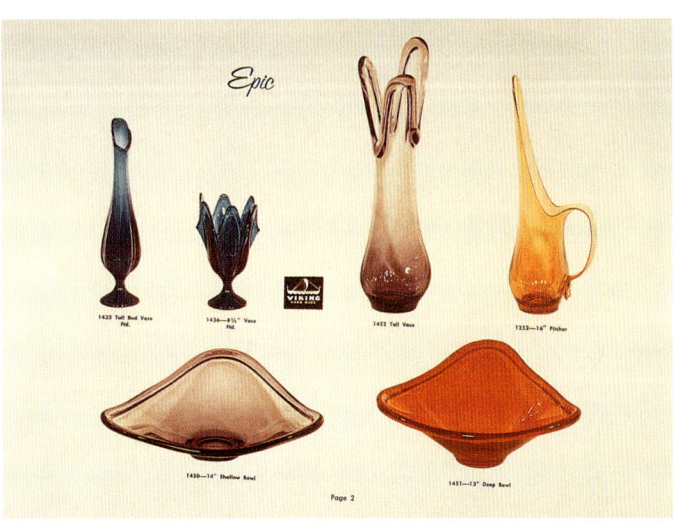

Viking Glass catalog "Epic," 1962. Note the #1252 pitcher and the three pieces with thick, rolled edges creating an extra thick lip at the rim. This was a circa 1960 practice used for a short time. It required extra time and exceptional skill, both increasing the cost at a minimal, but significant, visual difference to the finished product.

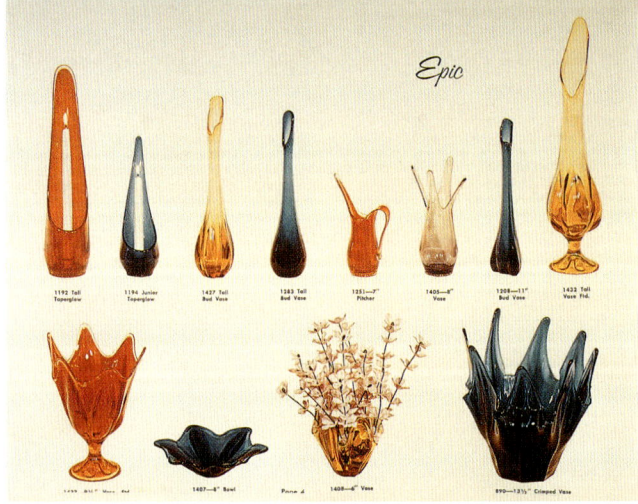

Viking Glass catalog page "Epic," 1962. Note the small swung pitcher, the use of the splayed out finish on the #1405 vase and the #890 vase. This vase form and the number are from the much earlier Christina line. The once crystal line has been made in color and, for this vase, the foot ground away to make it sit low and flat versus footed.

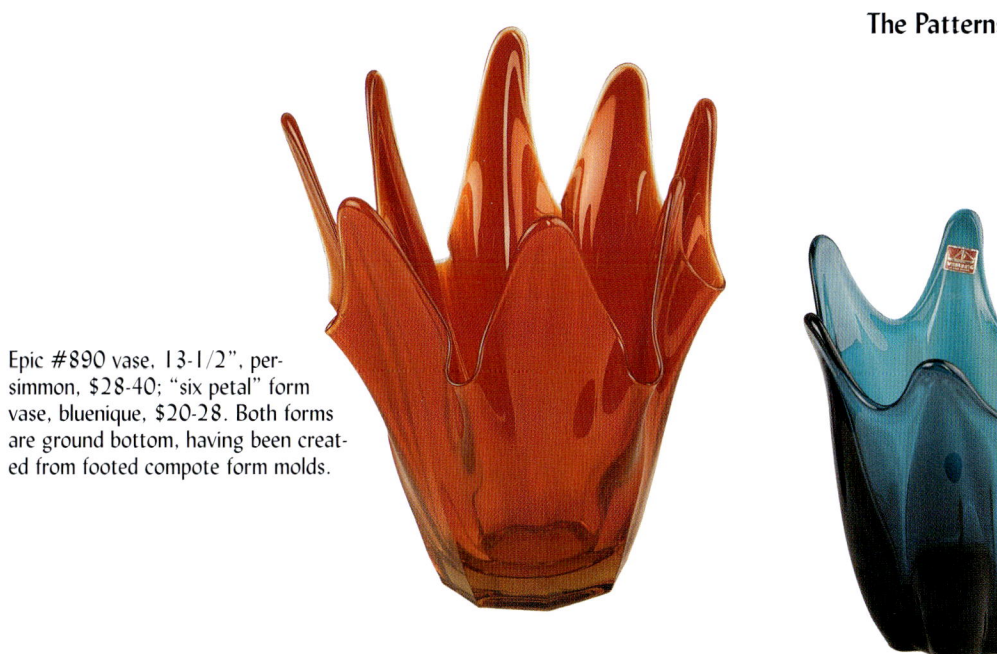

Epic #890 vase, 13-1/2", persimmon, $28-40; "six petal" form vase, bluenique, $20-28. Both forms are ground bottom, having been created from footed compote form molds.

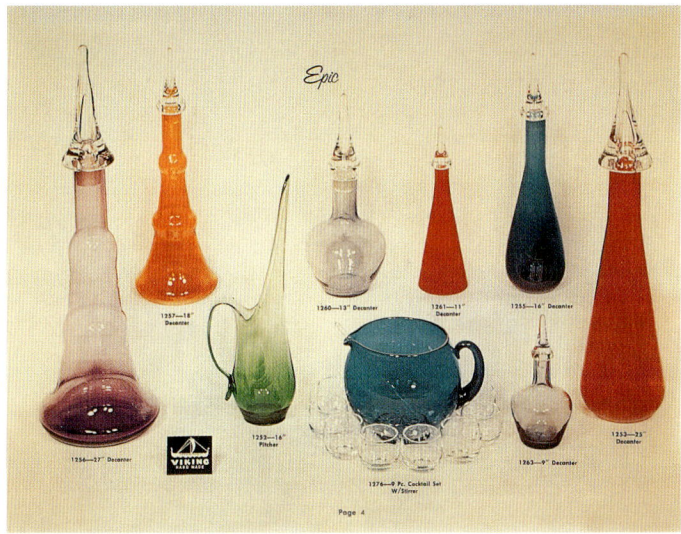

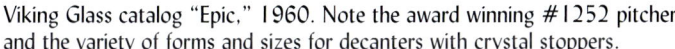

Viking Glass catalog "Epic," 1960. Note the award winning #1252 pitcher and the variety of forms and sizes for decanters with crystal stoppers.

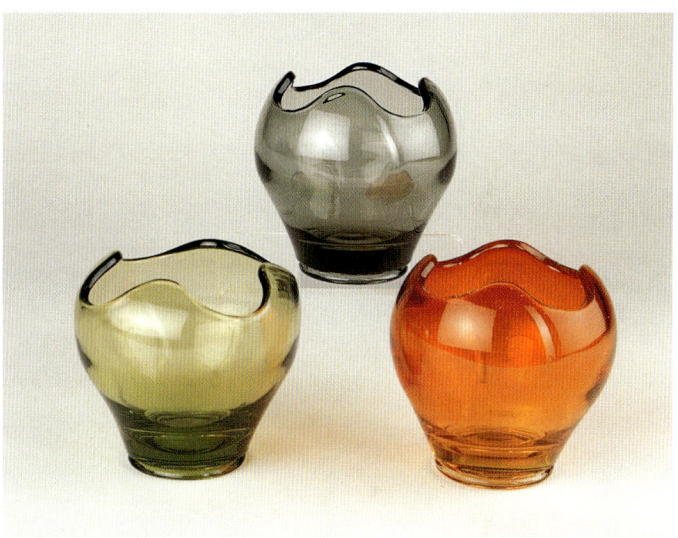

Epic rose bowl #1141, 3-1/2", avocado, $8-14; charcoal, $14-24; persimmon, $16-26, shown in 1960 catalog.

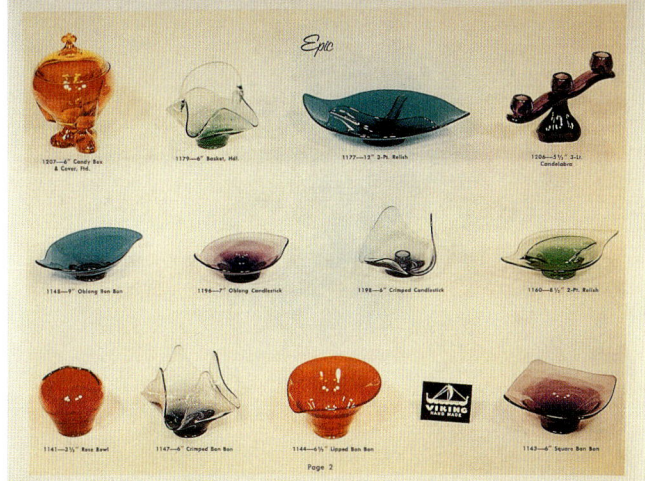

Viking Glass catalog page "Epic," 1960. Included here are a number of best selling forms that remained in the line for a long time, like the #1198 Oblong Epic bonbon. Also shown here is the illusive #1206 candelabra.

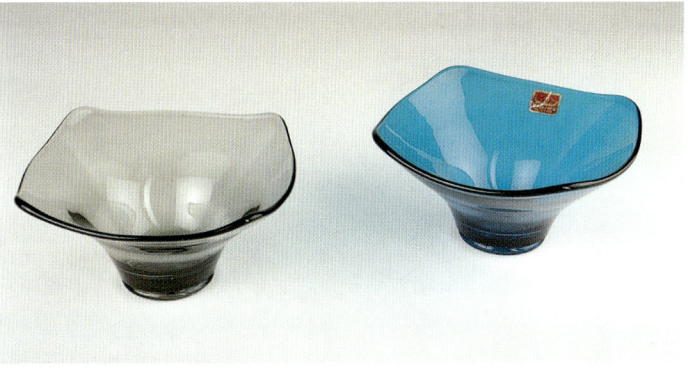

Epic square bonbon #1143 charcoal, $10-22; bluenique, $14-22, shown in 1960 catalog.

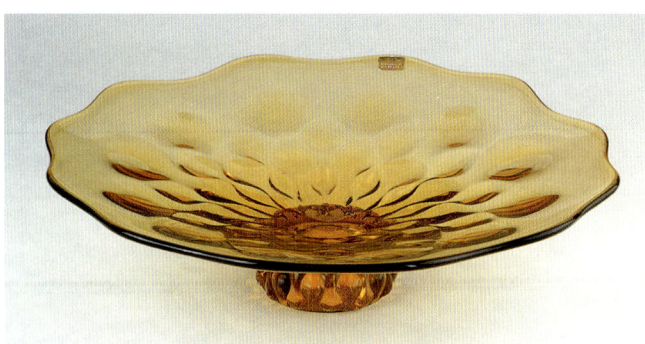

Epic "sculpted foot" low bowl, 14" diameter, 3-3/4" tall, amber, $16-22, shown in Sparkling Designs for '65 ad campaign. Other shapes with the same foot were produced.

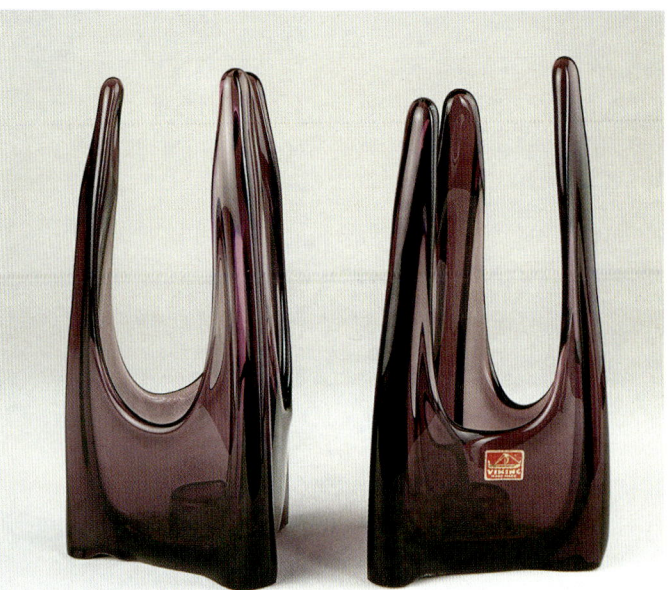

Epic "candle vase" #1222 amethyst, $22-34 each, shown in a February 1959 advertisement.

Epic bonbon 6" charcoal, $10-16; plate 11-1/2" charcoal, $10-18.

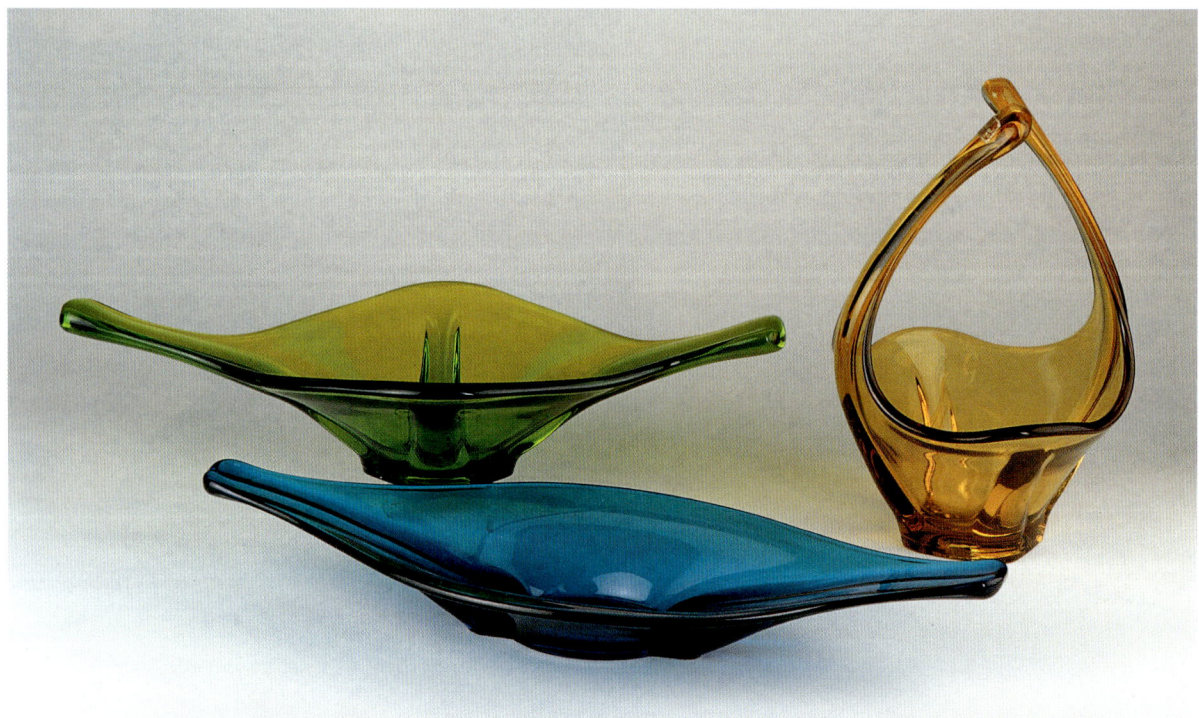

Epic bowl #6609, 18", avocado, $24-34; #1232 oval deep bowl, 20", bluenique, $28-42; amber basket from the same mold but with pulled up ends (see basket chapter for pricing). Note this and the #6718 crimped bowl shown earlier in this chapter are the only forms we believe resemble the "Italian styled" modern free-form shapes of the 1950-60s. All others found and similar are not Viking.

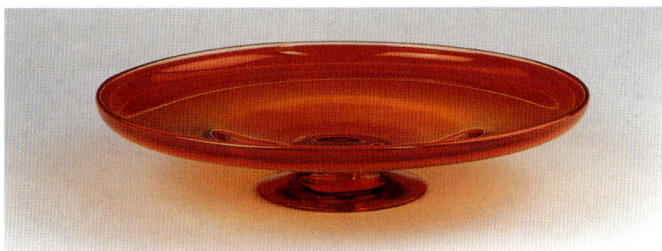

Epic cake salver or "gardenia bowl" #1442 shown in the 1962 catalog, 12" diameter, persimmon, $40-48. Part of a short-lived line of plain and simply elegant forms in the early 1960s.

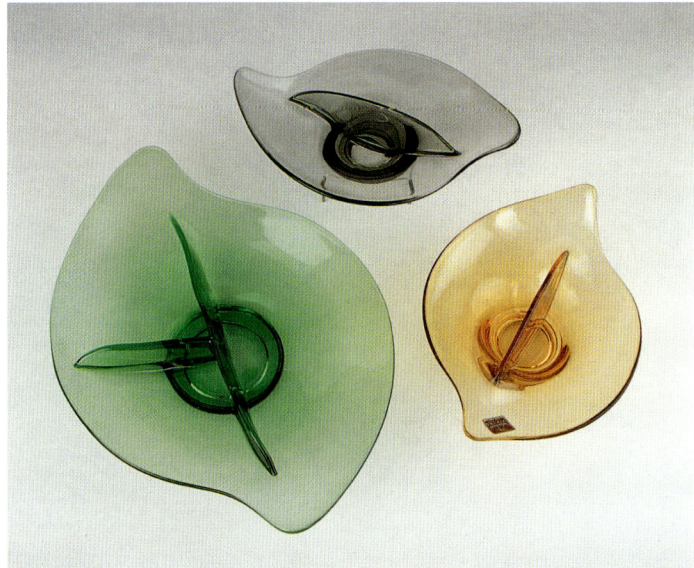

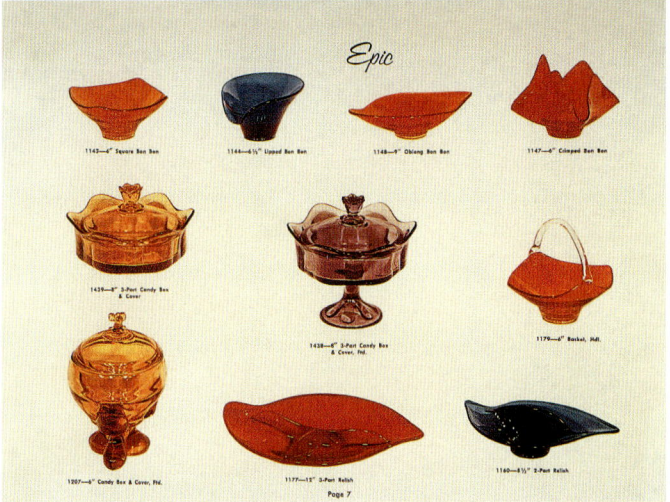

Viking Glass catalog page "Epic," 1962.

Epic Oblong three part divided relish #1177, 12", emerald green, $22-28, shown in the 1956-59 literature and 1962 catalog; two part divided relish #1160, 8-1/2", charcoal, $8-18; amber, $6-12, shown in catalogs from 1962-1968 and beyond.

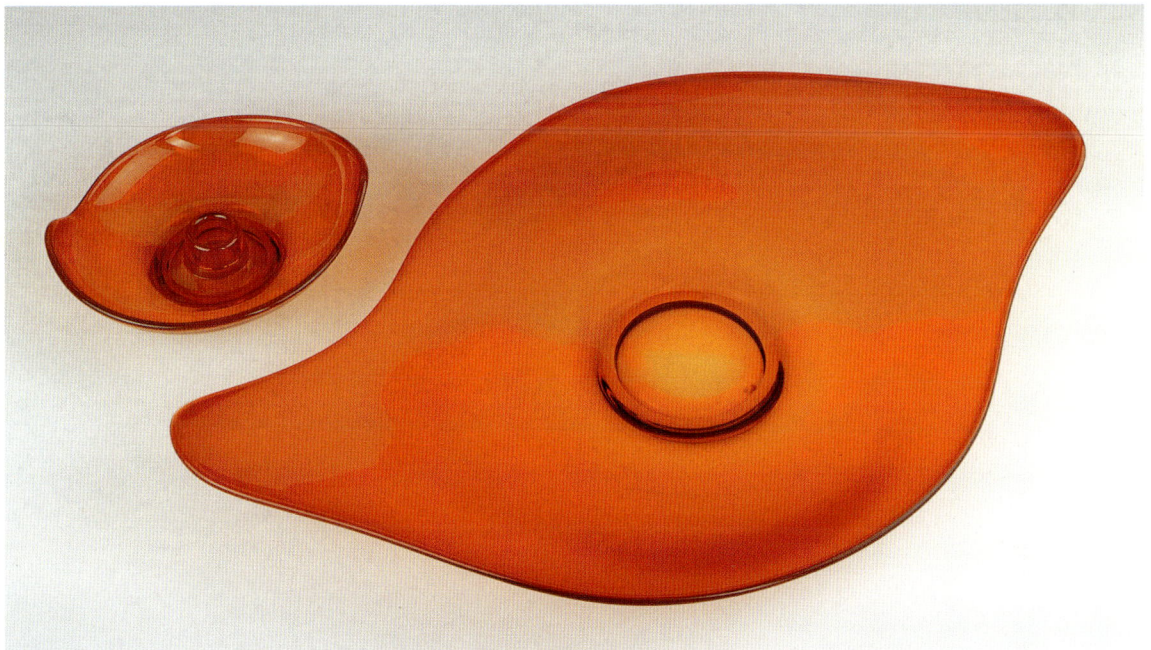

Epic Oblong shallow bowl #1186, 17", persimmon, $28-40; Oblong candle #1196, 7", persimmon, $16-22 each. These pieces were marketed together and today often appear as one bowl and two candle bowls as a "console set." The "Oblong" form sold well for Viking.

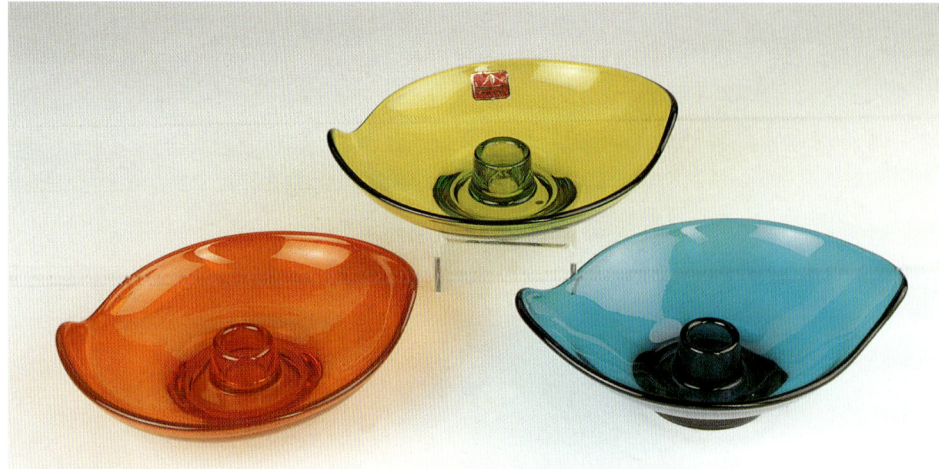

Epic Oblong candle bowl #1196, 7", persimmon, $16-22; avocado, $10-16; bluenique, $14-20 each.

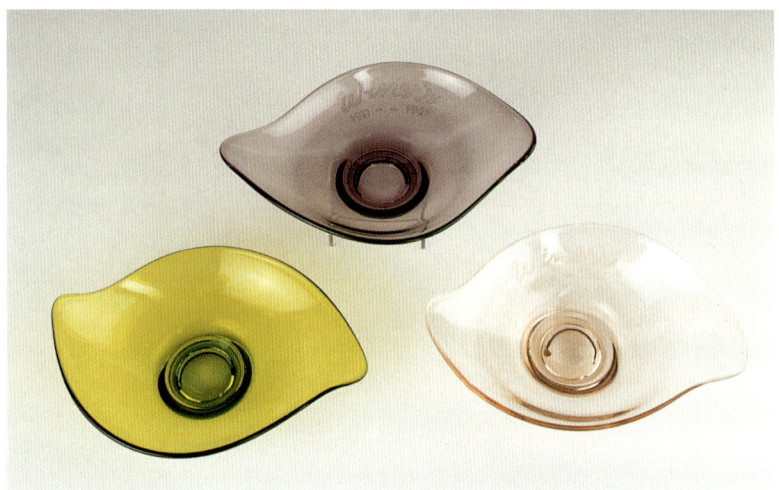

Epic oblong bonbon #1149, 9". Avocado, $8-12; amethyst, $10-18; cherry glo, $12-20. Cherry glow and amethyst shown engraved "Winer's 1911-1961," an anniversary promotion for a local New Martinsville business. Add $6 if etched as such with date.

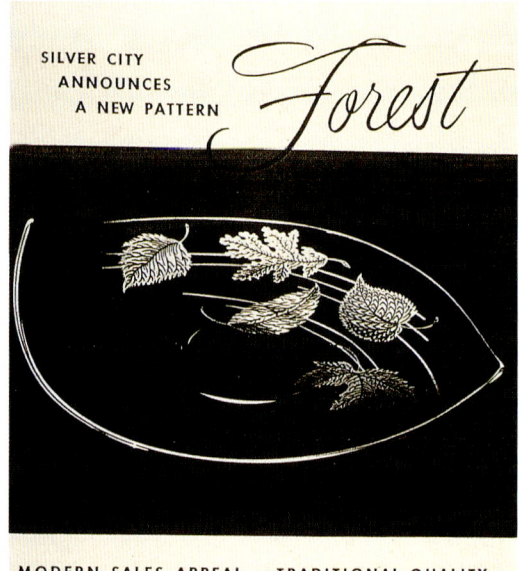

Epic oblong bowl with decoration "Forest" as a silver overlay by Silver City Glass. Viking glass decorated by another firm and then remarketed under their label.

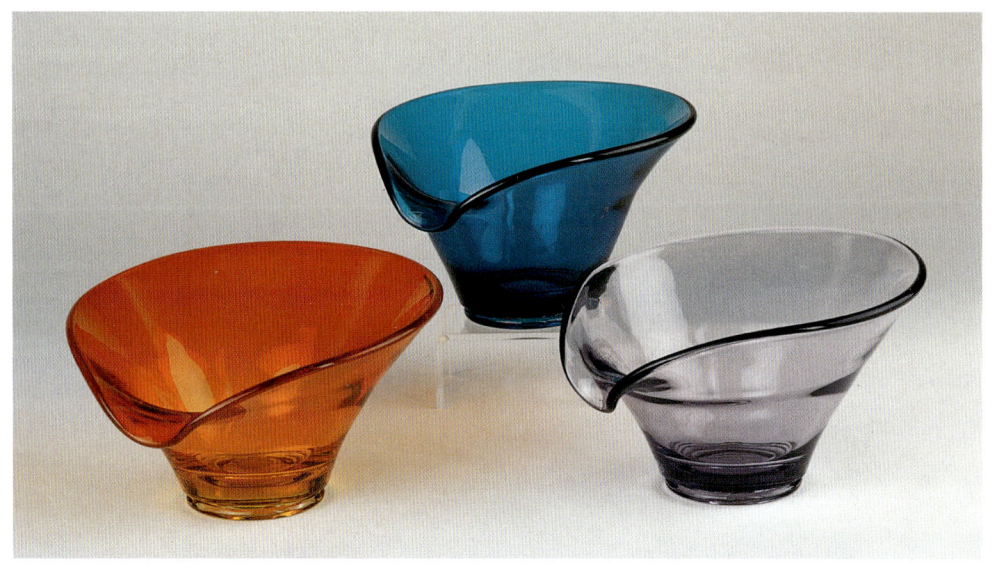

Epic lipped bonbon #1144, 6-1/2", persimmon, $14-22; bluenique, $12-18; teaberry, $20-32, form shown in the 1962 catalog.

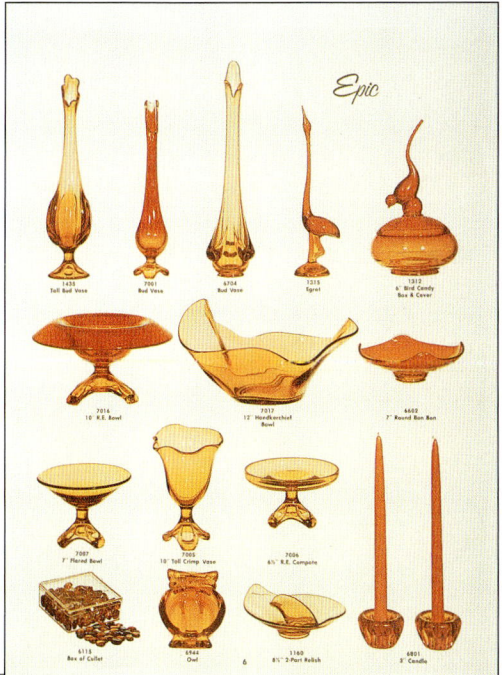

Viking Glass catalog "Epic," 1970, in amber and persimmon. Note that the loop footed pieces remain without decorative loops on their sides here and the foot is still the graceful, open underneath arching foot that touched the table at three points.

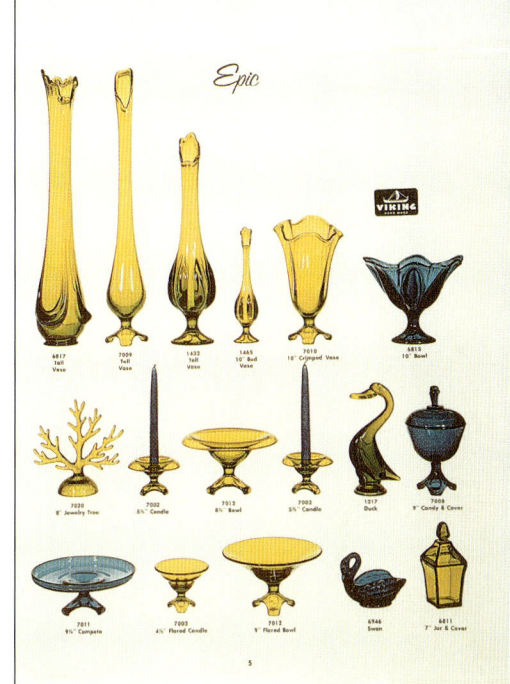

Viking Glass catalog "Epic," 1970. On this page note the difficult to find jewelry tree #7020, the swan and duck, and that the #7000 line has the arched, three point of contact foot.

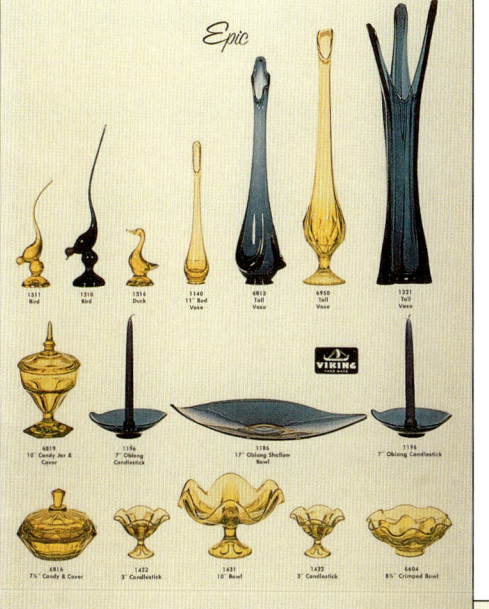

Viking Glass catalog page "Epic," 1970, in bluenique and lime. Note both #1311 and #1310 birds are offered.

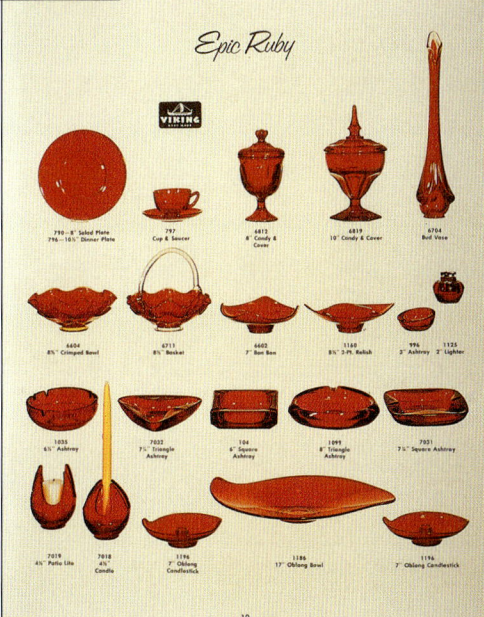

Viking Glass catalog page "Epic," 1970, in ruby. Noteworthy here is that even the #700 dinnerware line, which in 1970 and long before was produced without any name or pattern affiliation (later called Formal Classic), is tossed into the catch all line of Epic.

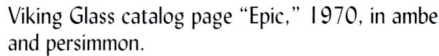

Viking Glass catalog page "Epic," 1970, in amber and persimmon.

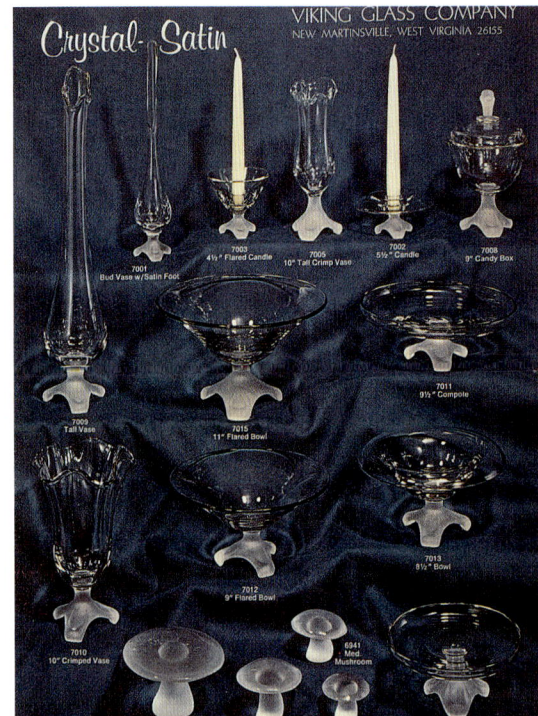

Viking Glass catalog page "Crystal Satin," 1970. Epic Drape, with the original three point foot. Note the mushrooms in crystal satin.

Epic Line Foot-Base Shapes

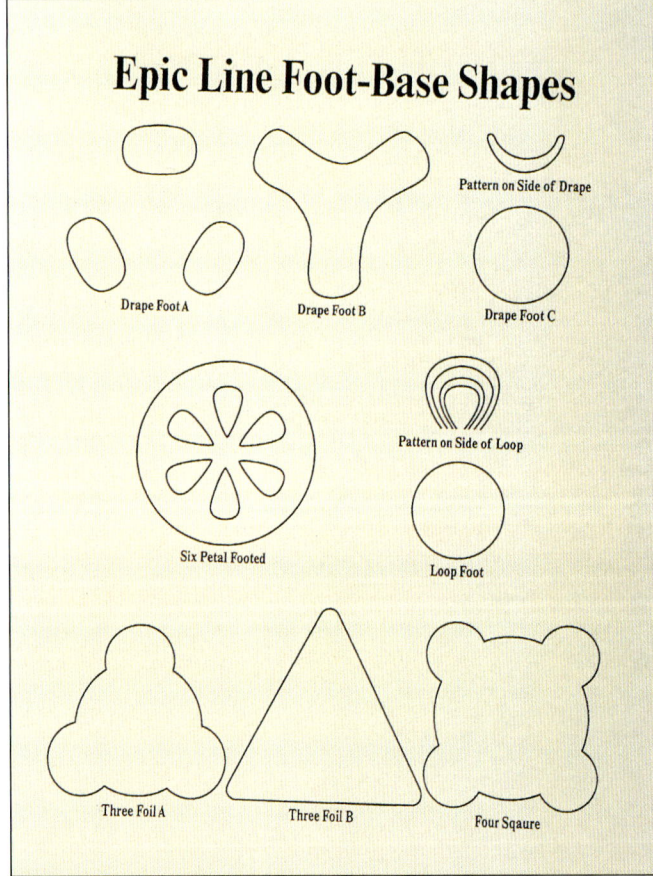

Drape Foot A

Drape Foot B

Pattern on Side of Drape

Drape Foot C

Six Petal Footed

Pattern on Side of Loop

Loop Foot

Three Foil A

Three Foil B

Four Sqaure

Devised by the authors is this chart to help distinguish and give names for easier reference to some of the endless forms used in the Epic line. While the practice of author naming is not ideal, it is necessary for those of us who do not easily recall line numbers alone. Shown here are the bases/feet on several beginning pressed shapes that were then manipulated to make swung vases, footed bowls, covered candy dishes, and other forms. Drape is shown in the original (used through 1970) and the later revised solid foot and the single round foot, also later. Six petal feet and bases are perhaps the most common in Epic. Three Foil One is the pre-1970 form and #2 is post 1970. Note: Loop was produced only for a short time around the early 1960s.

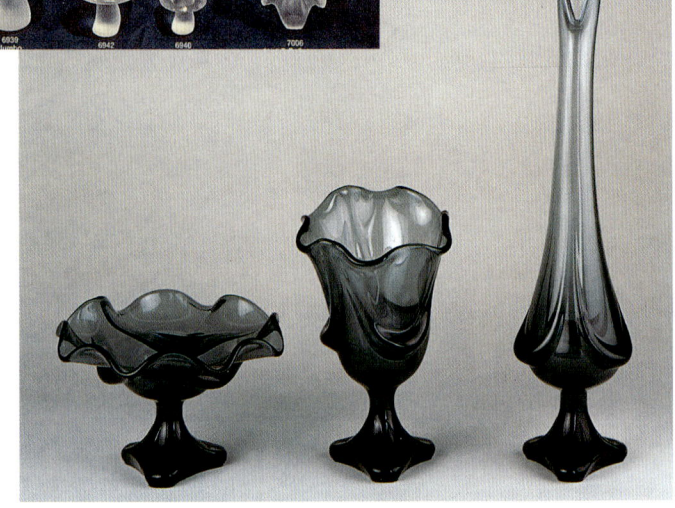

Epic Drape shapes after 1970. Note that the one arched three point foot is now a more solid "Y" foot. Charcoal pieces, $16-32 each.

FLAIR Line #800 is the reintroduced colored glass version of the earlier made Cristina shapes. It is shown in *China, Glass & Tableware*, December 1956. While the basic shapes of Flair are familiar as octagonal Christina forms, the tops of objects are now pulled in the free-form and "modern" shapes of the Epic line. In 1956 the line had these pieces:

Bowl, #810, 9-1/2"
Bowl, #811, 12"
Bowl, # 812, 9"
Bowl, shallow #814, 13"
Bowl, crimped #815, 18"
Candy jar with lid, footed #830, 9"
Compote, #840, 5" tall and 8" diameter
Compote, #842, 4" tall and 6" diameter
Compote, #843, 5"
Compote, #844, 4"
Plate, #854, 14"
Vase, crimped #883, 6"
Vase, crimped #890, 13-1/2"
Vase, footed #891, 11"

While the use of the Flair name fades, the use of the forms in the Epic line does not pass as quickly. The 13-1/2", #890 crimped vase remains through at least 1962. The crimped 18" bowl #815 remains in the line through 1960. The footed vase #891 is still in the line in 1957 as are the #879 vase, #843 compote, and #814 shallow bowl.

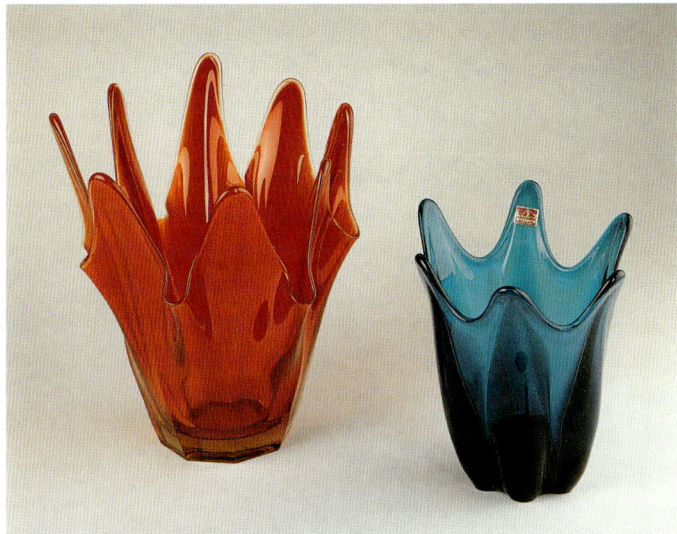

Epic crimped vase #890 Flair line persimmon, circa 1962, 13-1/2", $45-65; crimped vase, bluenique, 8-1/2", $38-50. Note that the #890 line is comprised of old Christina line pieces in color and ground to sit flat. Christina pieces are also shown in the Epic six petal line, treated in the same manner–ground to sit flat.

FLAMENCO was a line within a larger offering of two-tone pieces. First found in the December 1959 ads as a "new concept" two-hue crystal, Viking placed full-page ads in numerous national magazines promoting what they were confident would be the "Show-Stealer of 1960." It was not to be.

The ad copy in a full-page, color ad declared the "color flowed in—not on, but in—the glass!" It was noted as "available in all the shapes made so popular by Viking." (*China, Glass & Tablewares* December 1959) To date Flamenco has been found in a very limited number of shapes: largely free-form bowls and swung vases. It continued to be promoted in *Crockery & Glass Journal*, where in the February issue copy reads "the striking new Flamenco marries a brilliant persimmon or blue color with crystal for two-hued hand swung decorative and utility pieces." That seems accurate. In May the copy reads "Epic vase, 9" high, combines crystal with persimmon or bluenique color, $7.50. Also comes in two opalescent shades, $5.00." We have found no other examples or copy to suggest the Flamenco line extended beyond these four color treatments suggested in the ad copy above. There is some question about the inclusion of the opalescent as properly being in the Flamenco line; however, it was marketed at the same time and with other certain Flamenco items, so Flamenco for the purposes of this book includes:

Persimmon and crystal
Bluenique and crystal
Green shading to opalescent
Blue shading to opalescent

Flamenco was still being promoted in full page, full-color ads in the nation's leading homemaker magazines in July 1960. (*The Gift and Art Buyer*, July 1960) It was a phenomenal advertising campaign for a single line. And all indications are Flamenco sold moderately at best. Ex-Viking employees remember it as being produced for a short time.

Inside of the 1961 Viking catalog we used is stapled a note, on Viking Glass Company letterhead. It reads, in part: "Discontinued Items. Catalog Supplement. Page of Flamenco, Page of Green Opalescent." Flamenco briefly appears and was discontinued by the end of 1960, having been in production about one year or less. It was not a showstopper.

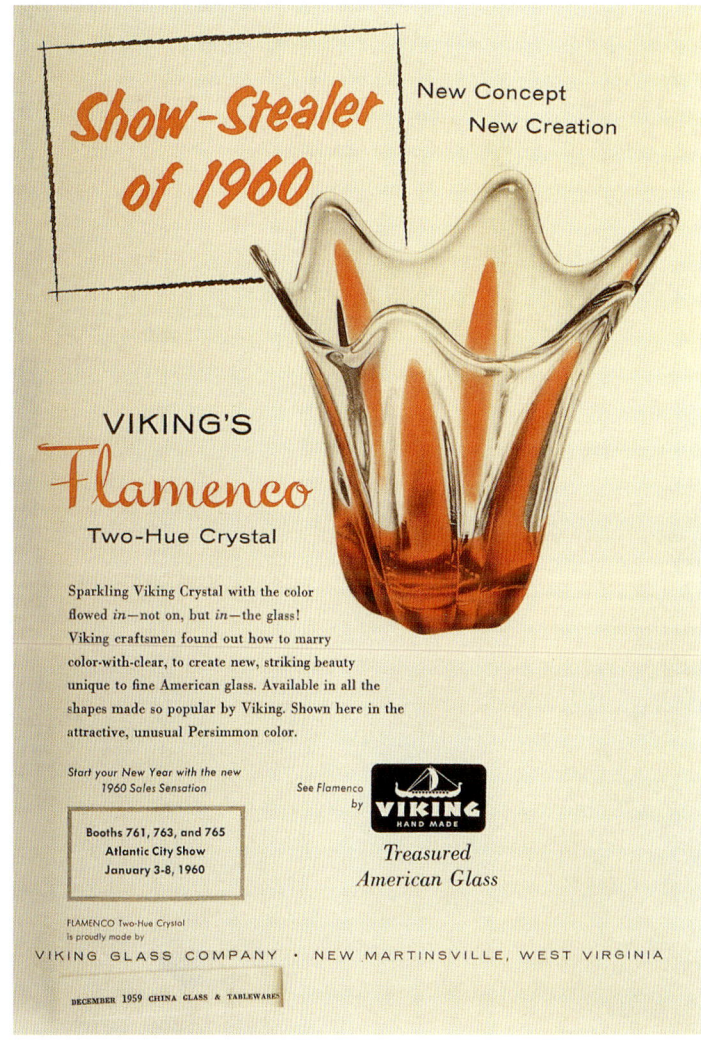

Viking advertisement claiming Flamenco to be the "Show Stealer of 1960." *China, Glass & Tableware*, December 1959.

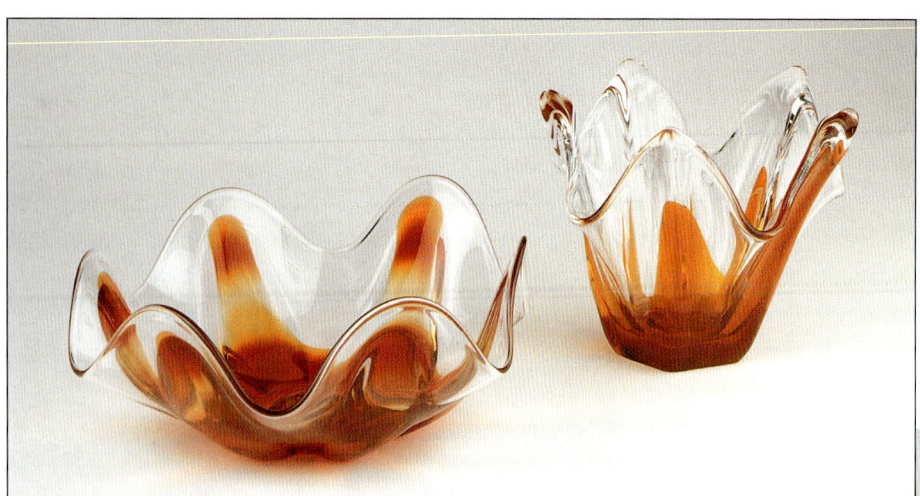

Flamenco persimmon and crystal bowls, 4-1/2" tall by 9-1/2" wide, $48-58; 6" tall by 7" wide, $54-64.

Flamenco bluenique and crystal bowl, 4-1/2" tall by 9 1/2" wide, $48-58; 6" tall and 7" wide, $50-60. Both with ground bases.

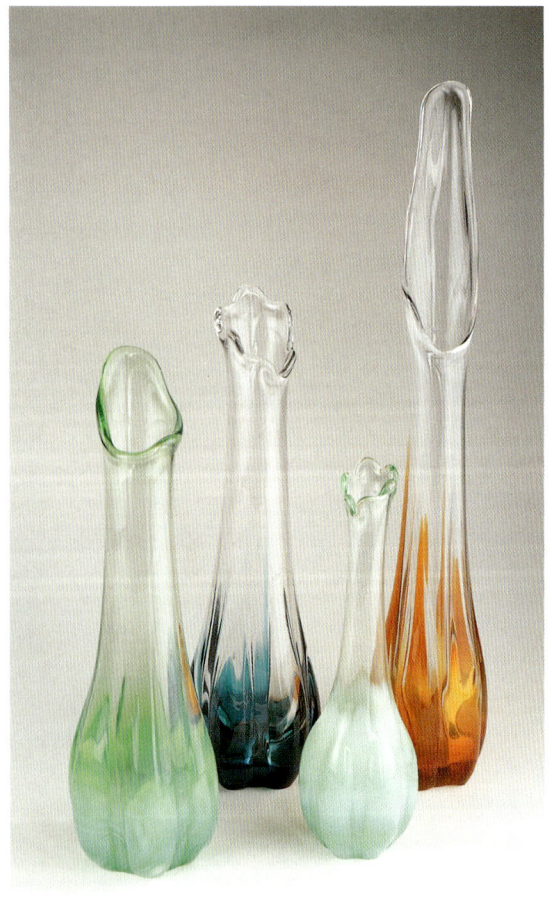

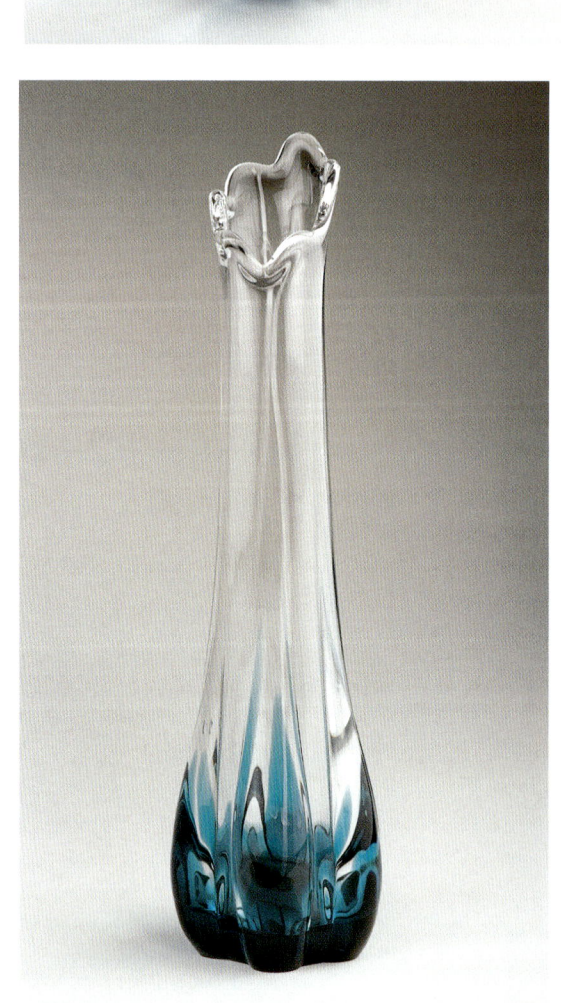

Flamenco swung vases, opaque green and crystal, 15", $58-76; bluenique and crystal, 15", $48-68; opaque green and crystal, 11-1/2", $54-72; persimmon and crystal, $52-68. All from Epic six petal molds ground flat at the base.

Flamenco bluenique and crystal swung vase, 15", ground bases, $48-68.

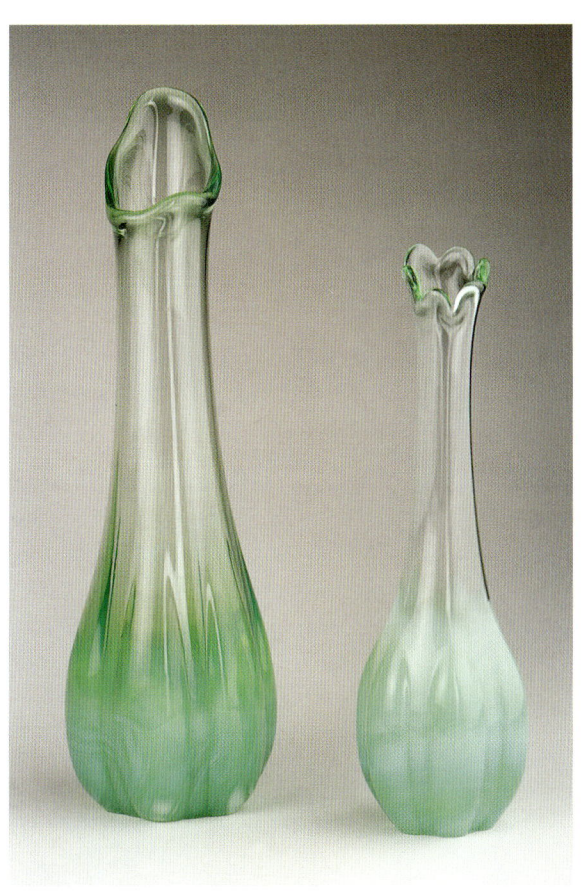

Flamenco opaque green and crystal swung vase, 15", $58-76; 11-1/2", $54-72.

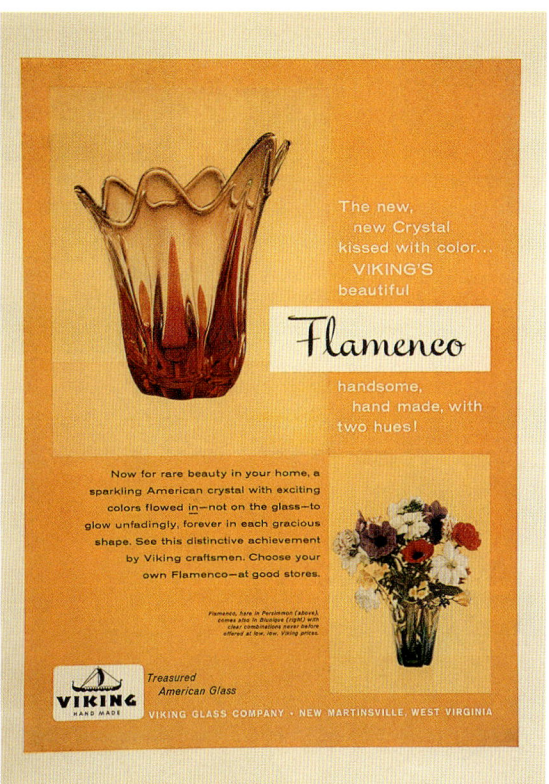

Viking advertisement for Flamenco, "kissed with color." Undated, circa 1960.

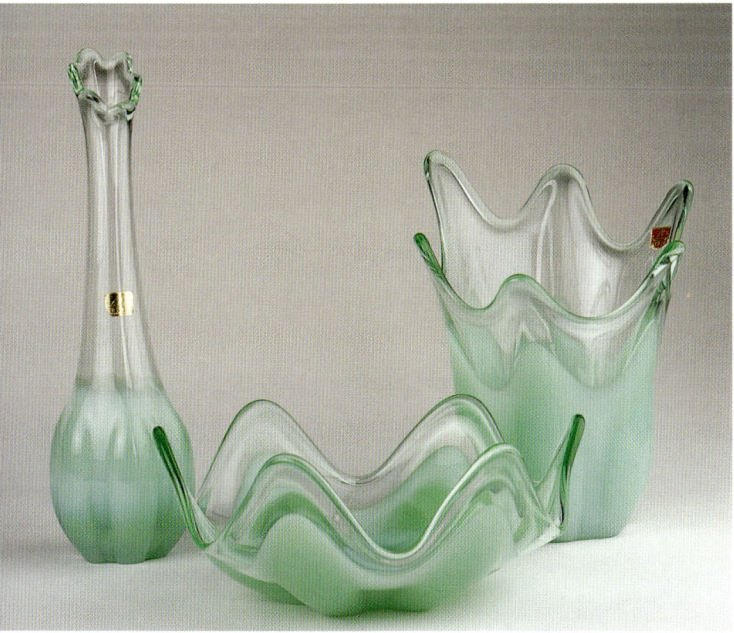

Flamenco opaque green and crystal swung vase, 11-1/2", $54-72; bowl, 9-1/2" by 3-3/4", $56-74; and vase, 8-1/2" tall by 7-1/2" wide (spun mould process), $58-78.

GEORGIAN Line #6900 is a line echoing early 1800s cut glass. The honeycomb-like facets were in fact originally hand cut facets covering an object's surface. Several glass manufacturers produced the century-plus later Georgian pressed glass variations. Viking is one of those. The pattern takes the name from the early Georgian period, when they were then believed to have been first popular. We first found Georgian in the Viking literature of 1953, where it appears on a price list. The "regular colors" offered in Georgian that year were crystal, amber, amethyst, evergreen, olive green, charcoal, colonial blue, harvest gold, and cherry glo. One could collect just Viking Georgian and have a splashy collection, it would seem! The circa 1955 catalog shows a 10 oz. low footed goblet, 12 oz. tumbler, 9 oz. tumbler, 5 oz. tumbler, and a 4 oz. sherbet. Interviews with ex-Viking factory employees resulted in repeatedly hearing that the Georgian molds, these original shapes, had come from some other factory and were not original to Viking. It was suggested but not confirmed that these had come from nearby Paden City Glass.

By 1956 the offerings in the Viking factory price list included eight Georgian colors: crystal, amber, amethyst, emerald green, Charcoal, colonial blue, cherry glo, and cobalt blue. Some of these Georgian colors are difficult to find today. The pieces available in 1956 were the same #69 items: tumblers 5 oz., 9 oz., 12 oz., and sherbet 4 oz. Listed but noted as made in only Crystal, amber, emerald green, and cherry glo is the 10 oz. low footed goblet. One might wonder why not all pieces were offered in all colors?

The 1960 catalog continues with the 4 oz. sherbet, 5 oz., 9 oz., and 12 oz. tumblers, and a 10 oz. footed goblet. Five shapes in seven colors: pink, charcoal, emerald green, amethyst, amber, ruby, and light blue. No plates, no pitchers, no bowls yet. All drinking vessels, and no colorless crystal.

Viking Georgian in the 1962 catalog includes ten shapes. Charcoal was no longer shown and the other colors remained unchanged.

> Bowl/nappy, 6"
> Bowl/nappy, 8"
> Goblet, 10 oz.
> Jug, 54 oz.
> Plate, salad 8"
> Plate, 9-1/2"
> Sherbet, 4 oz.
> Tumbler, flat 5 oz.
> Tumbler, flat 9 oz.
> Tumbler, flat 12 oz.

The 1963 catalog supplement had expanded Georgian to include seven new forms, an entirely new set of shapes. Even the seemingly familiar goblet form is offered in a dramatically restyled size and shape. Note that in 1962 it was the #69 – 10 oz. goblet and had a ringed stem. In 1963 the new goblet was the #6963 – 11 oz. goblet and had an entirely new faceted stem. As late as the 1968 catalog, both styles of Georgian goblet were offered, the 10 oz. ring stemmed goblet and the facet stemmed 11 oz. goblet.

The Georgian offerings featured in 1963 were dramatically new. The seven new additional forms included a tall, swung "bud" vase, a candy box with cover, a fluted compote and several additional stemware pieces, all with a very '60s look. It was also no longer just a tableware line, it was now a line of tableware and accessories, including pieces titled "Coupette." Georgian had arrived.

By the 1964 price list the Georgian line had grown considerably. Dramatically more pieces were offered but in only half as many colors and none of these were the same colors produced in 1956. Georgian was available by 1964 in avocado, bluenique, ruby, and honey, with the pieces offered in these four colors listed below:

> sherbet, 4 oz., #6901
> tumbler, 5 oz., #6902
> tumbler, 9 oz., #6903
> tumbler, 12 oz., #6904
> goblet, 10 oz., 36905
> salad plate, 8", #6907
> ice lip jug, 54 oz., #6908
> wine, 4 oz., #6910
> goblet, 11 oz., #6911
> ice tea, 13 oz., #6912
> sherbet, 6 oz., #6913
> candy jar with lid, #6918
> toothpick holder, #6919
> oil with stopper, 5-1/2 oz., #6921
> cream and sugar with lid, #6922
> juice jug, 32 oz., #6923
> candy box with lid, #6924

(Note: this is a different shape from the early #69 candy with lid.)

The 1967 and 1968 price lists feature the same four colors with the only change in offering being the discontinuance of the oil bottle only and no new pieces were added. The 1970 catalog, the last for the period covered by this book, featured seventeen items in Georgian, the same items as 1968, except the oil bottle with stopper had been discontinued. The 1970 colors for Georgian were identical to 1964: avocado, bluenique, honey, ruby, and with some pieces then in brown and cobalt.

A note on Georgian: Every glass company made it, well… almost every. Suffice it to say, many made it. Distinguishing one company's Georgian from another's is difficult, and in some colors and forms perhaps impossible. A Georgian pattern was made by Viking / Dalzell-Viking, Beaumont, Fenton, Cambridge, Paden City, Canton, Duncan Miller, Hocking / Anchor Hocking, Hazel-Atlas, Central, and Libby glass companies.

Several hundred pieces of known Viking Georgian were examined and none had a ground bottom. Thus, while sorting one manufacturer from another may be complex, pieces with ground bottoms were made by someone other than Viking.

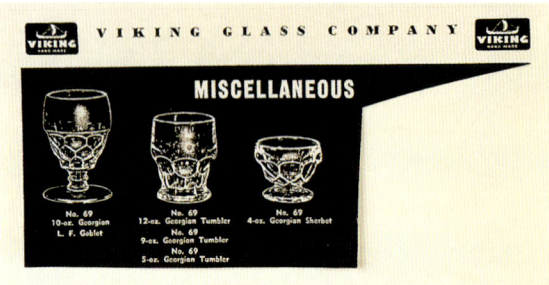

Viking Glass catalog illustration from 1956, a very short line at the time.

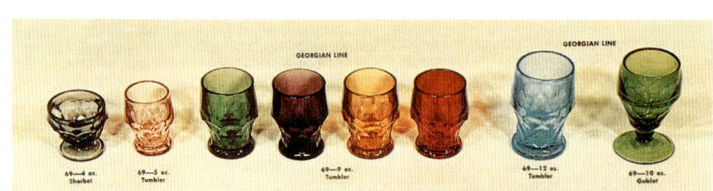

Viking Glass catalog illustration, 1960 catalog.

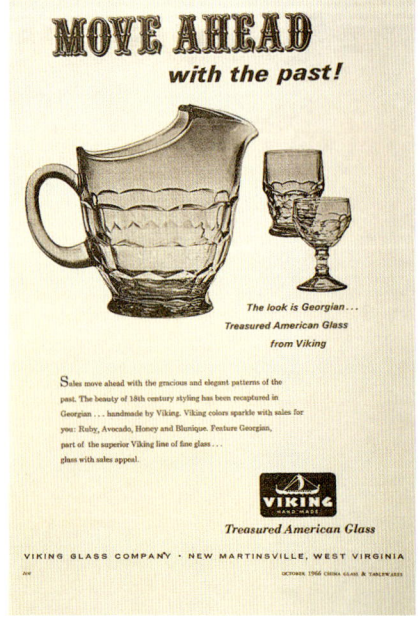

Viking Glass advertisement for Georgian, "Move ahead with the Past." *China, Glass and Tableware*, October 1966.

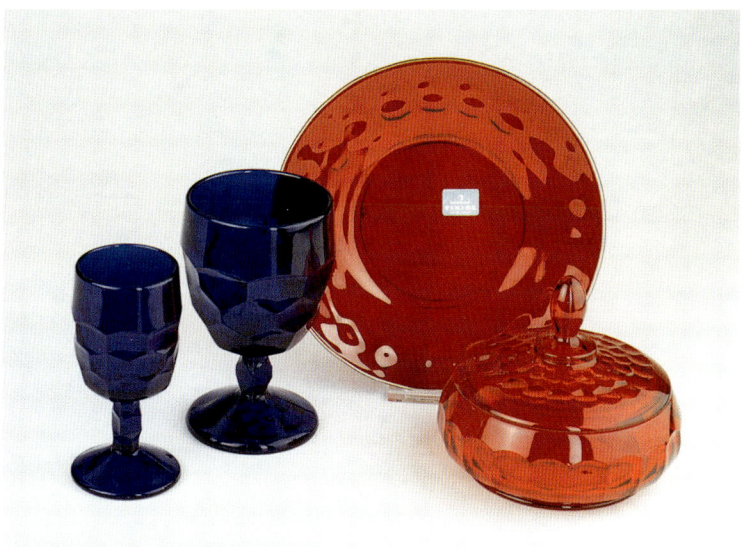

Georgian pattern wine goblet, 5", cobalt, $14-24; goblet, 5-3/4", cobalt, $16-24; salad plate #6907, 8", ruby, $14-18; candy with lid #6928 ruby, $28-38, appears in 1968 catalog.

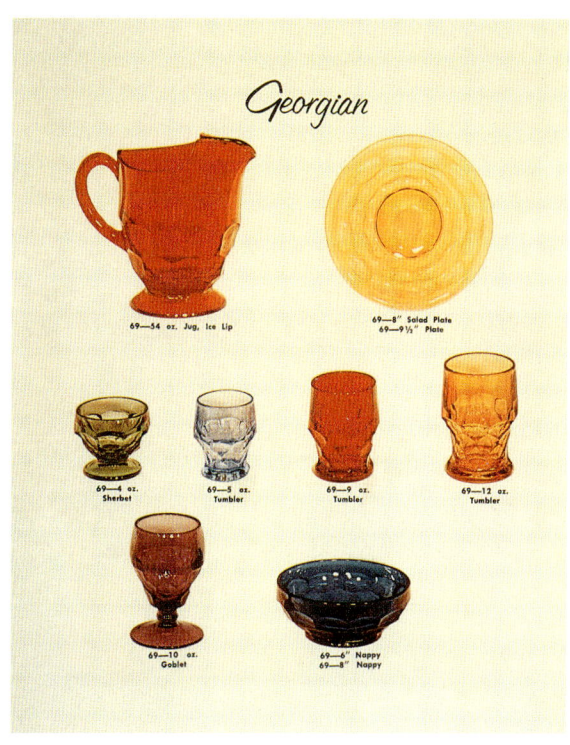

Viking Glass catalog page "Georgian," 1962.

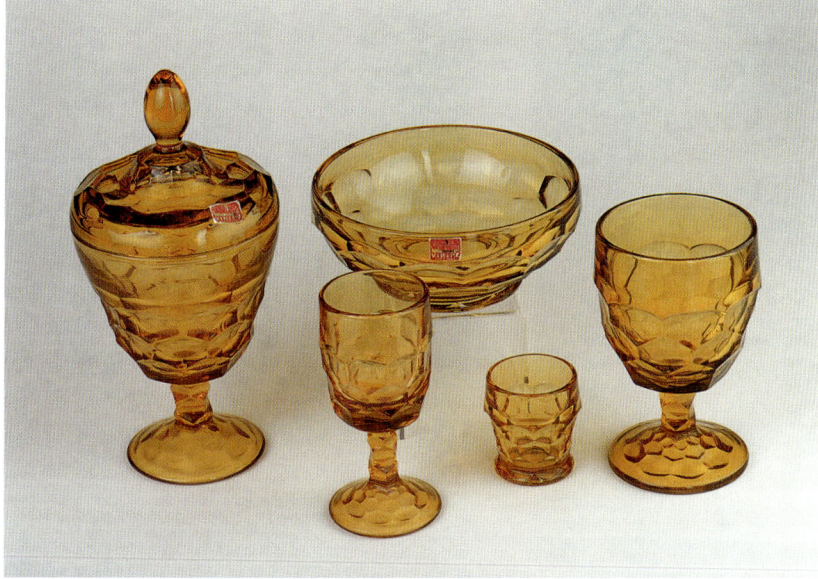

Georgian candy with lid #6918, $10-16; wine #6909, 7 oz., $6-12; bowl/nappy, 6", #69, $6-10; toothpick/whiskey #6919, $10-16; footed iced tea #6963, 13 oz., $8-14, all amber.

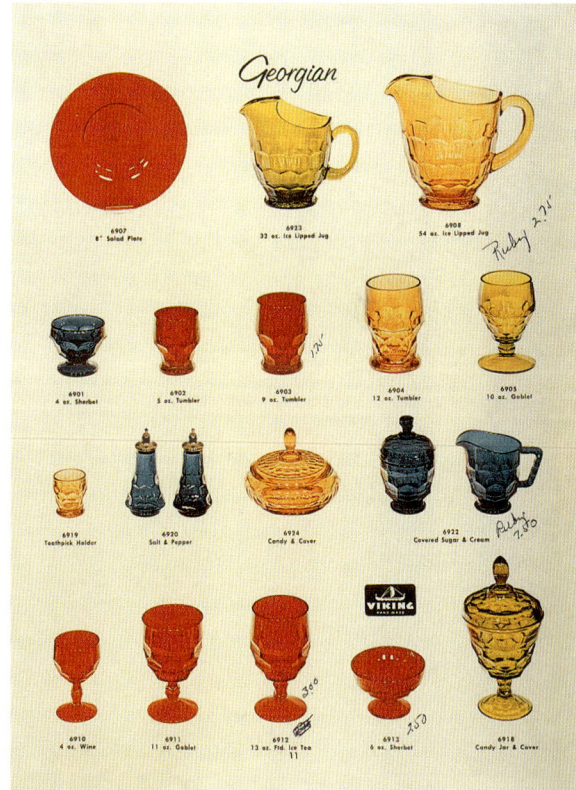

Viking Glass catalog page "Georgian," 1970.

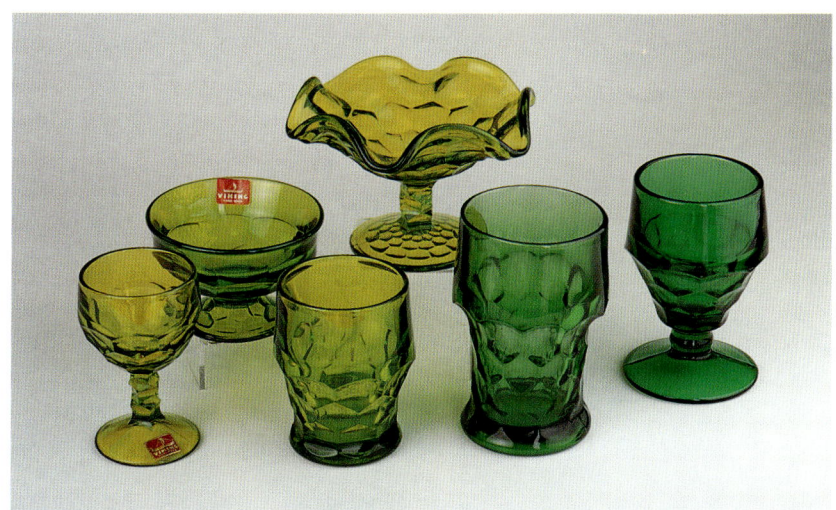

Left:
Georgian avocado wine #6909, 7 oz., $8-12; footed sherbet #6913, $8-12; tumbler #6903, 9 oz., $8-12; fluted small compote, $10-14; tumbler #6904, 12 oz., green, $12-16; low footed goblet, 6 oz., green, $14-16.

JANICE Line #4500: The form that would become Janice was shown by New Martinsville Glass in *China & Crockery Journal*, January 1940; but, the name Janice was not yet then in use. An advertisement in 1944 again shows the pattern but does not yet use the name. By the 1948-49 catalog, several pages of Janice were included and it is clearly labeled by that name.

The circa 1949-1951 price list offers Janice in an extensive fifty-six piece listing for crystal and the same fifty-six pieces in sky blue. This is the most extensive offering found of Janice. Colored Janice received its most extensive offering in this early 1950s era as well. Specifically offered in the price list found from this era are the following Janice colored pieces.

Ebony offerings were four pieces:

> Basket, 12" oval with crystal handle #4552
> Basket, 6" with crystal handle #4566
> Ice tub, 6", #4584
> Vase, 8" three toed #4527

Evergreen offerings in Janice were:

> Bowl, 12" oval with crystal swan handle #4551/ 1S
> Basket, 6-1/2" with crystal swan handle #4566
> Celery, 12" with crystal swan handle #4521
> Ice tub, 6", #4584
> Vase, 8" three toed #4527

Ruby Janice at this time included:

> Basket, 11" with crystal handle #4590
> Basket, 12" with crystal handle #4552
> Bowl, 12" oval #4551
> Bowl, 12" oval with crystal swan handle #4551/1S
> Candlestick, 5-1/2" one light #4554
> Celery, 12" with crystal swan handle #4521/1S
> Cup and saucer, #4580
> Goblet, Luncheon #4581
> Plate, 13" two handled #4529
> Plate, 8-1/2" salad #4579
> Sherbet, low # 4582
> Sugar and creamer, #4532
> Tumbler, 11 ounce footed #4592
> Vase, ivy 4" with peg (for use on a candlestick) #4578

One last note on the context of the 1949-51 price list regarding Janice is the mention of Janice Luncheon sets in 15, 21, and 27 piece sets. The type and number of each piece contained in a set are not listed on the price list. These were available in crystal, sky blue, and ruby.

The 1953 price list featured almost thirty crystal Janice shapes. Two pieces, the 8" flared vase and ice tub, were offered in Ebony and in Evergreen. While ruby is in the 1953 price list, there was no ruby Janice by this time and no other colored Janice was available in 1953. This is a dramatic change for the circa 1949-51 price list which offered extensive colored Janice.

The 1956 catalog and price list have no separate listing for Janice patterns. However, the #4536 two light candelabra and 4454 one light candlestick are there in the candlestick section.

In 1964 Janice was offered in a limited number of largely tableware shapes in the Viking price list, all apparently in crystal only. Celery, sugar and creamer, three toed 10-1/2" bowl, two and one light candlestick, five part divided relish, 14" rolled edge plate, individual size cream and sugar, and salt and pepper.

In 1970 Janice shapes shown in the catalog numbered nine: salt and pepper, individual and table cream and sugar sets, one and two light candlestick, five part relish, celery, 14" rolled edge plate, and three toed bowl. Janice in several forms appeared in the factory gift shop when the Dalzell-Viking factory closed in the 1990s. Some of the last production included earlier Janice forms in colors that had not been produced for decades such as ebony and ruby. Janice was the longest produced and one of the most used lines of forms. Perhaps Janice was challenged only by the Princess line of shapes as a widely utilized single line at Viking glass.

Pieces confirmed as produced in the period of this book in the Janice shape include:

> Basket, oval handled #4552, 12" width, 10" height
> Basket, handled #4566, 6-1/2" width, 9" height
> Basket, handled #4590, 11"
> Bonbon, #4518 two handled, flipped sides 3" height, 7" diameter
> Bonbon, #4524 two handled 6", 4" height, 6" diameter
> Bonbon, #4525 two handled 5-1/2" diameter, 4-1/2" height
> Bonbon, #4248 cupped 6"
> Bowl, flower, eight deep crimps #4574, 5-1/2" diameter
> Bowl, flared #4513, 12" width, 3" height
> Bowl, six deep crimps #4515, 12" width, 3-1/2" height
> Bowl, flared #4555, 13" width, 4" height
> Bowl, three toed, flared #4510, 11" width, 4" height
> Bowl, three toed flared #4511, 10-1/2" width, 4" height
> Bowl, three toed cupped #4512, 10-1/2", 4" height (1940s –1970)
> Bowl, oval bowl #4551, 12" width, 4" height
> Bowl, flared #4555, 13" diameter, 4" height
> Bowl, flared #4531, 9-1/2"
> Bowl, cupped #4535, 9-1/2"
> Bowl, two handled #4591, 9"
> Candelabra, two light #4457, 5" tall, 7" width
> Candelabra, two light #4536, 5" tall, 5" width (1940s and 1970)
> Candlestick, one light rectangular base #4585, 6" tall, 4-1/2" rectangular base
> Candlestick, one light round base #4554, 5" diameter (1940s and 1970)
> Candy box with cover, #4541, 5-1/2" diameter
> Celery, oblong #4521, 11" (1940s-1970)
> Cheese and Cracker, two pieces, tray and cheese stand # 4528, 11"
> Condiment set, five piece tray, two jars, two lids #4548
> Cruet/ oil bottle with ground stopper, #4583, 5 oz.
> Cream, sugar and tray, individual 3 oz., three piece, #4586
> (Same number continued in use in 1970, but C&S without a tray)

Cream, sugar, and tray, individual #4545 (also sold without tray)

Cream, sugar, and tray, table 6 oz., three pieces, #4532

(Same number continued in use in 1970 but C&S without a tray)

Cup and saucer, #4580

Goblet, luncheon, footed 8 oz., #4581

Goblet, luncheon, footed 11 oz., #4592

Ice Pail, braided glass handle #4589, 10" tall

Ice Tub, #4584, 6"

Jam jar with lid, #4577, height 6"

Jam jar with lid and under plate, #4577/20

Jug, berry cream #4576, height 4"

Mayonnaise set, three piece, #4522, width 6", height 4"

Nappy, two handled #4517, 6"

Oil bottle with glass stopped, #4583, 5"

Plate, #4529, 11"

Plate, rolled edge #4530, 11"

Plate, salad #4579, 8-1/2"

Plate (Torte), footed and rim edge #4556, 14" (1940s and 1970)

Plate (Torte), #4538, 15"

Plate (Torte), #4516, 13"

Plate, two handled #4529, 13"

Plate, two handled #4520, 7"

Platter, oval #4588, 13"

Relish, two part, two handled #4534, 6"

Relish, three part #4255, 7"

Relish, five part #4538 (1970)

Sherbet, low #4582

Vase, ball #4565, 8" diameter

Vase, Ivy with peg #4578, 4" diameter

Vase, Ivy, flat bottom #4575, 4" diameter

Vase, three toed flared "Rocket" #4527, 8"

NOTE ON JANICE: Pieces in this shape were made for decades after the period covered in this book, including additional shapes not made in this period, and thus not listed above.

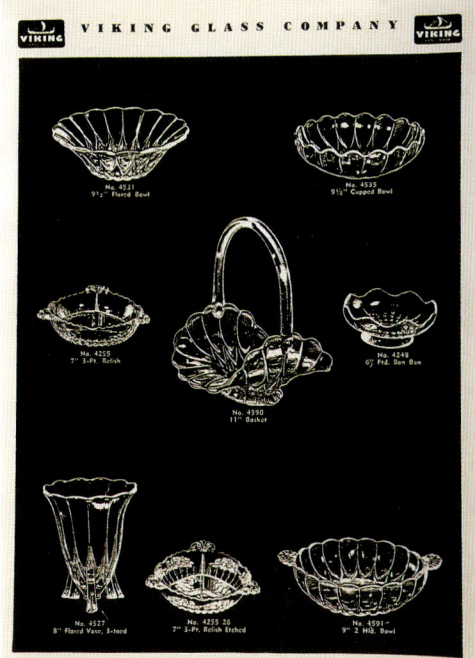

Viking Glass catalog page "Janice," 1948-49.

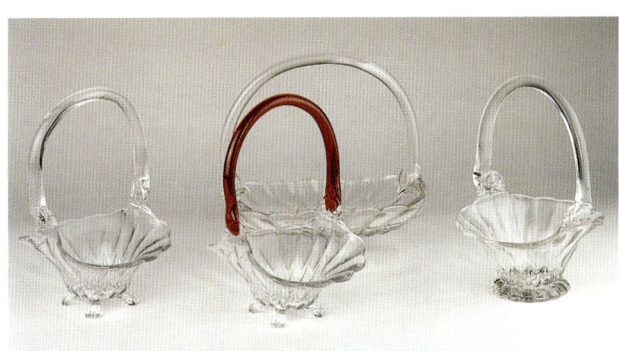

Janice pattern baskets: four toed, 9", all crystal, $30-40; four feet crystal with ruby handle, 9", $32-48; oblong all crystal (from celery dish), $30-42; flat bottom all crystal, $28-38.

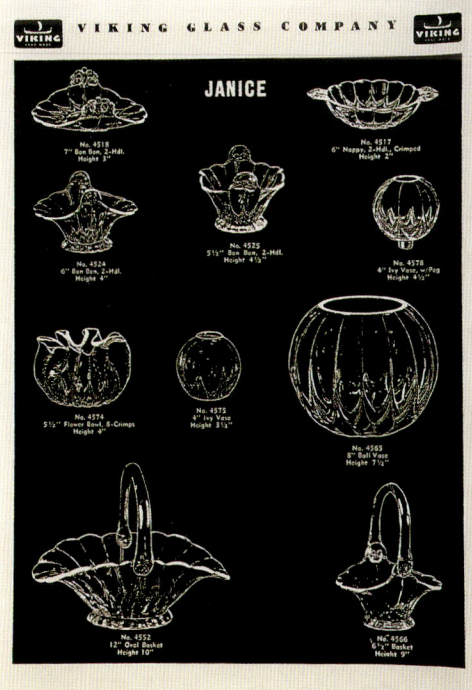

Viking Glass catalog page "Janice," 1948-49.

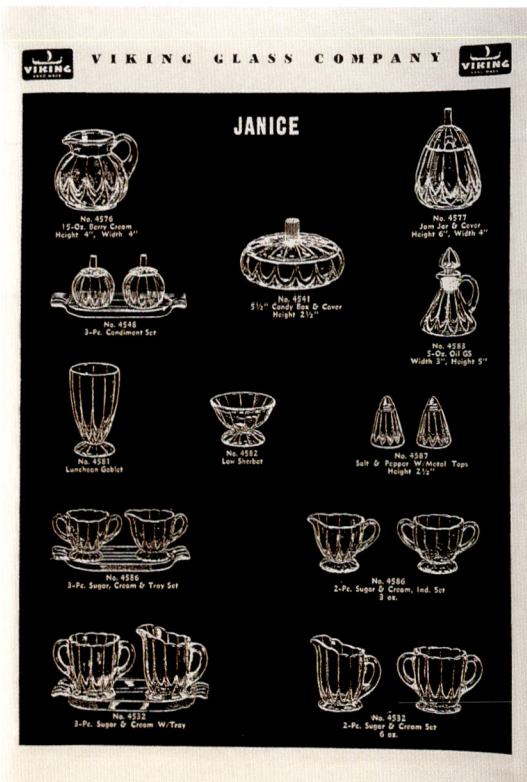

Viking Glass catalog page "Janice," 1948-49.

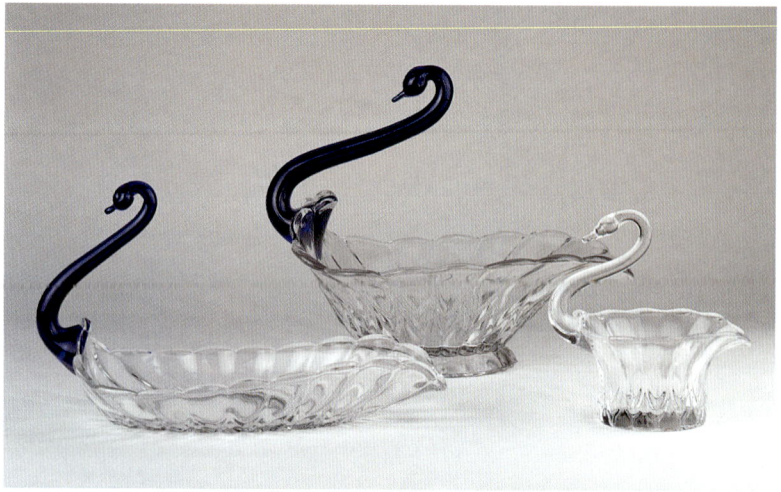

Swan handled Janice pattern bowls. Oblong celery with cobalt blue swan handles, 11", #4521-1/S, $48-68; oval bowl with cobalt swan handle #4551-1/S, $50-76; swan handled Janice crystal #4566, 6-1/2", circa 1950, $30-40.

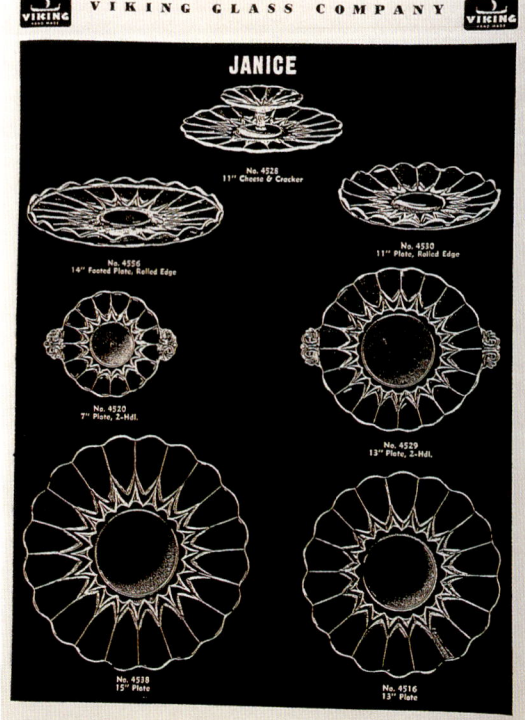

"Breakfast For Two" ad campaign in national magazines featuring Janice table setting. *House & Garden*, November 1947.

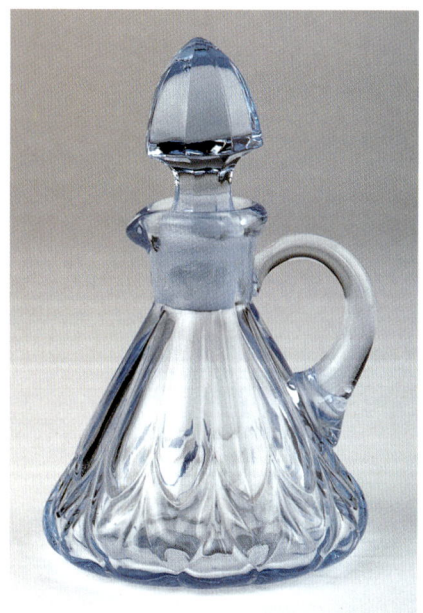

Janice pattern oil bottle with stopper, colonial blue #4583, 5", $26-38.

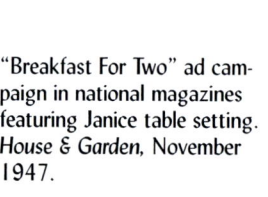

Viking Glass catalog page "Janice," 1948-49.

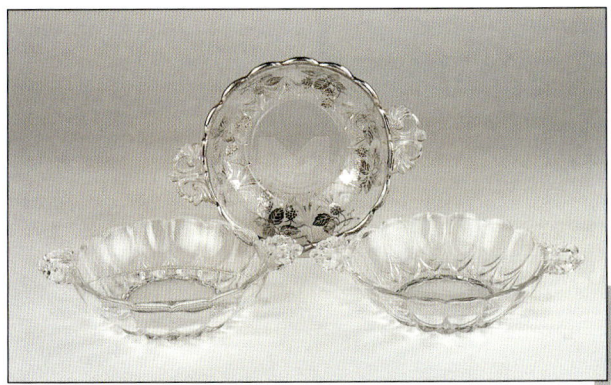

Janice pattern tab handled serving pieces that remained popular for decades include these. With sterling decoration or unknown cutting, $14-28; monogram cut, $8-12.

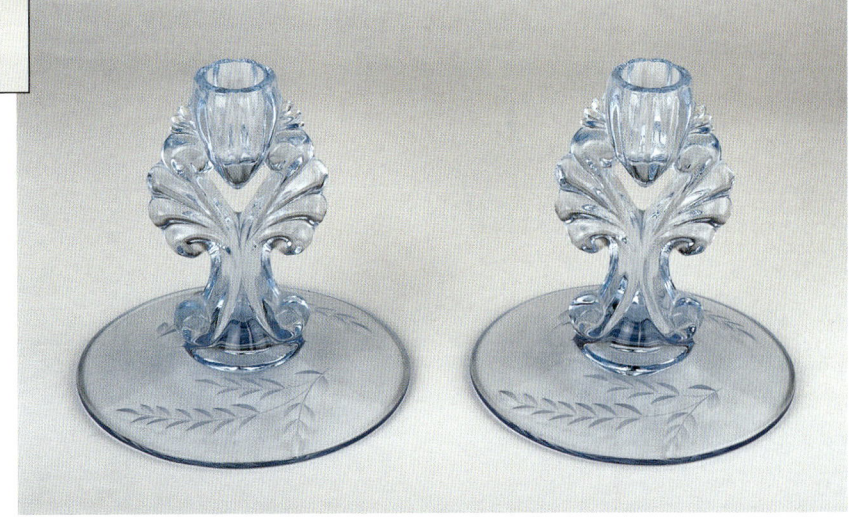

Janice pattern one light candlestick, 5-1/2", #4554 with unknown cutting, $20-32 each.

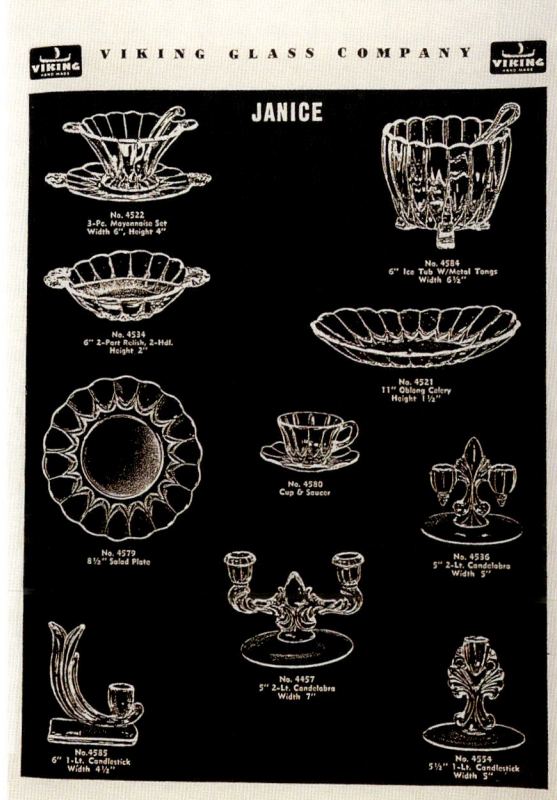

Viking Glass catalog page "Janice," 1948-49.

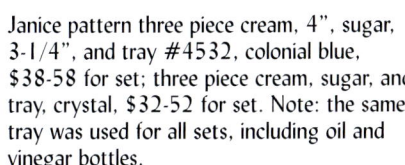

Janice pattern salad plate #4579, 8-1/2", ruby, $24-28; low sherbet #4582 ruby, $14-24.

Janice pattern three piece cream, 4", sugar, 3-1/4", and tray #4532, colonial blue, $38-58 for set; three piece cream, sugar, and tray, crystal, $32-52 for set. Note: the same tray was used for all sets, including oil and vinegar bottles.

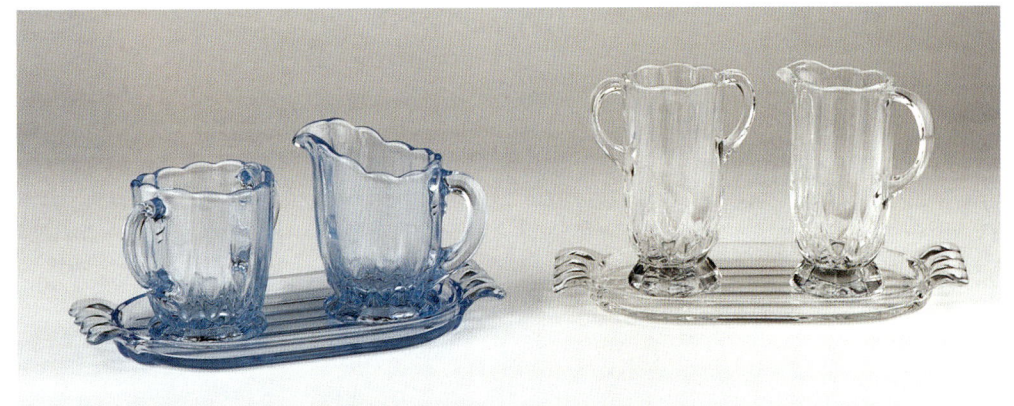

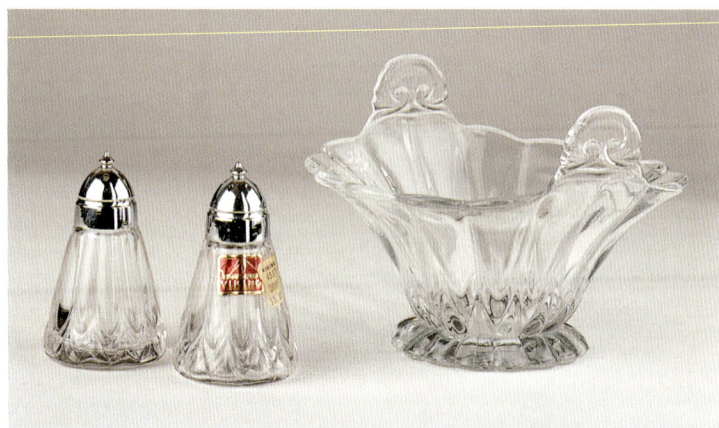

Janice pattern salt and pepper #4587, $12-18 set; bonbon #4525 crystal, $14-22.

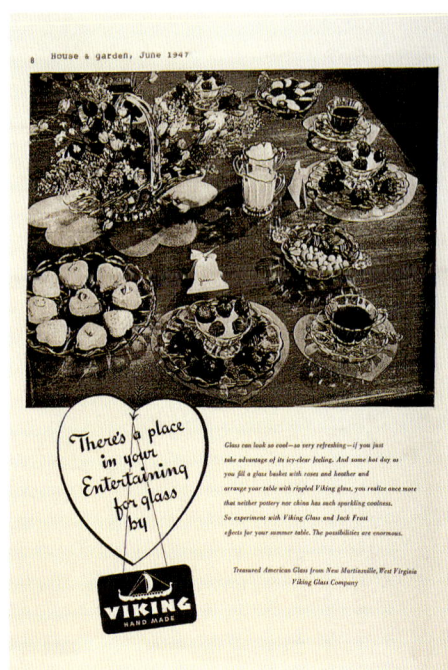

Viking Glass ad for Janice tableware appearing in *House & Garden,* June 1947.

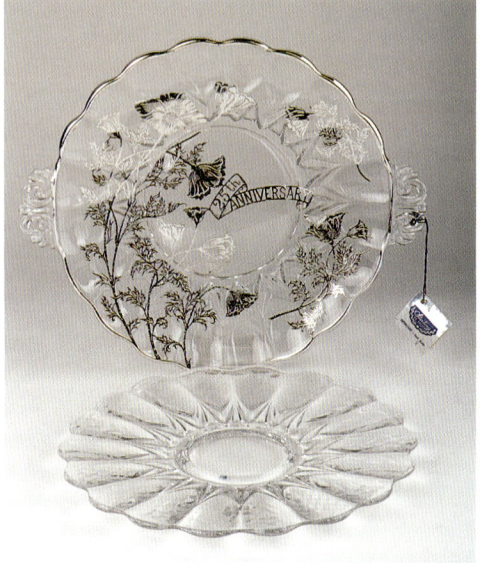

Janice pattern two tab handled plate with Silver City decoration "25th Anniversary" and original hand tag #4529, 11", crystal, $12-18 without hang tag; plate #4528, no handles, crystal with unidentified hand cutting, $10-16.

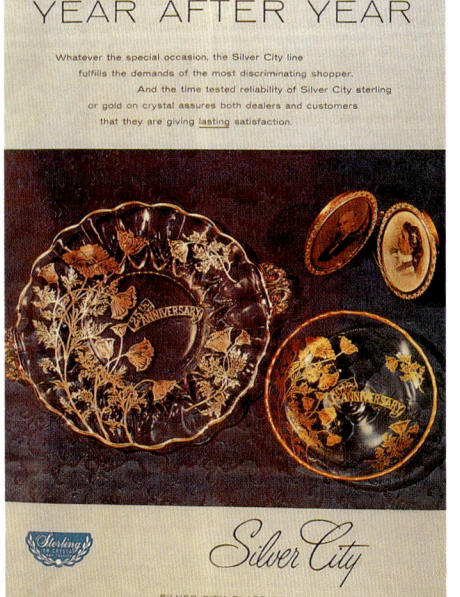

Advertisement for Silver City Glass Co., a Meriden, Connecticut, decorator of glass from diverse glass manufacturers. The plate illustrated on the left is the Viking 11", #4528; the other is not Viking. *Gift & Art Buyer,* April 1962.

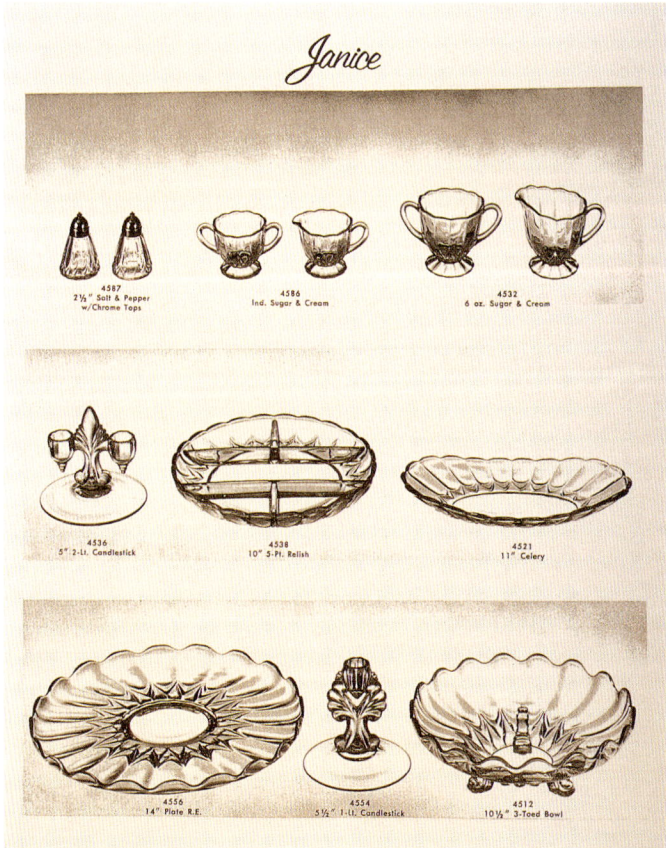

Viking Glass catalog page "Janice," 1970. This shows the items in the line at the end of the time period included in this book. While reduced to a few major shapes, the line was twenty-five years old in 1970, a well-used vehicle in the Viking offerings.

MOUNT VERNON line #1600 has first been found by us in the 1962 catalog. It has been reported that the line was first issued by New Martinsville Glass in crystal as early as 1932 and shortly discontinued by them. It appears to have not been produced again then until reintroduced in color in the 1962 line.

In this 1962 Viking catalog, pieces were given only a #16 designation, while later piece designations were expanded to pieces specific to 1600 numbers for each shape. Colors shown in 1962 were only amber and ruby. Pieces offered were:

    Bowl/sauce dish, 4"
    Cocktail, 3 oz.
    Goblet, 10 oz.
    Plate, salad, 8"
    Sherbet, 5 oz.
    Tumbler, 12 oz.
    The 4" sauce dish would later disappear and later still reappear.

By 1963 the Mount Vernon line appears in the catalog supplement with a "supplemental" new 12 oz. footed ice tea, a 3 oz. wine, a 9" covered candy, a 9-1/2" cake salver, and a 7-1/2" footed bowl. The colors shown in the catalog included amber, emerald green, ruby, and amberina.

In 1964 the price list has Mount Vernon available in avocado and ruby only. The offering was for seven shapes: goblet, sherbet, cocktail, wine, tumbler, footed ice tea, and salad plate.

Looking forward to the 1967 through 1970 catalogs and price lists, Mount Vernon appears in none of these, suggesting a short, mid-1960s original production period. The Mount Vernon shape was reintroduced later and in production at the time of Dalzell-Viking closing.

Known pieces in this 1960s era Mount Vernon include:

    Bowl, footed flared, 7-1/2"
    Bowl/sauce dish, 4"
    Cake salver, 9-1/2"
    Candy jar with lid, 9"
    Cocktail, 3 oz., #1603
    Goblet, 10 oz., #1601
    Ice tea, footed, 12 oz., #1606
    Plate, salad, 8", #1607
    Sherbet, 5 oz., #1602
    Tumbler, 12 oz., #1605
    Wine, 3 oz., #1604

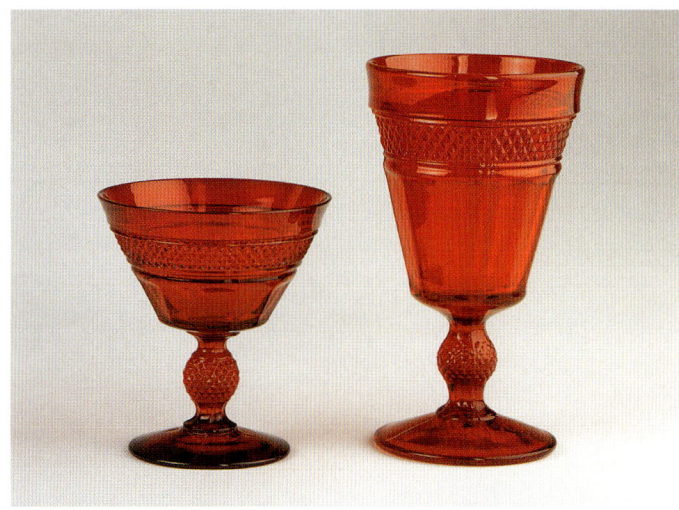

Mount Vernon pattern sherbet, 5 oz., #16 ruby 4", $14-24; goblet, 10 oz., #16 ruby 6", $20-28. *Compliments of Replacements, LTD.*

THREE TOED line No. 10 is a small but important line and made its appearance in the Viking offering circa 1951. It remained in production through the period of this book and beyond. It is important for two reasons: all the pieces except the flowerlites were etched with Viking's Prelude etching, and all pieces were sold in large quantities to both Silver City and Rockwell Silver companies. These firms purchased this line in crystal and in a number of colors for decorating. They applied silver and gold overlay designs. The first mention for this line is for the predecessor to the #1007 flowerlite shown in a June 1950 trade journal ad introducing "The newest VIKING exclusives: the line #550 Flowerette and the #549 Flowerlite." These 1950 versions are round, three legged bowls whose legs look like tree trunks and appear to have been made from or made to imitate an old mold from the Beaumont Glass Company of Morgantown, West Virginia. In the 1951 catalog there are shown the #551/1, 6-1/2" three toed bonbon and the #551/3, 7-1/2" three toed lemon plate with the same legs. These forms are from the same mold, simply tooled and formed differently when the glass was still hot. The Beaumont pieces of similar form were prone to chip on the feet so perhaps Viking produced a new mold or modified the Beaumont mold for the No. 10 line which features a teardrop-shaped "pad" on the bottom of each leg. In a June 1951 trade journal ad, the #1007 was finally introduced "To every woman who loves flowers, live with flowers…and Viking Glass." The #1007, humorously called "007" by the authors, were made in crystal, amber, ebony, cobalt blue, and evergreen. By the 1953 price list, there were six flowerlite or flowerette pieces in up to six colors and six other pieces in up to three colors and featuring the Prelude etching. Nine pieces in this line are found in the 1955 catalog. The 3-lite Flowerlites are gone and the final five pieces to appear in the line have been added.

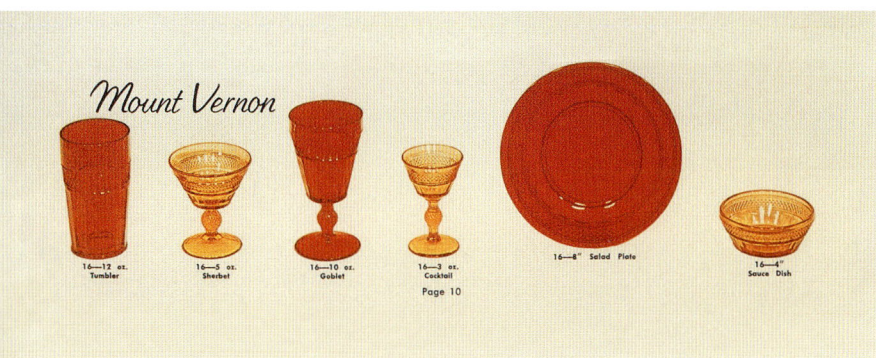

Viking Glass partial catalog page illustrating Mount Vernon pattern pieces, 1962.

The pieces in the line are as follow:

Bonbon, three toed 6", #1008
Bonbon, three toed, crimped 6", #1009
Bonbon, three toed, crimped 7", #1011
Bowl, three toed crimped 9", #1003
Bowl, three toed 10", #1090
Bowl, three toed 11", #1002
Cake Plate, three toed 11", #1091
Epergne, two piece 8", #1086
Epergne, two piece 7", #1088
Flower block, 3" flowerette #1006 (See below for explanations.)
Flowerette, 4-1/2" (bowl and flowerette frog insert) #1006
Flower block, 3" flowerlite #1007
Flowerlite, 4-1/2" (bowl and flowerlite frog) #1007
Flower block, 3-1/2" flowerette #999
Flowerette, 5-1/2" (bowl and flowerette frog) #999
Flower block, 3-1/2" flowerlite #1014
Flowerette, 5-1/2" (bowl and flowerette frog) #1004
Mayonnaise set, two pieces #1009/79
Plate, three toed lemon 7", #1010

The language of Frogs: Explanations:

Flower block = flower frog, the single piece of glass with holes for flower stems

Flowerette = three toed bowl with flower block/frog that does Not have a candle well center

Flowerlite = three toed bowl with flower block/frog that has a candle well in the center

Frog = flower block and flower frog are all used interchangeably.

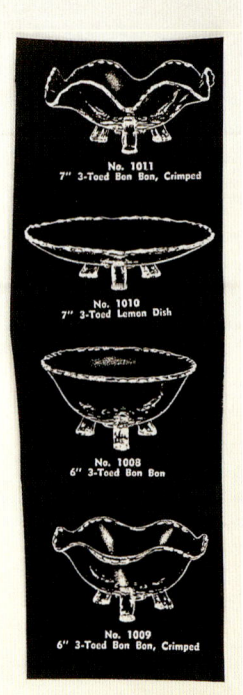

Viking Glass partial catalog page showing three toed items, 1956.

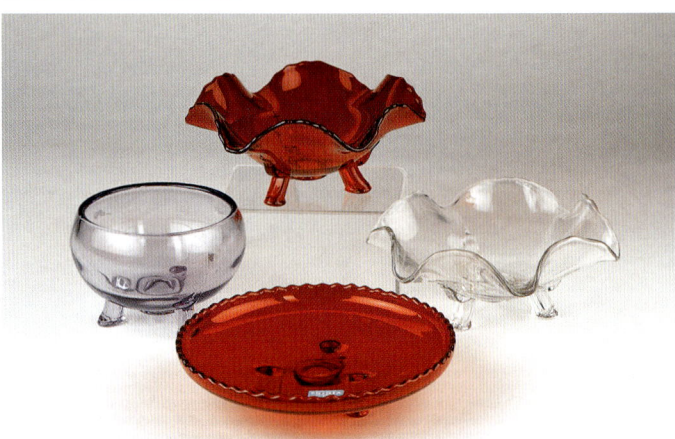

Three Toed shape items in Line #1000. It is suggested that this line, for simplicity's sake and to avoid confusion with an already called "Three Toed" line in Viking Epic, should be called Line #1000 or, for those who dislike numbers, Pam's Line. All the items shown were created from the same mold. Cupped bowl teaberry, $22-38; flat lemon dish (the original shape when pressed) ruby, $12-22; crimped bowl or bonbon in ruby, $12-20 and crystal, $8-12.

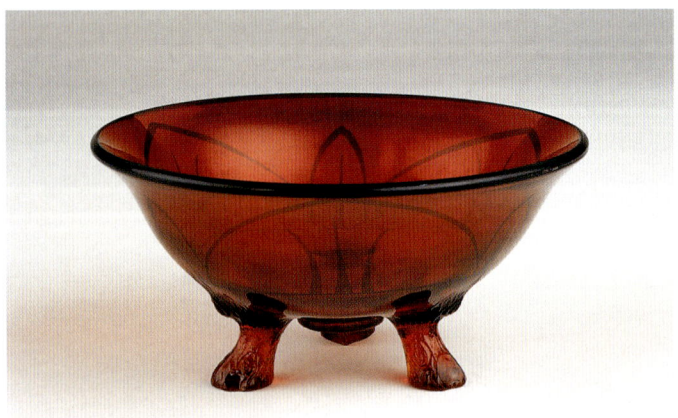

Beaumont Glass Co., of Morgantown, West Virginia's, style three toed bowl. This is either the form/mold used or copied by Viking for its original three toed pieces.

PRINCESS: *China, Glass & Decorative Accessories* in December 1951 noted, "a completely new line of tableware and flatware." It was Viking's new Princess line. Early sales must have been good because one year later, in December 1952, saw press releases citing the release of "new pieces" in the "Princess line of handmade glass introduced last January by Viking" (*Crockery & Glass Journal*). Added were seven shapes: celery tray, vinegar-oil, cigarette box, ashtray, double mayonnaise, butter dish with cover, and a small three-part relish.

A few early Princess shapes were quick to disappear from the line. From the early 1951 Princess supplement to the 1951 catalog, we learn of some pieces that did not have the common ribbon base but instead short, curled legs. These might prove difficult to identify as Princess as they lack this common foot decoration. These less common pieces include:

Bowl, salad, three toed 15", #5290
Cup, punch, three toed 5 oz., #5251
Plate, rolled edge, three toed 16", #5291
Punch set, ten piece bowl, ladle, and 8 cups #5250

By 1953 the price list has Princess in crystal offered in over fifty shapes representing an amazing expansion in a short time. Beyond the more extensive crystal offerings, evergreen, colonial blue, harvest gold, and amethyst Princess were available in 1953 in the forms of swans, ring holders, and the #5230 covered candy box only. The only other 1953 Princess offering was Charcoal in eighteen shapes.

The 1970 Viking catalog, the last year focused upon in this book, contained twenty-six Princess-shaped items.

Bowl, crimped, 10", #5207
Bowl, crimped, 8", #5211
Bowl, footed, 10", #5269
Bowl, salad, 10", #5203
Bowl, shallow, 13", #5201
Butter, oval with cover, 8-1/2", #5224
Cake salver, 11", #5226
Candlestick, 4-1/2", #5213
Candelabra, two light, 5", #5214
Celery tray, 10", #5249
Chip and dip set, 13", #5295
Compote, flared, 7-1/2", #5228
Compote, crimped, 7", #5231
Epergnette, 5", #5273
Mayonnaise set, three pieces, #5236
Plate, 14", #5216
Plate, (torte) rim edged, 14", #5217
Plate, rim edged, 11", #5220
Plate, 11", #5222
Plate, two handled, 12", #5223
Relish, five part oval, 13", #5287
Relish, three part two handled, 10", #5238
Salt and pepper, 3-1/2", #5242
Sandwich Tray, handled, #5243
Sugar and Cream, #5247
Sugar and Cream with tray, #5248
Tid Bit tray, two tier with chrome handle, #5243

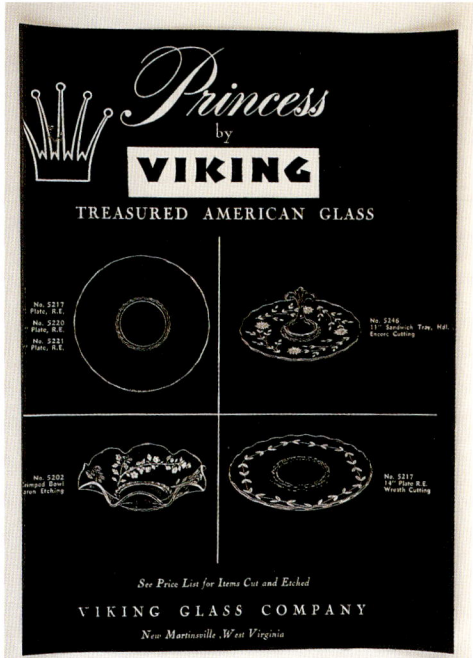

Viking Glass catalog supplement, first page for Princess section, 1950.

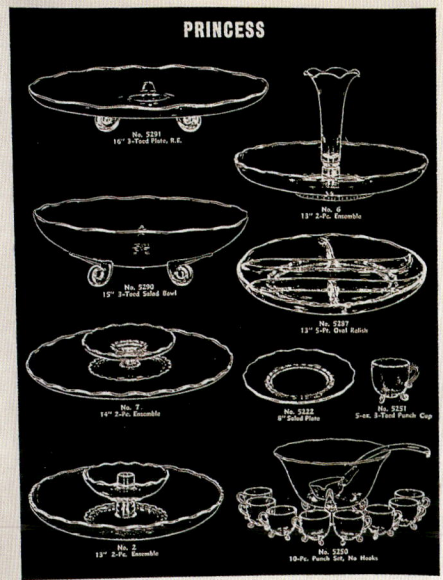

Viking Glass catalog page "Princess," 1956.

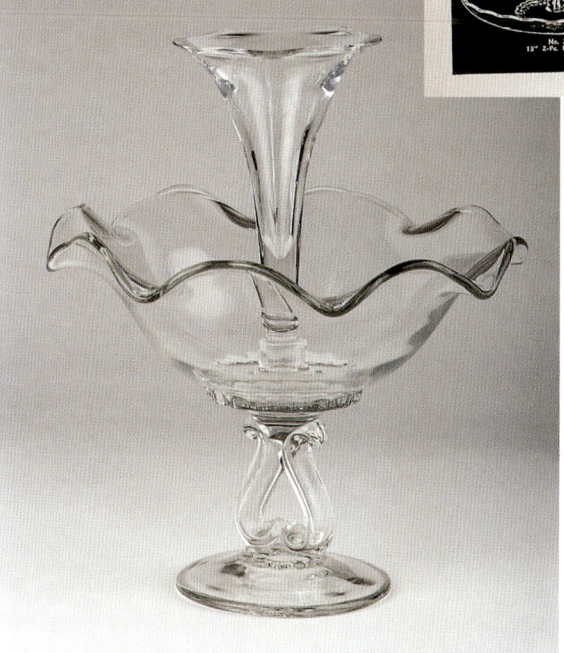

Princess pattern epergne #1084, two part crystal, 11", $48-58.

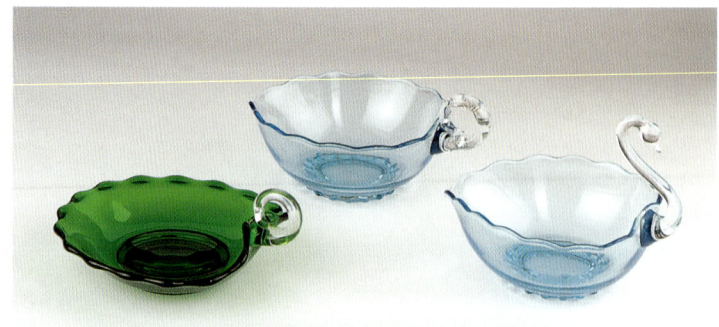

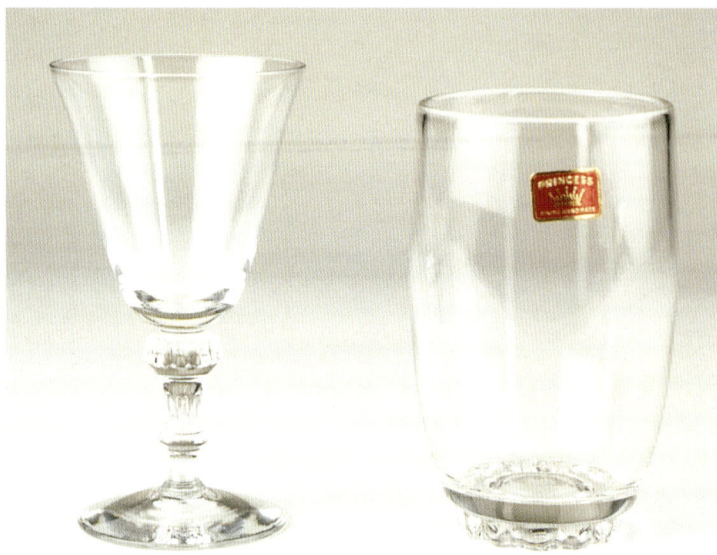

Princess pattern crystal ring handled bowl or nappy, evergreen, $16-26; crystal ring handled "heart shaped bowl" or nappy, colonial blue, $14-22; swan handled "heart shaped bowl" or nappy, colonial blue, $24-38. Note the similarity of edge on all forms, a useful Viking identification clue.

Princess pattern claret, 4 oz., #5200 crystal, $14-18; tumbler, 12 oz., #5261 crystal, $8-16. Both include the distinctive Princess ribbon or "cog" in their design.

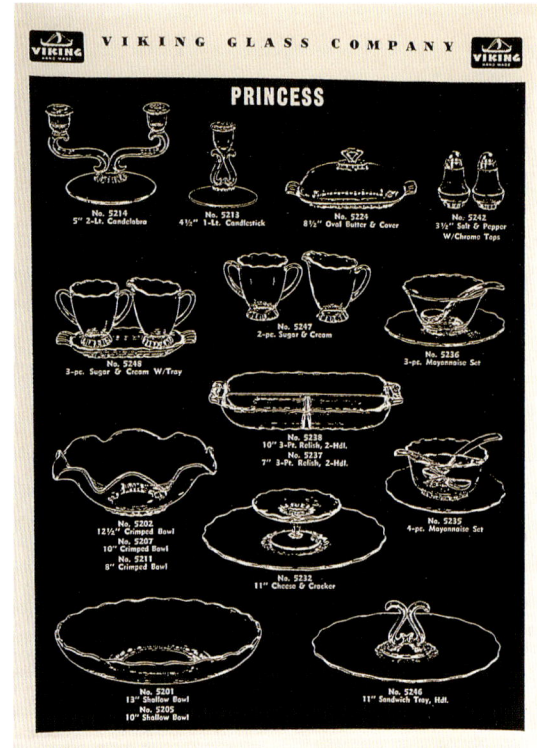

Viking Glass catalog page "Princess," 1956.

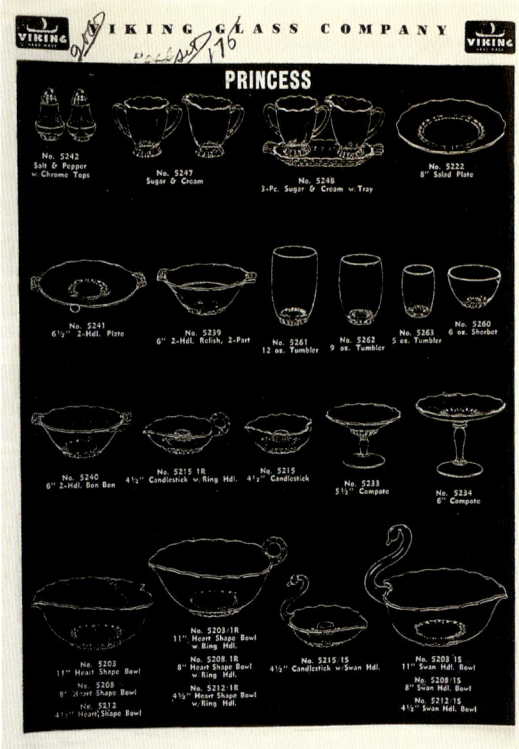

Viking Glass catalog page "Princess," 1948-49. See animal and Janice pattern chapters for related swan handled items.

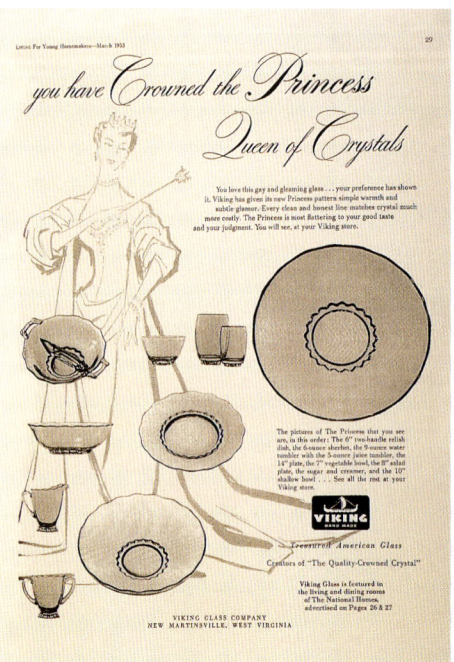

Viking Glass advertisement for "Queen of Crystals," the Princess pattern. *Living For Young Home-makers,* March 1953.

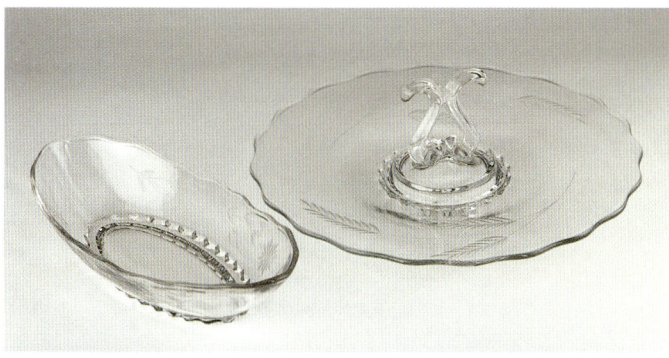

Princess pattern celery tray #5249, 10-1/2" with leaf pattern cutting, $14-18; Princess handled sandwich tray with wheat cutting #5246, 11", $19-24.

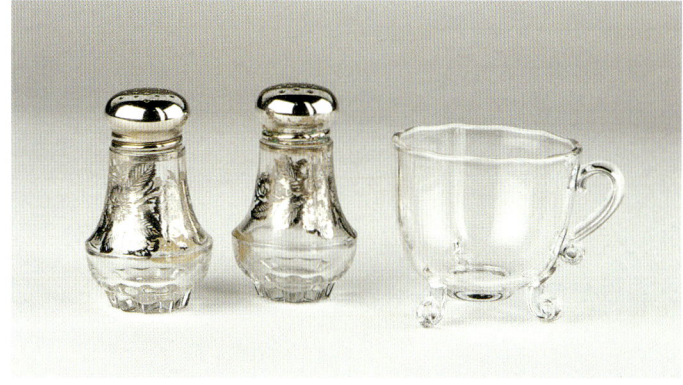

Princess pattern salt and pepper with sterling silver overlay decoration and "Silver City" label #5242, 3-1/2" pair, $18-28; punch cup three toed 5 oz. crystal #5251, $4-8.

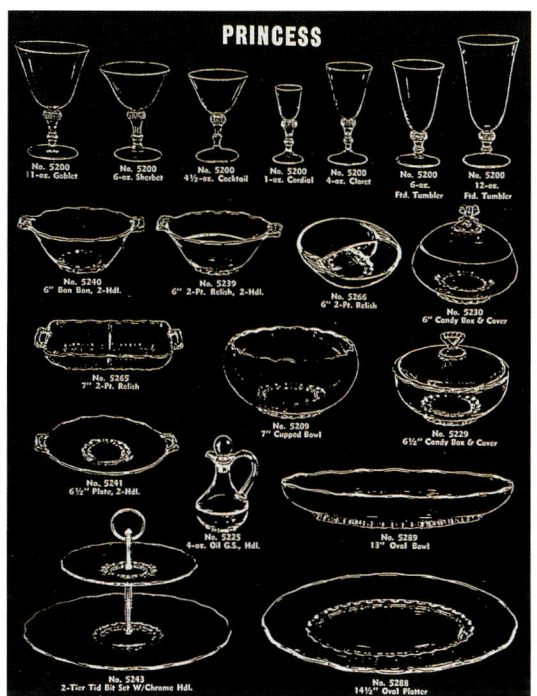

Viking Glass catalog page "Princess," 1956 catalog. The distinctive stemware line is shown here in its entirety.

The undersides of the Princess ruby pieces, showing where the subtle pattern that defines each as a part of the Princess line can be found.

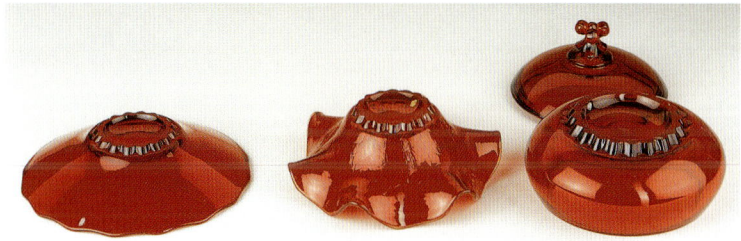

Princess pattern bonbon scalloped rim ruby, $26-36; crackle glass crimped bowl, 8", ruby, $30-40; candy box with lid #5230, 6", $44-58.

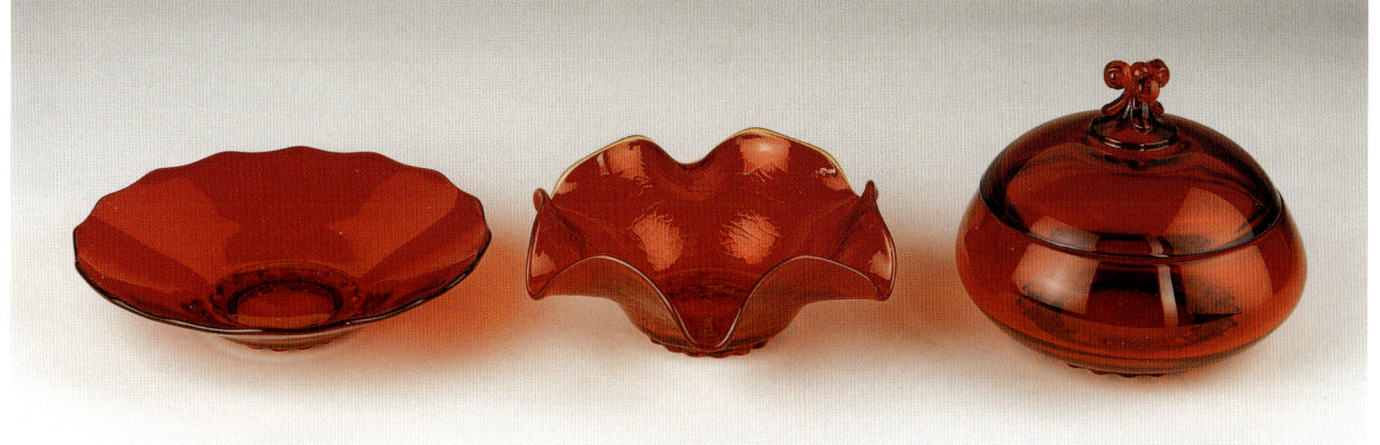

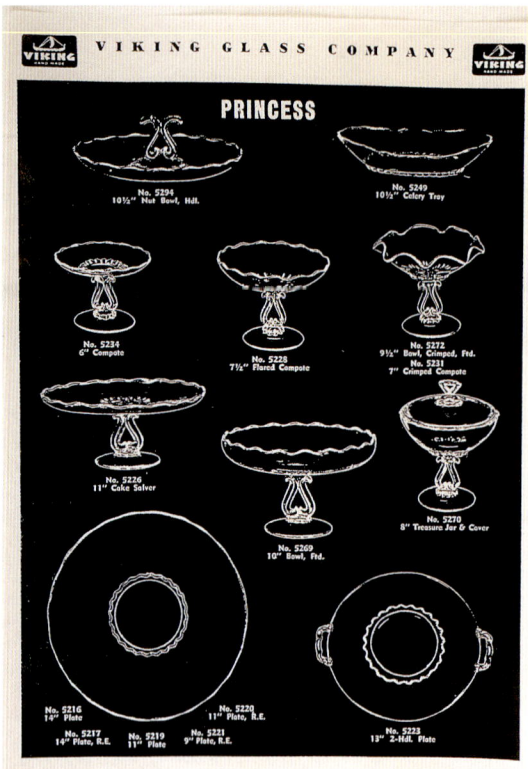

Viking Glass catalog page "Princess," 1956 catalog.

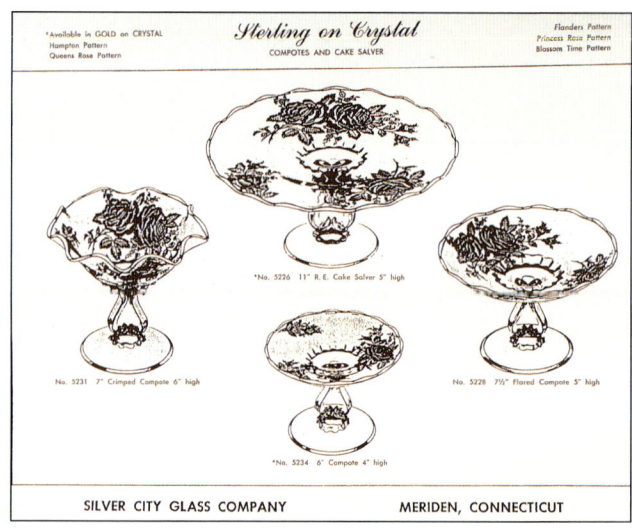

Catalog page from Silver City Glass Co., all pieces shown are Viking Princess blanks.

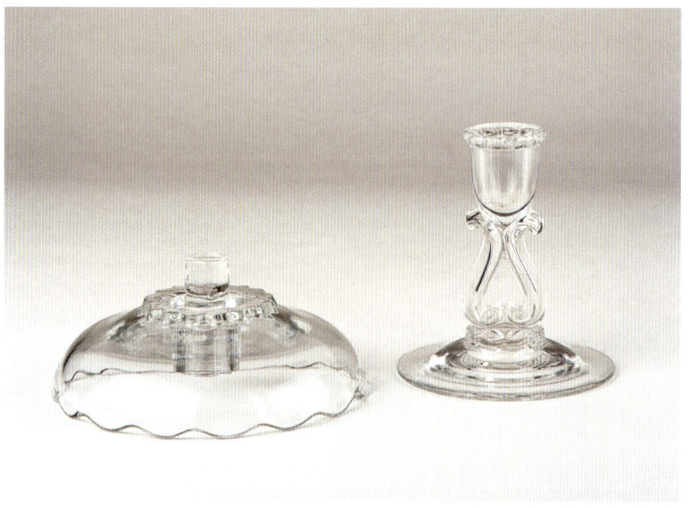

Princess pattern bobeche, shown upside down, and single candlestick, 4-1/2", #5213, $12-18 each.

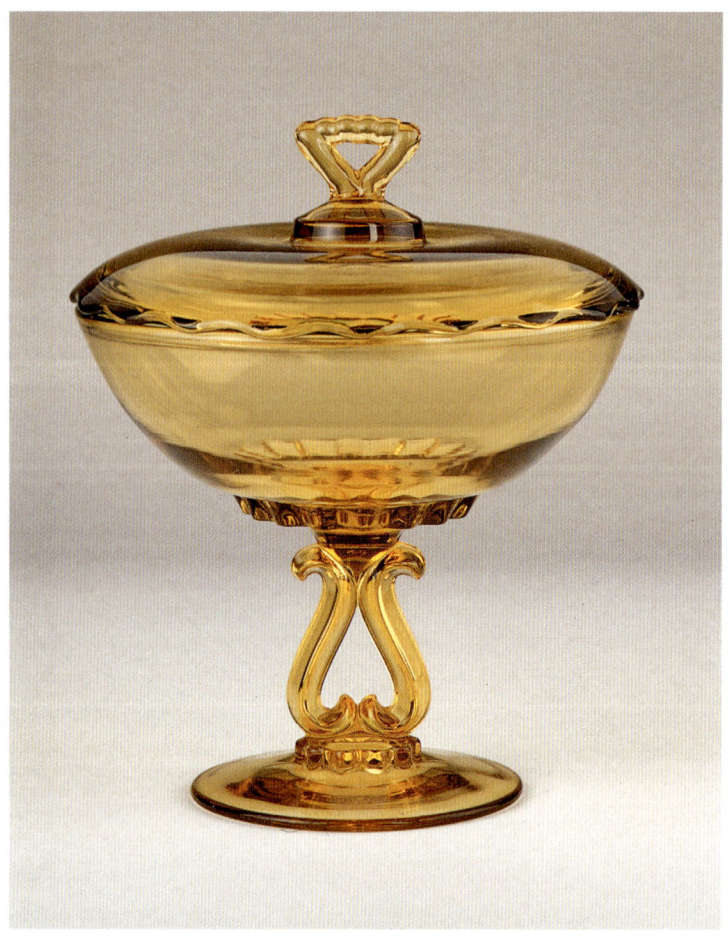

Princess pattern "treasure jar with lid" #5270 amber 8", $30-38.

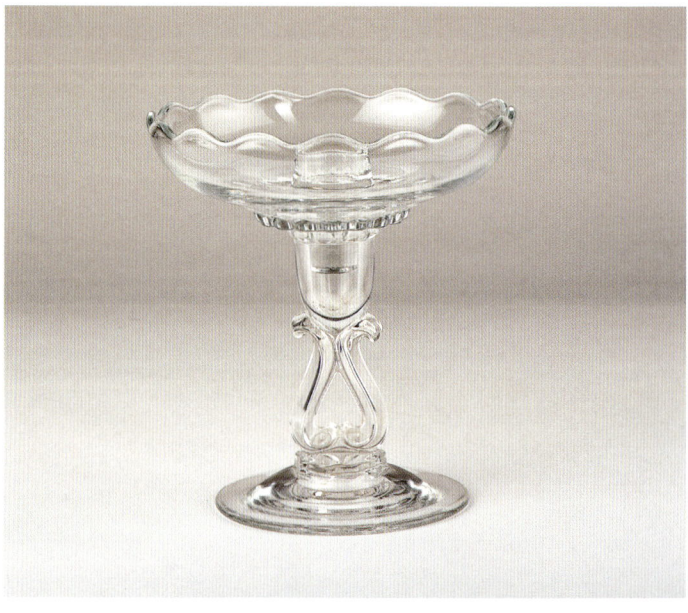

Princess #5213 candlestick with bobeche in place, $24-38.

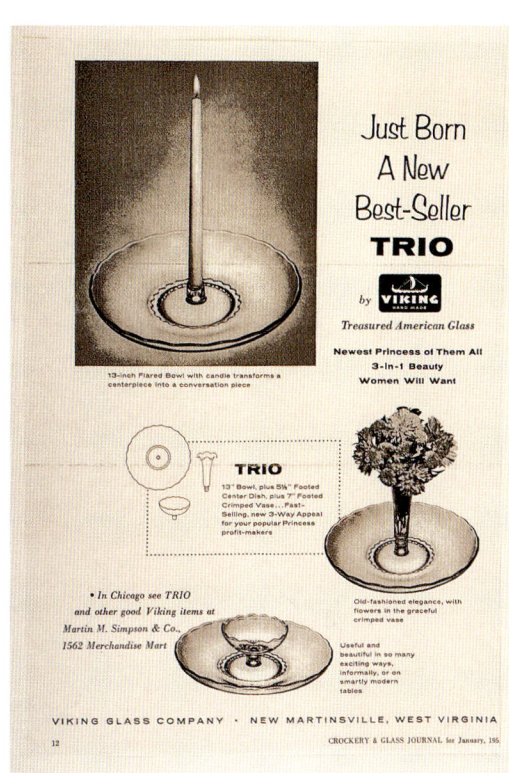

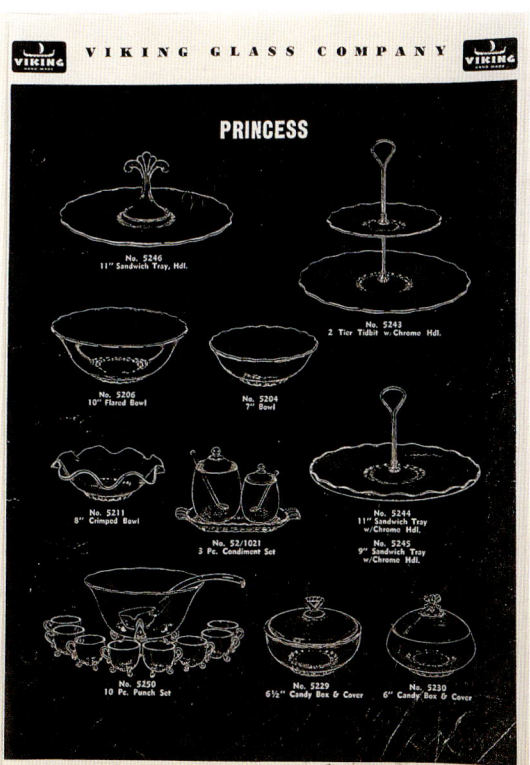

Viking Glass catalog page "Princess," 1950. Note the #5230 candy box shown here in ruby and the three toed punch cups.

Princess pattern "new" three piece Trio. A variation on the then very popular interchangeable piece candle bowl/ flower/serving piece. *Crockery & Glass Journal*, January 1955.

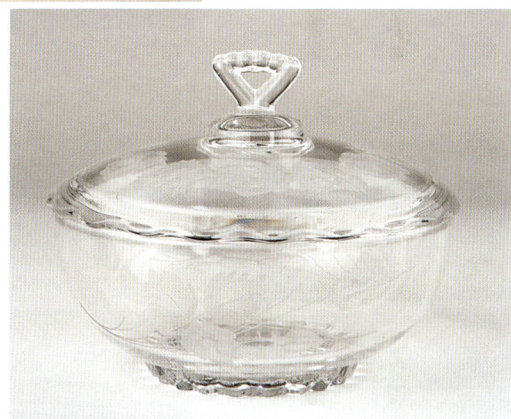

Princess pattern candy with lid #5222, 6-1/2", unidentified hand cutting decoration, $20-34.

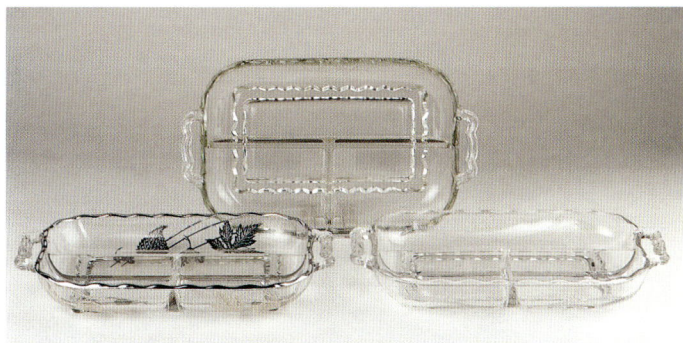

Princess pattern three part relish #5238 with handles, 10". Sterling silver overlay decoration, $14-26; hand cut monogram, $8-16; and unidentified hand cutting, $12-20.

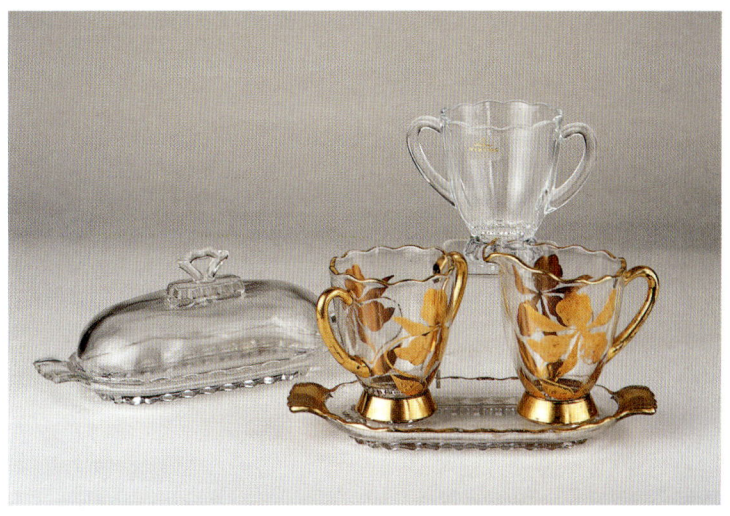

Princess pattern butter with lid #5224, 8-1/2", $19-28; three piece creamer and sugar with tray #5248 with gold floral decoration by Silver City, $18-34 set.

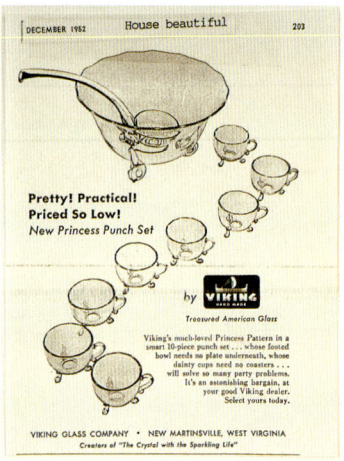

Princess punch bowl advertisement, *House Beautiful*, December 1952.

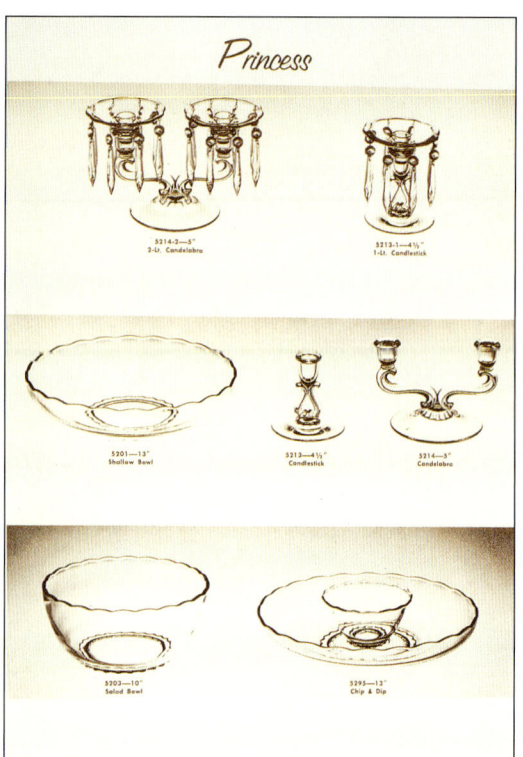

Viking Glass catalog "Princess," 1970, available items in the Princess pattern, as shown in the last catalog during the time period covered in this book.

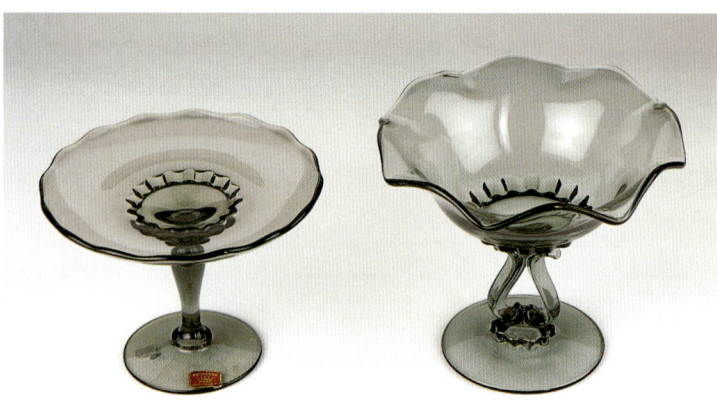

Princess pattern charcoal, footed lemon dish #5234, 6", $22-32; crimped compote #5231, 7", $22-38.

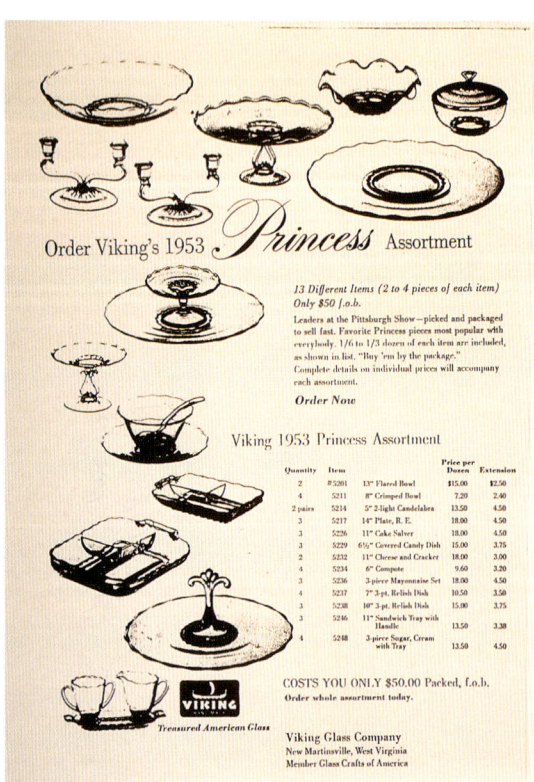

Princess pattern assortment, 1953. *China, Glass & Decorative Accessories*, March 1953.

PRINCESS PLAZA is sometimes known as Princess Square and is similar in form to the better known Princess shape. It includes the ribbon-based design of Princess but adds square ribbon motif feet or bases on most pieces. Princess and Princess Plaza shapes are easily confused and can be attractively interchanged or mixed. Princess Plaza is not included in the January 1953 price list but makes an appearance in the tableware press (*Crockery & Glass*) in February of 1955 where it was shown and indeed called Princess Square. By late 1955 Princess Plaza was being advertised in full-page ads in *House Beautiful*. The 1956 price list features twenty-eight Princess Plaza shapes. Nine new shapes were introduced into the line in 1960, but by the 1962 catalog only fourteen shapes were offered.

It was no longer offered by the 1964 price list, having a production period of less than ten years.

> bowl, 13" shallow #5501
> bowl, 16" shallow #5503
> bowl, 19" shallow #5505
> candlestick, 4-1/2" one light #5513
> candlestick, 4-1/2" one light with bob & 8 prisms #5513-1
> candelabra, 5" two light #5514
> candelabra, 5" two light with 2 bob & 16 prisms #5514-2
> candelabra, 6-1/2" three #5515
> candelabra, 6-1/2" three with 3 bob & 24 prisms #5515-3
> epergne, 6-1/2" with 2 bob, 16 prisms & peg vase #5516
> plate, 14" rolled edge #5517
> plate, 18" rolled edge #5518

plate, 11" rolled edge # 5520
Banana boat, 12" footed #5522
Bowl, round with prisms #5521, 11"
Bowl, footed 11", #5523
Cake salver, 12", #5524
Bowl, footed 12", #5525
Cake salver, 11", #5526
Cake salver, 13", #5527
Compote, flared 7-1/2", #5528
Cheese and cracker, 11", #5532

Cake salver, #5533, 9"
Candy box with lid, #5534, 7"
Compote, flared #5535, 7"
Mayonnaise set, three piece #5536
Salt and pepper, #5542
Sugar and creamer, # 5547
Sugar and creamer, individual #5548
Sugar and creamer, individual with tray #5549
Punch set, fifteen pieces #5550
Punch cup, 5 oz. # 5551

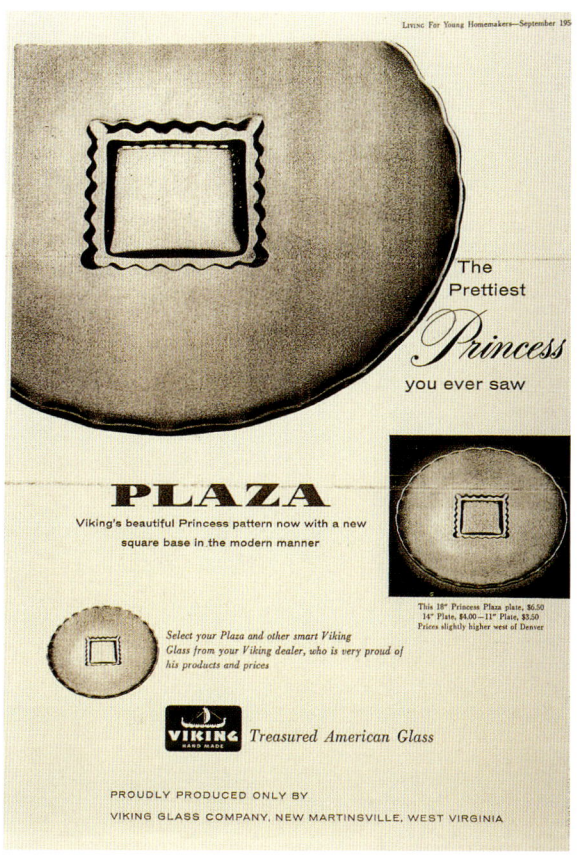

An advertisement for the "new" Princess Plaza. *Living For Young Homemakers*, September 1956.

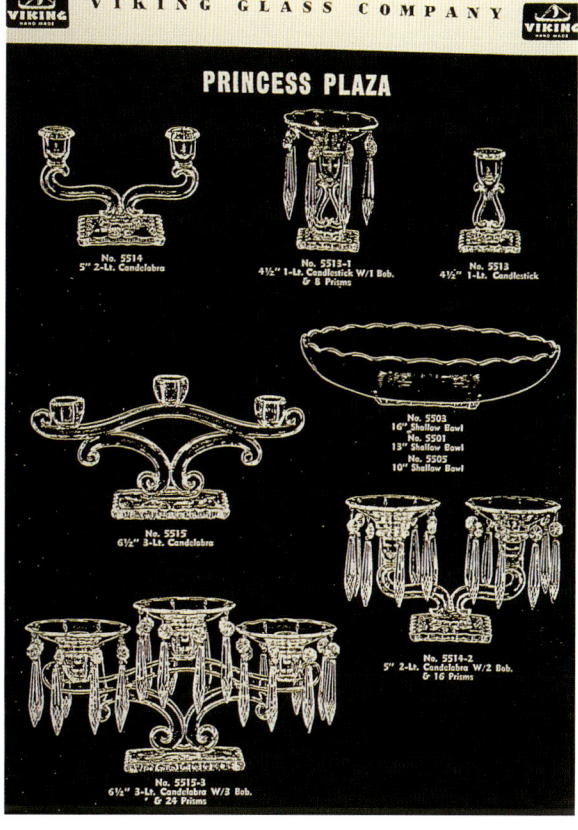

Viking Glass catalog page "Princess Plaza," 1956.

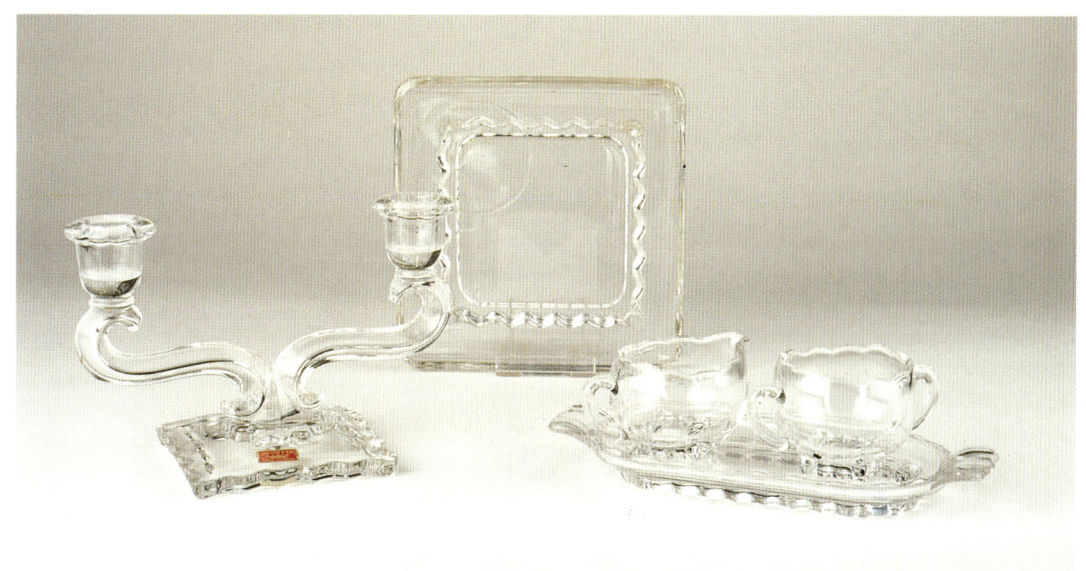

Princess Plaza pattern two light candelabra #5515, 5", $25-38; snack tray with cup indentation, $6-10; individual cream and sugar with tray three piece set, $28-38.

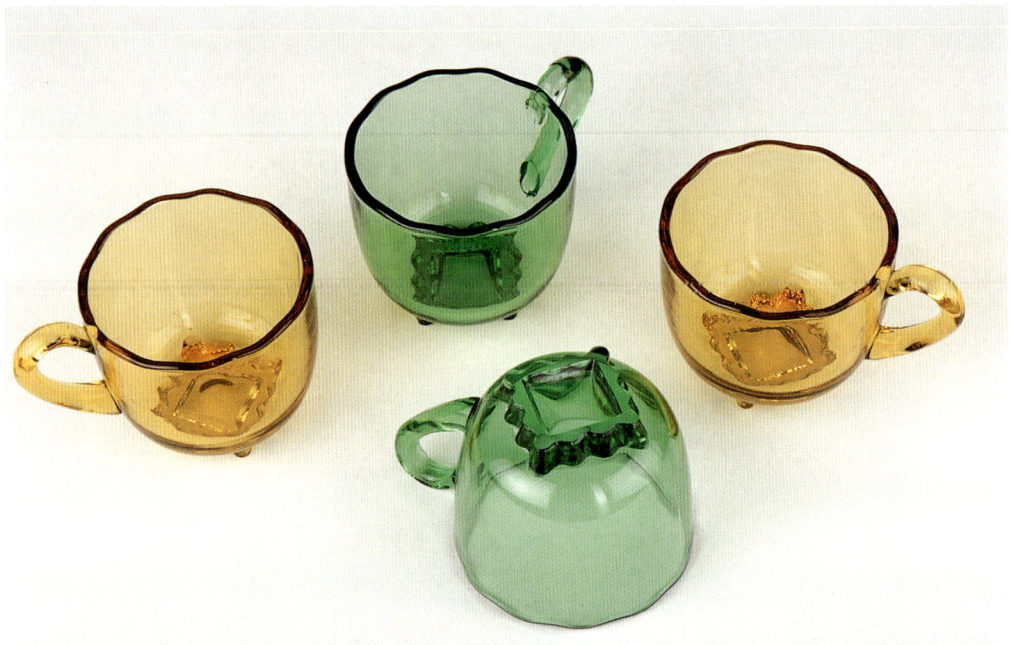

Princess Plaza pattern amber and green punch cups, $8-12 each. Note the square base distinguishes it from the more common Princess line.

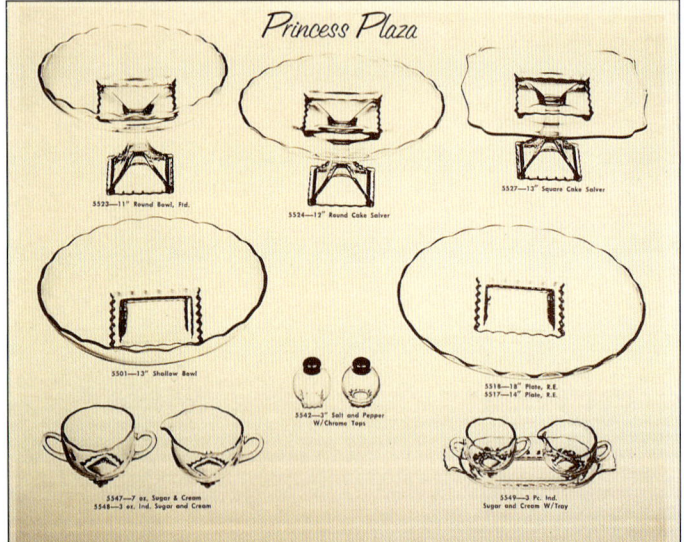

Viking Glass catalog page "Princess Plaza," 1962.

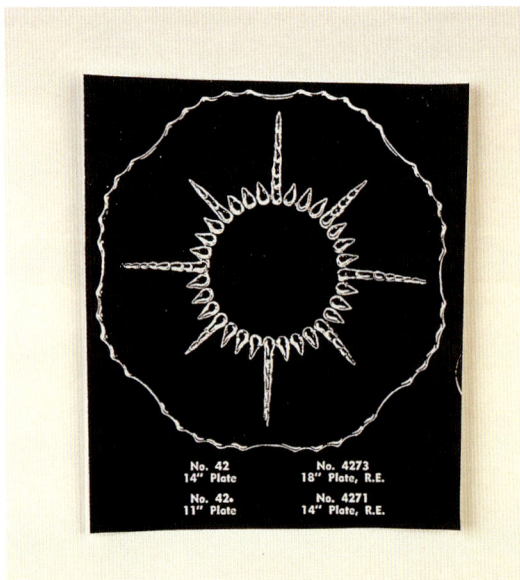

RADIANCE, line #42: We first find Radiance mentioned when *Crockery & Glass Journal* in January of 1937 wrote, "introducing Radiance new, different." This is one of several patterns begun by New Martinsville and continued by Viking after 1944. Radiance has a circle of "pulsating looking ray" on the base of the objects. It was widely used for decoration, particularly acid plate etching.

Radiance was not only continued by Viking but the line was increased during the Viking years. At least sixteen additional Radiance shapes were created by Viking, for a total of over forty Radiance shapes.

While colorless crystal Radiance is the most common Viking Radiance color, it was produced in color before Viking's time, by Viking, and, in limited pieces, until the closing of Dalzell-Viking decades later. Viking produced Radiance in ruby, evergreen, amber, ebony, and crystal. Large punch sets with flared bowls and evergreen or ruby punch bowl under plate and ruby or evergreen handled punch ladles were introduced by Viking, never having been made by New Martinsville Glass. It is safe to assume that Viking, due to length of production and increased piece types, made far more Radiance in color and crystal than did New Martinsville Glass. New Martinsville's Radiance production spanned eight years, a portion of which were the years when New Martinsville was in financial Receivership and the "crystal only years" of World War II. Radiance by Viking is likely that which is most often found.

Viking Glass catalog illustration for a large plate that well illustrates the design elements of Radiance patterned pieces.

Bonbon, footed #34248, 6": 1948, in line in 1953, and gone by 1956

Bowl, ball or 5 qt. punch #4221, 9": 1945

(Ebony and evergreen in 1950 and 1953) gone by 1956

Bowl, flared #42, 10": 1945, in line in 1951, and gone by 1956

Bowl, flared #4265, 11": 1945

Bowl, flared #4211 crimped 12-1/2": 1945 (evergreen 1953). In line 1962 and 1968

Bowl, flared #4213, 13": 1945, in line in 1951 and gone by 1956

Bowl, flared #4272, 13-1/2": 1948 (Viking creation) gone by 1956

Bowl, flower footed #4279, 6": 1953 (Viking creation, evergreen in 1953)

Bowl, flower footed #4280, 9": 1953 (Viking creation, evergreen in 1953)

Bowl, nut handled #42, 10-1/2": 1953

(Old New Martinsville shape reintroduced for Prelude etching in 1953)

Butter with lid, #42, 6": 1948, in line 1962

Cake salver, #4274, 11": 1951 (Viking creation) gone by 1956

Candy box with lid, three part #42, 7": 1945, in line in 1953 and gone by 1956

Candy box with lid, #4289: 1953 (Viking creation, amber, evergreen, and ruby)

Candy box with lid, #4287: 1956 (Viking creation) in line 1962

Celery, oval, #42, 10": 1945, gone by 1956

Cheese and cracker, #42, 11": 1945, in line in 1953, and gone by 1956

Compote, #4720, 7": 1948 (Viking creation, evergreen in 1953) gone by 1956

Cup, punch handled, 5 oz., #4278: 1951 (Viking creation)

Lazy Susan, three piece includes 18" torte plate #4273: 1962 (Viking creation)

Mayonnaise set, three pieces #42: 1945, in line in 1953, and gone by 1956

Plate, #42, 11": 1945

Plate, #42, 14": 1945

Plate, rolled edge #4721, 14": 1948 (Viking creation, evergreen in 1953)

Plate, rolled edge #4273, 18": 1951 (Viking creation, evergreen in 1953)

Plate, #42, 18": 1953

(Old New Martinsville shape reintroduced for Prelude etching in 1953)

Punch set, fifteen pieces #4275: 1951

Punch set, fifteen piece, no plate #4276: 1956

Punch set, Deluxe (with chrome lazy susan) #4275-1/2 : 1951

Punch set, eleven piece #4288: 1953 (Viking creation, evergreen base & ladle)

Punch set, eleven piece #4285: 1956 (Viking creation)

Relish, three part #4226, 7": 1948, gone by 1951

Relish, three part #4255, 7": 1948, in line in 1953, and gone by 1956

Relish, two part #4222, 7-1/2": 1945

Relish, two part #4223, 8-1/2": 1945, gone by 1948, and did not return to line

Salt and pepper, #42, 3": gone by 1951

Sandwich tray, handled #42, 11": 1953

(Old New Martinsville shape, reintroduced for Prelude etching in 1953)

Sugar, cream (four toed) and tray, #42: 1945, in line in 1962, and 1970 without tray

Tidbit set, four piece, three tier revolving #4281: 1956 (Viking creation)

Tray for sugar and cream, #42: 1945, gone by 1948, and did not return to line

Vase, flared #42, 10": 1945, in line in 1953, and gone by 1956

Vase, flared, eight crimp #4243, 10": 1945

Vase, flared #42, 12": 1945

Vase, eight crimp #4230, 12": 1945

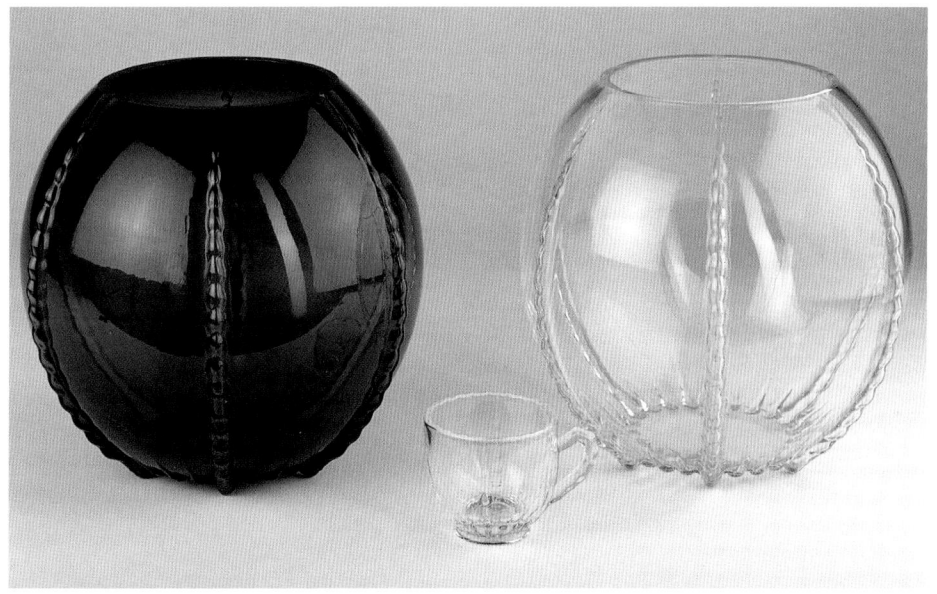

Radiance pattern ball vase or punch bowl #42, 9" evergreen, $68-88 and crystal, $48-58, with punch crystal cup, $4-9 each.

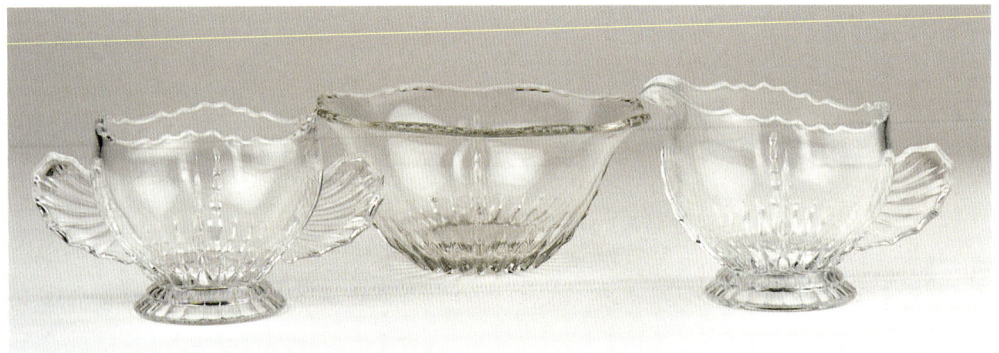

Radiance pattern #42 creamer and sugar, crystal, $8-16 each; mayonnaise bowl, crystal, $8-14.

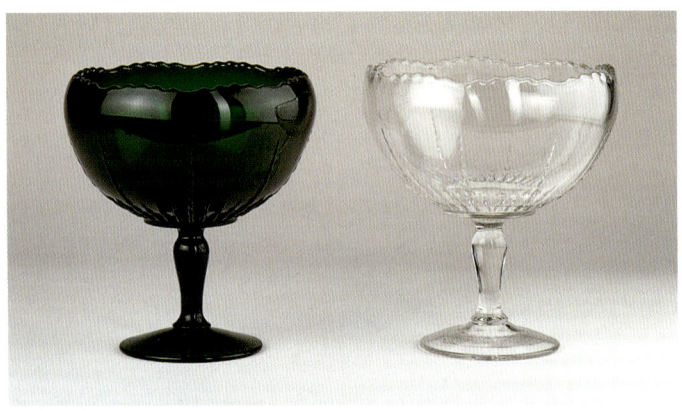

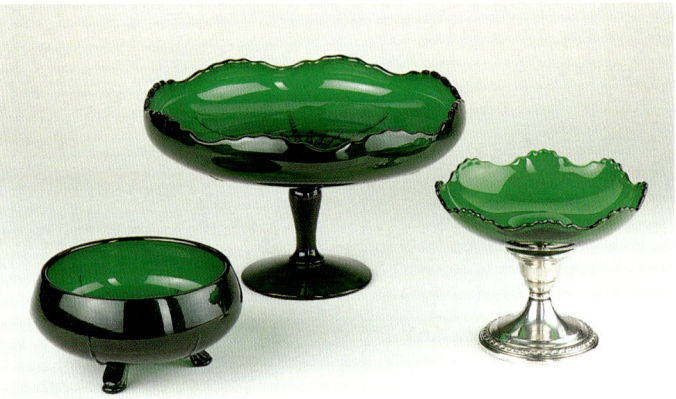

Radiance pattern candy box with lid, missing lid #4289 evergreen, $12-26 as shown; compote "flower bowl" 6" tall evergreen, $48-64; bowl with sterling base (marketed by a silver company) evergreen, $30-45.

Radiance pattern compote or "flower bowl" in catalogs, #4280, 9" tall evergreen, $48-68; crystal, $18-28. Shown on the 1953 price list.

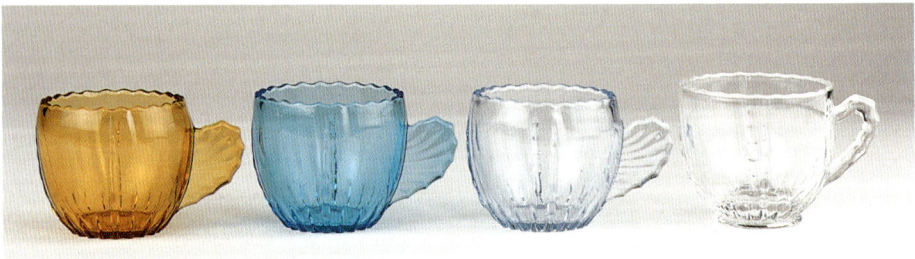

Radiance pattern punch cups, 5 oz., #4278, amber, $4-6; sky blue, $8-14; colonial blue, $8-12; and crystal, $4-6 each. Note the solid handles and the later, redesigned open handles.

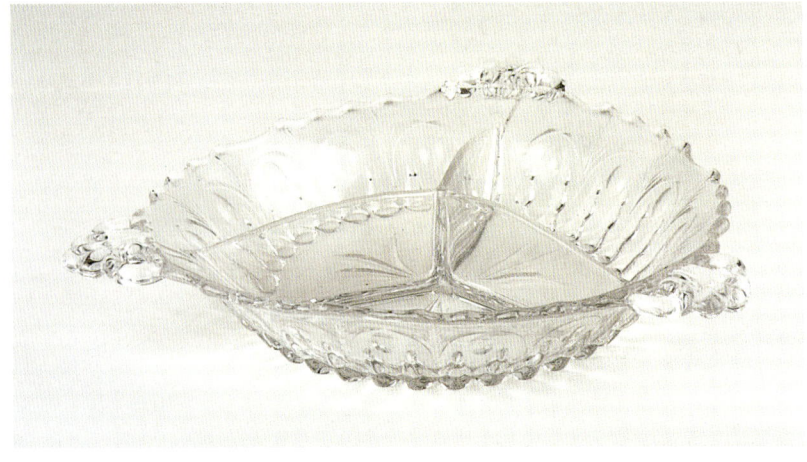

Radiance pattern three part relish #4255 with unknown hand cutting, 7", $14-24.

SCROLL Line #1900 was first found in a September 1954 *Crockery & Glass Journal* ad as an oval double flowerlite candle/floral bowl. Then it appears in *Crockery & Glass Journal*, December 1955 with the note, "Viking Glass ... is planning to add a number of new items to its Scroll line. Illustrated in this 1955 promotional was a "new Oval Scroll" mayonnaise bowl with ladle. It was available in crystal, amber, green, and amethyst. An ad in the magazine *Living For Young Homemakers* in 1955 illustrates the Scroll console set with the illusive scroll candlestick and notes they were available in the "new satin finish." The Viking 1956 price list has an offering of ten Scroll shapes. In 1956 Scroll was available "plain or crackled" and in nine "colors," four of which are satin. The authors have yet to see crackled pieces of Scroll. Pieces produced in Scroll include:

        Bowl, oval #1957, 10"
        Bowl, oval #1958, 11"
        Bowl, oval #1970, 6-1/2"
        Bowl, oval #1975, 6"
        Bowl, oval #1974, 5"
        Plate, oval #1951
        Bowl, two handled, oval #1973, 7"
        Cream and sugar, oval #1972
        Candlestick, oval #1976, 2"
        Gravy boat, #1978, 6"
        Flowerlite, double #1048, 6-1/2"

In 1962 the #1049 candy from the Scroll line was reintroduced. Actually, this was the same item number, and perhaps the same mold, but it was dramatically reworked. The new piece #1049 was indeed oval in shape, but it had no foot (thus no Scroll) and candleholders had been added at both ends of the bowl. It was offered with and without the oval flower frog from the #1048 bowl and frog set. The #1048 also reentered the line in 1962. No later or additional Scroll use was found.

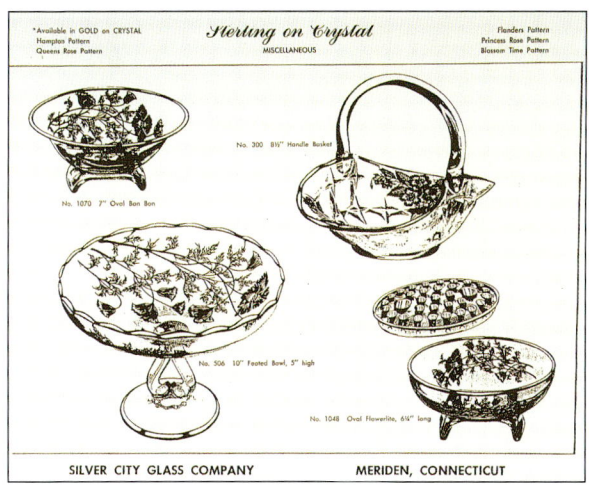

Silver City Glass Co. catalog page showing the use of a #1057 Scroll oval bowl for their silver decoration "Flanders." Undated catalog, circa 1960.

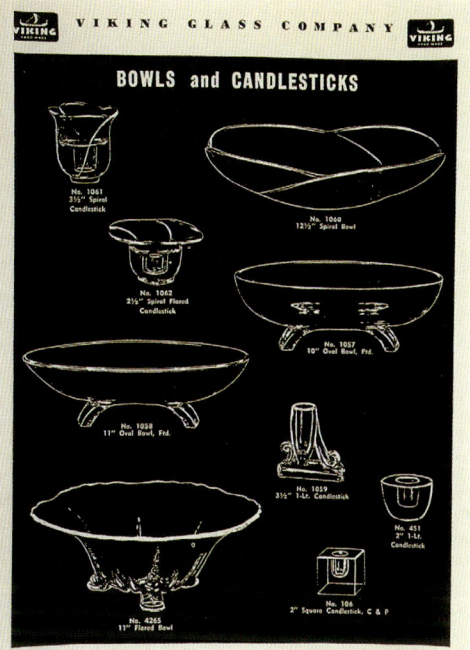

Viking bowls and candlesticks page from the 1956 catalog. Note: one light scroll #1059 candlestick.

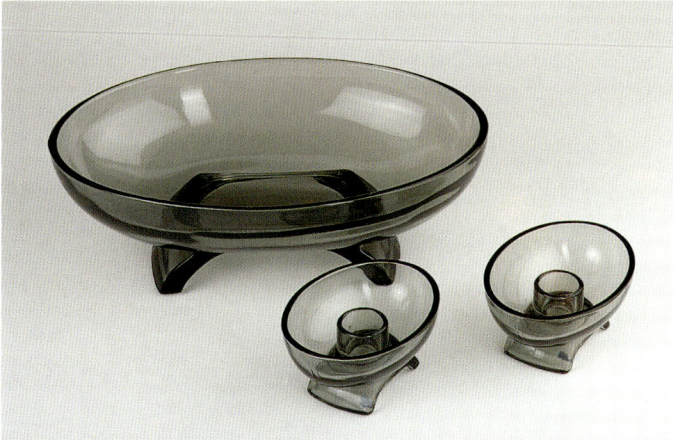

Scroll pattern charcoal oval footed bowl #1057, 10", $22-32; candlesticks, 2", $20-28 each.

Advertisement for a three piece console set in the Scroll pattern. Noted as made in crystal, amber, emerald, and cherry glo. *House and Garden*, November 1955. *Image compliments of Tom Felt.* Note the forms shown: an open, single scroll candlestick and the other candlestick in a bowl form with two scroll foot, both Scroll pattern sticks.

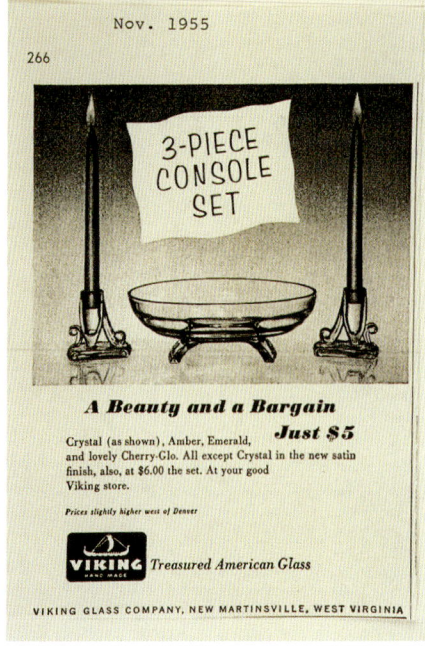

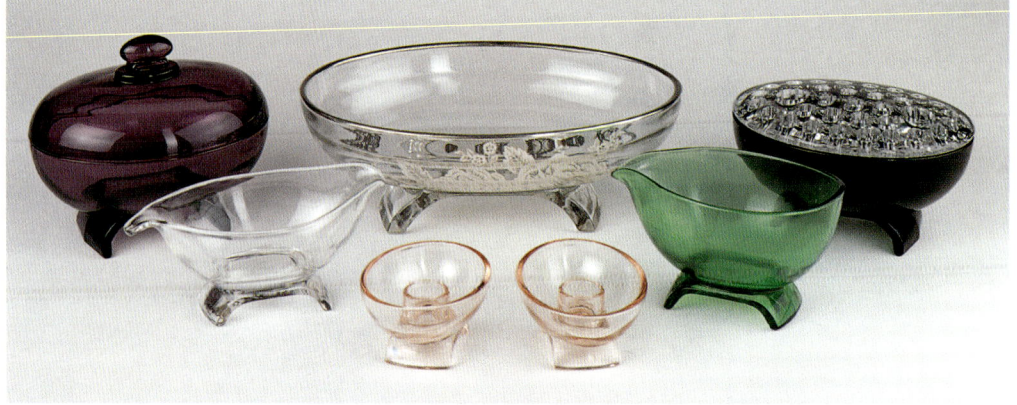

Scroll pattern oval candy box with lid #1049 amethyst, 6-1/2", $28-38; creamer #1072 crystal, $12-16; candlestick #1067 cherry glo, $20-28 each; oval bowl #1057 crystal with silver decoration, $18-28; gravy boat, 6", #1078 green, $18-28; ebony double flowerlite with crystal frog #1048, 6-1/2" (see Flower bowl chapter for various color pricing).

TEARDROP, Line #4400 is a pattern begun by New Martinsville Glass in the early 1940s. It was continued by Viking in 1944 and produced for some years after that. It appears on the 1945 Viking price list. Called only #4400 by company literature, in visual elements it resembles New Martinsville's Radiance in many ways. However, Teardrop/Line 4400s rays are solid, tapering, and thus teardrop-like. Radiance rays are interrupted and repeating.

Much of the teardrop pattern found has been acid etched to impart a surface pattern or decoration. The predominant etchings found on Teardrop shapes are Prelude and etching #29.

By early 1953 only four pieces of Teardrop remained on the price list: #4457, 5" two light candelabra; #44, 7-1/2" candy box with lid; #44 two handled 12" plate; and #44, 11" salver. The candelabra alone remained in the Viking line by 1956 and it remained through 1970. The pieces made over time in this line by Viking include:

> Bowl, cupped salad #4463, 11"
> Bowl, cupped three toed #4460, 12"
> Bowl, handled nut #44, 10-1/2"
> Bowl, flared #44, 10"
> Bowl, flared #4454, 12"
> Bowl, flared #4456, 13"
> Bowl, flared three toed #4459, 12"
> Cake salver, #44, 11"
> Candelabra, two light #4457, 5"

> Candy box, three part with lid #44, 7-1/2"
> Cheese and cracker, #44, 11"
> Mayonnaise set, three piece #44
> Plate, #44, 11"
> Plate, torte #44, 14"
> Plate, two handled #4462, 11"
> Plate, footed, rolled edge #4461, 13"
> Plate, flat #4464, 13"
> Sandwich server, center handled #44, 11"
> Sugar, creamer and tray, three pieces #44

THREE FOILS is one of several shapes with the Epic line. It was referred to as Three Foils in a *China, Glass and Tableware* ad of February 1957. Only two pieces of this shape survived to the 1962 catalog and none remain in the line by 1964.

> Bowl, #1201, 11"
> Bowl, #1202, 11"
> Vase, #1203, 10"
> Vase, #1204, 12"
> Bowl, #1211, 13"
> Bowl, #1212, 12"
> Vase, #1213, 13"
> Vase, #1214, 13"
> Vase, #1215, 22"
> Vase, #1216, 6-1/2"
> Rose bowl, #1217, 6-1/2"

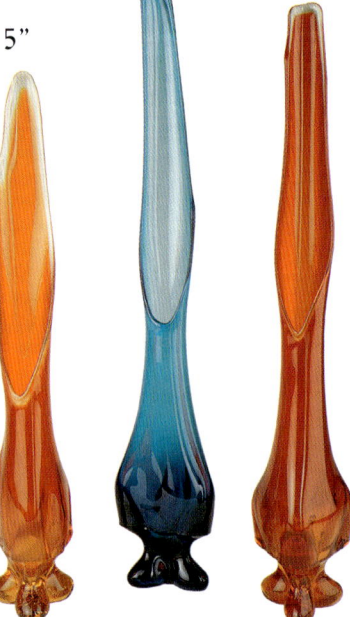

Epic Three Foil swung vases #1220, 19"-22", persimmon, $24-36; bluenique, $20-32. Featured in *House Beautiful*, October 1958.

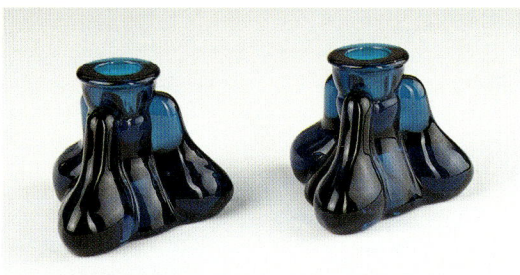

Epic Three Foil #1210 candlesticks 3-1/2" tall, bluenique, $24-34 each. Shown in the 1963 Viking Glass catalog supplement.

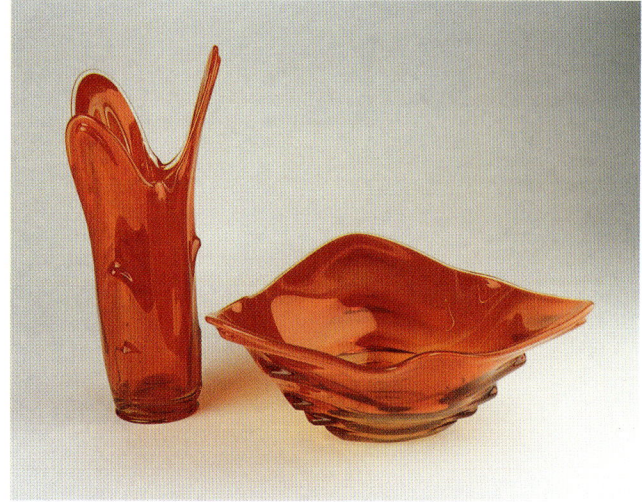

Tundra pattern vases, flared #6654, 10", persimmon, $30-42; bowl flared #6653, 12-1/2", persimmon, $45-58.

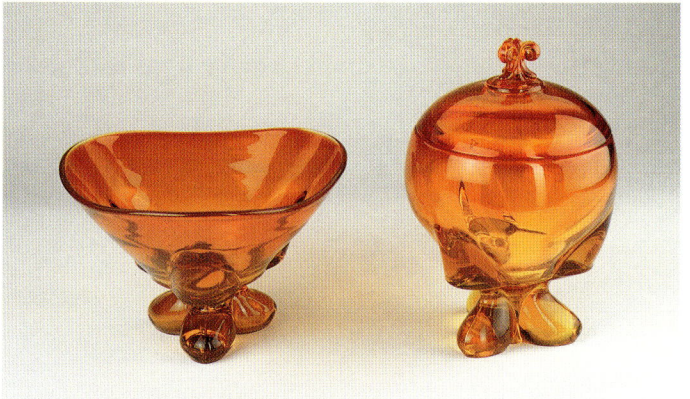

Epic Three Foil #1209 flared bowl, persimmon, $28-34; #12207 candy bow with cover, 6", persimmon, $30-40. Note that both are created from the identical mold.

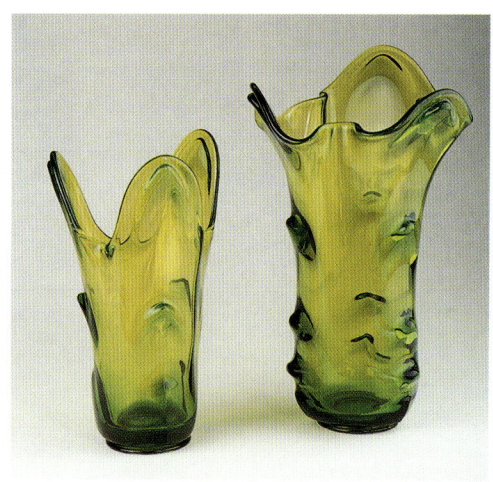

Tundra pattern vases, flared #6651 avocado 7-1/2", $22-34; swung vase, 13", avocado, $28-42.

TUNDRA was a "new" line when mentioned in the December 1966 *China, Glass & Tableware*. It is found only in vases and bowls. With striking tongues of glass accenting the exterior of Tundra forms, it is a strikingly handcrafted and modern line. Factory employees reported it did not sell particularly well. Found in the 1967 catalog are these Tundra pieces in avocado, bluenique, honey, and persimmon:

- Bowl, #6650, 9"
- Vase, #6651, 7-1/2"
- Vase, tall, #6652, 13"
- Bowl, #6653, 12-1/2"
- Vase, flared, #6654, 10"
- Vase, tall, #6655

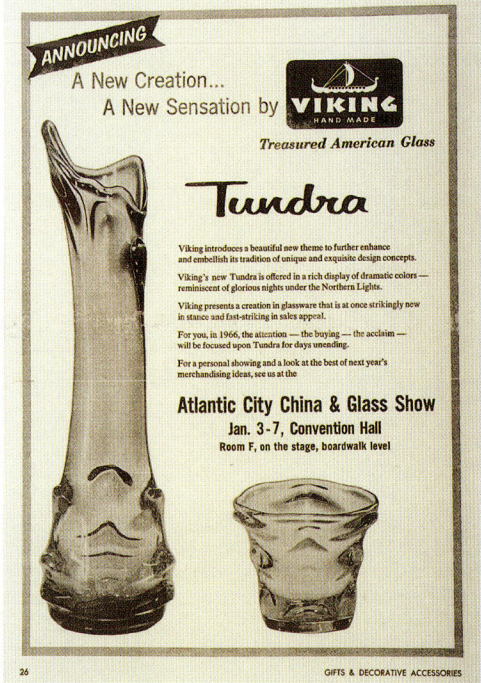

"Announcing A New Creation … A New Sensation by Viking. Tundra." Advertisement in *Gifts & Decorative Accessories*, 1965.

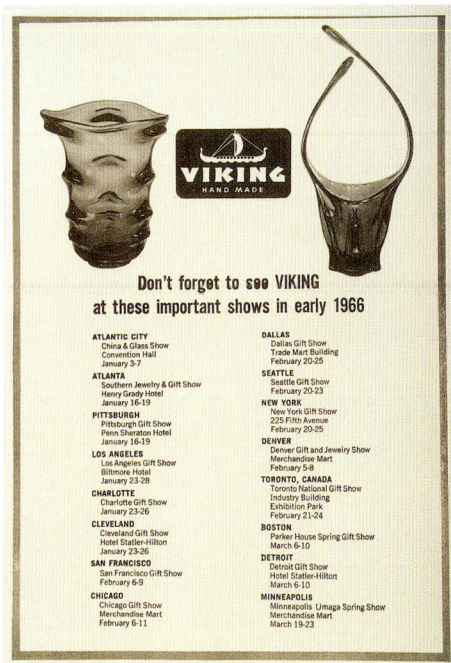

Advertisement for a 1966 trade shows with Viking featuring Tundra as one of the two patterns. *China, Glass & Tablewares,* January 1966.

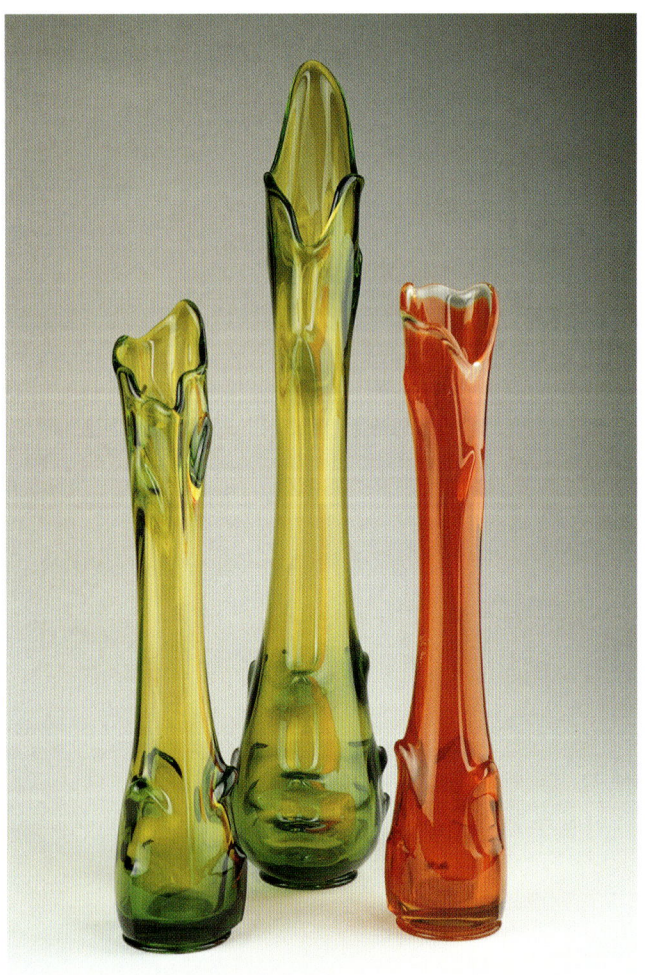

Tundra line vases. Swung vase #6652 avocado 13", $22-32; "tall" #6655 avocado 23", $32-46; swung vase #6652 persimmon 13", $28-38.

Viking Classics

This grouping is an eclectic list of some very plain, predominantly "round" shapes with no visible pattern. They were used largely for cutting and etching, as well as for gold and silver decorating by others. The 1962 catalog titled this ware "Round Dinnerware." Its validity as a group of shapes or patterns was confirmed when Dalzell/Viking made a line called "Formal Classics" in crystal, cobalt, ruby, black, and evergreen using many of these very same, long dependable molds. With simple gold bands it was a high market item. This list includes some of the forms used later to constitute this classic dinnerware and it includes a number of similar and related forms used only in earlier periods and largely for decorating.

Manufacturing objects for others in the trade to decorate was a large part of the Viking business for many years. Here are some, only some, of these classic and often round shapes gleaned from the literature:

Bowl, nappy #172, 3-1/2" (ca. 1948-1950)
Bowl, nappy #173, 4-1/2" (ca. 1948-1950)
Bowl, nappy #17, 4-3/4" (ca. 1948-1950)
Bowl, eight crimps #480, 5-1/2" (ca. 1945-1950)
Bowl, fruit, #954, 4-1/4" (ca. 1948-1955)
Bowl, soup #955, 6-1/2" (ca. 1948-1955)
Bowl, round #426, 8" (ca. 1948-1950)
Bowl, bulb #778, 4" (ca. 1945-1955)
Bowl, round #439, 9" (ca. 1948-1950)
Bowl, round salad #787, 10", Sonata etch (ca. 1948-1955)
Bowl, round #449, 10-1/2", Rock crystal engraved (ca. 1945-1950)
Bowl, two handled #973, 10-1/2" (ca. 1948-1955)
Bowl, shallow #484 72, 3-1/2" (ca. 1945-1950)
Bowl, eight crimps #482, 12" (ca. 1945-1955)
Bowl, rolled edge #493, 12" (ca. 1945-1955)
Bowl, shallow round #702, 12-1/2" (ca. 1945-1948)
Bowl, shallow round #703, 12-1/2" (ca. 1945-1948)
Bowl, with Marie, eight crimps #707, 12-1/2", pansy cut (ca. 1945-1955)
Bowl, shallow #784, 12-1/2", Sonata (ca. 1948-1955)
Bowl, #455, 14" (ca. 1948-1955)
Bowl, shallow #783, 15" (ca. 1948-1955)
Butter with lid, oval #957, 6-1/2" Prelude and Sonata (ca 1948-1961)
Coaster or ashtray, #414, 3" (ca. 1945-1955)
Cup and saucer, #797 Round Dinnerware list 1962 (ca. 1948-1970)
Cup and saucer, after dinner #798 (ca. 1948-1955)
Egg cup, double #779, 4" (ca. 1948-1962)
Jar, horseradish with ground stopper, 5 oz., #403 (ca. 1955-1970)
Plate, crescent bone #490, 5-1/2" (ca. 1945-1950) later used by Dalzell-Viking
Plate, crescent salad #1093, 7-1/2" (ca.1955-1970)

Plate, bread and butter #791, 6" Prelude (1948-1962)

Plate, salad #976, 7" Prelude (1950-1970)

Plate, salad # 790, 8" Prelude, ruby in 1970 (ca. 1948-1970)

Plate, dinner #796, 10-1/2" Prelude, ruby in 1970 (ca. 1948-1970)

Plate, round #450, 13" Rock Crystal engravings (ca. 1945-1950)

Plate, two handled #972 (ca. 1948-1955)

Plate, torte #785, 14" Sonata (ca. 1948-1955)

Plate, torte #781, 16" (ca. 1948-1955)

Plate, rolled edge torte #782, 16" (ca. 1948-1955)

YESTERYEAR is a term at Viking that causes confusion. It was introduced in March 1957 (*China, Glass and Tableware*) and, like Epic, was a marketing line of diverse shapes. Epic was the modern and abstract form against which the traditional pressed and historic shapes of Yesteryear were contrasted. With these two lines Viking was attempting to target two distinct audiences, contemporary and traditional. Originally the Yesteryear line was composed largely of old molds reintroduced. With time, new pieces and even entire patterns were created to fit in the Yesteryear line. There are no firmly set or similar shapes, patterns, or piece types in the original Yesteryear line.

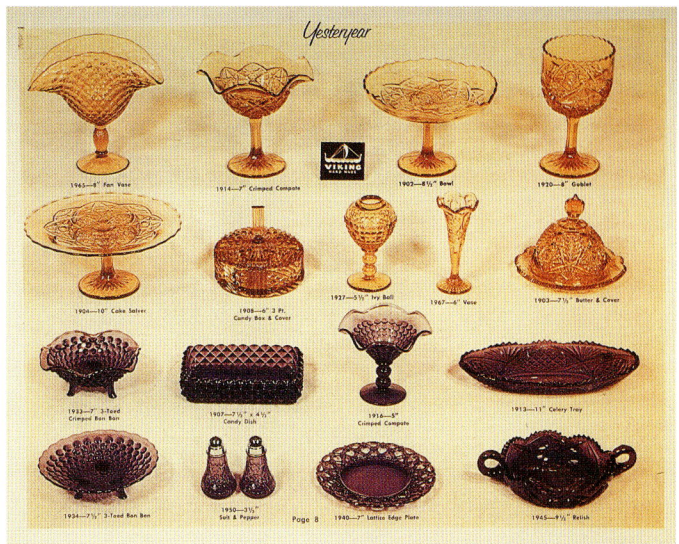

Viking Glass catalog page "Yesteryear," 1960. Amber and amethyst.

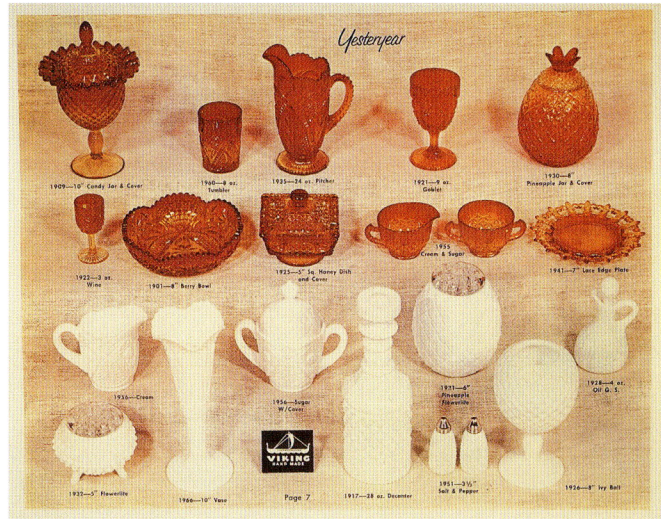

Viking Glass catalog page "Yesteryear," 1960. Amberina and milk glass.

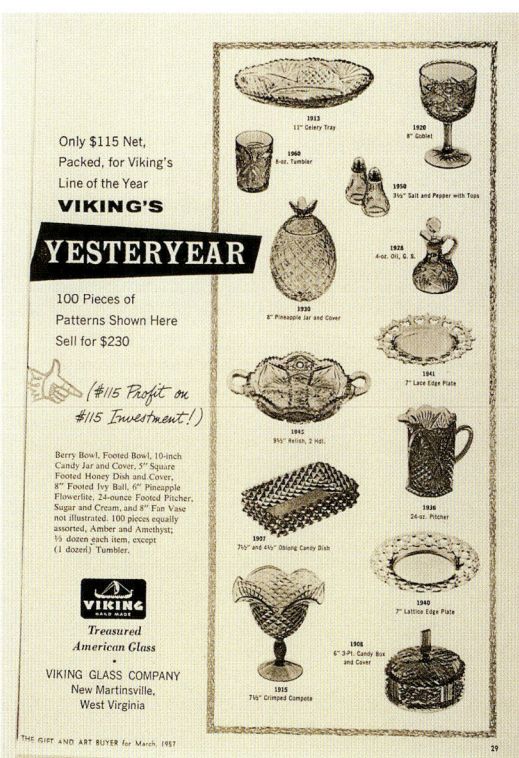

One of several advertisements, many being two full pages, for Viking's Yesteryear line. *The Gift & Art Buyer*, March 1957.

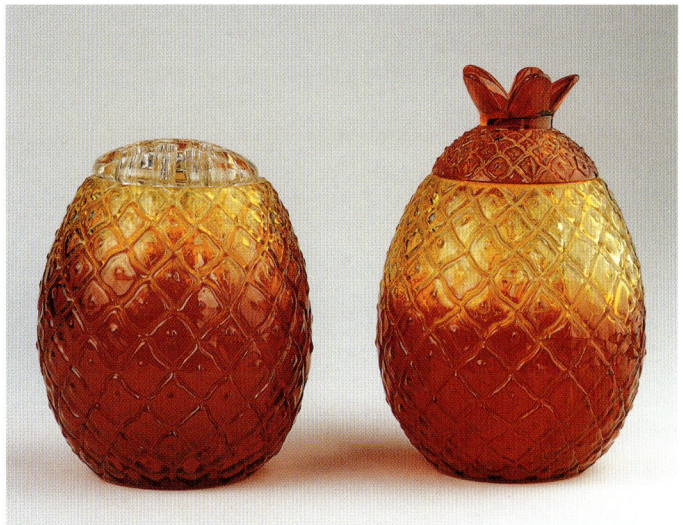

Yesteryear line pineapple amberina with crystal flower frog, $55-68; pineapple jar with lid, #1930 amberina, $52-68.

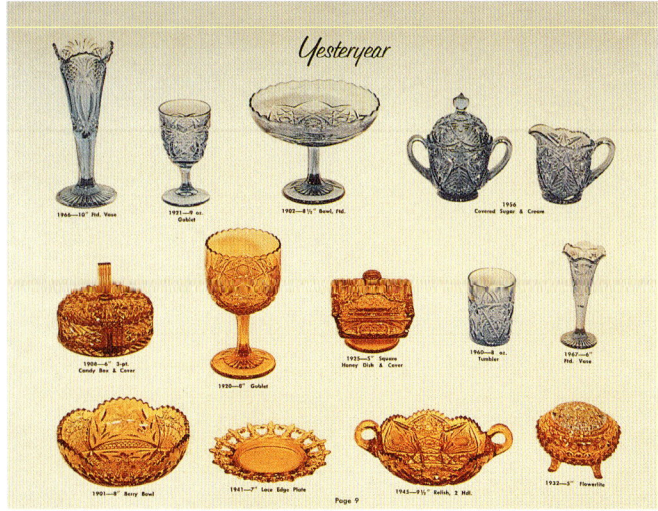

Viking Glass catalog page "Yesteryear," 1962. Colonial blue and amber.

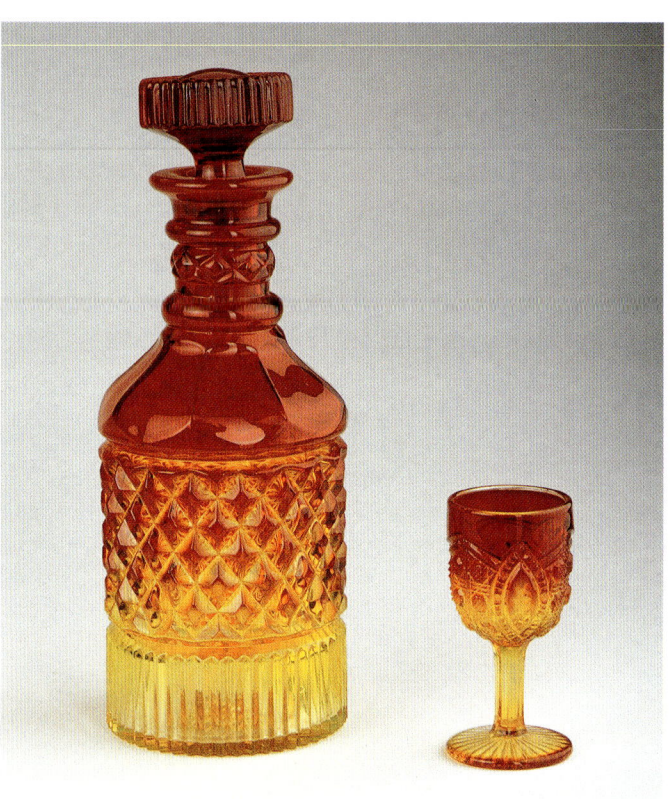

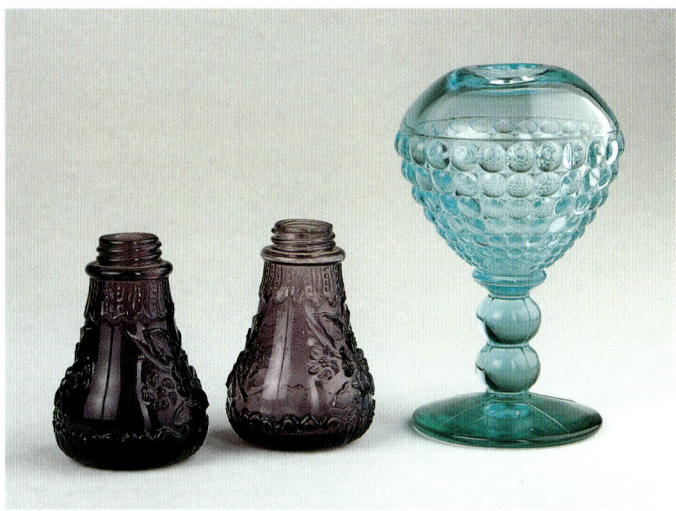

Yesteryear line salt and pepper #1950 amethyst, $8-16 pair with tops, shown in 1962 catalog. Yesteryear line footed ivy ball, colonial blue #1927, 5-1/2", $18-26.

Yesteryear line decanter #1917 with stopper, 28 oz., amberina, $48-62; cordial #1922, 3 oz., amberina, $14-22, shown in 1962 catalog. Note the decanter form is found in the circa 1950s catalog in crystal.

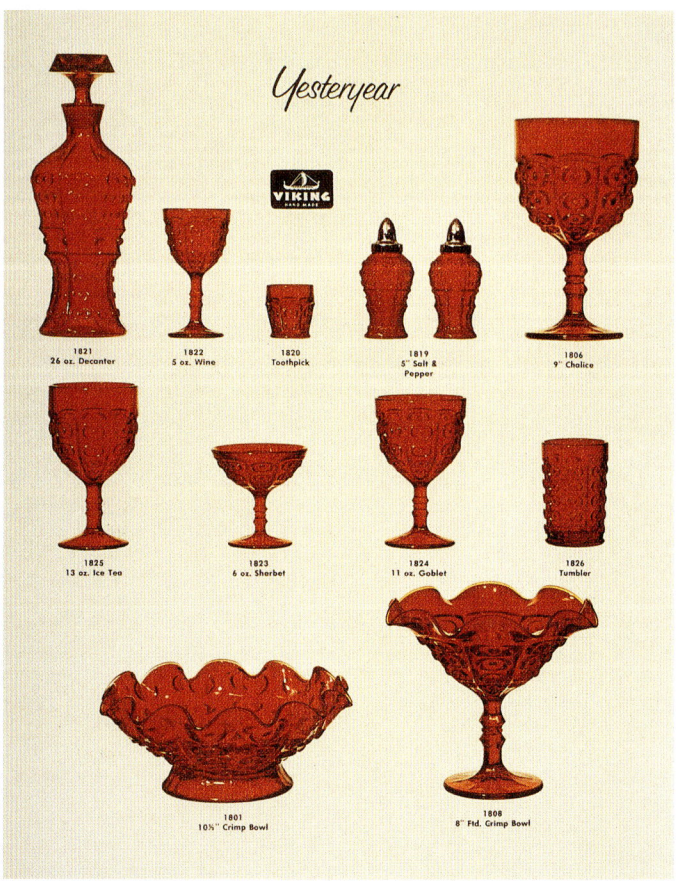

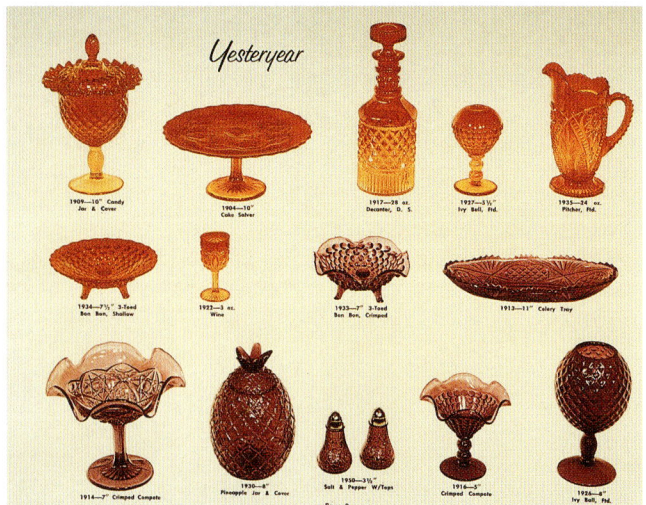

Viking Glass catalog page "Yesteryear," 1962. Amberina and amethyst.

Viking Glass catalog page "Yesteryear" all ruby pieces, 1970, the last year covered by this book.

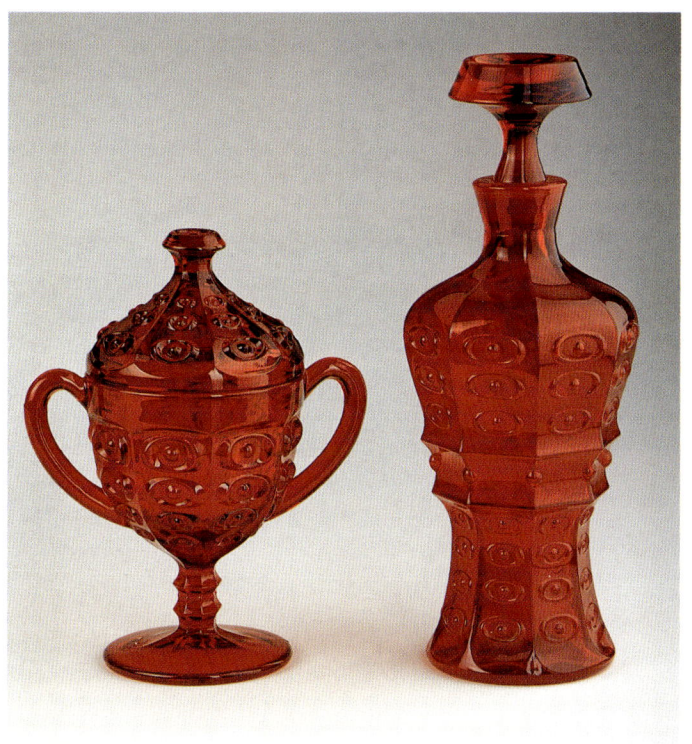

Yesteryear line "bull's-eye" sugar bowl with lid #1811 ruby, $20-28; decanter #1821 with stopper, 11", ruby, $48-68.

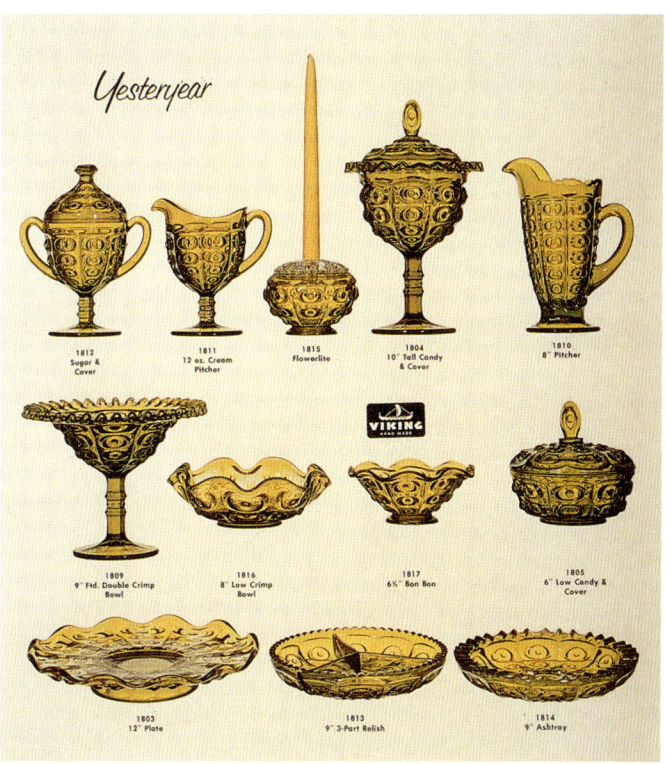

Viking Glass catalog page "Yesteryear" all avocado pieces, 1970 the last year covered by this book

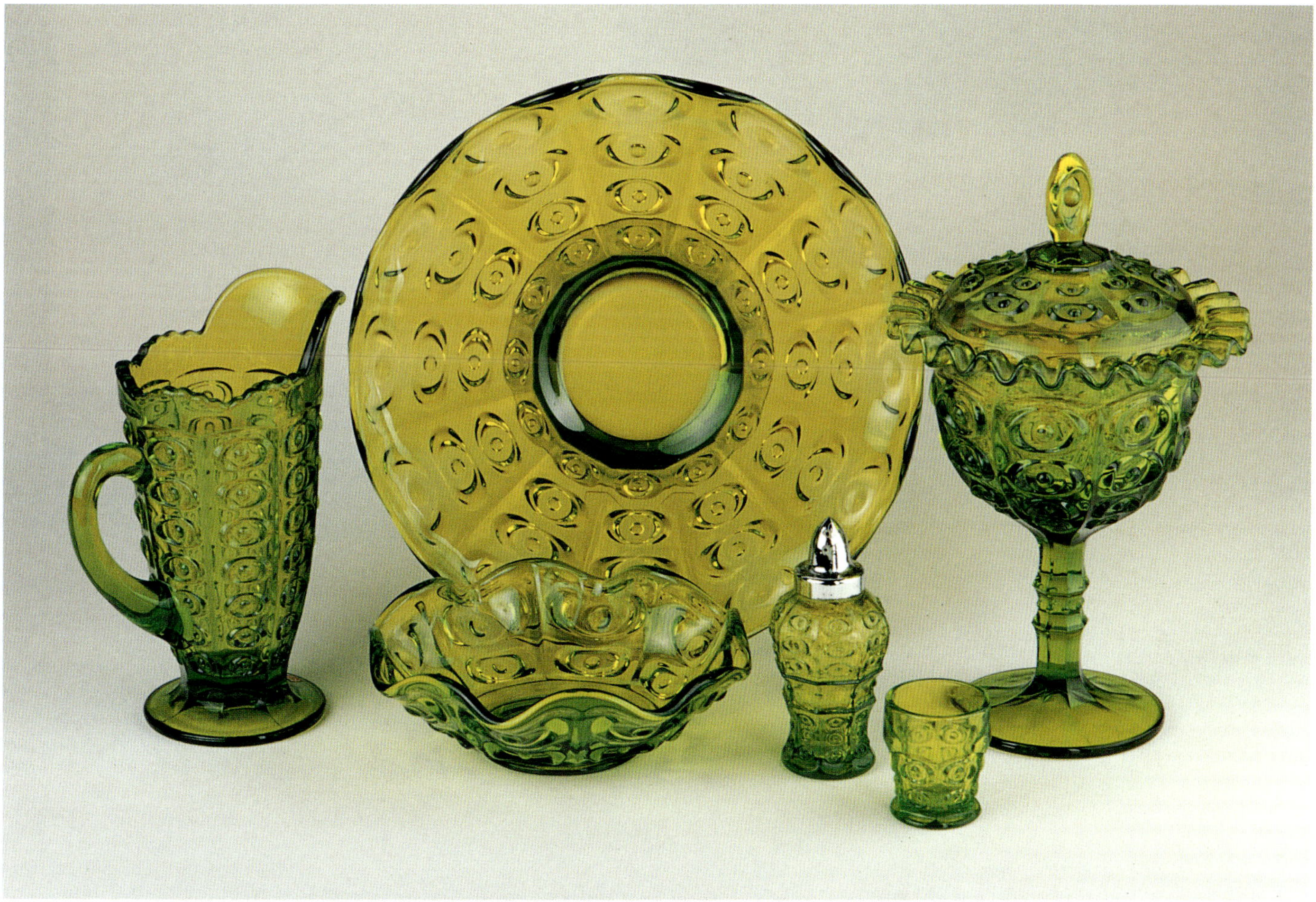

Yesteryear line "bull's-eye," all in avocado. Pitcher #1810, 8", $20-28; low crimped bowl, 8", $10-18; footed cake plate #1803, 12", $22-32; salt shaker #1819, $5-8 each; toothpick/whiskey #1820, $8-14; tall candy with lid, $20-28.

The Cuttings, Etchings, and Decorations of Viking 1944-1970

These are the "cold shop" works done on the already cooled glass blanks.

Viking had at times a large and extensive acid and plate-etching department. Interviews with ex-employees stated that at times as many as thirty-five people worked in decorating and it may have infrequently risen to as large as fifty employees. When there was work to be done, persons were pulled from other parts of the factory to meet demand. Sometimes the work required night shifts to supplement production.

BANFORD is one of the "Rock Crystal Engravings" found in the 1948-49 catalog. Two pages including seventeen shapes are featured in the catalog's two-page spread. The Banford cut is shown in *Crockery & Glass Journal*, December 1947 and *House and Garden*, November 1948.

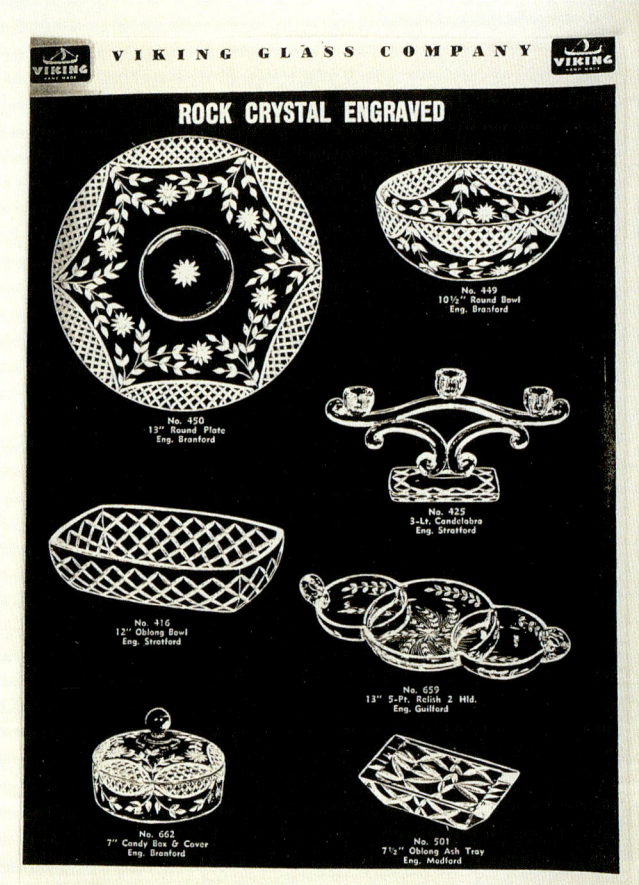

Viking Glass catalog page "Rock Crystal," 1948-49. Largely in the Branford pattern with limited examples of Stratford, Medford, and Guilford patterns.

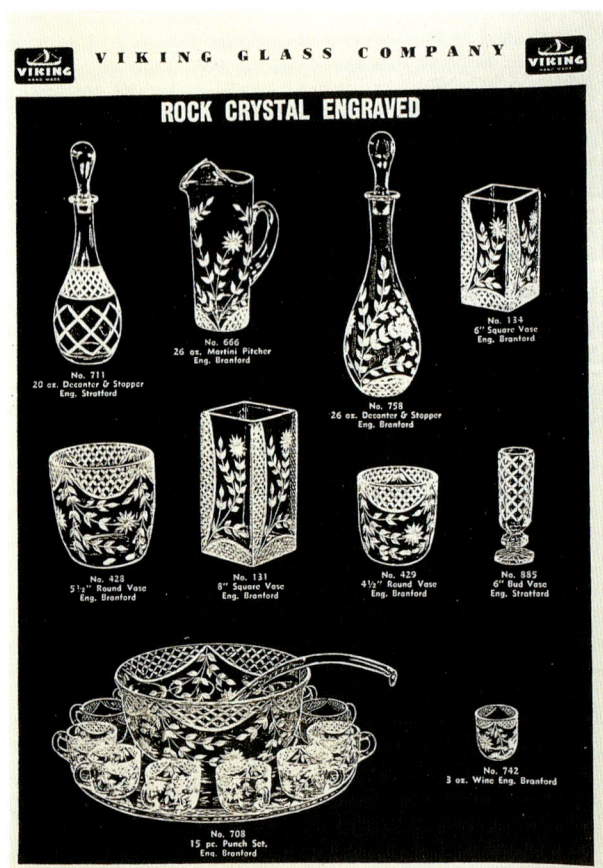

Viking Glass catalog page "Rock Crystal," 1948-49. All in the Branford pattern except one bud vase cut in the Stratford pattern.

CANTERBURRY Etch 10-31 NM originally continued by Viking BECOMES Rhapsody in Blue in Viking catalogs of the later 1940s era. (Measell, 1994, 199)

CORONET cutting was also at times referred to as the Encore cutting, 1953 price list. See Encore.

CUT PEARL was a short line produced for a short time. A July 1958 press release noted the introduction of "handmade and finished glass serving dishes with half olive and miter cutting around the outside edges. The celery dish retails for about $4. Line is called Cut Pearl." Nothing else is known of this line.

ENCORE cutting is featured on the 1956 price list, where nineteen pieces are listed.

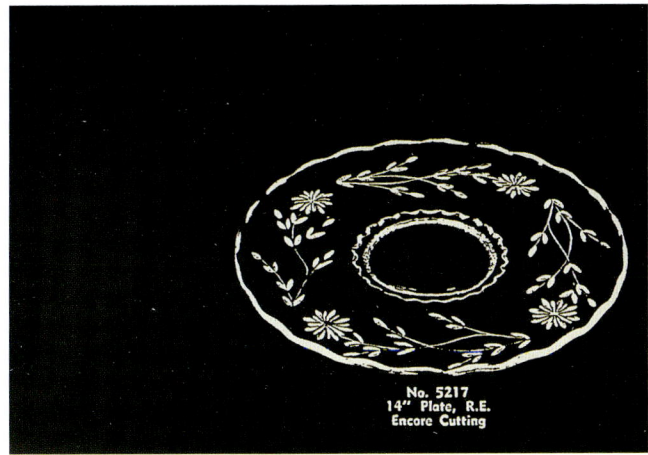

Viking Glass partial catalog page illustration for the Encore cutting, 1956.

ETCH #26 appears on the Viking April 1945 price list but no name is given and only the number designation identifies it. Today this etch is called Meadow Wreath, see that entry.

ETCH # 29 is popularly called Florentine, see that entry.

FERN engraving (gray cutting): the 1947 catalog shows this engraving on Radiance vases and console sets.

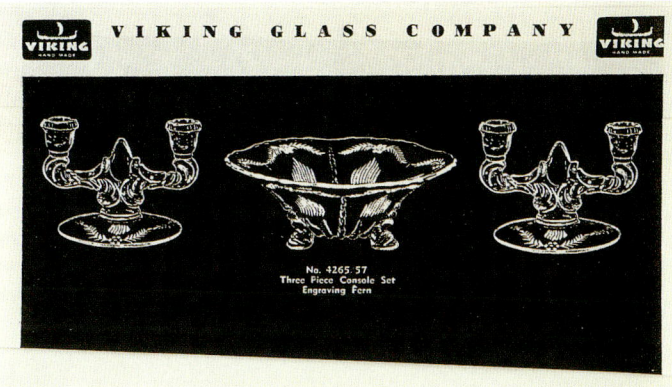

Viking Glass partial catalog page illustration for the Fern "engraving," 1948-49.

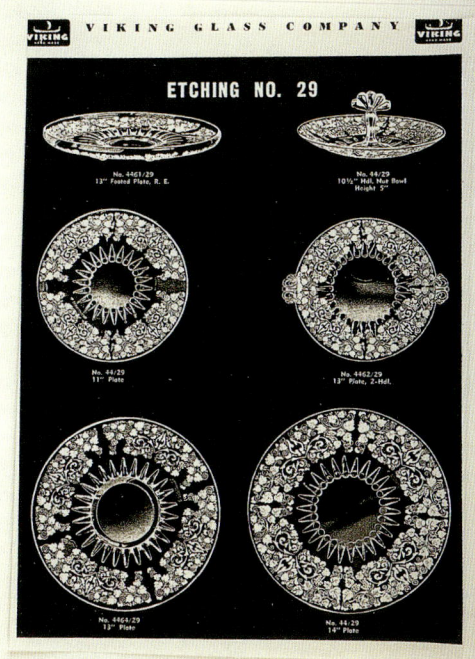

FESTIVAL was an early Viking cutting about which only the name is known.

FLORENTINE is an acid plate etching. It was originally New Martinsville Glass etch #29. The #29 pattern was continued in production by Viking Glass. The January 1948 Viking catalog illustrated twenty-two pieces of etch #29. It was a decoration used predominately on the teardrop line.

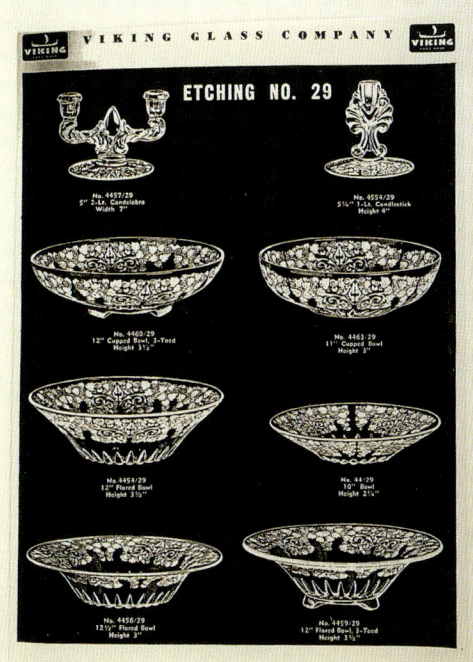

Viking Glass catalog page "Etching No. 29," 1948-49.

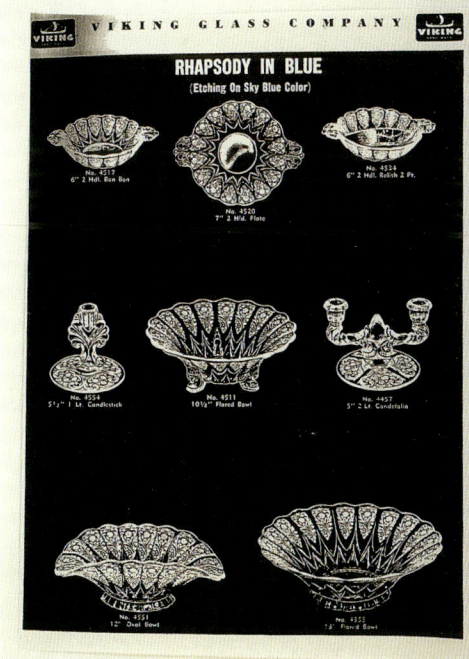

Viking Glass catalog page "Etching No. 29," 1948-49.

Viking Glass catalog page "Etching No. 29," 1948-49.

GUILFORD was a "Rock Crystal" cutting found in the 1948-49 catalog and illustrated on the same page as Bradford, see the page illustrated there.

HEATHER was an early Viking Glass cutting about which nothing else is known.

INSIGNIA etch: January 1953 price list, on six items, all vases or ashtrays or a cigarette box. This is a very coat of arms looking lion decoration.

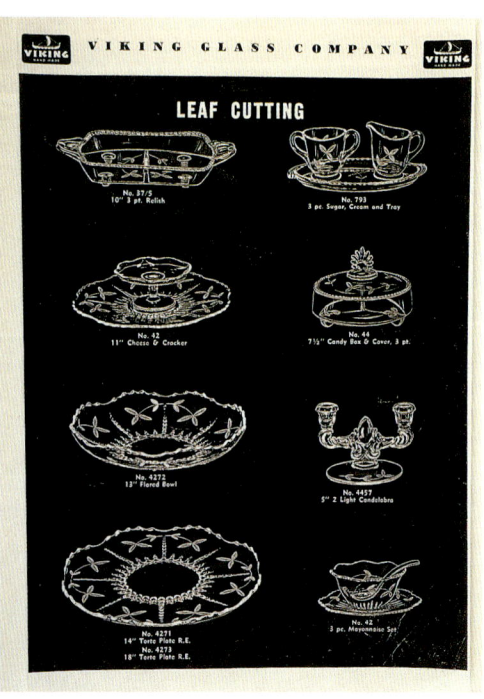

"Faces Beaming Vases Gleaming" two part advertisement appearing in *House Beautiful*, May 1951. The crystal covered cigarette box, ashtray, and vases are etched with the lion decoration "Insignia." An example of this pattern was turned down by Dean when he loudly announced a few years back it was "Not American Made, possibly Swedish, clearly European." No piece was on hand to use in the book due to this false assumption.

LEAF Cutting: 1953 price list features twenty-six items with this cut.

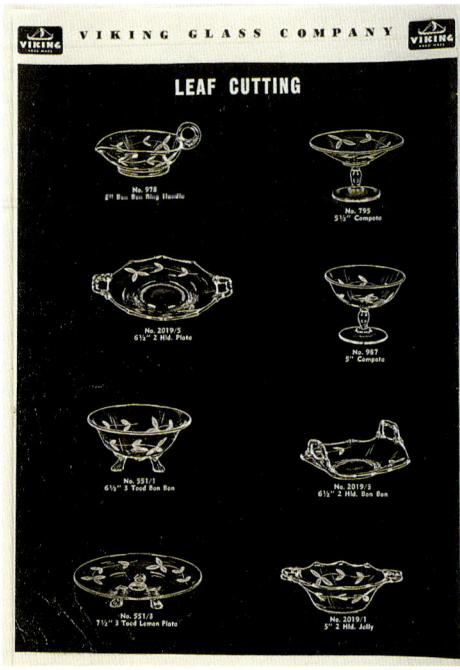

Viking Glass catalog page "Leaf Cutting" on plain shapes, 1950-51.

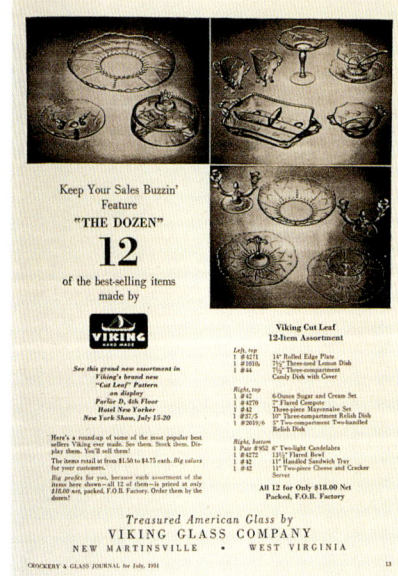

Advertisement for twelve item Leaf Cutting Assortment, *Crockery & Glass Journal*, July 1951.

Viking Glass catalog page "Leaf Cutting" including several Radiance blanks, 1950-51.

MARSHALL cut: alternate rays of wheat and parallel lines. Shown in one of the circa 1940s catalog on candlesticks, etc. in Janice forms.

MEDFORD was a "Rock Crystal" cutting appearing in the 1948-49 catalog. See the Bradford catalog illustration.

MEADOW WREATH etching #26 was introduced in December 1938 by New Martinsville Glass. It was continued by Viking Glass and appears in 1945 on twenty Radiance shaped pieces and other relishes and a candleholder. In the January 1948 catalog it appears on twenty-six shapes. All items with numbers beginning with 42 are the Radiance shaped blanks.

    Bowl, flared #42/26, 10"
    Bowl, flared #4213/26, 13"
    Bowl, flared three toed #4265, 11"
    Bowl, crimped #4211/26, 12-1/2"
    Candelabra, two light #4457/26, 7" width
    Candlestick, #4554/26, 5-1/2" tall, 4" base
    Candy box, 3-part with lid #42/26, 7"
    Celery, #42/26, 10"
    Cheese and cracker, two part #42/26, 11"
    Mayonnaise, three piece set #42/26
    Plate, torte #42/26, 14"
    Plate, torte or cake #42/26, 11"
    Relish, two part #4223/26, 7"
    Relish, three part round #4226/26, 7"
    Relish, three part, two handled, oblong #37/26, 10"
    Sugar and creamer with tray, #42/26
    Sugar and creamer, no tray #42/26
    Vase, round top #42/26, 12" tall
    Vase, round top #42/26, 10" tall
    Vase, eight crimps top #4230/26, 12" tall
    Vase, eight crimps top #4232/26, 10" tall

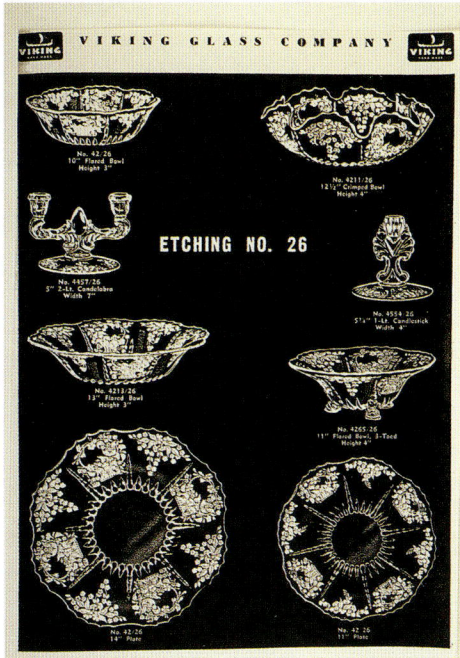

Viking Glass catalog page "Etching No. 26," 1948-49. Radiance blanks.

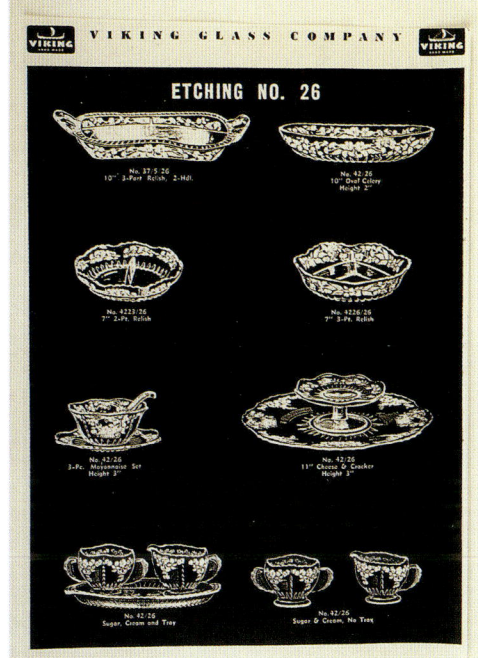

Viking Glass catalog page "Etching No. 26," 1948-49. All but one is a Radiance blank.

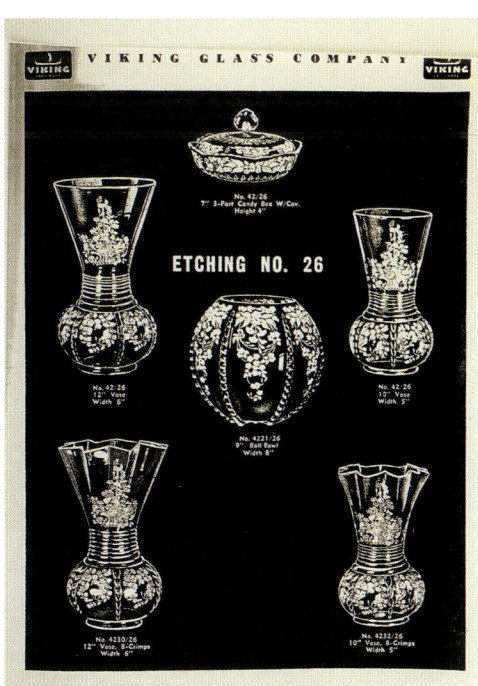

Viking Glass catalog page "Etching No. 26," 1948-49. All on Radiance shaped blanks.

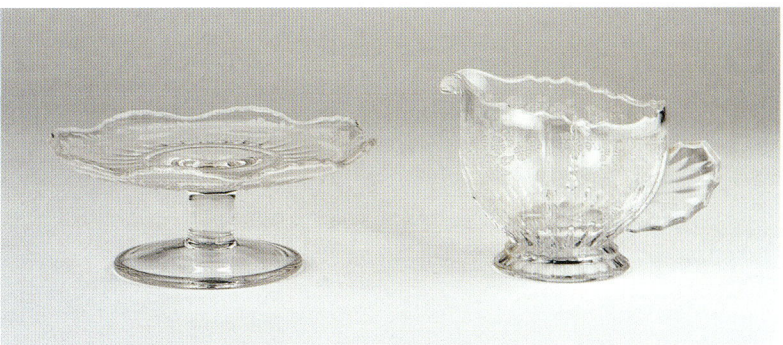

Radiance pattern cheese compote #4226 decorated with "Meadow Wreath" etching #26, 5-1/2" diameter, crystal, $12-22; #42/26 creamer, crystal, $12-20.

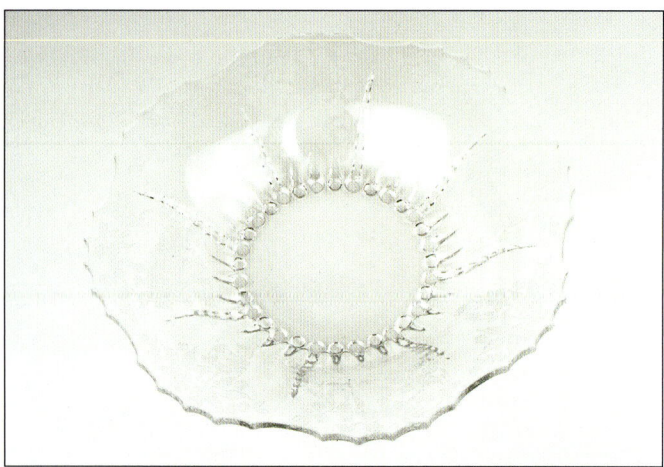

Radiance pattern flared bowl #4213/26 decorated with "Meadow Wreath" etching #26, 13-1/2", $36-48.

MELODY cutting: "new cutting on Princess shape" July 1954 *Crockery and Glass Journal*. C&GJ April 1949 melody cut on plain candlestick illustrated c. 1940s catalog offerings on sixteen shapes, by 1956 there were twenty-four pieces with this decoration.

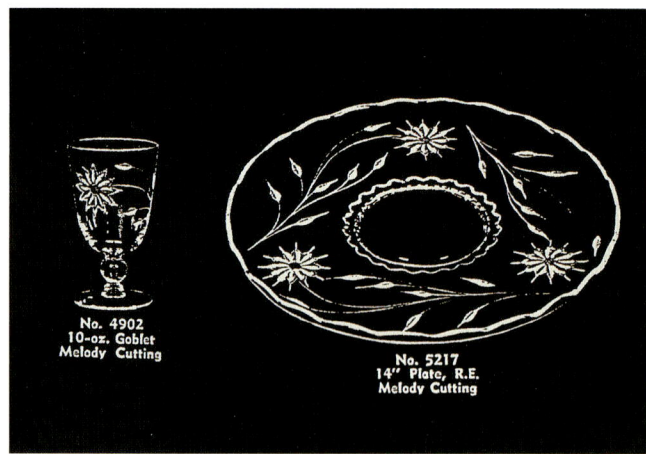

Viking Glass partial catalog page "Melody Cutting," 1956.

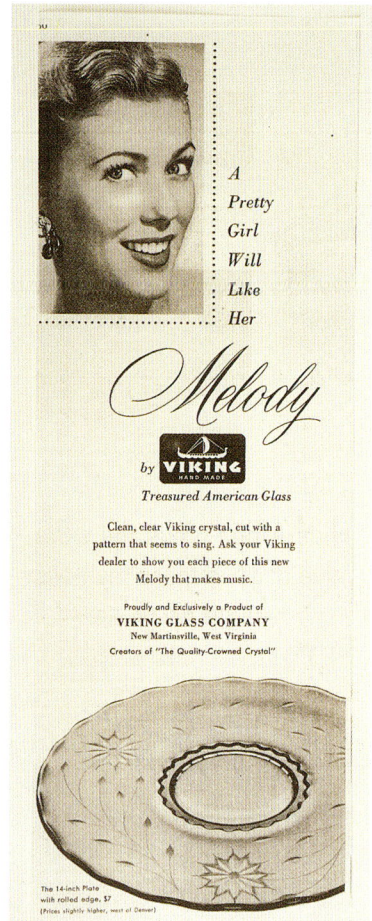

Melody pattern glamour advertisement appearing in national magazines in October 1954.

PANSY is an engraving (gray cutting) shown in the 1948-49 catalog. It is featured on Radiance vases and console sets on seven shapes.

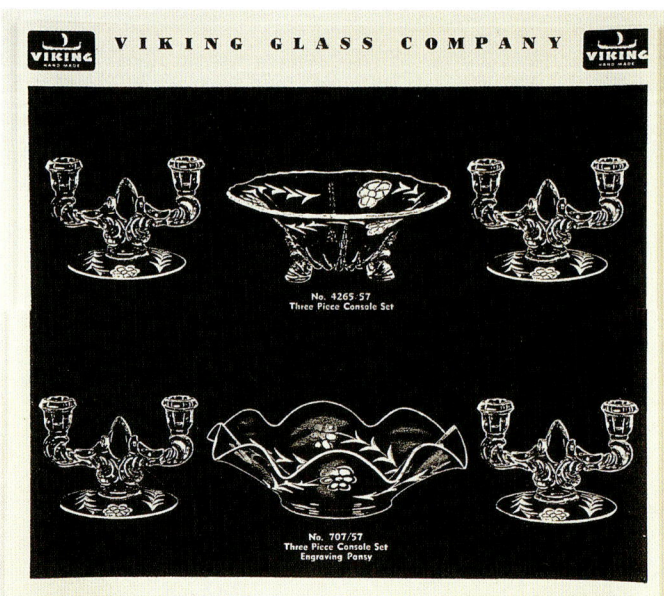

Viking Glass partial catalog page "three piece consol sets in Engraving Pansy," 1949-50.

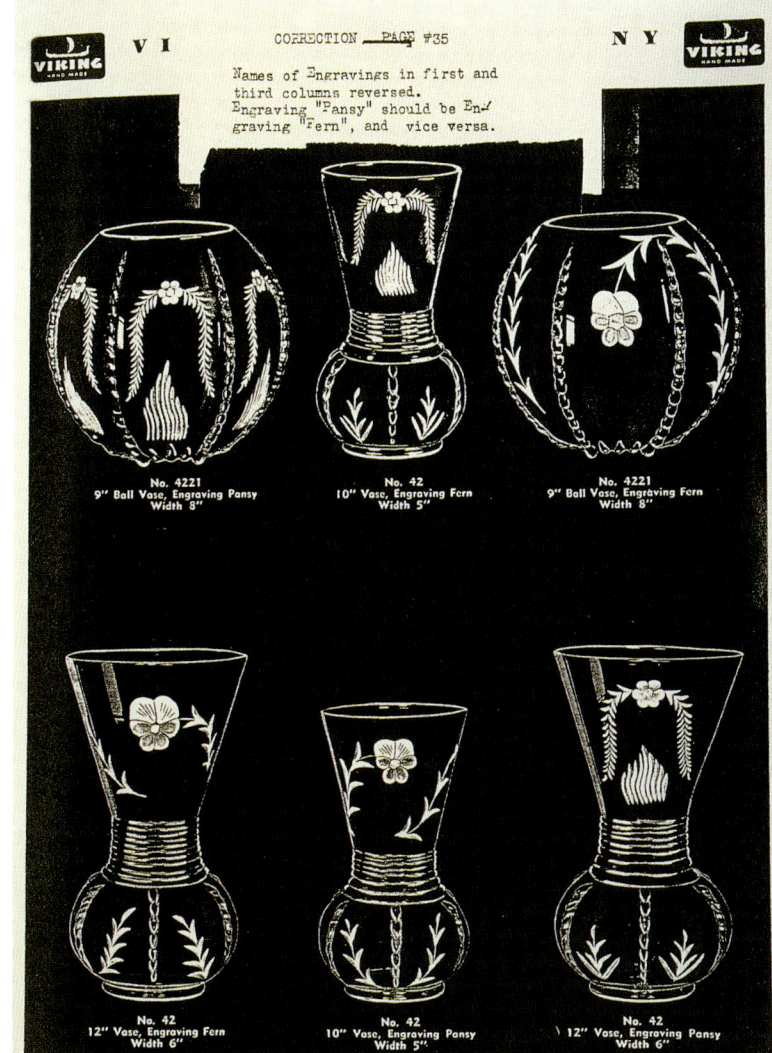

Viking Glass catalog page Pansy and fern engravings (gray cuttings) with inverted captions and original note explaining the inversion. 1948-49.

PRELUDE plate etching is first found in December of 1948 as it is featured in an advertisement in *China, Glass & Decorative Accessories, House Beautiful,* and other publications. It was called "lovely new Prelude etch" in the ads. It appeared frequently in ads in popular magazines such as *House & Garden* (November 1949) and *House Beautiful* (June 1949). These were often full-page, prominent, and expensive ads appealing to the middle class and well to do across the US.

On the 1956 price list, Prelude shapes numbered eighty-four, an amazing number. By 1968, thirty-seven Prelude decorated shapes remain on the Viking price list. In 1970, there are thirty-five Prelude items on the price list.

Bonbon, three toed, crimped #1009, 9" (1970)
Bonbon, three toed, crimped #1006, 6" (1970)
Bowl, footed #5269, 10" (1970)
Bowl, shallow #5201, 13" (1970)
Bowl, three toed # 1090, 10" (1970)
Bowl, three toed #1002, 11" (1970)
Bowl, three toed, crimped #1003, 9" (1970)

Butter, oval with cover #5224 Princess 8-1/2" (1970)
Candelabra, two light #952, 6" (1970)
Candelabra, two light #4457, 5" (1970)
Candelabra, two light #5214, 5" (1970)
Candlestick, one light #4554, 5-1/2" (1970)
Cake salver, #5226 Princess 11" (1970)
Celery tray, #5249 Princess 10-1/2" (1970)
Compote, flared #5228 Princess 7-1/2" (1970)
Cruet, oil bottle with ground stopper #980 (1970)
Lemon plate, 3 toed #1010, 7" (1970)
Mayonnaise set, three piece #5236 (1970)
Plate, cake three toed #1091, 11" (1970)
Plate, salad #790, 8" (1970)
Plate, salad #976, 7" (1970)
Plate, #5219, 11" (1970)
Plate, torte rolled edge #5217 Princess 14" (1970)
Plate, two handled #5223, 12" (1970)
Relish, three part two handled #5238 Princess 10" (1970)
Relish, five part oval #5287 Princess 13" (1970)
Salt and pepper, #13, 3-1/2" (1970)
Salt and pepper, #986, 3-1/2" (1970)
Sandwich tray, handled #5246, 11" (1970)
Sugar and Cream, #42 (1970)
Sugar and Cream, #5247 (1970)
Sugar and Cream with plain tray, #5248 (1970)
Tid Bit tray, two tier with chrome handle #5243 (1970)
Vase, bud footed #1154, 10" (1970)
Vase, footed #1106, 11" (1970)

Prelude Stemware is a complex matter. In the 1948-49 catalog, four Prelude etched stems appear, all with a line and item numbers of #4900. They are mouth blown, handmade, pulled stems. The list includes a 9 oz. water goblet, a 6 oz. tall sherbet, a 3-1/2 oz. cocktail, and a 12 oz. footed tumbler. Simple, but not for long.

In early ads, a pressed stem with no known line number is shown. This stem was likely pressed and decorated at Viking. However, the need for a thinner, more "elegant" stemware line seems likely to have led Viking to look outside of their abilities to produce such a line of glass. In 1956, two distinct Prelude etched stem lines exist. The now #4901 line and a ball stemmed #4902 line, eight shapes in #4901—the ladies leg pulled stems—and seven items in the ball stem. Remember, the price lists note all stemware was F.O.B. Morgantown, West Virginia. The etching plates from Morgantown Glass survive, although that company closed in the 1970s. Etching plates are the large metal slabs on which the artwork is carved. Once prepared, the plates are used in creating the delicate acid etched pattern for decorations like Prelude. On the surviving Morgantown etching plates are found several examples of the Prelude pattern giving good reason to believe Morgantown was producing the thin mouth blown stemware parts of the Prelude line for Viking.

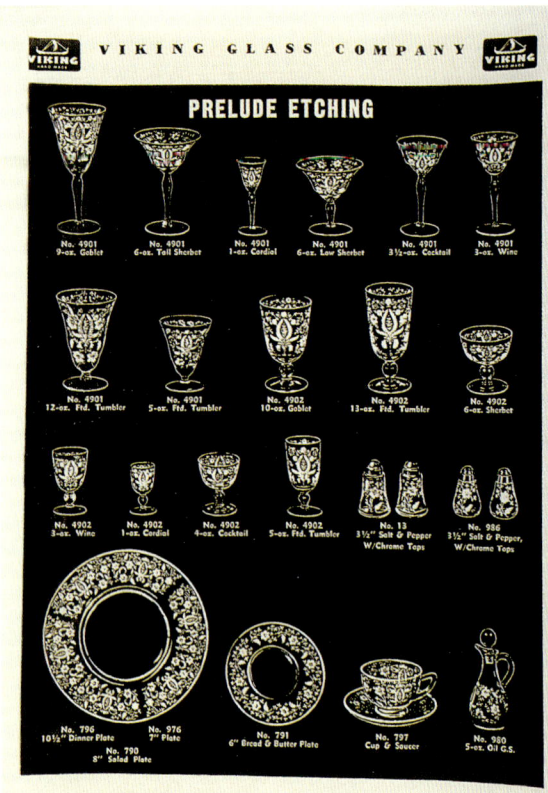

Viking Glass catalog page "Prelude Etching," 1956. Note the presence of both handmade stem lines #4901 with a pulled ladies leg stem and #4902 with a ball stem.

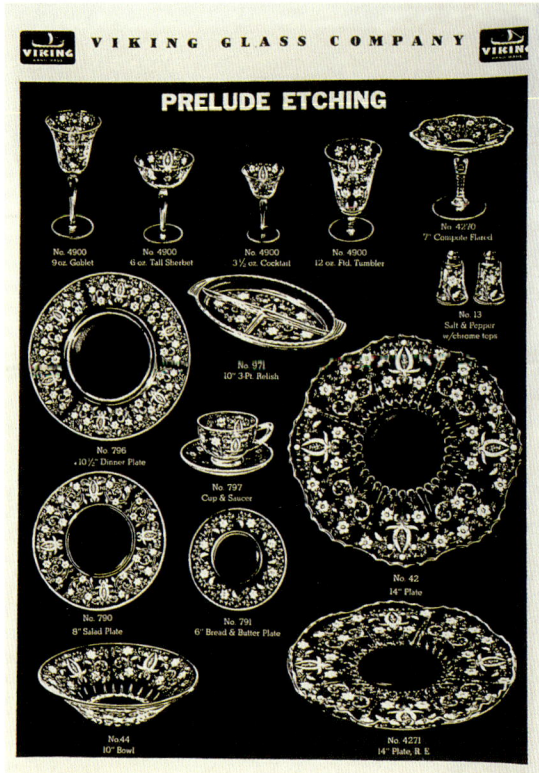

Viking Glass catalog page "Prelude Etching," 1948-49. Note that the line was much smaller than the similar but more extensive page from 1956.

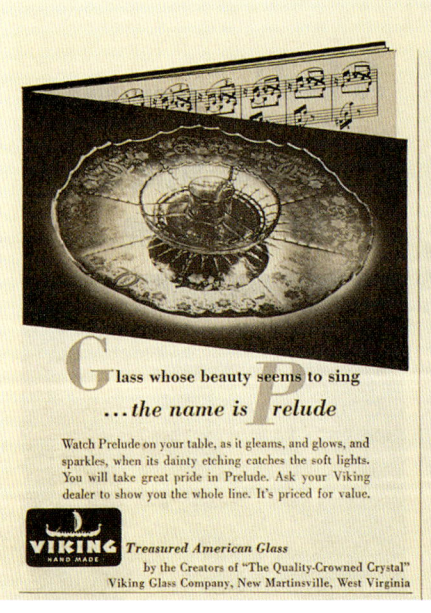

Prelude ad appearing in national magazines circa 1950s.

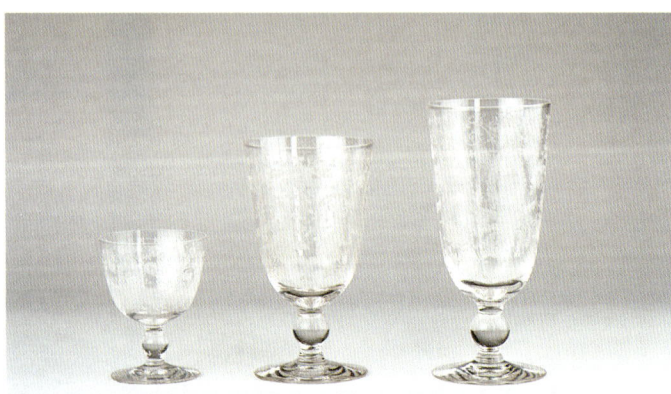

Prelude etching ball stem line #4902 cocktail, 4 oz., $10-18; footed tumbler, 5 oz., $12-22; footed tumbler, 13 oz., $14-26.

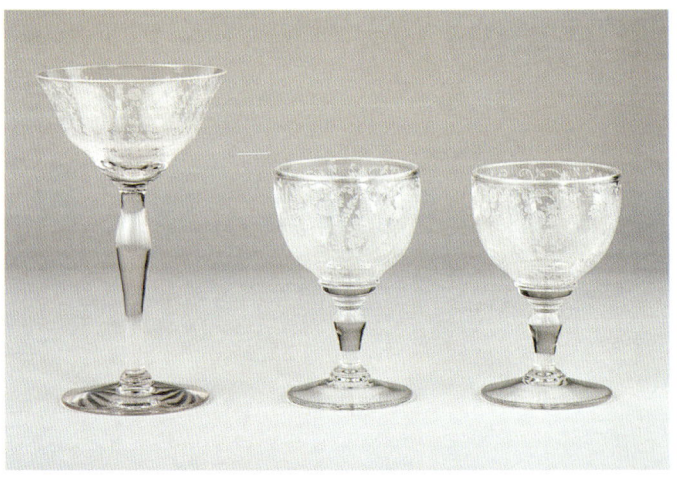

Prelude etching on a pulled stem ladies leg cocktail, 5-1/2", beside the earlier form of Prelude on a pressed stem, shown in the undated ad nearby. See text for suggestions that thin, mouth blown stems were a Morgantown product while this earlier hand pressed stem was likely a Viking piece made in New Martinsville.

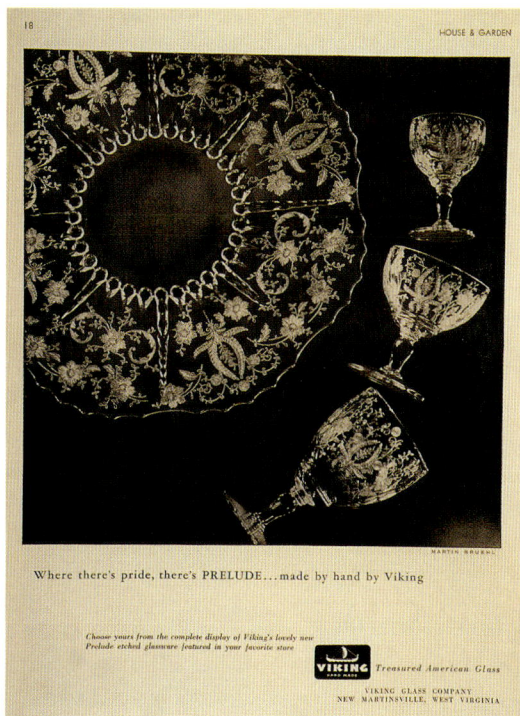

Ad for Prelude showing the hand pressed stems on which the etch first appeared. *House & Garden*, undated circa 1940s, pre-1948?

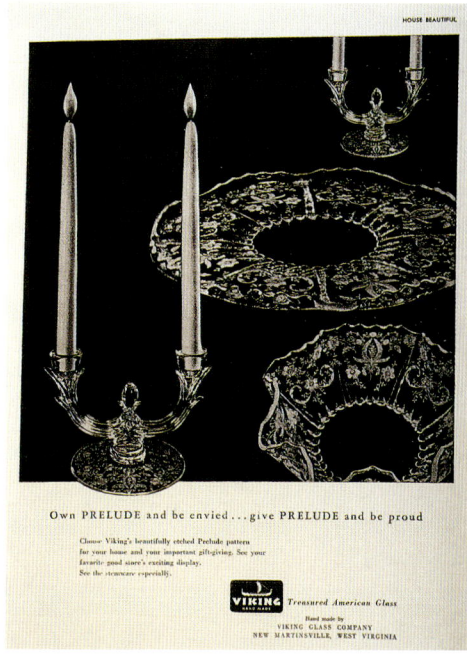

Prelude advertisement appearing in *House Beautiful*, November 1949. Advertising for Prelude decorated Viking was a long term and major national campaign.

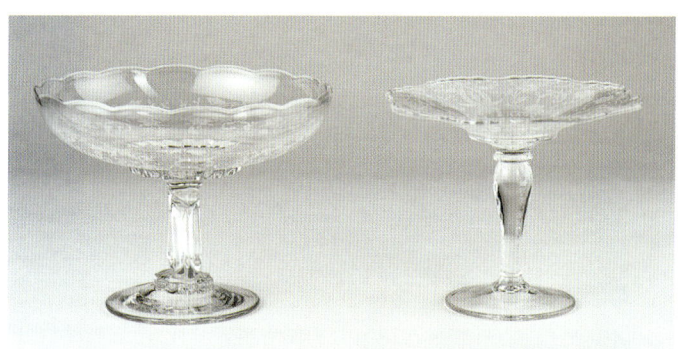

Prelude etched decoration on Princess pattern compote #5228, 7-1/2" crystal, $26-38; compote #4270, 7" crystal, $24-38.

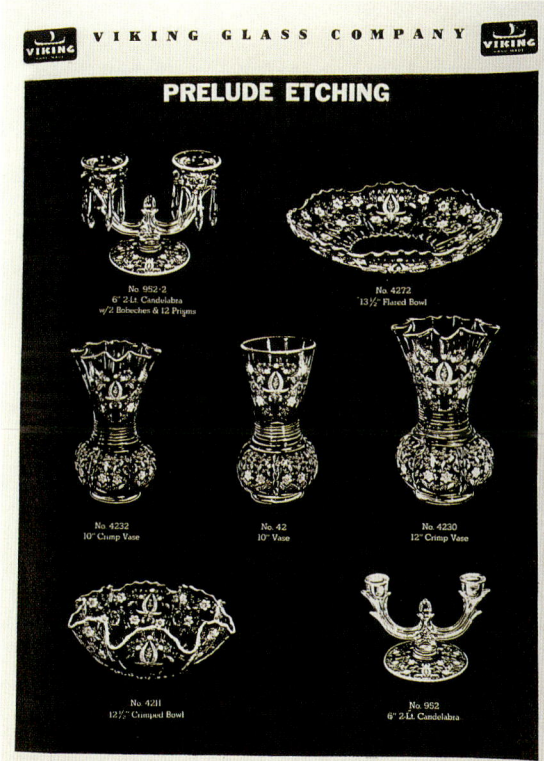

Viking Glass catalog page "Prelude Etching," 1948-49.

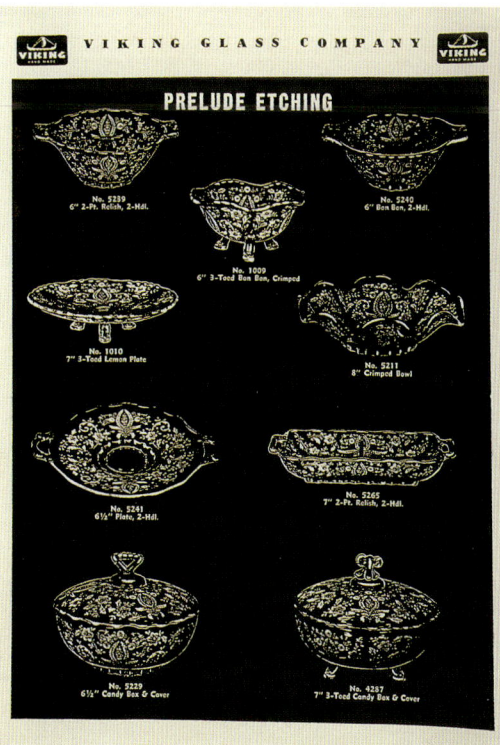

Viking Glass catalog page "Prelude Etching," 1956.

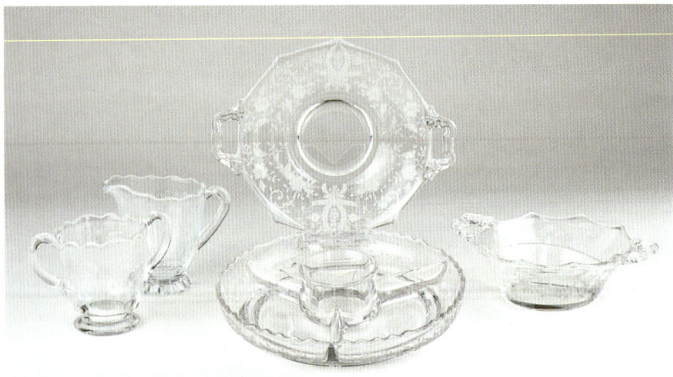

Prelude etching sugar and creamer #5247 on Princess shape crystal, $12-22 each; two part divided relish #2019/6, 5", $19-26; round shrimp server #100 crystal, $30-38; two handled plate #2019/5 crystal 6-1/2", $18-24.

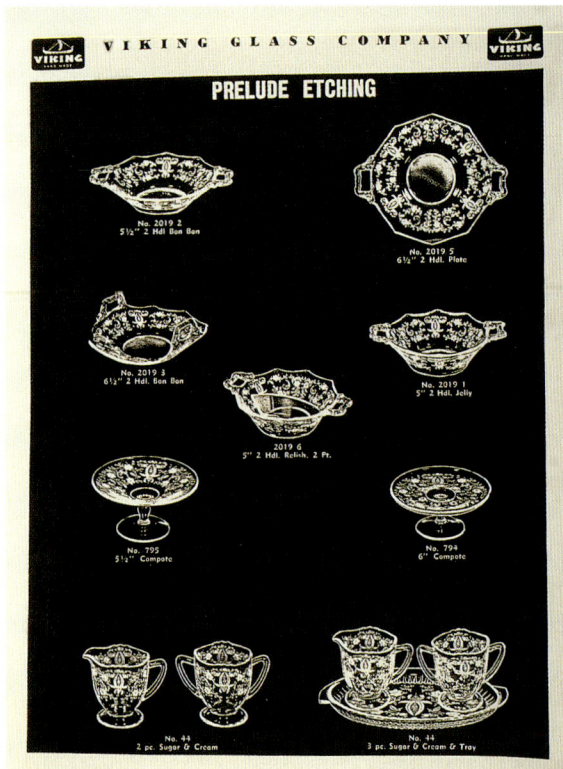

Viking Glass catalog page "Prelude Etching," 1948-49.

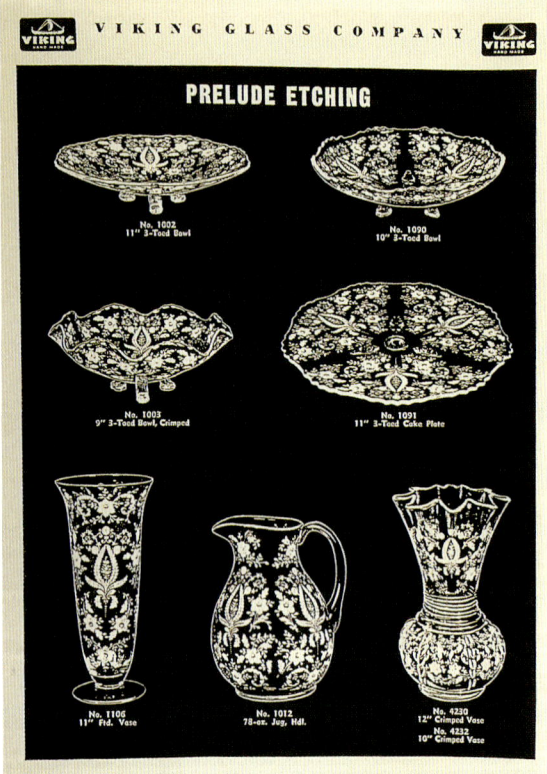

Viking Glass catalog page "Prelude Etching," 1956.

"Good-looking glass, isn't it?" asks this Martin Bruehl ad agency advertisement that appeared in *House and Garden* in June 1949.

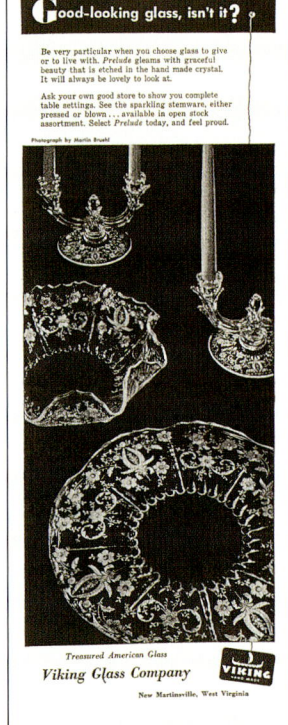

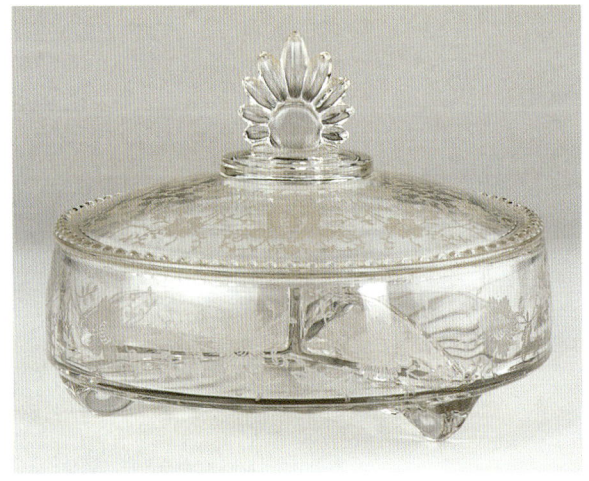

Prelude etched decoration on three part candy box with lid, #44, 7-1/2" crystal, $48-62.

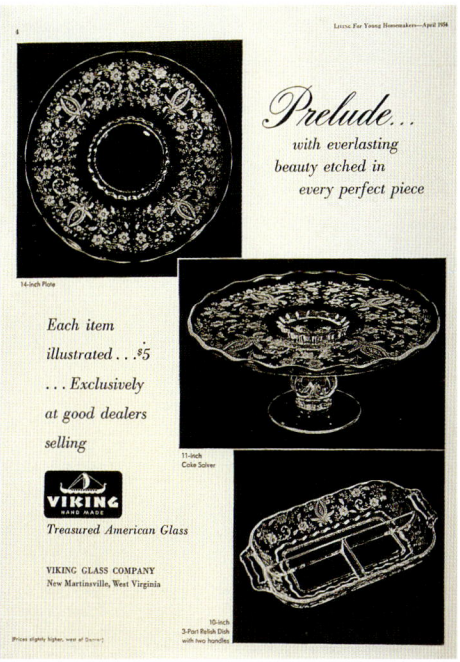

Prelude advertisement. *Living for Young Homemakers*, April 1954.

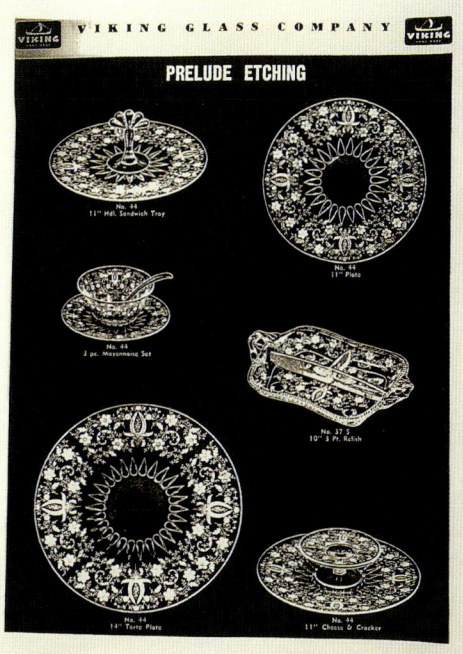

Viking Glass catalog page "Prelude Etching," 1948-49.

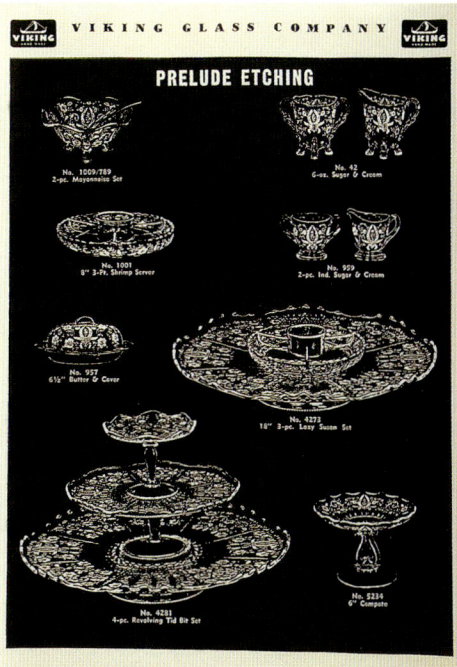

Viking Glass catalog page "Prelude Etching," 1956. Interesting pieces include the "Lazy Susan Set" using the shrimp server as a center element and the four piece revolving tidbit tray, a sure disaster if revolved too quickly! These two were short-lived pieces in the Prelude line.

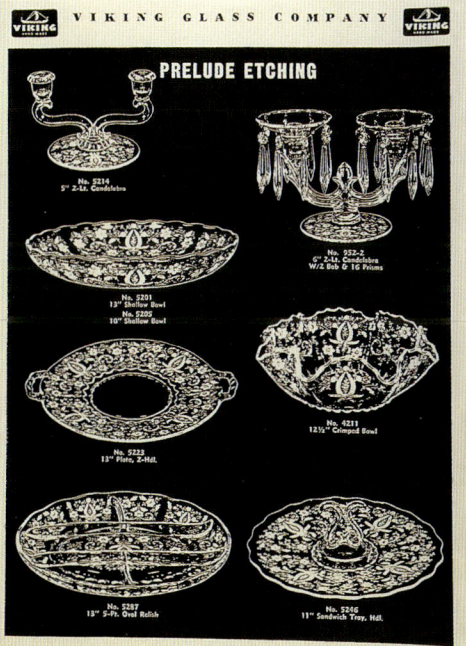

Viking Glass catalog page "Prelude Etching," 1956.

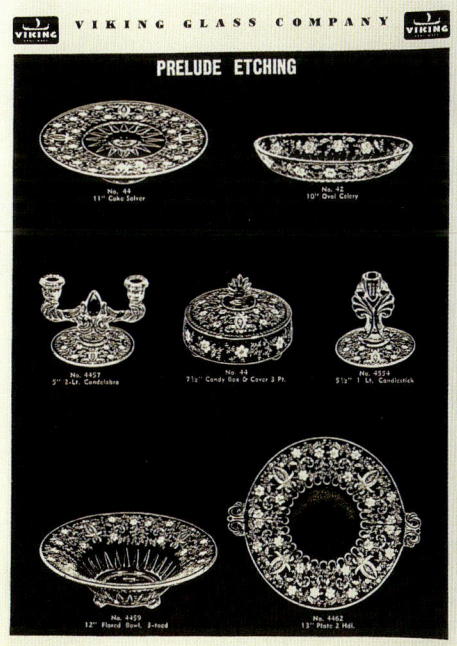

Viking Glass catalog page "Prelude Etching," 1948-49.

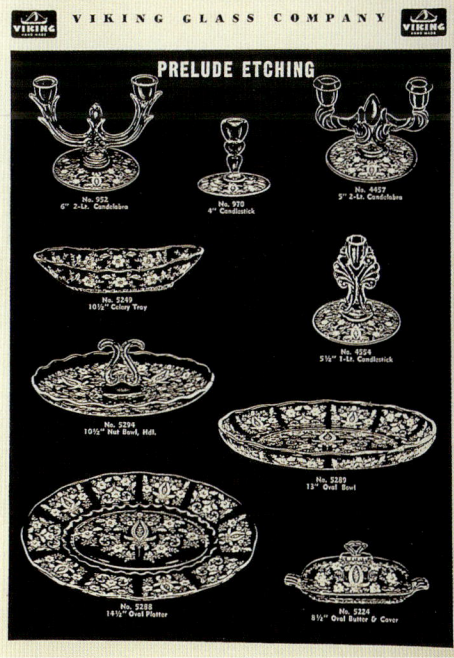

Viking Glass catalog page "Prelude Etching," 1956.

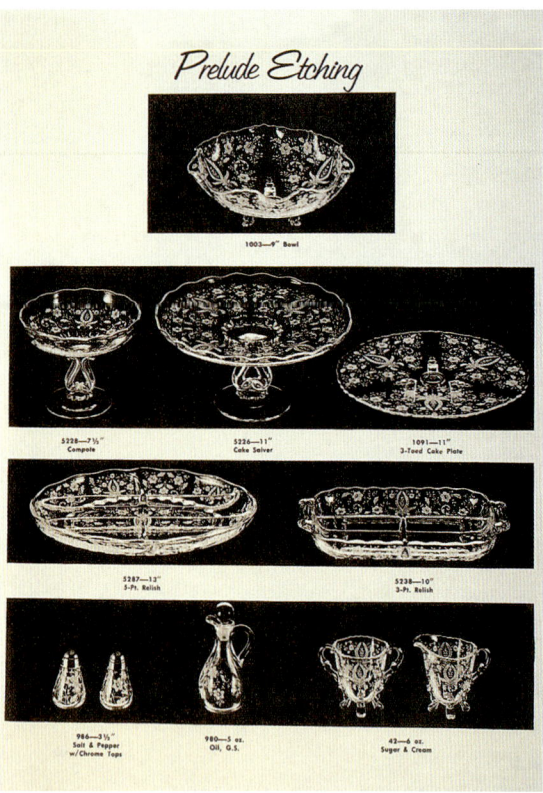

Viking Glass catalog page "Prelude Etching," 1970.

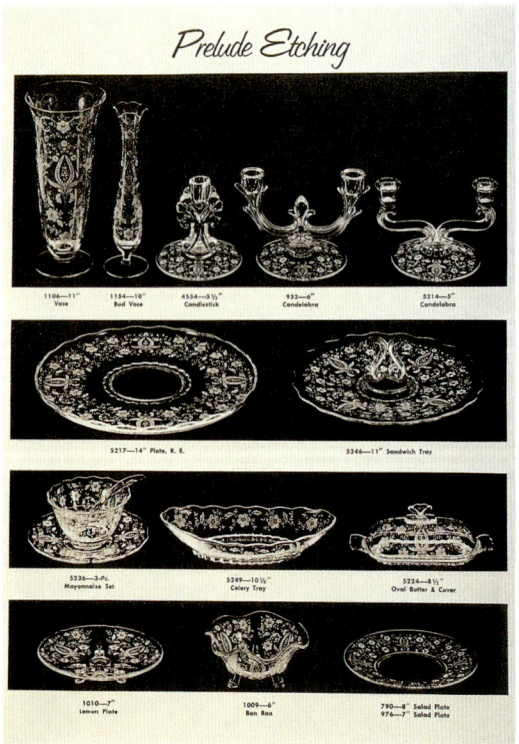

Viking Glass catalog page "Prelude Etching," 1970.

REMEMBERANCE rock crystal engraving (a cutting) is on the 1956 price list where it is offered on twenty-one shapes.

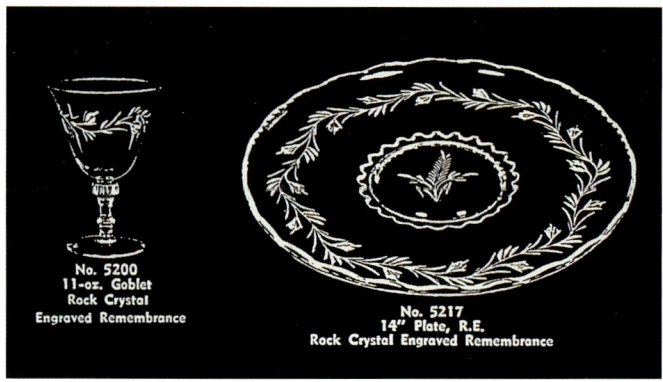

Viking Glass partial catalog page "Rock Crystal Engraved Remembrance," note the Princess stemware, 1956.

RHAPSODY IN BLUE is an acid plate etching on Sky Blue colored blanks. In the 1947 catalog it appears on two pages, all on the Janice blank. It is another etching begun by New Martinsville and continued by Viking. But there is a difference. New Martinsville made it on crystal and it was their etch #31 Canterbury. Viking made it only on Sky Blue and changed the name and number. The two could not easily be confused.

    Bonbon, two handled #4517, 6"
    Bowl, flared dolphin footed #451, 10-1/2"
    Bowl, oval #4551, 12"
    Bowl, flared #4555, 13"
    Candlestick, one lite #4554, 5-1/2"
    Candy Box with lid, #4541, 5-1/2"
    Celery, oblong #4521, 11"
    Cheese & cracker, #4528, 11"
    Mayo set, three piece #4522
    Plate, two handled #4520, 7"
    Plate, two handled #4529, 13"
    Plate, torte, rolled edge #4556, 14"
    Relish, two handled, two part #4534, 6"
    Sugar, creamer, and tray, three pieces #4532

ROCK CRYSTAL ENGRAVED is a style and not a specific pattern. It refers to lightly cut designs on the glass, many were left gray or unpolished. In this manner are the cuttings Branford, Stratford, Guilford, and Medford. In 1956, twenty-one pieces of Rock Crystal were offered for sale by Viking.

ROSE OF SHARON is an acid plate etching announced as "new" and offered on Princess shapes in *China, Glass & Decorative Accessories* in December 1951. Not surprisingly, its line number is #52, typical of many Viking line numbers that begin with the year the line was first introduced. The 1952 price list has twenty-eight items in this decoration and it appears also in the 1953 price list. It is shown in the 1956 catalog. Available Rose of Sharon pieces include:

    Bowl, flared #5201, 13"
    Bowl, crimped #5202, 12-1/2"
    Bowl, Shallow #5205, 10"
    Bowl, flared #5206, 10"

Bowl, crimped #5207, 10"
Candelabra, two lite #5214, 5"
Plate, #5216, 14"
Plate, rolled edge #5217, 14"
Plate, #5219, 11"
Plate, rolled edge #5220, 11"
Plate, two handles #5223, 13"
Cake salver, #5226, 11"
Cake salver, #5227, 8"
Compote, crimped #5231, 7"
Cheese and cracker, #5232, 11"
Compote, #5233, 5-1/2"
Compote, 35234, 6"
Mayonnaise set, three pieces #5236
Relish, two handled three part #5237, 7"
Relish, two handled three part #5238, 10"
Relish, two handled two part #5239, 6"
Bonbon, two handled #5240, 6-1/2"
Plate, two handled #5241, 6-1/2"
Salt and pepper, #5242, 3-1/2"
Sandwich tray, center handled #5246, 11"
Sugar and cream, two piece #5247
Sugar and cream with tray, three piece #5248

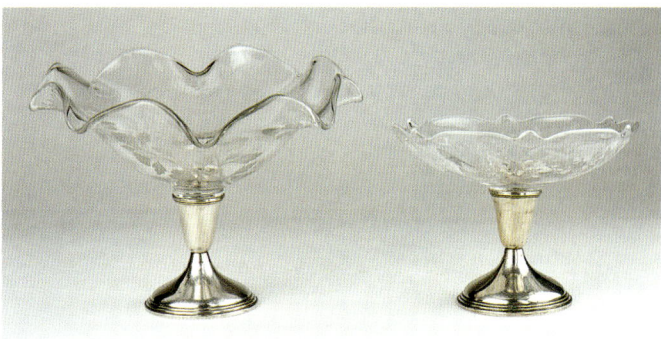

Rose of Sharon etchings on sterling silver based crystal compotes, $40-58 each.

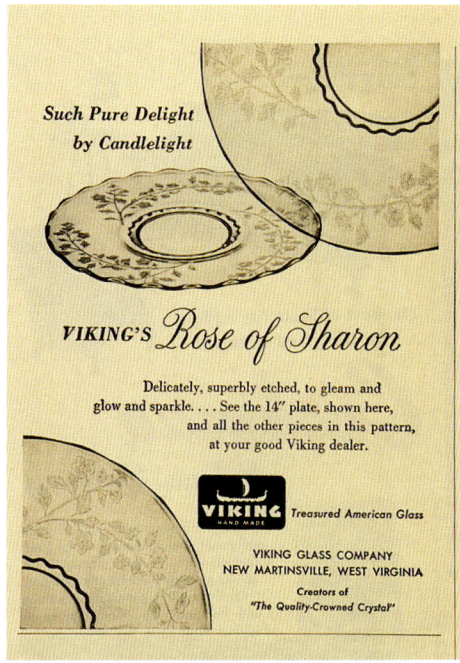

"Sure Pure Delight by Candlelight" ad for Rose of Sharon appeared in *The American Home*, October 1953.

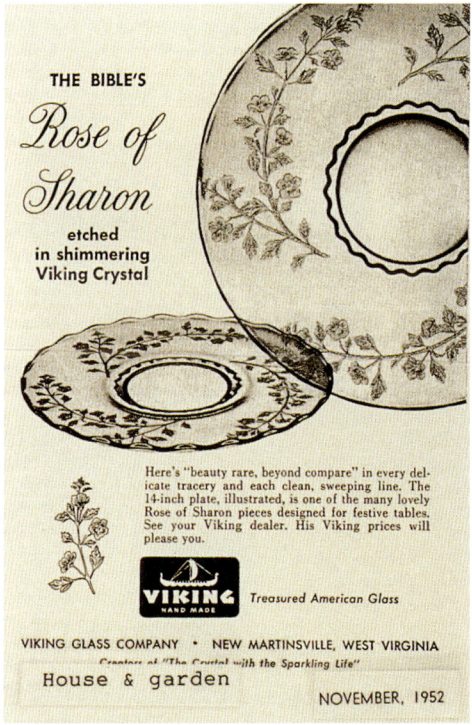

"The Bible's Rose of Sharon etched in shimmering Viking Crystal" reads this November 1952 *House and Garden* advertisement.

SONATA: "a brand new etching scheduled to appear after the first of the year and due at the Pittsburgh show," December 1948, *China, Glass & Decorative Accessories*. Sonata appears in the Viking catalog of 1949. It remained in the catalog until circa 1951. At least twenty pieces were illustrated in 1949. These are:

Bonbon, #2019/2 two handled 5-1/2"
Bonbon, #2019/3 two handled 6-1/2"
Bowl, salad #787, 10"
Bowl, shallow #784, 12-1/2"
Butter, oval with lid #957, 6-1/2"
Candlestick, one light #970, 4"
Candelabra, two light #952, 6"
Candy box with lid, #662 three part 7"
Celery, #951, 11-1/2"
Cheese and cracker, #794, 11"
Jelly, two handled # 2019/5, 5"
Mayonnaise, three piece #788

Mayonnaise, four piece #789
Plate, two handled #2019/5, 6-1/2"
Plate, cake or torte #786, 14"
Plate, cake or torte rolled edge #785, 14"
Relish, three part #958, 10"
Relish, three part #971, 10"
Relish, two handled, five part #2019, 6-1/2"
Sugar, creamer, & tray, #793

STARLIGHT: "new" cutting as featured in *China Glass & Tableware* for February 1957.

STRATFORD: a 1948-49 era "Rock Crystal" pattern, see the page illustration for Bradford.

SYLVAN is a decoration on Princess as featured in *China & Glass* in February 1953.

TIARA: "new" cut shown in the *Crockery & Glass Journal* of October 1955. The 1956 price list has eighteen shapes offered as "rock crystal engraving."

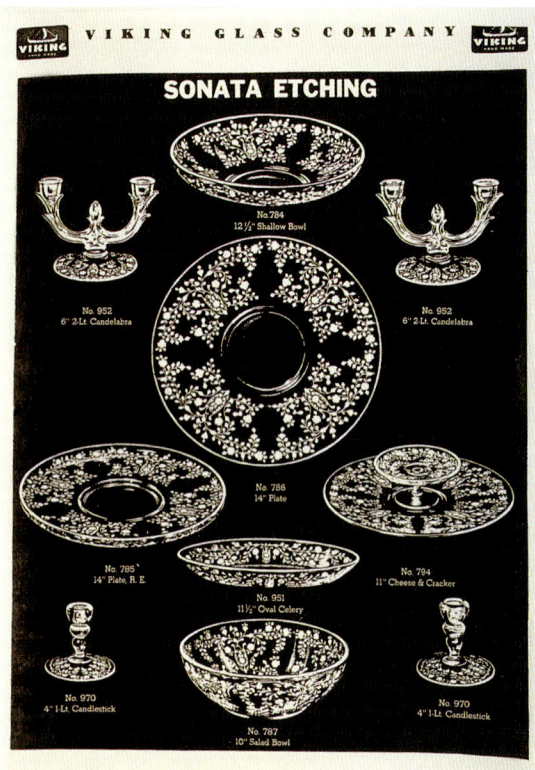

Viking Glass catalog page "Sonata Etching," 1948-49.

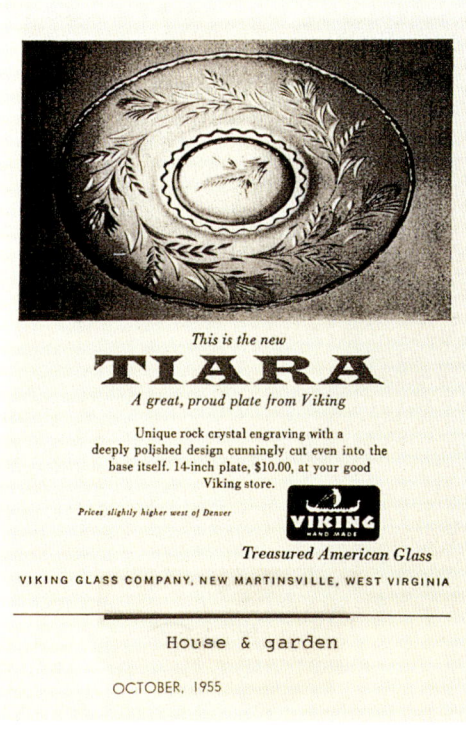

Announcing the new "Tiara rock crystal engraving" a hand cut, polished design. *House & Garden*, October 1955.

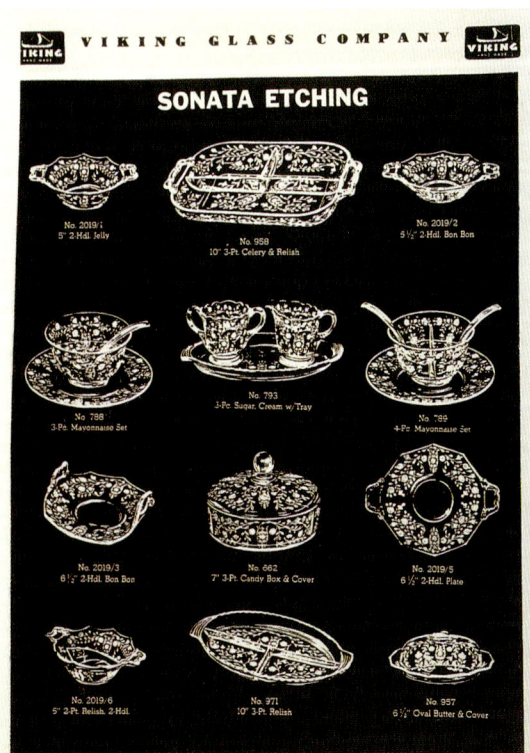

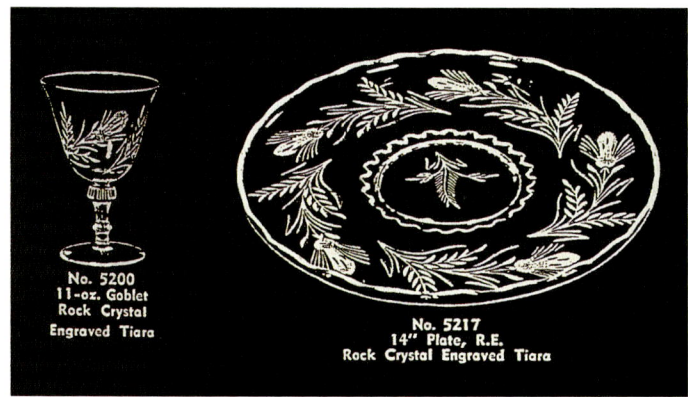

Viking Glass partial catalog page "Rock Crystal Engraved Tiara," 1956. Note Princess line stemware.

Viking Glass catalog page "Sonata Etching," 1948-49.

VIKING STAR was an early Viking Glass cutting.

WHEAT cut was shown in *House Beautiful*, November 1953, as "new." Quoted as "Viking introduces Wheat," *Crockery & Glass*, July 1953, provides an illustration. Wheat is shown in early catalogs on the Princess shapes.

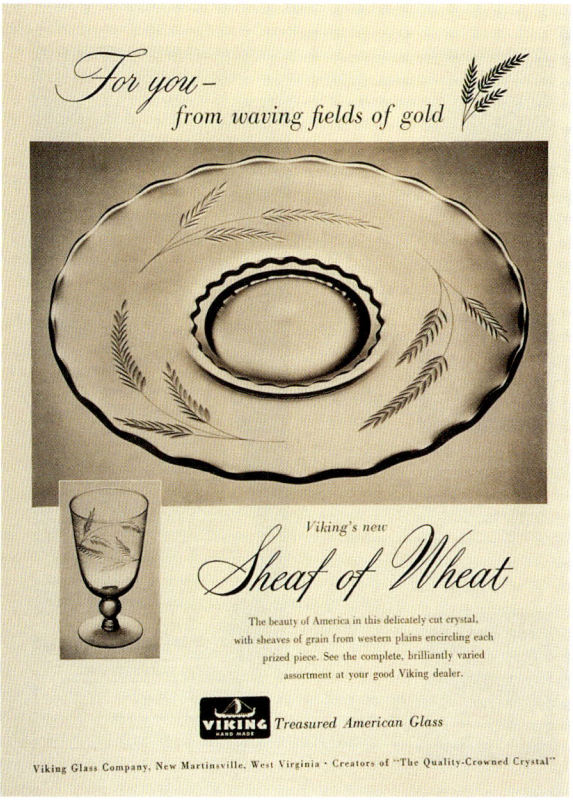

The new "Sheaf of Wheat" was also called Wheat at times. Here as shown in October 1953, *House & Garden*.

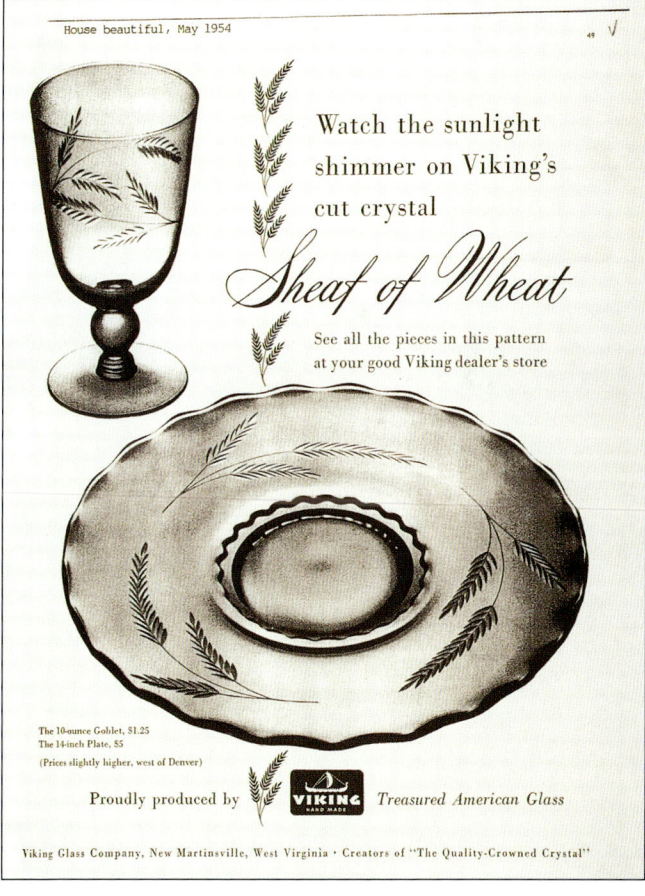

Sheaf of Wheat goblet and 14" plate, *House Beautiful*, May 1954. *This ad, like several others, was shared by Tom Felt.*

WREATH: 1951 catalog supplement on Princess blanks shown on catalog cover.

Viking "Confusables" and Want-to-be Glass

There are endless shapes and forms on the collectible market that might at first glance appear to be Viking. There are endless pieces being offered on-line, in shops, and elsewhere, and called Viking that are not. Some of this is lack of information, some just bad guessing; some are intentional attempts to misrepresent. Viking, with its "modern" and "mid-century" appeal, is fast becoming collectible and, as the number of buyers increase, some prices may increase, and some Not Viking will be sold as Viking. Here are quick notes on Viking – specific to this time period, but generally correct for all Viking production.

If the color looks wrong, it probably IS wrong for Viking. L.E. Smith Glass made very similar forms in slightly different colors and Fenton Art Glass in the 1960s made strikingly similar colors in very different forms. These two companies produced some of the "most likely to be confused with Viking" American glass.

In this period we find no free hand or off hand glass in the line. Some pieces were produced at the Viking factory, as they always are at any handmade glass factory. These were not in the catalog, line, or wide production. We heard tales of and saw awe-inspiring examples of completely hand-sculpted pieces made at Viking by specific artisans or as experimental objects by artisans who came for short time periods. None of these off hand and free-formed pieces were placed into regular production as far as we could learn. No Viking glass formed without the aid of molds or presses appears in literature, catalogs, or other sources for this time period.

Later, after buying Rainbow Glass and operating that facility as a second factory, some off hand animals, etc. were in the line. These animals are indistinguishable from what Rainbow made for years prior to becoming Viking II. Pilgrim Glass, Scandia Glass, and other companies made these identical, sometimes paper labeled, and often-indistinguishable free-form, small animals. Beware. This driven point about no free hand glass means that pre-1970 Viking shapes began as pressed shapes and were then pulled, crimped, swung, or otherwise manipulated by hand by individual artisans into the desired abstract form. If it looks entirely free-formed, it may indeed be all formed without

molds and is, if so, not Viking of the period this book covers. A significant amount of the free-formed looking glass offered as Viking was imported. It is often Italian glass of skill and quality, but not Viking. Beware. Learn the shapes and colors of Viking.

By 1970 Viking had largely developed the shapes and forms that would be signature Viking glass. After 1970 several distinctly pressed patterns enter the line, Country Craft, cabbage, etc. These are obvious and distinctively patterned. However, the basic Viking forms for abstraction and the "modern" look are in place before 1970. The Epic "free-formed" look, created by spun molds and the literally swung glass lines, thus retain the basic shapes and look of Viking. This method to create free-formed pieces is in common practice by the end of 1970. Many individual forms were already discontinued by 1970. If a piece of glass seems not to resemble the forms shown in this book or to be a identifiable post-1970 pattern, it very likely is not Viking. Remember, Viking began with one form and could make numerous diverse objects from the same basic building block beginning shape. Learn to look for distinguishable characteristics and these "building blocks." Vikings bases and feet are often the best visual clues. See the details in the Epic chapter.

If it has a pontil, the scar on the base formed when the hot glass was held for shaping, it is NOT Viking of this era.

Viking of this period, excluding the thin stemware made for Viking by someone else in Morgantown, West Virginia, is not thin walled glass. It remains heavy and fashioned in the 1940s "Viking" or Scandinavian manner of thick crystal.

Few pieces contain more than one color. Amberina, the two tone Flamenco, and some pieces with color applied handles are the exceptions in the Viking line. Multicolored pieces are very likely NOT Viking.

What follows are a few examples of possible items that you might confuse with Viking. This is by no means all of the pieces similar to Viking. You might ask, how did we come to have these? Some we purchased along the path of collecting and research, believing them to be Viking but now know differently. Even with caution, you too may make attribution mistakes.

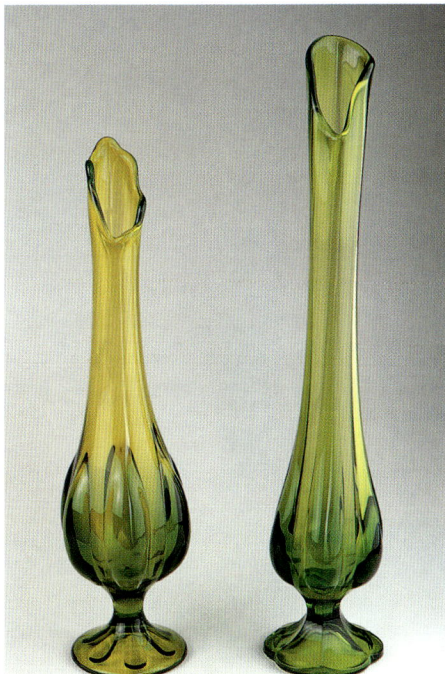

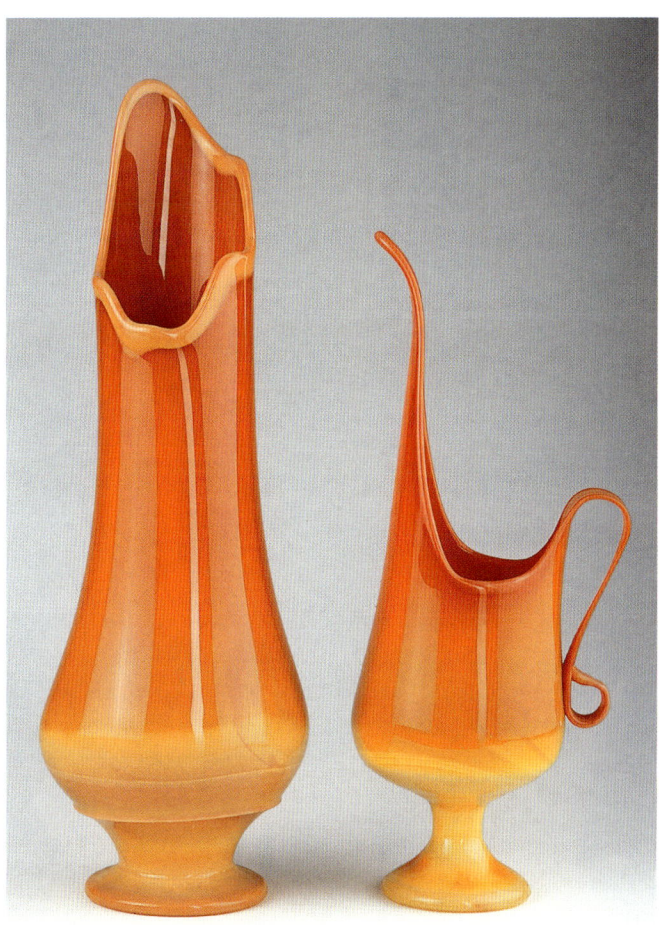

Viking six petal Epic swung vase in avocado and similar color and form, believed to be an L. E. Smith Glass Co. product. Easily confused.

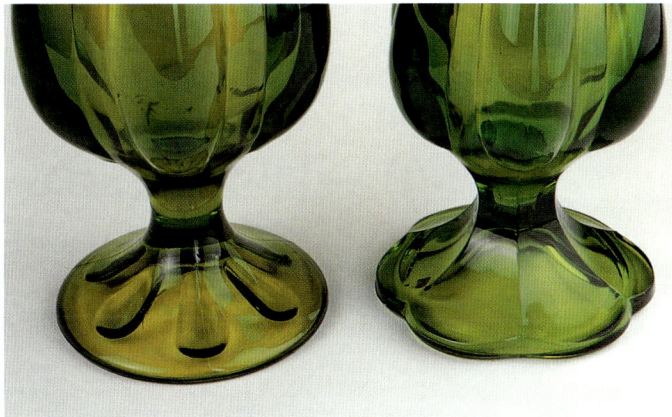

Forms in Smith Glass bittersweet color. Similar to Viking form but Not Viking in color or form.

Base close up of two similar swung avocado vases. Note: the round foot with petal is Viking on vases, compotes, covered candy boxes, and other forms. The petal shaped base is NOT Viking on any vase, compote, covered candy, or other form in any color.

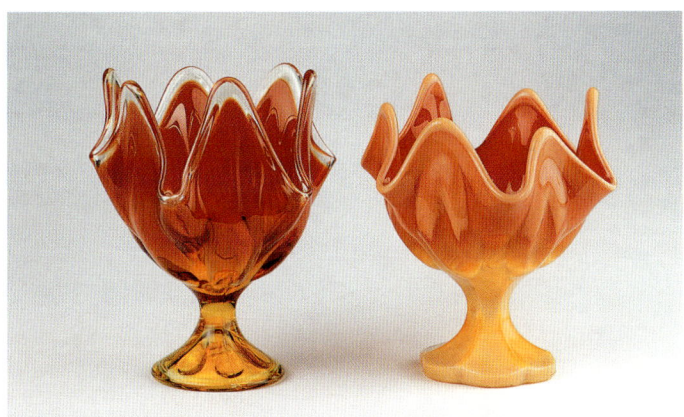

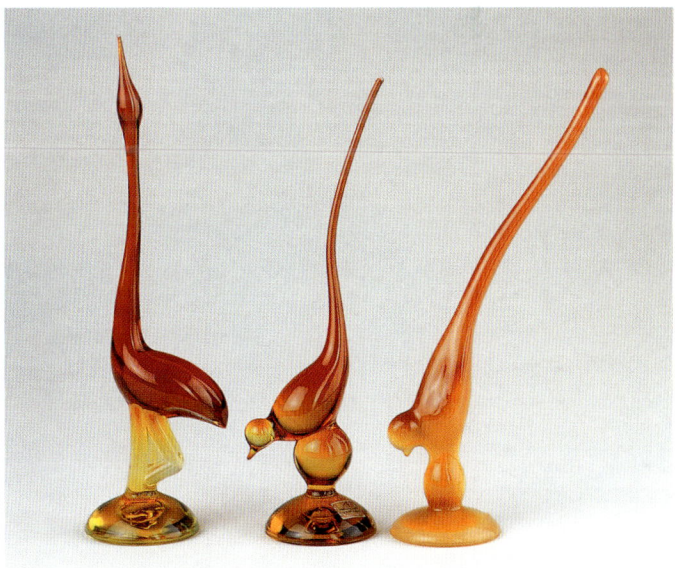

Confusing color and form. Left is Viking six petal Epic in Persimmon. The other is L. E. Smith bittersweet color in a similar form. This color, bittersweet, resembles nothing Viking made. Smith's bittersweet has often, in fact predominately, been incorrectly labeled as Viking on the secondary market at the time of this writing.

Birds. Left to right: Viking egret, Viking #1311 long tailed bird, L. E. Smith bird in bittersweet color. Smith birds were produced in other colors closer to Viking than the example shown. The actual distinctions between Viking and Smith birds are many. Easiest is that the Smith bird has features, such as wings and feathers, visible on the body. Viking, being very modern, is smooth, with detail of no kind, being sculptural and more abstracted.

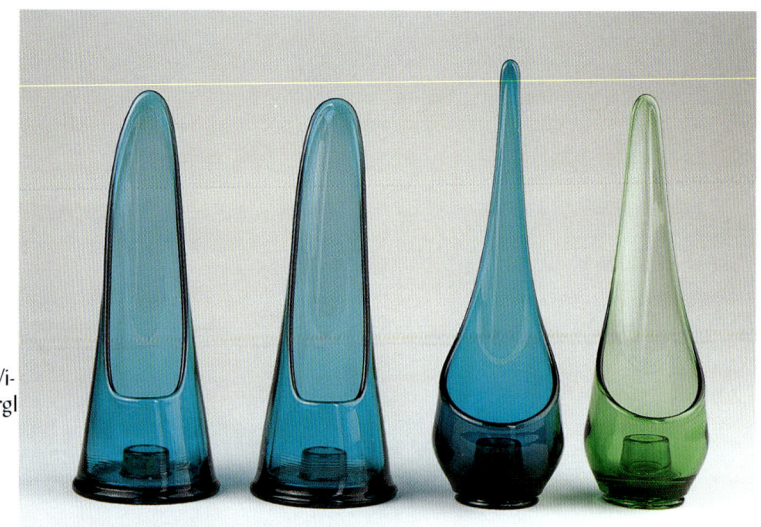

Left: the set in a blue color is Not Viking but resembles the Viking Tapergl set on the right.

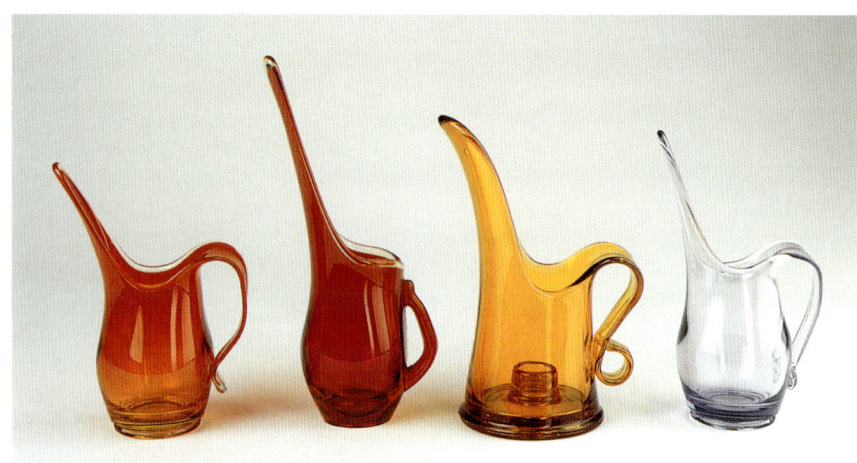

Pitchers, left to right: Viking persimmon and form; Not Viking red - not Viking form; Not Viking yellow- amber with candle well; and Viking teaberry. The maker of the taperglow-like candlesticks in this section also produced the yellow amber candle well pitcher shown here, see similarities in ringed foot/base.

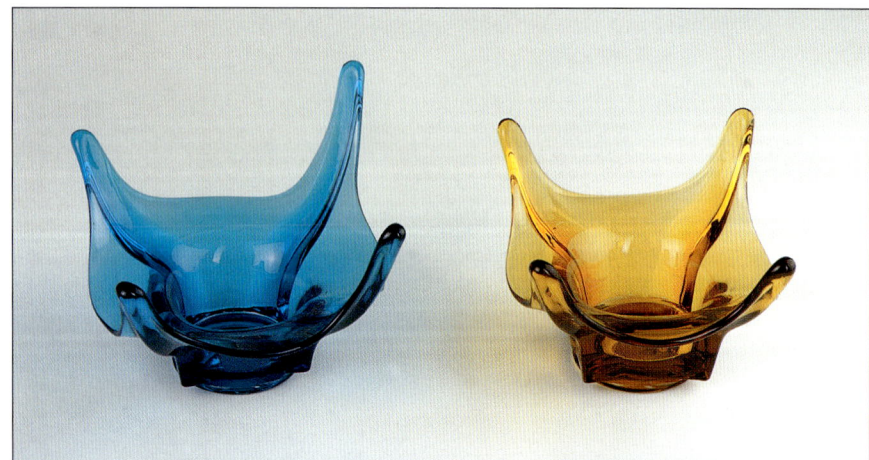

Bowls in Viking-like color and seeking to imitate the spun mold process abstractions, but these are Not Viking.

Swans confuse people. They need not. These close-ups show the distinguishing detail. Left is a colonial blue Viking swan showing where the hand applied swan handle is attached. Note that there is not a pronounced point or "V" here. The right swan is a Duncan and Miller Glass Co. swan; note the pronounced point where the neck and body join.

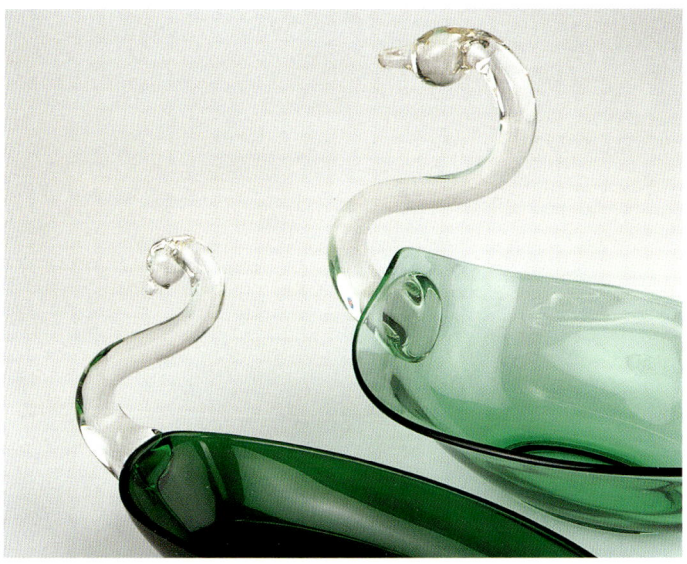

Same lesson on swan bowls as previous, different size and colors, still the illustration is to make clear that Viking swans have no pronounced point where body and neck join, Duncan & Miller swans have "That point." Get the point!

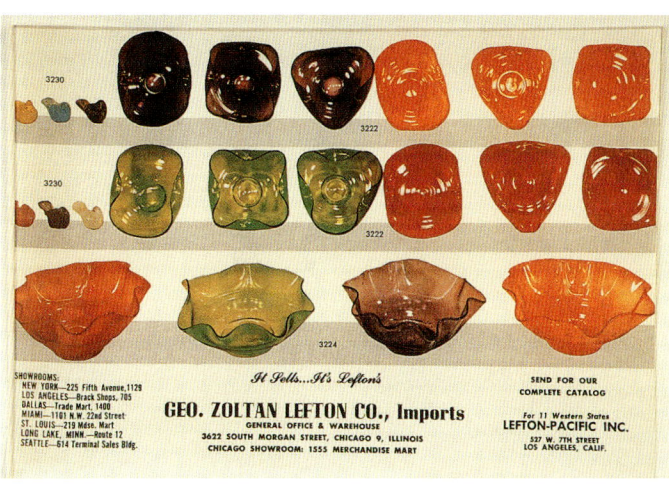

A page of 1950s colorful imports that might be confused with or labeled on the secondary market as Viking.

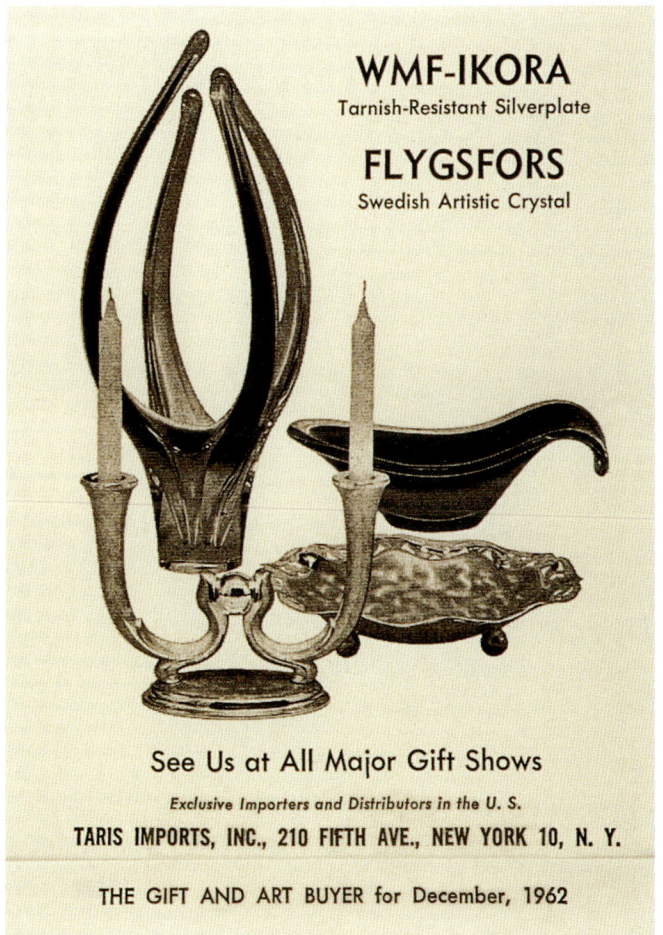

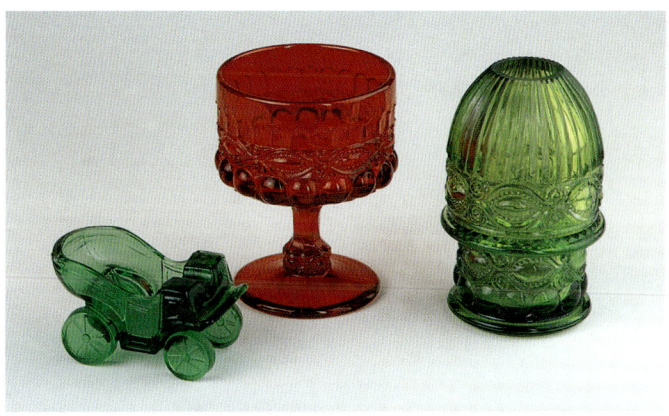

A short note to state that New Martinsville Glass before Viking and Viking for many years provided large quantities of glass for glass marketer L. G. Wright and his company. These are Wright molds and forms that were *possibly* made at Viking. Production records for Wright at the West Virginia Museum of American Glass show well over a dozen glass houses producing items for Wright. Viking and Fenton Art Glass™ were consistently two of the top suppliers to Wright.

Imported glass of the 1950s and early 1960s is often marketed as Viking and, depending on the audience, Viking is found on the secondary market as Venetian, Scandinavian, etc. Note the wild handled basket vase and its resemblance to the Viking basket vase shown in the basket and Epic chapters.

The Hands That Made the Glass...

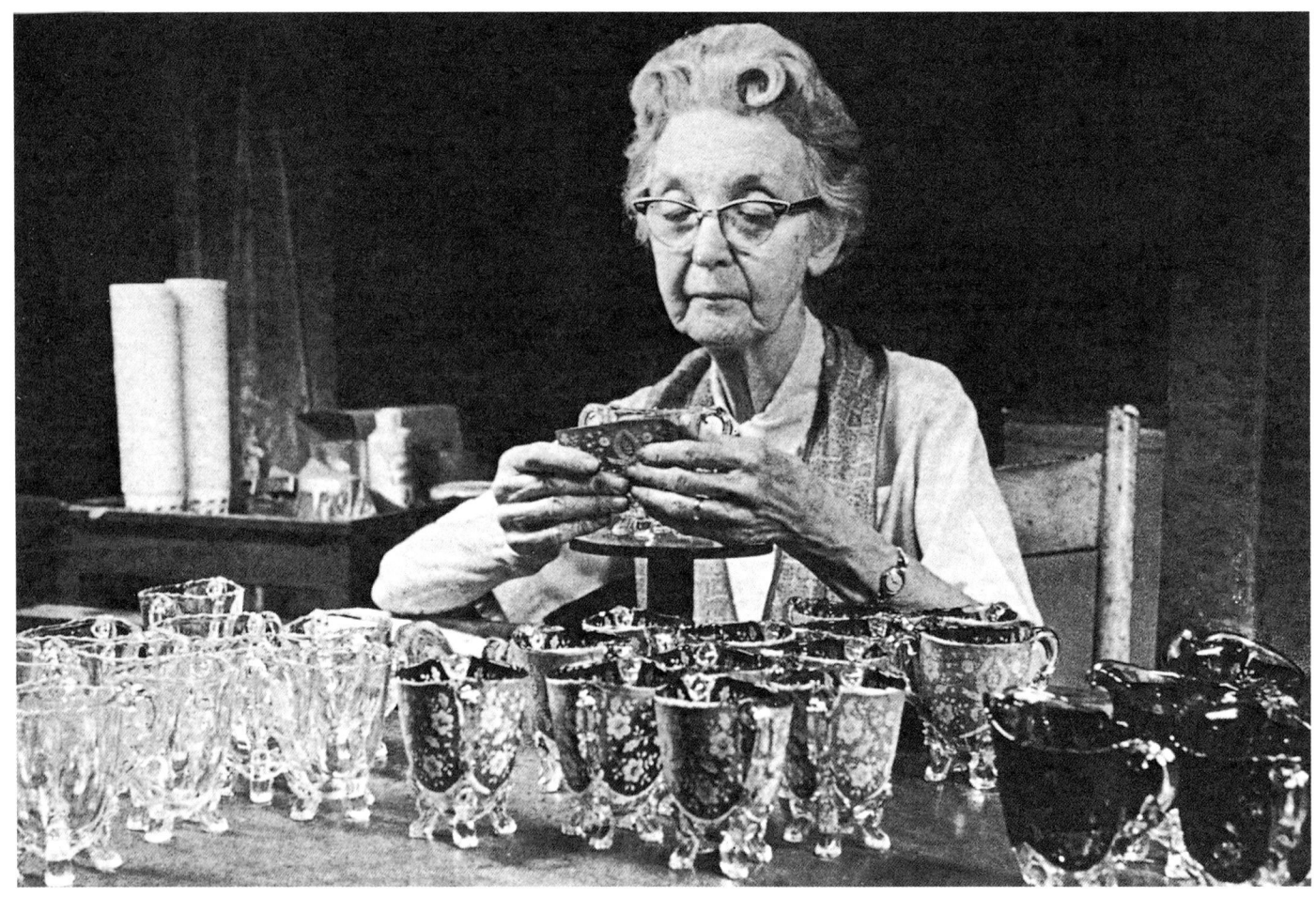

Skilled hands at Viking applying the paper to transfer a wax image onto the glass as part of the steps in creating an acid plate etching on a piece of crystal.

While it is impossible to name all the folks who have worked at Viking in its several reincarnations spanning decades, it seems just and right to pay tribute to the men and women who have worked there. These men and women have hands with great skill, artistic and sharp eyes for design and quality, gentle hands that carefully packed, and sharp minds that created endless designs and shapes for our enjoyment. These are the folks whose lives were, for a short time or a long time, a part of the processes that allow us to today enjoy this beautiful product. As collectors, we see objects—glass is light and color—objects to be desired, sought, obtained.

For the hundreds of people whose lives revolved about the glass factory, it was often like one extended family, with joys and hardships. Outlet manager of many years Goldie Smith told us, "I loved every minute of it—I never awakened when I didn't want to go to work." Following are the names of those who appear on one of the ledgers of American Flint Glass Workers Union Local 510 of New Martinsville. Please read through the list below, say the names, hear the trends of the same family name as it appears and reappears. Notice the large number of women represented in the Union. These women were joining the labor force in historically large numbers in the mid-1940s to do work that in all prior times of peace would have been most often done by men. These ladies abilities and willingness to work allowed Viking to continue in tough times.

These men and women are the artisans and support staff responsible for creating the glass and helping move it from West Virginia to the corners of the earth. These names represent the workers from August 2, 1942 through April 5, 1947, the height of the Second World War. Here are some of the named and unnamed individuals and the family names as small tribute to the many who made this glass:

Anderson, Burnett
Anderson, Marie
Anderson, Boyd
Anderson, William
Auten, Arthur
Auten, Cleona
Anderson, Lona
Ater, Allie Lee
Angus, William H.
Arnett, Mildred
Anderson, Violet

Barth, Wm. E.
Barturg, James
Bugle, Arthur
Bugle, William
Brookover, Fred
Bugle, Riley
Bland, Bernice
Butler, Anna
Bugle, George
Blair, Robert
Billeter, James
Brookover, Clara
Burch, Ella
Barth, Henry
Barret, Retha
Burge, Charles
Blake, Irma
Bartung, Amos
Barth, Joseph
Beckett, Bertha
Burgess, Glenn
Beegle, Clarice
Beegle, Russell
Beegle, D. Lewis
Brookover, Ed
Blair, Trilby
Bowen, Mearldean
Bowen, Roy

Coen, Gertrude
Coleman, Edna
Crawford, Hobart
Carroll, Frank
Crist, James
Chaplin, Paul
Conley, Etta
Chaplin, Edna Mae
Crothers, Mary
Cumbridge, Wilbur
Carpenter, James
Carpenter, Ida
Carroll, Marie
Clark, Elizabeth
Cross, Alice
Clegg, Delcia
Cannon, Mildred
Clegg, Charles
Conroy, Steve
Cramblett, Edna
Carroll, Esther
Cutright, William
Cutright, Genova
Cross, Irvin
Crebar, Gertrude E.
Chaplin, Carl
Calvin, Gertrude
Coen, Frank
Carpenter, Henry Vernon
Clegg, Florence

Crawford, J. Ila
Crawford, m McCoy Juanita

Dalrymple, John
Dalrymple, John Jr.
Dalrymple, Lara
Delancy, Lora
Debille, Mabel
Durig, Edna Rose
Duke, Clyde
Duke, Thurman
Duke, Greg
Danner, Lynskey Eloise
Davis, Susan
Davis, Imogene
Davis, Thelma
Dennis, Harry
Dalrymple, Helen
Duty, Arthur
Davis, Nora
Dawson, Mary
Dennis, Luthur
Dennis, Melvin
Dennis, Walter
Dennis, edgar L.
Dyer, Langwell Ida Mae
Dick, Ralph Jr.

Edge, Myrtle
Edward, Paul
Ensminger, Ernest
Edgar, Mary F.
Eller, Anbea (?)
Ensminger, Henry
Eller, Sherman

Frye, Robert
Faucett, Buelah
Folger, Grace
Forbes, Bernard
Frye, Dave
Ferrebe, Edna
Fox, Mildred
Fox, Rex
Fitzgerald, Melba
Frazer, Herman

Goddard, Ina
Greathouse, Okey
Garrison, Taylor Lora
Goddard, Anna
Goddard, John
Gebring, John
Glendenning, Iris (?)
Glendenning, Betty Jane
Greathouse, Ora Y.
Gray, Andrew

Hinzman, Pearl
Hinzman, William
Haskins, Lee
Howell, Ernest
Howell, Theodore
Howell, Chester
Huffman, Lewis
Hostutler, Blanche
Hansan, Bethel
Haught, Delia
Howell, Franklin
Hartline, Leland
Howell, Joseph W.

Hill, Mannian Dorothy
Heinzman, Chloye
Heinzman, Betty
Hoffer, Geneva
Hawkins, Mamie
Heinzman, Martha
Haskins, Blanche
Howell, Joseph
Hartman, Glennan
Hostutler, Mildred
Howell, Otto
Hoover, Mary
Heinzman, Howard
Harman, Jake
Harman, Floyd
Heinzman, Charles
Harman, Moynelle
Haskinson, Nadie
Howell, Harry
Hammel, Jack
Huffman, Sherman
Howell, Roosevelt
Harter, Herman
Haskins, Eugene
Herman, Laura Ruth
Haskins, James
Huggins, Joseph E.
Hartline, Francis
Hartline, Cacil
Hartline, James A.
Heinzman, Bertha
Huffman, Eugene
Hartline, Martha R.
Huffman, Perry
Howell, Charles A.
Hartline, Patricia

Ice, Ray William

Jackson A. W.
Jacobs, Jack
Jakes, Herman
Johnson, Rebecca
Jobes, Joseph
Johnson, Mildred
Jobes, Leonard
Johnson, Ila Jane
Johnson, Chas. H.
Johnson James
Johnson, Richard
Jobes, Dewar

Kirkhart, William
Kosher, Harold
Kuhn, Mary J.
Kavanagh, Georgia
Kauffman, Alta
Kocher, Emma
Kauffman, Ray
Kincaid, Edna
Kirkland, Ellsworth
Kirkhart, Alma
Kay, Kathryn
Kirkhart, Wilma
Kirkhart, Velma

Lyons, Grimm Ruby
Lewis, Thomas
Lively, David
Lemons, Marjorie
Lohr, James

Lipscomb, Bernard
Lowell, William
Lemans, Mary
Longwell, Thos.
Longwell, John Albert
Lemasters, James
Lohr, Clarence
Leheu, John (?)
Lemasters, Albert
Litman, Edward
Lennox, Melvin
Loy, Garnet
Litman, Virginia
Loy, Helen
Lemans, Wanda
Leasure, Junior
Leasure, Nancy
Longwell, Helen
Loy, Hazel
Leasure, Robert
Loy, Arch
Long, Dale
Loy, Walter
Lemasters, Jess
Ladd, Raymond
Lemasters, Dimple
Lewis, Mary Lorrain
Loy, John
Lovall, Margie
Loy, Gladys
Loy, Amos E.
Litman, Velma
Longwell, Gladys
Lancaster, Mary
Lively, Mase
Loveall, Willard
Loy, Paul
Loy, Ruby
Lemasters, Geo.
Longwell, Bernard
Lipscomb, Hazel
Lively, Edna

McCoy, John
McCoy, Gertrude
McCoy, Blair Esther
McCoy, Clarence
McEldowney, Emma
McCoy, Juanita
Mason, Carl
Mason, Cora
Miller, William
Mason, Oliver
Martin, Clifford
Minger, James
Minger, Thomas
Minger, Lawrence
Mulligan, John
Miller, Anna L.
Miller, Clovis
Moellendick, Curtis
Mulligan, Rose
Myers, Susanna
Moore, Charles
Myers, John
Miller, Gordon
Morris, Annabell L.
Morris, Nettie
Miller, Elsie
Morgan, Jack
Morris, Velma

Miller, Francis
Morris, Paul
Morris, Margaret
Morris, Betty
Morris, Grace
Miller, F.E.
Moellendick, Florence
Mason, Charles
Martin, Waneda
Miller, Willa Mae
Morrison, Harols
Morris, Willima
Morris, Anna L.L.
Morris, Hermione
Morris, Charles Jr.

Nice, John
Neely, Garnett
Nolan, Betty
Neff, Harold
Nice, Earl
Nolan, David
Nelson, Francis
Nolan, George
Nice, Ruth
Nice, Clem
Nice, Jess
Nice, Floyd
Nichols, Wright Patty
Nice, Mandy A.
Nice Wanda
Nice, Evelyn G.

Oblinger, Helen
O'Neil Ralph
O'Neil Lucy

Platt, Messick Opal
Potts, Charles
Pickett, Pearl
Potts, Mildred
Potts, Roy
Potts, Irwin
Prunty, Herman
Pyles, Irene
Pyles, Kathryn
Prunty, Arch
Phillips, Mary
Pegg, Berneda
Poole, Donald
Pyles, Sheldon
Potts, Ida
Phillips, Mabel
Pairdy,Wykes Sarah
Phillips, Grace

Potts, Louise
Palmer, Olive J. Cross
Palmer, Mary
Pryar, William
Pyles, Wilson
Powell, Lorena
Pittman, Louise
Potts, Irma
Pyles, Pearl
Potts, Walter
Powell, Oma
Powell, Lockwood
Pyles, Amos
Pyles, Georgia
Prunty, Wesley
Powell, Mildred L.
Petty, Forest
Potts, Mont
Powell, David

Quinn, Jack

Ripley, Nellie
Resseger, Jacob
Resseger, George
Resseger, George Jr.
Resseger, John
Ruble, Harold
Robinson, Hoy
Richter, James
Ritz, Frank
Roberts, Martha
Rice, Viola
Ruble, Delphia
Robinson, Florence
Rice, Robert
Resseger, Mae
Resseger, Louise
Richards, Daniel
Reed, W.R.
Rice, J.W.
Resseger, Minnie
Ruble, Louise
Repco, Vernice
Robinson, Margaret
Ruble, Wilma Jean
Riggenbach, Fred
Roberts, Mary E.
Robinson, James
Ruble, Earl
Repco, Irma Potts
Robinson, Herbert

Shreves, James L.

Sidenstricker, Ed
Smith, Lelia
Smith, Adam
Snyder, Dan
Starcher, Julia
Straswider, Presley
Suter, Alfred
Suter, Ralph
Shuman, Mildred
Shepherd, Vera
Schuster, Kathryn
Snyder, Stanley
Smith, Zelma
Shepherd, Juanita
Skinner, Sherman
Stackhouse, Marian
Scully, Gladys
Smith, Delbert
Stackhouse, Audrey
Shepherd, Hazel
Staggers, Lenora
Slaven, Betty Jane
Sinert, Harold
Sellbach, La Meta
Schaffer, Audrey
Sarner, Leone
Smith, Elva
Schnidler, Ella M.
Shreve, Pearl
Sickles, Howard
Sidell, C.R.
Septer, Justice
Smith, Leroy
Smith, Harold A.
Smith, Eva
Smith, Arnold
Schaffer, Chester

Tuttle, Opha
Thomas, Dora
Thomas, Ralph
Travis, Otis
Travis, Mildred
Travis, Carrie
Travis, James
Tedron, Ann
Tedron, Pearl
Truex, Arvilla
Travis, Everett
Truex, Clifford
Tippin, Elmo
Thomas, Roy
Toomey, Thos.
Travis, Betty

Thomas, Leroy
Thomas, Benjamin F.
Tustin, Paul
Thompson, Roy
Thompson, George
Travis, Harry
Thomas, Glenna
Tuttle, Sidna
Thomas, Sherman
Travis, George

Underwood, Nina Lee

Van Camp, Elyn

Whiteman, B.E.
Whiteman, Lina B.
Wayman, Helen
Workman, Robert
Wagner, Wanda
West, Florence
Wetzel, Goldie
Watkins, Kenneth
Wilson, Goldie
Wyke, Paul
Wright, Patty
Wise, Mary
Woods, Edna
Woods, Boyd
Woods, Faye
Williamson, Lawrence
West, John
Williams, Anna
Wells, Clinton M.
Weltz, Russel R.
Whiteman, Mildred
Willison, Anna
Wood, Elwood M.
Wilkson, Geo
Wychoff, Tom

Yeager, Ray
Young, Emery
Yoho, Mary
Yoho, Ora
Yoho, Wesley
Yeager, Wallace
Yeager, Foster
Yocum, Kathryn
Yeager, Marie

Zohund, Dorothy (?)

"I worked there, I met my wife when she was working there, and my grandma worked there. My grandma's 98 now."

Robert Cross
Proving the sense of
community in the glass house

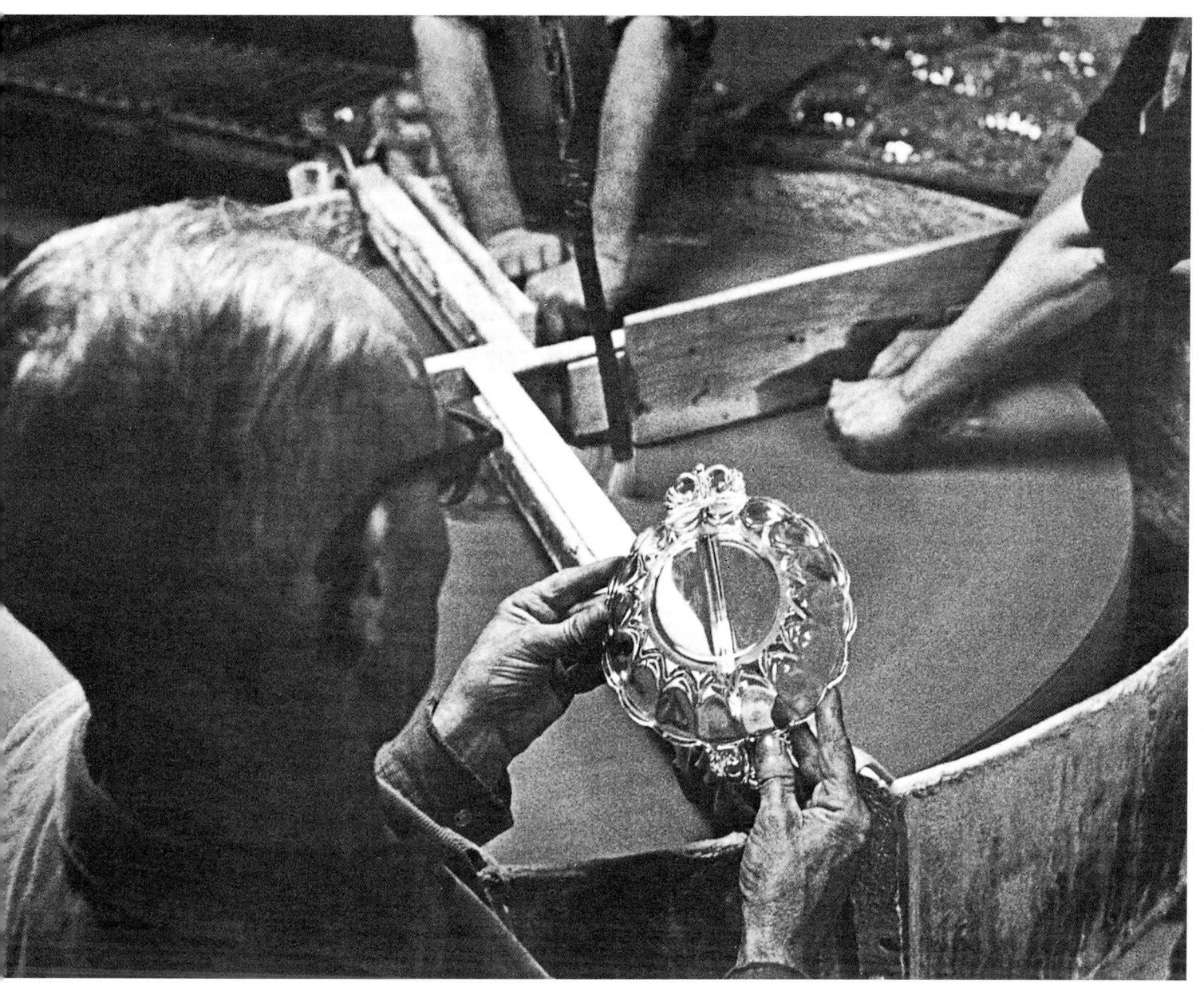

Skilled hands at Viking grinding the bottom of a Janice bowl to insure a flat, smooth, and level finish.

Bibliography

Coe, Debbie and Randy. *Elegant Glass Early, Depression, & Beyond.* Atglen, Pennsylvania: Schiffer Publishing, Ltd., 2001.

Measell, James. New Martinsville *Glass, 1900-1944.* Marietta, Ohio: Antique Publications, 1994.

Viking Handmade Glass. Company catalog January 1948 original loose bound black and white 54 pages. Collection of West Virginia Museum of American Glass

Viking Handmade Glass. Company catalog January 1950 original loose bound black and white 32 pages plus 1 page supplemental. collection of Rock Wilson

Viking Handmade Glass. Company catalog January 1950 supplemented to Jan 1951 catalog original loose bound black and white 36 pages plus 4 page Princess supplement. collection of West Virginia Museum of American Glass.

Viking Handmade Glass. Company catalog January 1956 purchased photocopy loose bound black and white, Princess page A1-7, Prelude pages B1-8, Misc. pages c1-8

Viking Glass Company Treasured American Glass. Catalog circa 1957, microfiche F-9087 loaned by Corning Museum of Glass.

Viking Glass Company Treasured American Glass. Catalog 1958, microfiche F-9141 loaned by Corning Museum of Glass.

Viking Glass Company Treasured American Glass. Catalog 1959, microfiche F-8931 loaned by Corning Museum of Glass.

Viking Glass Company Treasured American Glass. Catalog 1959, color and black and white, original 23 pages. Author's collection, gift of Jeff Conover.

Viking Glass 1962 Catalog. Color and black and white original 27 pages. West Virginia Museum of American Glass collection, gift of Jeff Conover.

Viking Glass 1963 Catalog Supplment. Color 4 pages. West Virginia Museum of American Glass collection, Tony Tomazin collection purchase.

Viking Glass 1967 Catalog. Black and white photocopy. Collection of Fenton Art Glass.

Viking Glass Catalog. 1968 black and white photocopy, 19 pages with accompanying price list. Corning Museum of Glass.

Viking Glass Catalog. 1969 black and white photocopy, 19 pages. Corning Museum of Glass.

Viking Glass Treasured American Glass 1970. Original color and black and white company catalog, 25 pages. Collection of Replacements, Ltd.

Viking Glass Company Price List for "last six months of 1946," 1950, January 1953, January, 1956, 1964, 1967, 1968, 1970.

Index